E-Commerce and Intelligent Methods

AF849547

Dear MyCopy Customer,

This Springer book is a monochrome print version of the eBook to which your library gives you access via SpringerLink. It is available to you at a subsidized price since your library subscribes to at least one Springer eBook subject collection.

Please note that MyCopy books are only offered to library patrons with access to at least one Springer eBook subject collection. MyCopy books are strictly for individual use only.

You may cite this book by referencing the bibliographic data and/or the DOI (Digital Object Identifier) found in the front matter. This book is an exact but monochrome copy of the print version of the eBook on SpringerLink.

Studies in Fuzziness and Soft Computing

Editor-in-chief
Prof. Janusz Kacprzyk
Systems Research Institute
Polish Academy of Sciences
ul. Newelska 6
01-447 Warsaw, Poland
E-mail: kacprzyk@ibspan.waw.pl
http://www.springer.de/cgi-bin/search_book.pl?series=2941

Further volumes of this series can be found at our homepage.

Vol. 85. D. Rutkowska
Neuro-Fuzzy Architectures and Hybrid Learning, 2002
ISBN 3-7908-1438-5

Vol. 86. M.B. Gorzałczany
Computational Intelligence Systems and Applications, 2002
ISBN 3-7908-1439-3

Vol. 87. C. Bertoluzza, M.Á. Gil and D.A. Ralescu (Eds.)
Statistical Modeling, Analysis and Management of Fuzzy Data, 2002
ISBN 3-7908-1440-7

Vol. 88. R.P. Srivastava and T.J. Mock (Eds.)
Belief Functions in Business Decisions, 2002
ISBN 3-7908-1451-2

Vol. 89. B. Bouchon-Meunier, J. Gutiérrez-Ríos, L. Magdalena and R.R. Yager (Eds.)
Technologies for Constructing Intelligent Systems 1, 2002
ISBN 3-7908-1454-7

Vol. 90. B. Bouchon-Meunier, J. Gutiérrez-Ríos, L. Magdalena and R.R. Yager (Eds.)
Technologies for Constructing Intelligent Systems 2, 2002
ISBN 3-7908-1455-5

Vol. 91. J.J. Buckley, E. Eslami and T. Feuring
Fuzzy Mathematics in Economics and Engineering, 2002
ISBN 3-7908-1456-3

Vol. 92. P.P. Angelov
Evolving Rule-Based Models, 2002
ISBN 3-7908-1457-1

Vol. 93. V.V. Cross and T.A. Sudkamp
Similarity and Compatibility in Fuzzy Set Theory, 2002
ISBN 3-7908-1458-X

Vol. 94. M. MacCrimmon and P. Tillers (Eds.)
The Dynamics of Judicial Proof, 2002
ISBN 3-7908-1459-8

Vol. 95. T.Y. Lin, Y.Y. Yao and L.A. Zadeh (Eds.)
Data Mining, Rough Sets and Granular Computing, 2002
ISBN 3-7908-1461-X

Vol. 96. M. Schmitt, H.-N. Teodorescu, A. Jain, A. Jain, S. Jain and L.C. Jain (Eds.)
Computational Intelligence Processing in Medical Diagnosis, 2002
ISBN 3-7908-1463-6

Vol. 97. T. Calvo, G. Mayor and R. Mesiar (Eds.)
Aggregation Operators, 2002
ISBN 3-7908-1468-7

Vol. 98. L.C. Jain, Z. Chen and N. Ichalkaranje (Eds.)
Intelligent Agents and Their Applications, 2002
ISBN 3-7908-1469-5

Vol. 99. C. Huang and Y. Shi
Towards Efficient Fuzzy Information Processing, 2002
ISBN 3-7908-1475-X

Vol. 100. S.-H. Chen (Ed.)
Evolutionary Computation in Economics and Finance, 2002
ISBN 3-7908-1476-8

Vol. 101. S.J. Ovaska and L.M. Sztandera (Eds.)
Soft Computing in Industrial Electronics, 2002
ISBN 3-7908-1477-6

Vol. 102. B. Liu
Theory and Praxis of Uncertain Programming, 2002
ISBN 3-7908-1490-3

Vol. 103. N. Barnes and Z.-Q. Liu
Knowledge-Based Vision-Guided Robots, 2002
ISBN 3-7908-1494-6

Vol. 104. F. Rothlauf
Representations for Genetic and Evolutionary Algorithms, 2002
ISBN 3-7908-1496-2

Javier Segovia
Piotr S. Szczepaniak
Marian Niedzwiedzinski
Editors

E-Commerce and Intelligent Methods

With 67 Figures
and 35 Tables

Springer-Verlag Berlin Heidelberg GmbH

Assoc. Professor Javier Segovia
Universidad Politécnica de Madrid
Facultad de Informática
Campus de Montegancedo
28660 Madrid
Spain
fsegovia@fi.upm.es

Assoc. Professor Piotr S. Szczepaniak
Technical University of Lodz
Institute of Computer Science
ul. Sterlinga 16/18
90217 Lodz
Poland
office@ics.p.lodz.pl
or
Systems Research Institute
Polish Academy of Sciences
ul. Newelska 6
01-447 Warsaw
Poland

Assoc. Professor
Marian Niedzwiedzinski
University of Lodz
Systems Analysis and
Design Department
ul. P.O.W. 3/5
90-255 Lodz
Poland
mariann@krysia.uni.lodz.pl

ISSN 1434-9922

DOI 10.1007/978-3-7908-1779-9

Library of Congress Cataloging-in-Publication Data applied for
Die Deutsche Bibliothek – CIP-Einheitsaufnahme
E-Commerce and intelligent methods: with 35 tables / Javier Segovia ... (eds.). – Heidelberg; New York: Physica-Verl., 2002
(Studies in fuzziness and soft computing; Vol. 105)

This work is subject to copyright. All rights are reserved, whether the whole or part of the material is concerned, specifically the rights of translation, reprinting, reuse of illustrations, recitation, broadcasting, reproduction on microfilm or in any other way, and storage in data banks. Duplication of this publication or parts thereof is permitted only under the provisions of the German Copyright Law of September 9, 1965, in its current version, and permission for use must always be obtained from Physica-Verlag. Violations are liable for prosecution under the German Copyright Law.

© Springer-Verlag Berlin Heidelberg 2002
Originally published by Physica-Verlag Heidelberg in 2002
MyCopy version of the original edition 2002

The use of general descriptive names, registered names, trademarks, etc. in this publication does not imply, even in the absence of a specific statement, that such names are exempt from the relevant protective laws and regulations and therefore free for general use.

Hardcover Design: Erich Kirchner, Heidelberg

www.springer.com/mycopy

Preface

This book covers significant recent developments in the field of Intelligent Methods applied to eCommerce. The Intelligent Methods considered are mainly Soft Computing Methods that include fuzzy sets, rough sets, neural networks, evolutionary computations, probabilistic and evidential reasoning, multivalued logic, and related fields.

There is not doubt about the relevance of eCommerce in our daily environments and in the work carried out at many research centers throughout the world. The application of AI to Commerce is growing as fast as the computers and networks are being integrated in all business and commerce aspects. We felt that it was time to sit down and see how was the impact into that field of low-level AI, i.e. softcomputing. We found many scattered contributions disseminated in conferences, workshops, journal, books or even technical reports, but nothing like a common framework that could serve as a basis for further research, comparison or even prototyping for a direct transfer to the industry. We felt then the need to set up a reference point, a book like this.

We planned this book as a recompilation of the newest developments of researchers who already made some contribution into the field. The authors were selected based on the originality and quality of their work and its relevance to the field. Authors came from prestigious universities and research centers with different backgrounds.

The book is divided into five parts. The first one is a general exposition of the eCommerce framework, and the next 4 cover the research contributions ranging from Neural Networks, Bayesian Networks, Fuzzy Logic, Evolutionary Programming, Agents and Case Based Reasoning, applied to a various number of problems in eCommerce such as:

- Customer Service and Support,
- Negotiation and Trading Strategies,
- Logistic Design and Support,
- Inventory Optimisation
- e-CRM,
- Customer and/or Product Profiling and Personalization
- Customer Modelling and Segmentation
- Product Search and Matching
- Trust and Security in payments and transactions

Our hope and wish is that the reader will find in this volume many motivating and enlightening ideas that will help him to contribute to this field of Intelligent Methods applied to eCommerce.

J. Segovia, P.S. Szczepaniak, M. Niedzwiedzinski
Editors

Contents

Part 3. Evolutionary Programming

Part 4. Fuzzy Logic

Part 5. CBR and Agents

Part 1 Foundations of Electronic Commerce

Barriers to Global Electronic Commerce

Marian Niedwiedzinski

Department of Systems Analysis and Design, University of Lodz, 3/5 P.O.W. St., 90-225 Lodz, Poland, mariann@krysia.uni.lodz.pl

Abstract. This chapter addresses factors, which play limiting role in international trade. There were discussed main barriers in general with an emphasis on procedural barriers. These barriers are connected with archaic, paper-based bureaucracy consuming a lot of efforts, time and money. They can be eliminated or reduced by multi-aspect trade facilitation.

1 Introduction

The diagram below shows my general understanding of the problem.

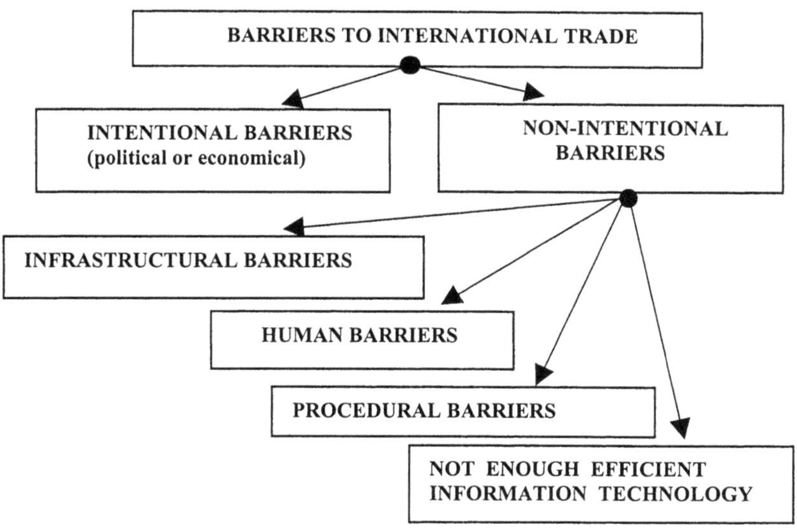

Fig. 1. Barriers to international trade

The globalization of production and the liberalization of trade form new terms in the world economy. The environment of international trade is beginning to change due to a new political situation and due to recent developments such as globalization, progressive reductions in tariff rates, the advance in electronic trading techniques. So, eliminating from our consideration the first (intentional one) and the last (not enough efficient information technology) barriers, one can imagine the following "filters", limiting the scale of international trade existing at present.

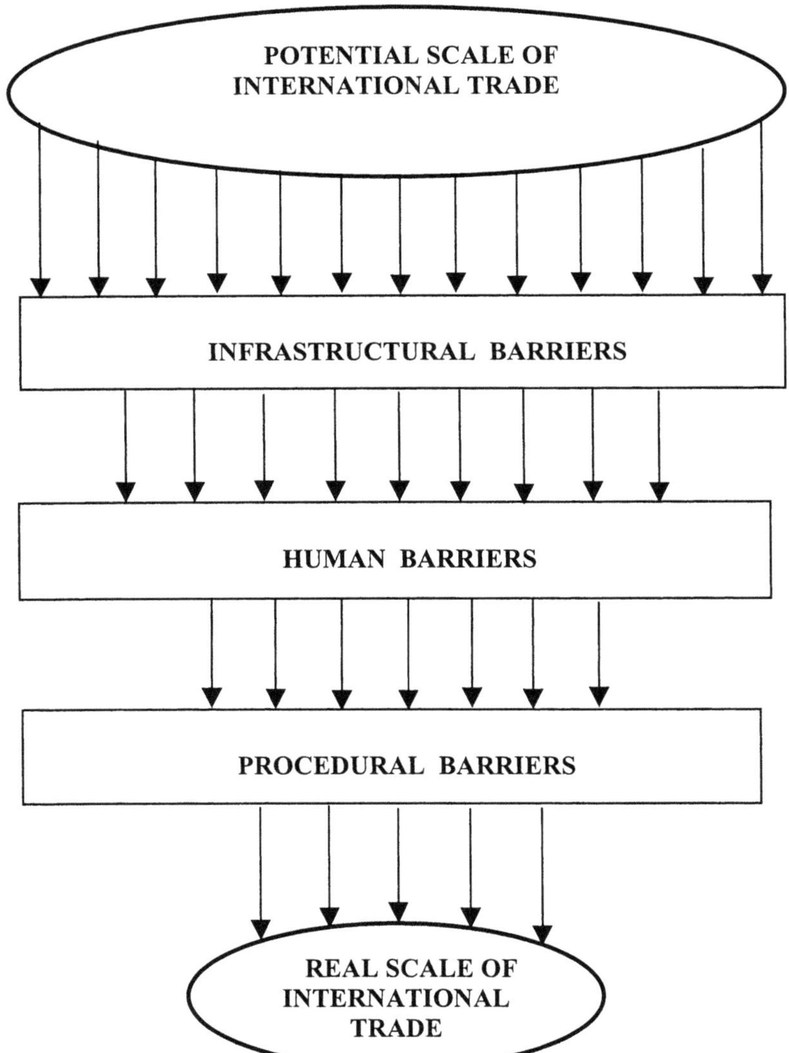

Fig. 2. Limiting effect of barriers to international trade

Arrows symbolize opportunities in trade flows blocked by particular barriers.

Reasons of eliminating from our considerations the first and the last barriers mentioned above are as follows.
The first barrier (intentional one) is not much active any more as a political situation has globally changed. Man-made barriers arising from policy reasons (to protect society, national economy and other political goals) like for example: prohibitions, import restrictions, special incentives or restrictions on exports, preferential national treatment etc. are less and less important.
The last barrier (not enough efficient information technology) is not a critical factor any more as present technological developments enable international trade partners to communicate in a very fast and effective way. New information technologies make comparison of offers and ordering itself a matter of minutes.

So, one should concentrate on barriers in the middle of the figure 1:
- Infrastructural barriers;
- Human barriers;
- Procedural barriers.

2 Infrastructural barriers

As regards infrastructural barriers one can list the following three typical groups.
Barriers connected with a general level of security of doing business in a selected country:
- Security of business people;
- Security of goods;
- Security of payments etc.

Barriers connected with banking and insurance area:
- Lack of reliable banking and insurance system;
- Small number and power of banks;
- Small variety of banking products and services;
- Quality and costs of banking services;
- International acceptability of banking and insurance services;
- Lack of reliable currency system;
- Level of inflation;
- Lack of governmental guarantees of payments.

Barriers connected with transportation of goods:
- Lack of adequate transportation facilities;
- Old and poorly maintained vehicles;
- Poor road conditions;
- Poor packing of goods (lack of palletization and containerization);
- Lack of standardization of transport vehicles and unit loads;
- Lack of use of bar-coding and Unique Reference Number;

- Poor organization of storage areas;
- Poor handling of cargo;
- Limited professional organization;
- Poor organization of Customs area at border crossing points.

3 Human barriers

As regards human barriers one can list the following:

- Bad motivations of people engaged in international trade (corruption);
- Lack of competencies of people engaged in international trade;
- Knowledge of languages; (It was estimated that a significant part of business opportunities are lost due to language problems. So, it seems necessary to provide native language interfaces to trade systems and documents including native alphabets and writing styles.)
- Lack of trust and ethics of people operating in international trade area;
- Different cultures and traditions represented by partners from various countries;
- Heterogeneity of business partners;
- "Rational ignorance"; (It occurs when business partners remain uninformed because the expected costs of becoming informed exceed the expected benefits.)

To eliminate the problem of "rational ignorance" the concept of trade points was created. Trade point is a source of trade-related information, which provides actual and potential traders with data about business and markets opportunities, potential clients and suppliers, trade regulations and requirements. Participants of foreign trade (e.g. customs, banks, chamber of commerce, freight forwarders, transport and insurance companies) are connected with trade points to provide all necessary services for trade transactions. All trade points are interconnected in a worldwide electronic network to increase participation of traders, in particular SMEs, in the emerging global electronic commerce.

4 Procedural barriers

As regards procedural barriers one can list as follows:

- Outdated laws and regulations;
- Excessive bureaucracy;
- Too many documents,
- Outdated commercial practices;
- Lack of co-ordination between Government entities and the private sector;
- Lack of clear rules,
- Limited number of qualified civil servants;
- Lack of regulation concerning taxation in e-commerce;

The numbers below show how important is the problem of bureaucracy in international trade and what is the scale of it.
Based on statistics from 1995 and estimations made by UN experts active in ITPWG (International Trade Procedures Working Group) one can calculate as follows [5].

- Total international trades $28 000.000.000.000
- Estimated percent transaction costs 5%
- Transaction costs $1.400.000.000.000
- Estimated percent savings 50%
- Total savings $700.000.000.000

So, about $700.000.000.000 lost in 1995 due to bureaucratic problems. It is enough to discuss the problem of bureaucracy more deeply.

New information technologies are changing business including international trade. EDI as a way of replacing traditional paper documents by their electronic equivalents is only a part of the problem. The other necessary part is trade facilitation, which means eliminating (or limiting) bureaucracy and contains harmonization, simplification, standardization and rationalization of procedures used in international trade. By the way, it contains also making the international trade procedures more transparent.
International trade by its very nature is currently more difficult and error prone than dealing with an equivalent domestic consignment. This is due to a number of reasons including a greater number of official and commercial participants, more complicated and time consuming payment processes, the geographical distance over which the goods must travel, the physical and documentary checking, special documentary requirements connected with protection of the environment and endangered species etc. Possible frictions, extra costs, differences in regulations and uncertainties connected with foreign trade additionally limit trade flows. This prevents some businesses from trading on an international basis. This applies particularly to small and medium size enterprises (SMEs). That is why, some 90% of global trade is being done by large business organizations, which have the administrative and legal resources to cope with international trade transactions. The level of international trade could easily be extended if such international markets were made more accessible to small or medium size enterprises. The challenge in supporting these smaller organizations is to provide facilities for identifying market opportunities, as well as to conduct international trade transactions in a way that is easy yet safe and trustworthy.
It is especially important for developing countries and countries in transition. As in developed countries (like for example in Italy), SMEs take part up to 50% of total export [6].

5 Trade facilitation

So, it is necessary to make efforts, to ensure progressively that the international trade process can be undertaken in a similar way to that required domestically.
To be effective the processes of such trade facilitation must cover the totality of the international trade transaction. It should impact on the processes, which take place both before and after the purely physical movement of the goods. This ensures that processes such as the order and payment processes, which take place independently of the movement of the goods, are covered. Facilitation activities should be approached in a co-ordinated manner to ensure problems are not created in one part of the transaction chain by introducing solutions to another part.

International trade has long been important but it is only relatively recently that the significance of trade facilitation has been realized. The participants who include manufacturers, importers, exporters, freight forwarders, carriers, ports, airports, banks, insurance companies, public administrations, chambers of commerce etc. have joint and separate interests in the simplification of trade procedures.
Buyer and seller need to see their agreement for the sale and purchase of goods accomplished with the minimum of complication and cost and with no more formalities than are proportionately necessary to complete the sales contract.
The service providers associated with the movement of the goods want to be able to do so on behalf of their clients with the minimum of complication, linked to the effective operation of their transport and handling resources.
The service providers associated with payment want to finance and facilitate payment for their customers' trade transactions by means which, whilst meeting individual requirements as closely as possible, will give proper weight to prudent precautions against loss or misunderstanding.
Both commercial and administrative management are becoming more aware of the increased efficiency, reduced costs and better customer service that can be obtained from adopting trade facilitation techniques. At a company level, the adoption of trade facilitation techniques, such as the use of the aligned documents has yielded procedural and economic benefits. At a macro economic level, the adoption of trade facilitation techniques can be useful to greater economic activity.
All together leads to a number of benefits which result in:

- An open and efficient trading process,
- Stronger relationships with trading partners,
- Better co-ordination of the trade transactions,
- Promoting of best practices, especially - use of international standards,
- Reduced burdens of bureaucracy,
- Reduced transaction costs,
- Reduced and more understandable (to users) procedures,
- Reduced time,
- More effective transaction controls,
- More trustworthy international trade, by means of more reliable controls,
- Easier accessibility for SMEs to international trade.

Moreover, there is also the "lost opportunity" factor – a difficult to count loss of trade due to the overly complicated requirements of international trade.

There are two main steps of trade facilitation:
1. Developing International Trade Transaction (ITT) framework;
2. Business procedures analysis.

The reason for developing ITT framework is to provide a graphical representation of international movements of goods. The ITT frameworks provides a comprehensive and easy to understand overview of the procedures, parties and information flows associated with import/export transactions. This enables the ITT framework to be used as an educational tool, to advise decision-makers of the formulation of international trade policy and provide practical guidance to enterprises wanting to engage in international trade. Individual National/Regional frameworks are now being developed by individual countries to show a graphical representations of the international trading process for their own country/region.

The purpose of the business procedure analysis is to describe functional business processes, to identify constrains that adversely impact on the mission and objectives of international trade, and to propose appropriate changes to those business processes. Business procedures analysis serves as a catalyst to facilitate international transactions through the rationalization of processes and information flows. The diagram below shows both perspectives of trade facilitation activities.

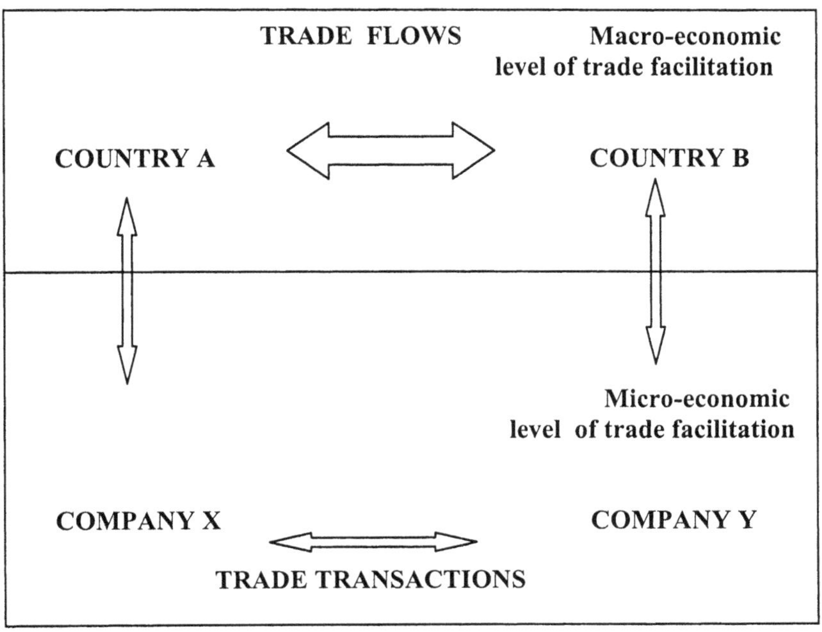

Fig. 3. Macro- and micro-economic levels of trade facilitation [1]

The process of rationalization of trade procedures includes the following parts.

- Analyzing and understanding the key elements of international transactions and working for the elimination of constrains, using functional models (requirements specifications) and diagrams;
- Simplifying, streamlining and standardizing functional business processes through the use of value chain principles and structural analysis;
- Proposing to resolve overlaps, redundancies and bottlenecks;
- Promoting best practices through governments, industry, and associations.

The leading and coordinating role in trade facilitation plays CEFACT (The Center for Trade Facilitation and Electronic Business) – a specialized body within the UN/Economic Commission for Europe. Its field of activity is shown below.

	Activity level					
Activity type	**A** Meta-Standards	**B** Standards	**C** Guidance	**D** Conformance & Certification	**E** Implementation	**F** Facilitation Measures
I Environment	Languages, Practices	Laws	Business guidelines	Courts, Tribunals	Contracts	Agreements
II Business Activity-Models	Modeling languages	Business scenarios	Recommended practices, conventions	Multilateral agreements, test definitions	Business Applications	Recommendations
III Information Modeling	Modeling languages	Message Standards	User guidelines	Test definitions	Actual data	Implementation guidelines
IV Technology	Tools, Techniques	Interoperability standards	Profiles	Test definitions, interoperability standards	Software, hardware	Recommendations (e.g. ITU, ISO)

Fig. 4. Activity framework of CEFACT [1].

The following specialized agencies and other intergovernmental and non-governmental organizations are also active in trade facilitation:

- Inter-Governmental Maritime Consultative Organization (IMCO);
- World Trade Organization (WTO);
- European Economic Community (EEC);
- Custom Co-operation Council (CCC);
- Central Office for International Railway Transport (OCTI);
- International Chamber of Commerce (ICC);
- International Air Transport Association (IATA);
- International Union of Railways (UIC);
- International Organization for Standardization (ISO);
- International Chamber of Shipping (ICS);
- International Federation of Freight Forwarders Associations (FIATA);
- International Railway Transport Committee (CIT), and many others.

It is not an easy task to built a global electronic village in the real context of international trade. As one can easily see, it is so much to do in the field, that it is impossible to do everything at once.
So, it is necessary to have a long term strategy of eliminating barriers from international trade. This strategy should consist of the following steps:

1. permanent monitoring of existing barriers (in a particular country or region);
2. identification of the most critical barrier (which is a bottle-neck of trade);
3. efforts to eliminate the most critical barrier;
4. return back to the first step.

No doubt that the future of global electronic commerce will be really excellent.
At present however, businessmen planning their activities in this field should understand and take into consideration numerous barriers mentioned above, which exist yet.

References

1. CEFACT (1997) Work Program and a Proposed Methodology for its Development and Continuous Updating. United Nations, Geneva, pp19, 23
2. Economic and Social Council (2000) Facilitation Measures related to international Trade Procedures. United Nations Geneva
3. Economic Commission for Europe (2000) Simplification.com. United Nations New York and Geneva
4. ITPWG Workshop on Trade Facilitation (2001) Transport & Trade Problems faced by Developing Countries. UNCTAD Geneva
5. Lee R.M.(1999) Bureaucracy Made Easy: eProcedures for Global Trade. Proceedings of the 12th Electronic Commerce Conference, Bled, pp 547

6. United Nations Conference on Trade and Development (1997) Services Infrastructure for Development and Trade Efficiency Assessment, Geneva, pp 12
7. Trade Point Review 1999 – 2000 (2000) United Conference on Trade and Development Geneva
8. World Customs Organization (2001) Electronic Commerce Strategy for Customs. Brussels

Foundations of Electronic Data Interchange

Hanna Niedwiedziska[1] and Marian Niedwiedzinski[2]

[1]Technical University of Lodz, Institute of Computer Science, Sterlinga 16/18, 90-217 Lodz, Poland, hnied@ics.p.lodz.pl
[2]Department of Systems Analysis and Design, University of Lodz, 3/5 P.O.W. St., 90-225 Lodz, Poland, mariann@krysia.uni.lodz.pl

Abstract. This chapter addresses sources of electronic commerce, which are mainly connected with electronic data interchange (EDI). To have a clear picture how electronic commerce works, it is necessary to call to mind some basic information about EDI: its components, its fundamental benefits and standards.

1 Electronic Commerce

Commerce is the marketing and exchange of goods and services between buyers and sellers over distances and borders. It can be the flow of trade between countries, the transactions between companies or the relationship between customer and tradesman.

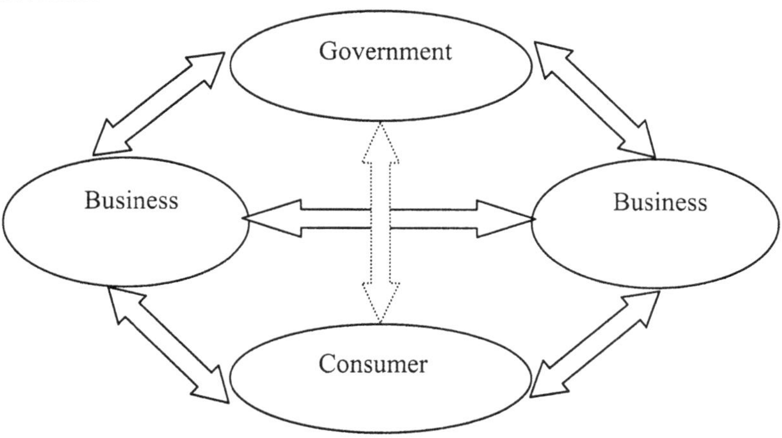

Fig. 1. Main actors and relations within electronic commerce [1].

Communication and information technology has evolved very rapidly over the last quarter of the 20th century. The base of electronic commerce is telecommunications network (in particular the Internet) and the tools like electronic mail, WWW, smart cards, electronic data interchange or automated data capture and bar code.

Sometimes Electronic Commerce is defined as doing business electronically. Electronic Commerce is a general term for the conduct of business with the assistance of telecommunications and tools based on telecommunication. The shortest definition of EC is “doing business without the paperwork” [5].
The Web, being a human–to-machine interface where data are entered for one transaction, does not solve the problem of the machine-to-machine interchange of existing data: that is done by EDI. The two technologies therefore complement each other. That is why it is necessary to present in introduction some basic information concerning Electronic Data Interchange.

2 Electronic Data Interchange

Paper documents have been the basis of all business through out the centuries. Today, a lot of documents are prepared on computers. This way requires great work, brings about duplications of operations, mistakes and numerous corrections. In today's world of business and technology there is, however, a paperless way to interchange data. Data may be moved electronically at very high transmission speed between computers. This way is named Electronic Data Interchange (EDI).
EDI as a paperless business communication method was preceded by few previous methods of operating with data. The diagram below shows this progress.

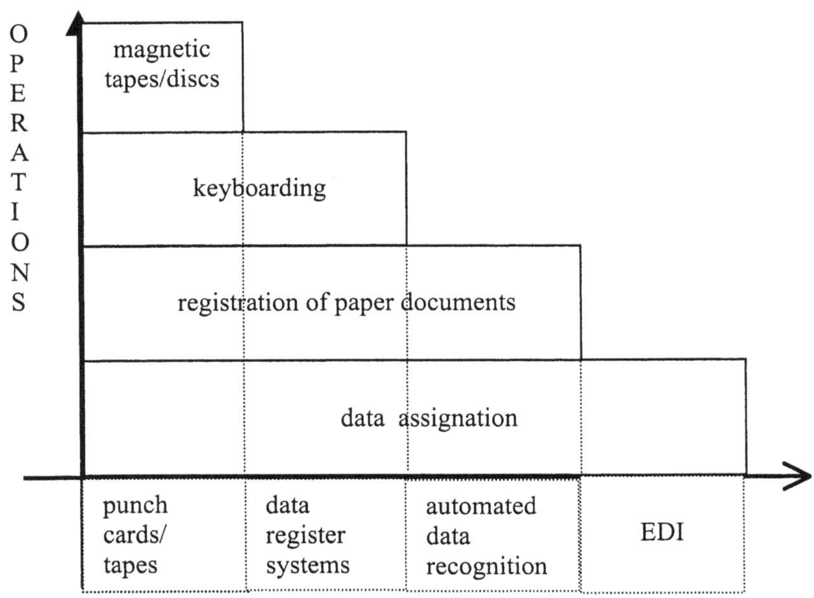

Fig. 2. Main phases of progress in methods of data input [4].

Electronic Data Interchange may be defined as the transmission of business data in a structured, electronic format from a computer application in one business to a computer application in another.
The transfer can be done through a direct computer link or through a modem in telecommunication network. EDI is communication between applications, it can occur between computers if each of them can accept identical data formats. The data or information from the computer system of the sender causes specified actions in the computer system of the receiver. An EDI system gets data from an application and translates them into one of the flexible formats defined by the EDI standard. The data are processed by the EDI system and sent according to the agreed communication method. The receiver can interpret the message and translate it into the format, which is used by his own system.
Electronic Data Interchange is possible thanks introduction public electronic document standards. These documents are called EDI messages and are available for most business functions. Currently there are development groups for trade, transport, customs, industry, finance, insurance, construction, tourism, health care and other public services.
EDI systems are very different from the data communication systems, which cause only transmission of data without further actions from the computer system. They are different from electronic mail (e-mail) which must be read by the receiver and which does not make use of standardised document formats. There is no agreement needed between the sender and the receiver relating to the way of processing mail. In case of Electronic Data Interchange, the co-ordination of the format and the contents of data are necessary. Each element of data is standardised. The computer, which receives them, can understand and realise automatically various operations, for example: modify the databases, start some procedures or make the output documents.

2.1 Components of Electronic Data Interchange

Electronic Data Interchange requires the following basic components:

- EDI translation software - executes the basic function of converting data to a standard electronic format or translating data from a standard electronic format;
- Computer hardware - it may be a PC, mini or mainframe computer. The choice of a computer depends on many factors including other data processing needs and requirements. To start up EDI, a PC system is the best because of its lower cost, simple installation and minimum hardware requirements;
- Telecommunication services - like telephone network services, phone connection, public VAN (Value Added Network), private EDI networks or Internet.

2.2 Benefits of Electronic Data Interchange

There are numerous advantages of using EDI, of which the most important are:

- Faster and more efficient exchange of information - data is introduced only once, there is much less duplication of data, EDI eliminates dependence on the mail, which can be slow and unreliable.
- Elimination of errors - EDI makes it possible to avoid errors, which can be made during manifold input data or during edition of the paper documents.
- Unlimited time of work - EDI gives possibility to do business 24 hours a day, 7 days a week independently of time zones, which enables constant up-to-date information supply at a lower expense rate.
- Elimination of language barriers in business - EDI makes use of its own, "new language" in business (standard electronic messages) and makes it possible for the users to be active on all markets.
- Use of the Just-In-Time method in manufacturing and retailing for quick response to the market.
- Reduction of payment barriers and shortening of transaction time.
- Reduction of costs and manual work associated with paper handling, data entry, transcription, manual sorting and other operations involving paper documents.
- Higher competitiveness of firms using EDI.
- Easy extension of business activities from a local market to a global one.

2.3 Standards of Electronic Data Interchange

The notion of standard determines the base of Electronic Data Interchange. Standard documents must be converted into a predefined format so every computer can easily understand them. In EDI, the phrase-predefined format is not used. Instead, standard or data standard is used. A standard strives to define all data elements that should be contained in a standard business document. This includes naming or identifying them as mandatory or optional. In addition, standardisation sequences the data elements in a preestablished order that is understandable to all computer systems. To establish standard EDI transactions, industry and special agencies have combined efforts to develop common data formats.

A good choice of EDI standard is very important. Selecting a wrong type of standard could be very costly. When a company or industry decides to implement EDI, one of the first questions asked is "What standards should be used ?".

There are four categories of standards: proprietary, industry, national and international. The first EDI systems were local systems. They concerned some trade transactions like orders or customs declarations. They were closed, because they did not respect the data structure in other users' programs. They are proprietary standards. They reflect computer file formats that are specific to one company. The standard was designed by defining data specific to one company and incorporating those data into the standard.

Some time after, the industries began to consolidate their standards efforts. Industry standards have been made. These are the standards, which can be compatible for all industry participants. For example:

- ODETTE in automotive industry,
- SWIFT in banking,
- CEFIC in chemistry,
- EDIFICE in electronics,
- EANCOM in trade.

The next groups of standards are national standards. These standards are connected with one country or with a group of countries. For example:

- TDI, TRADACOMS in Great Britain,
- SADBEL, ICOM in Belgium and Luxembourg,
- SEDAS in Austria,
- GENCOD in France,
- SEDAS, SINFOS, MADACOM in Germany,
- ANSI X12 in USA, Canada and Australia.

In 1985 the United Nations established the EDIFACT Committee to develop one world-wide EDI standard - United Nations / Electronic Data Interchange for Administration, Commerce and Transport. UN/EDIFACT is an international standard, which defines structures according to which computer documents have to be prepared and standardises business documentation in a business language common for all countries in the world.

EDIFACT covers standardisation in the following main areas:

- Syntax rules - rules governing the structure of an interchange and its functional groups, messages, segments and data elements. They are independent of the type of computers, applications or communications protocols.
- Data elements - the smallest units of information within a message. A unique identification tag, data element name, data description and representation can identify them.
- Segments - the immediate units of information in a message. A segment consists of a pre-defined set of functionally related data elements, which are defined by their sequential position within a set.
- Messages - logically grouped segments required for the type of message transaction covered.

References

1. Economic Commission for Europe (2000) Simplification.com. United Nations New York and Geneva, pp 3
2. Niedwiedziska H. (1995) Variety of EDI Standards. Proceedings 3rd National Conference EDI, ód, pp 291-295

3. Niedwiedziska H. (1996) EDIFACT – EDI standard of the Future. Scientific Bulletin of ód Technical University, ód, pp 39-48
4. Niedwiedziski M.(1989) An evaluation of computer investments in companies. State Economic Editor Company, Warsaw, pp 106
5. Raman D.(1996) Cyber Assisted Business. EDI-TIE B.V. Hoofddorp

Some Legal Aspects of Electronic Commerce

Agnieszka Grudzińska-Kuna[1] and Magorzata Ziemecka[2]

[1] The College of Computer Science, 17a Rzgowska St., 93-008 Lodz, Poland, agkuna@krysia.uni.lodz.pl
[2] Department of Systems Analysis and Design, University of Lodz, 3/5 P.O.W.St., 90-225 Lodz, Poland, mlziem@krysia.uni.lodz.pl

Abstract. To take the opportunities that electronic communication via open networks brings with it, business community needs clear, stable, secure and trustworthy environment. Creating secure and trustworthy environment required both technical and legal solutions.
This chapter addresses selected legal aspects of electronic commerce. They cover major legal issues connected with choice of jurisdiction forum and applicable law, protection of data and intellectual property rights, concluding electronic contracts.

1 Introduction

Global, open networks and electronic commerce as a platform created on theirs basis offers great opportunities for business and consumers. Using Internet provides users with virtually unlimited access to information in terms of new distribution channels and broad range of sources. Information has become a commodity. It can be digitally produced, distributed, sold in fast, cheap and simple way.
Electronic commerce enables new methods of business conducting. It implies new trades procedures by enabling to contract electronically between previously unknown parties. It also brings with it new business to business and business to consumer relations. Openness and global nature of electronic commerce bring about increase of cross-border transactions.
Furthermore, in electronic environment it can be observed emerging of new business processes, which lead to new business models.
Thus electronic commerce contribute decisively to improvements in business efficiency, competitiveness and job creation.
To take the opportunities that electronic communication via open networks brings with it, business community needs clear, stable, secure and trustworthy environment. Creating secure and trustworthy environment required both technical and legal solutions.

This chapter addresses selected legal aspects of three areas of electronic commerce, which raise the major legal issues. These areas are as follows:

- Internet based electronic commerce – jurisdiction and applicable law, intellectual property rights, domain name system regulation, data protection;
- Paperless environment – electronic contracts, digital signature, consumer protection;
- Business environment – taxation.

2 Jurisdiction and Applicable Law

The international nature of electronic commerce raises questions, which concern some of the new modalities used for achieving an offer and acceptance in the on-line environment. Electronic contracts may involve parties from different parts of the world who may have not met each other earlier. They know each other only via communications on-line. For these reasons parties drafting contracts must be thoughtful about certain terms, such as disclaimers, choice of law and jurisdictional forum, consumer protection, limitation of liability issues and questions of mandatory local law. There are three possibilities of solving this problem:

1. International private law – a national law regulating the jurisdiction and competence of different laws in international issues from national point of view.
2. International contracts – regulate relations between states and their laws and have validity among signed countries and are subject to fulfilment.
3. International laws – often created by international organisations (EU or UN). Whether this law is binding for the members or voluntary depends on the structure of the organisation.

Some issues arise in the context of private international law [29]:

- jurisdiction to adjudicate a dispute at a particular location.
- the law applicable to the dispute, which also referred to as choice of law or conflicts of law,
- the recognition and enforcement of judgements in courts in foreign jurisdictions.

Jurisdiction raises the question which national court or arbitration tribunal will hear the dispute. When there is no term concerning jurisdiction in a contract, a national court will decide if it has jurisdiction over the case in accordance with its own national rules of law. So it is recommended that e-business partners should stipulate in their contract court or arbitration panel, which will have jurisdiction over a dispute arising from their contract and law, which will apply to this dispute. Arbitration clauses are usually used in international business dealings They allow avoiding submitting disputes to a state court and national rules of procedure that at least one of parties will not be acquainted with. Arbitration may not be necessary when countries are linked by treaties, which define courts having jurisdiction and facilitating the recognition of state court decisions. However such rules do not exist in most countries and they still accord privileges to their own nationals to submit dispute to their national courts (in the absence of a clause in a contract).

A cross-border transaction is arisen the question of applicable law, which is the law that parties to a contract can choose to govern the contract or the law that is applied when parties have not made a choice of law. There is a distinction between transactions concerning only businesses (B2B) and those concerning also consumers (B2C).

In B2B transaction the principle of the autonomy of the parties to a contract is functioning. It means that parties have the freedom to choose which law will govern their contract. This principle is recognised in most countries and also in the Rome Convention of 19 June 1980 on the law applicable to contractual obligations. When the parties have not specified applicable law in their contract, the jurisdiction responsible for the case will have to decide which law is applicable. It should be noted that each country has its own guiding rules with regard to choice of law. However there are two solution that are most commonly applied in this case [11]:

1. The applicable law will be the law of country of the seller.
2. The applicable law is that of the place of the signing of the contract.

In B2C transactions sellers should express an exclusive jurisdiction on their web sites and in their contracts. Web site owners should make sure that their preferences regarding applicable law and jurisdiction are valid and enforceable. So it must be clear where the contract is formed. There are specific rules applicable to contracts for the supply of goods or services to a consumer providing that one of the following conditions is met [2]:

1. The consumer has received in his home state a specific invitation addressed to him by advertising before the conclusion of the contract and he takes, in his home state, all the necessary steps to conclude the contract.
2. The supplier has received the consumer's order in the country where the consumer is domiciled.
3. The consumer travelled from his country to another country one where he gave his order to buy a good, provided that the consumer's journey was arranged by the seller for the purpose of inducing the consumer to buy.

The seller and the consumer can contractually designate a competent court in this particular contract, but some conditions should be well-defined [2]:

- a clause must have been entered into after the dispute has arisen, or
- the consumer is allowed to bring proceedings in courts other than those located in his country or the defendant's, or
- courts of the same country where the consumer and the supplier are located are designated.

The Brussels Convention, which is the relevant law for jurisdiction, is now proving to be adequate for electronic commerce. The European Union adopted a Regulation on jurisdiction and the recognition and enforcement of judgements in civil and commercial matters in December 2000. This Regulation will replace the Brussels and Lugano Conventions and provide rules for determining the competent court in case of international disputes, concerning e-commerce transactions within EU. The Regulation provides special rules for parts of contracts involving consumers. For example, a consumer could decide to sue a supplier before the courts of his own Member State whenever the supplier takes activities towards the consumer's Member State. So the sellers will have to face proceedings in any of the EU Member Sates in the case they do not put on their web site a disclaimer to exclude certain countries.

3 Intellectual Property Rights

The international character of electronic commerce raises questions for the nature of intellectual property law. The digital economy has the impact on the intellectual property system, namely, copyright and related rights, patents and trademarks, which are confronted with new issues created by EC. The evaluation of electronic commerce and its relationship with intellectual property is therefore likely to be an intensive and ongoing process, which will require vigilant monitoring of developments.

According to Intellectual property rights (IPR) creative work is a kind of property. The owner can use, rent and sell his rights over the property. He is also given an exclusive right over the use of his work in a certain period of time.

A kind of property right attached to the original work is a copyright. It prohibits copying someone else's work without his permission. It has the power over the right to copy the work even up to 70 years after the author's death. This period of time can differ depending on the kind of property being protected (books, musical compositions, photographs, films, sculpture, maps, advertisements, web page paintings, computer programs, databases). To people who are involved in musical and audio-visual creation (actors, singers, musicians, producers, and broadcasting organisations) neighbouring rights are granted. The related rights are in power for 50 years after the performance, fixation or first transmission. In Europe registration, copyright note or other formal acts are not required for copyright protection.

The Bern Convention is the most important international agreement for the protection of creative work. Over 120 countries have ratified it. Other agreements are International Regulatory Framework and EU Regulatory Framework. The European Commission Proposal for Directive of 10 December 1997 deals with reproduction and distribution rights, communication to the public rights, and legal protection of anti-copying and rights management system. Member States are obliged to inform network operators about exceptions from the reproduction right, like hidden copies stored on Internet servers. They can also offer a recompense for private copying according to their local law traditions and practice. The adaptation of the existing IPR European framework to the on-line environment is the directive's aim. It should be done in co-operation with international commitments, because such co-operation will stimulate creativity and innovation by ensuring that all protected by the copyright property law are equally protected throughout the single market. It will make cross-border trading with protected goods and services possible, with special attention to new electronic products and services, both on and off-line. Fair recompense must be also given to the authors if their work is used for private copying, photocopying, and illustrations for teaching and scientific research.

Member States are required to provide two types of technological adjuncts to the protection of copyright and related rights [29]:

- "anti-circumvention" provision – relates to need of rights holders to rely on technological measures to protect their work against infringement,
- "rights management information" – provides legal support to network-based rights management systems.

The WIPO Copyright Treaty (WCT) and the WIPO Performances and Phonograms Treaty (WPPT) were concluded at WIPO in 1996.

The directive on the legal protection of databases aims to ensure that appropriate and not varying level of databases protection will be a mean of securing the author's remuneration. It protects databases which contents suggest maker's own intellectual and creative work. Note that it only protects the databases, not the contents. The directive covers rental and lending right and certain rights related to copyright, protection of computer programmes and the term of protection of copyright, but it excludes protection of computer programmes used in making and operating the databases that can be accessed by electronic means. The protection rights are in power for 70 years after the death of the author. The new economic right protects large investments made in obtaining, verifying or presenting database's contents, and it lasts for 25 years from the 1 January of the year that follows the database's completion.

Trademarks protect signs that vary goods and services of one enterprise from those of other enterprises. Usually a registration is necessary. The offered protection has no time limit. Trademarks can be also used as metatags. They are not visible on the web site, but exist as a keyword in the page's HTML code. They enable the search engines to list a web site in response to a search. The more there are metatags hidden in the code the higher will the engine rank the site in the search results. Some trademark holders have challenged the unauthorised use of their trademark as a metatag. Well-known marks are given a special treatment and protection, because fame attracts attention. This protection was well established in the Paris Convention.

Patents are protections stimulating innovation and invention in technology. They protect the investments and the development of new technologies, and so give the inventors means to finance their research and work. The time of the protection is usually 20 years. USA patents don't have force in the EU, and also business models can be patent in USA but not in EU.

Shapes and appearance developed industrially are protected by industrial designs. Registered industrial designs are protected for about 10 to 15 years.

Unlawful acquisition of company's intellectual portfolio and other commercial practises are prohibiting by competition law. EU and international competition law can vary in different countries. Internet is not included in this set of laws.

4 DNS Regulation

Historically domain names were created for host identification purpose. Contrary to the numerical IP address, domain name is easy to remember. Domain names are organised in hierarchical structure of inverted tree. Each domain that branches from the root is called top-level domain (TLD). TLDs are used globally but their number is limited. Currently, these generic TLDs are: .com, .net, .org, .edu (exclusive to American universities), .gov, .mil, (exclusive to American government), .int and country code TLDs such as .us, .uk, .pl etc. From technical point of view DNS is a distributed database, which is query in order to translate domain name into IP address.
Because of its form domain name can reflect company name or product so that its holder can be easy recognised to Internet users. Therefore the main legal issues arising from domain names are related to trademarks. While domain names must be unique, trademarks may be identical if the companies are in different industries or in different geographic area. On the other hand domain name can be register in a bad faith. For example to sell the domain name to the company, whose brand it reflects. Speculative registering also often aims at disrupting the business of competitor or confusing its consumers. Such abusive registration of trademarks owned by third party is called cybersquatting.
Historically DNS has been co-ordinated by the Assigned Number Authority (IANA) located at University of Southern California. Since 1993, under co-operative agreement with National Science Foundation (NSF) Network Solution Inc.(NSI) has been the exclusive provider of domain name registration services for gTLD.
US government control under DNS and increase of trademark disputes entailed widespread dissatisfaction in Internet community and international authorities with the manner in which DNS has been run. In response to this, on the basis of US White Paper issued in June 1998, the Internet Corporation for Assigned Names and Numbers (ICANN) was created. It is non-profit public benefit California corporation, successor to IANA. It is ICANN responsibility *inter alia* to co-ordinate the management of the DNS, to allocate of IP address spaces.
In 1999 World Intellectual Property Organisation (WIPO) issued its Final Report on the Internet Domain Name Process. The Final Report contained set of recommendations concerning discouraging cybersquatters, dispute resolutions, exclusions for certain "famous" trademarks from domain name registration and addition of new gTLDs. ICANN supported implementation of WIPO recommendations in its Uniform Domain Name Dispute Resolution Policy (UDRP). UDRP establishes institution of an administrative proceeding to provide fast and inexpensive method to resolve cybersquatting cases.
In July 1999 a quorum of gTLD Registrars including NSI adopted of standard agreement for all gTLD DNS registrations that would effectively achieve a uniform dispute resolution procedure as recommended by WIPO.
At European Union level, the European Commission and the Member States participate in the work of the Governmental Advisory Committee (GAC). The GAC

has already provided the ICANN with advice on questions such as dispute resolution, geographical diversity and policies for ccTLD Registries. The Commission also encourages the Members States to participate in ICANN.
As far as domain name regulation is concerned the Commission aims at preparing code of conduct or other appropriate instrument to address abusive registration domain names and developing of alternative dispute resolution (consistent with WIPO recommendations) appropriate for TLD Registries operating in EU. Furthermore creation of legal framework for the new top level domain ".EU" might facilitate the establishment of clear Europeanwide guiding principles that would entail a "de facto" harmonisation of some national practices [4].

5 Data Protection

Although Internet has made it easier for the corporate marketing departments to collect data about customers and visitors to web sites, there are some rules that must be followed in collecting and using this information. The EU Data Protection Directive 95/46/EC of 24 October 1995 and the Telecommunications Data Protection Directive 97/66/EC of 15 December 1997 are regulations that need special attention. The free flow of data in the Union, and at the same time guarding the most basic rights and freedoms of individuals are the aims of the Data Protection Directive. It enables and prohibits any kind of interception or surveillance of electronic messages. Member States must decide under which conditions the processing of personal data is legitimate. According to the directive personal data can be gathered only for clearly named, lawful, and easy to understand purposes and must be used in a way that matches those purposes.
Personal data collection and processing is possible only if the individual has explicitly agreed or if some law allows it. Data must be processed only in purposes agreed during its collection and shouldn't be kept longer than it is necessary. Data must be secured from any unlawful or accidental destruction or loss. Before transferring to a third party an agreement must be made with the data subject. The customer must have access to personal data concerning him and can make a request to delete or correct it, if it is not complete, accurate or kept up to date, or to opt him out of the processing operation or certain uses of the data. The request must be granted in an appropriate period of time.
If the risk presented by processing the data or its nature is high so must be the security level. If the personal data is used in direct marketing the individual can disagree with the processing of data. Also payment systems must compliance with the data protection principles.
Although there are several security systems available, it should be kept in mind that detecting surveillance or interception is very difficult.
If the level of data protection in a country is inadequate, the Data Protection Directive forbids transfer of data to that country. In USA a data protection office does not exist in the government, so the level of data protection is not sufficient. But blocking the data flow to the USA is unreasonable. On 26 July 2000 the Euro-

pean Commission adopted a decision on the adequacy of the data protection in the US with the EU Data Protection Directive, which entered into force on 1 November 2000. The Safe Harbour is intended only in the USA, but there are, and will be, agreements with other countries.
At the beginning of 1999 the Council Decision authorising the Member States, on behalf of the European Community, to approve unanimously the adoption of the recommendation of the protection of privacy on the Internet by the Committee of Ministers of the Council of Europe came into force. It carefully considers the right of individuals to be informed whenever their data are being processed, and the circumstances in which data may be transmitted to third parties, especially when they are used in direct marketing. The decision also ensures compatibility between:

- the Directive 97/66/EC of the European Parliament and of the Council of 15 December 1997 (processing of personal data and protection of privacy in the telecommunication sector);
- the Directive 95/46/EC of European Parliament and of the Council of 24 October 1995 (protection of individuals with regard to the processing of personal data and on the free movement of such data).

6 Electronic Contracts

Contract is formed when one party makes an offer and the other party accepts this offer. The exchange of consents gives legal effect of the contract and changes the status of rights and obligations of involved parties. For example: placing an order notifies the supplier of intention of the client to enter contractual relationship. The acceptance of the order by supplier (by acknowledgement) creates an obligation of supplier to dispatch goods and the obligation of the receiver to pay for them. Both parties have also the obligations for the fulfilment of import and export formalities, tax declaration, etc. (if they are from different countries).
National law often requires a written document or even specific form of written document for validity of the contract.
Being involved in commerce activities from time to time gives rise to legal disputes. This happens, when parties disagree on the certain terms or conditions of the contract, or when a specific issue has not been taken into account. Even existence of the contract can be disputed. Specific concerns hereby rise about rights and protection of the consumers.
In electronic commerce both making and accepting an offer is done via open telecommunication network. This poses several questions:

- What constitutes an offer?
- What information must be available to the consumer and before the conclusion of the contract?
- How could an offer be accepted?
- In what language should terms and condition of the contact appear?
- Which national law is to be applicable law?

Most commerce laws were written before even businesses engaged in on-line commerce, therefore they did not adequately cover relationships and obligations in electronic commerce environment. However there has now been a wealth of regulatory development in this field at global, European Union (EU) and national level. Because of global character of electronic commerce international initiatives are of great importance. These regulations are supposed to be adapted to national laws.

One of the forms that facilitate implementing legislative reforms at national level is model law. Model law is intended as a recommendation for national legislators. For instance the United Commission on International Trade Law (UNCITRAL) created in 1996 the Model Law on Electronic Commerce. It offers national legislators a set of internationally accepted rules, which show how legal obstacles of development of electronic commerce could be overcome. It contains 17 Articles governing legal implications of electronic messages. These Articles also contain three specific provisions for electronic commerce. UNCITRAL Model Law has been incorporated in many legal systems (e.g., in Singapore, France, Colombia, the Republic of Korea, and the US State of Illinois).

Furthermore UNICITRAL is drafting Uniform Rules for electronic signature in order to ensure security of, and confidence in electronic transactions.

For the growth of international electronic trade, ability of businesses to enter into contractual relationships on-line, both with consumers and other organisational partners is critical. At European level Directive on Electronic Commerce (2000/31/EC) provides a legal framework within which contracts may be concluded on line. Under the Directive information society services[1] can be provided throughout the European Union if they comply with the laws in their home Member State. The E–Commerce Directive establishes rules in following areas: definition of where operators are established, transparency obligations for operators, transparency requirements for commercial communication conclusion and validity of electronic contracts, liability of the Internet intermediaries and on-line dispute settlement.

According to this Directive, Member States must ensure that their laws allow for contracts to be concluded electronically and that any obstacles, for example, requirement of handwritten form, are removed.

E-commerce Directive also seeks to make the contractual process more transparent. Therefore service provider should communicate "comprehensibly and unambiguously" prior to the placement of the order, at least the following information

- the different technical steps needed for concluded the contract;
- the language available for conclusion of contract;
- the technical means for identifying and correcting input errors;
- whether the contract will be archived and accessible;
- terms of contract and general condition in the way that allows recipient to store and reproduce them.

---

[1] Under E-commerce Directive this term is used in the meaning of Article 1.2. of Directive 98/34/EC as amended by Directive 98/48/EC.

The supplier should also incorporate on his web site an explicit clause of the applicable law. When parties have not chosen the applicable law, the governing law is that of the country with which the contract is most closely connected. In B2B contracts, in almost all cases, it is the country of establishment of the provider of goods or services. In case of information society services provider it is usually place where the business is legally registered. It is not necessarily the same place, where his web site is located.

On the other hand, in business to consumer contracts in absence of choice of law under a contract, the governing law is that of the country in which the consumer normally lives.

Furthermore, the consumer must be communicated in writing or in another durable medium such as by electronic mail among the others things about:

- address to which complaints can be addresses,
- after-sales services and guarantees;
- conditions and procedures for exercising the right of withdrawal.

This must be done in good time during the performance of the contract, or at latest at the time of delivery.

A crucial text for performing electronic transaction is Article 14 of the Vienna Convention which defines terms "offer" and "invitation to make offers" This Article implies a question whether general offer on the seller' s web site should be considered as a binding. Answer to this question is provided by Article 3.2.1.of Electronic Commerce Agreement"[2] which states:

"A message constitutes an offer if it includes a proposal for concluding a contract addresses to one or more specific persons which is sufficiently definite and indicates the intention of the sender of the offer to bound in case of acceptance. A message made available electronically at large shall, unless otherwise stated therein, not constitute an offer"

Regarding above definition the first step in forming an electronic contract should be an offer made by the purchaser. To protect the consumer the E-commerce Directive specifies that if the supplier accepts an offer he has to acknowledge its receipt without undue delay and by electronic means.

6.1 Interchange Agreement

Another example of bringing greater legal certainty to electronic commerce cross border transactions is contractual solution. Before conducting a transaction, involved parties enter into interchange agreement in which they accept common rights and obligations and another technical, legal and organisational terms and conditions concerning electronic communication between them. They can rely on law of such a contract in their e-commerce-based transactions.

Interchange agreement derives from using Electronic Data Interchange (EDI) technology. EDI usually took place between business partners who have long history of trading with each other. Exchange of data was possible after prior estab-

---

[2] Approved in March 2000 by UN/CEFACT

lishing of communication system. EDI Agreement was necessary in those cases, where there was no established legal framework. Such an agreement has to concern three aspect of interchange of electronic documents: technical, legal and security. Compared to the normal business agreement EDI Agreement includes more control and data security issues e.g.:

- processing and acknowledgement of receipt of messages;
- security of messages;
- confidentiality and protection of personal data;
- recording and storage of messages;
- admissibility of evidence of messages.

First standard interchange agreement was developed by International Chamber of Commerce in 1987. It was called UNICID[3] Rules. Since than, both The European Commission and United Nations have put forward their models of EDI Agreement[4].

Afterwards, many developed countries have produced their own variants of these standard agreements.

There are two main concerns on contractual solution.

Firstly, it can be obsolete due to recent development of legal regulations at both international and national level.

Secondly, development of telecommunication infrastructure and Internet, in particular, has changed the nature of electronic business communication. It has become more rapid and accidental. Trading partners that have no previous dealing with each other often engage in commercial trade. In such a situation it is impossible for them to negotiate interchange agreement before the e-transaction.

Returning to the first issue it is argued that contractual solution can help to overcome conflict of law problems [15]. These problems arise because of different degree to which different countries adopt their national systems. Of course cross border transactions for many years has sometimes implied conflicts between national laws. But nowadays perhaps it is a problem of scale.

Because of openness and global nature of electronic commerce, the volume of cross border transaction has considerably increased compared to the pass. To meet these new requirements Legal Working Group of UN/CEFACT has devised a form of modified interchange agreement which will permit complete strangers to establish a contractual relationship on agreed terms using initial exchange of messages [15]. This new form is called Electronic Commerce Agreement (E-Agreement).

E-Agreement is intended to serve business-to-business partners. Therefore it does not incorporate any provisions relating the consumer protection. The E-Agreement provides the framework of basic provisions for conclusion of subsequent e-transaction in sound legal environment. It is concluded by exchange of the Instrument of Offer and Acceptance by electronic means. Both instruments should be recorded and stored by each party.

---

[3] The Uniform Rules of Conduct for the Interchange of Trade Data by Teletransmission.

[4] UN version is called Recommendation 26 of UN/CEFACT

In instrument of offer "proposer" offers to enter into commercial contractual relationship. Instrument of offer contains the term under which he is prepared to do it. Among the other things it includes proposed form of communication, communication standards, software, TPPs, definitions of basic notions concerned with transaction such as an offer, receipt and conclusion. Instrument of offer specifies also law that shall govern both E-Agreement and E-Transaction.
Developing of Electronic Commerce Agreement is the first step, the next is to develop software to facilitate its use by business users in the national and international environment.

7 Digital Signature

Electronic commerce offers great opportunities for business and consumers, but it also brings with it significant risks. Commercial transaction requires the security such as:

1. Document authentication,
   Authentication means possibility to verify true sender of document.
2. Integrity,
   Integrity ensures that document is not modified by an unauthorised party.
3. Non-repudiation,
   Non-repudiation proves that the documents were exchanged. This prevents any refusal of receipt from the involved parties.
4. Confidentiality.
   Confidentiality prevents unauthorised access to an exchange document.

Traditional commerce is heavily based on performative documents that cause a change in the status of rights and obligations of the involved parties. These paper documents have to be signed personally to develop legal relevance and commitment. With the ongoing shift of traditional commerce to electronic, traditional documents become electronic or digital ones. Paperless nature of electronic documents causes some fears of the parties related to fulfilling the security requirements. Therefore there is a strong need for implementing technical and legal solutions, that replace in virtual world the psychical security of the paper-based world. It is important that these solutions to be trustworthy and consumers have confidence with them. Cryptography is effective tool for addressing above concerns in electronic environment.
Two important applications of cryptography are digital signatures and encryption. Digital signatures can help to prove the origin of data (authentication) and verify whether data has been altered (integrity). Encryption can help keeping data and communication confidential.
Electronic signatures based on "public key cryptography" are called digital signatures.
Technically speaking, digital signatures are usually created and verified by asymmetric cryptographic techniques similar to those used for encryption. Two complementary keys are generated and assigned to a user. One of them is used for

generation of a digital signature (it is a private key) whereas the other is used for verification of such a signature (it is a public key). It is of course crucial that the private key cannot be computed from the public key.
Contrary to cryptography used for confidentiality purposes, digital signature is a kind of seal, which is annexed to the data and leaves the content of electronic document intact.
With the help of the sender's public key, the recipient can find out whether the signed data has been altered and check that the public and private key of the sender are a complementary key-pair. Even the smallest change of the data would be discovered immediately.
There is no relation between digital signature and someone's personal signature. One can have several key pairs corresponding to his roles. Moreover he is not obliged to communicate under his name – he can choose a pseudonym, which safeguards his anonymity in transactions.
Keys may be allocated to private persons, legal persons or entities without legal status (e.g. department of an enterprise, working group or server).
Coherence between content of electronic document and digital signature is realised by applying hash functions. Hash functions are mathematical one-way functions, where some variable-length message is transformed into fixed-length hash. It is not possible to draw a conclusion from the hash value to the initial input message. Digital signatures are created by applying the private key not onto message itself but onto output stream of the hash value.
Verification of the authenticity and integrity of data does not prove the identity of the owner of the public key. Reliable information on the identity of the key owner can be given either by key owner himself or confirmed by a third party (e.g. a person or institution mutually trusted by both parties). In the context of digital signatures these third parties are called certification authorities (CA).
Main task of CA, which can be either public or private, is to issue relevant certificate. Certificate is a document which:

1. Identifies the CA issuing it,
2. Names, identifies or describes an attribute of entity or individual that is subscriber of certification,
3. Contains the subscriber's public key,
4. Is digitally signed by the CA issuing it [7].

CAs offer a range of certificates, graded according to the level of inquiry used to confirm the identity of the subject of the certificate. For example from personal information provided in on-line registration process through appearance in person, presenting registered credentials to thorough investigation.
CAs issue several types of certificates: indetifying certificates, authorising certificates, transactional certificates and time stamps.
An identifying certificate binds the name of subject of certificate to its public key. An authorising certificate certifies attributes of the subject other than identity, such as address, age, different kinds of membership etc. A third type of certificate, the transactional certificate attest to some fact about transaction. In this case CA works as a notary service.

A time stamp is a cryptographically unforgeable digital attestation that a document was in existence at a particular time.

Public key system can operate at a national or an international level, where thousands or millions of keys are involved. Therefore in order to fulfil the requirements of free accessibility of public keys and to facilitate their use in such an environment, automatic key management is necessary. This can be achieved by creating Public Key Infrastructure (PKI). PKI is based on three fundamental elements:

- certification authorities,
- repository of public keys, certificates and Certificate Revocation Lists (CRLs)[5,]
- management functions.

Certificate authority itself must be reliable, so the certifier may need to be certified. This issue can be addressed by both hierarchy of certificate authorities and a system of cross-certified authorities. On the top of a hierarchical structure (root of the tree) there are authorities, which create the overall guidelines for the entire PKI and establish policy for all certification authorities within their domain. Beneath CAs operate. They are expected to certify the public key of the users according to established policy. At the lowest level of hierarchy there are local registration authorities. They act as an intermediary between CA and a user. They can for example receipt enquiry for certificate on behalf of CA. In hierarchy, authorities at the higher level certificate public keys belonging to the authorities at beneath level. Cross-certification occurs within the same level.

Owing to strong demand for cryptographic services and products, concerns are expressed that abuse of cryptography by criminals or terrorists would make it increasingly difficult to fight against crime or prevent criminal and terrorist activities. These arguments implied some control measures of using cryptography. There are two main regulation schemes: export/import controls and lawful access to encryption keys. Whilst the export control measures are internationally widely applied, the second concept generates considerable controversy.

The underlying principle of this approach is to require that products and services incorporating encryption allow access to the respective keys. This would permit government agencies to decrypt a ciphered text. There are few different technical and institutional ways to provide key access. The two most known concepts are key escrow and key recovery. Generally speaking, these concepts imply that copies (escrow concept) or information (recovery concept) about relevant keys are given either directly to government agencies or to TTPs. In discussion on encryption regulation the weak points of these concepts are stressed. The most critical ones are:

- Any involvement of a third party in confidential communication increases its vulnerability;
- The costs associated with key access scheme can be very high;
- Key access schemes can be easily circumvented.

Above discussion of implementation cryptography in the context of electronic commerce has proved that using PKI with qualified certificate is the most secure

---

[5] CRLs are "hot lists" of cancelled certificates

and private way of signing an electronic document from technical point of view [18]. The next step is to gain public support and approval for the use of the technology. It means to make consumers recognise the technology as trustworthy and secure sufficiently to conduct electronic transaction. To achieve the aim, technical implementations require legal adjustment for their acceptance and accommodation into the legal system. In the current situation the most important legal problems are connected with recognition of digital documents signed with digital signature as an equivalent to written form and their recognition as evidence in legal proceedings in case of dispute resolution. Therefore there is extremely important for international organisation as the European Union or the United Nations to establish a legal framework for using electronic signatures. At European Union level Directive on Electronic Signatures (2000/31/EC) addresses this issue. This directive differentiates between following:

- „advanced electronic signature" and "electronic signature".
- "qualified certificate" and "certificate".

Advanced electronic signature must be uniquely linked to the signatory. It identifies the signatory and is linked to the data to which it relates in such a manner that any change of data can be detected. Advance electronic signature is created using means, which are under sole control of signatory.

"Electronic signature" serves as a method of authentication of data, to which is attached. Electronic signature is less secure than advanced one, as it does not have to be "uniquely link" to the signatory.

"Qualified certificate" is a certificate which meets the specified requirements and is provided by certification service provider who also fulfils specified requirements.

Under E-signatures Directive advanced electronic signature must be treated in the same manner as a handwritten signature if it is supported by qualified certificate and created by a "secure-signature-creation-device". It is also admissible as evidence in legal proceedings. On the hand electronic signatures cannot be denied legal effectiveness solely on the ground that it is in electronic form, not based upon qualified certificate or not created by secure signature creation device.

Moreover E-signatures Directive ensures that Member States will not make provision of certification services subject to prior authorisation, although they may introduce or maintain voluntary accreditation schemes aiming at enhanced levels of certification-service provision.

8 Consumer Protection

Legal provisions for consumer protection differ between European Union Member States. Although they are all meant to protect the consumer, a clear, common set of consumer protection standards still does not exist in Europe, so before e-commerce grows to large-scale, mechanisms to protect the consumers have to be developed.

Even though shopping in the cyberspace gets more and more popular every day, some matters still concern the consumers and stop them from buying in cyber markets. Potential buyers wonder whether it is possible not to receive the ordered merchandise, or if it can turn out to be defective. They also ask questions if credit cards are opened to misuse once their number has entered the Web, and whether bought programmes can damage or infect computers and systems.
The international nature of the Internet environment makes it hard to decide which court would have jurisdiction over a given transaction and which court should see to that the sued and judged cyber-shop follows the verdict. And another problem arises: would an unsatisfied customer from Europe fly to Japan to obtain his satisfaction? Well, it probably depends on the value of the bought product, but in most cases the answer is no.
Unless customer are assured of the existence of mechanism to lodge complains and address grievances as at the presence of a universal dispute resolution and redress system they will hesitate to shop on the Internet. Technological solutions, which could be achieved by industry self-regulation, are needed. Government input should be based on simple and predictable legal tools [14].
Chat room tips and instant messages are the most efficient means of on-line promotion. Web sites and e-mails can rival with the standard off-line promotion, like billboards, magazine ads, theatre previews and television commercials. Analysing how off-line and on-line promotion influence entertainment consumption gives an impression that perhaps one day Web promotion will be more effective and popular than the one on television.
An absolutely necessary part of financing electronic business and growth of new, free charged services is commercial communications. In the interest of consumer protection and fair-trading they must meet a number of clear demands.
The consumer should know that the message is commercial as soon as he receives it, especially by e-mail. The advertiser must respect opt-out lists, which are lists of people who have explicitly marked that they don't wish to receive unsolicited commercial e-mails, and opt-in lists in which an earlier permission of the recipient is required before sending of unsolicited commercial message. The Electronic Commerce Directive gives Member States the right to authorise and prohibit the sending of unsolicited commercial communication by e-mail [2].
The Organisation for Economic Co-operation and Development (OECD) Committee on Consumer Policy in April of 1998 has started to develop a set of basic guidelines to protect consumers taking part in e-commerce and not to create barriers to trade and provide a framework and a set of principles.
Governments, businesses, consumers and their representatives are the main actors of effective consumer protection, but nothing should stop any party from exceeding the guidelines or adopting more stringent provision to protect consumer online.

9 Taxation

The Internet is a truly global phenomenon. The challenges posed to tax systems by the Internet are real. The allocation of taxing rights must be based upon mutually agreed principles and a common understanding of how these principles should be applied. Tax authorities must respond by reaching globally consistent approaches to taxing these activities via the Internet.
The Internet opens up possibilities to improve the administration of tax systems but also opens up new avenues for tax evasion and avoidance. From the perspective of tax legislator these developments may challenge many of the traditional concepts embedded in tax laws and tax treaties.
Effective enforcement of tax laws requires accurate identification of a party and evidence that can be linked to the party. In fiscal matters this equates to identifying a taxpayer, obtaining evidence of income and linking the income to the taxpayer.

9.1 Indirect Tax

Cross-border transaction must comply with specific indirect taxation rules like Value Added Tax (VAT) and withholding taxes. Payment of VAT is determined based on what, where and to whom goods and services are sold. There are important considerations for indirect taxation, for example when different rates of tax apply to goods and to services. So, a product in physical form may attract one rate of tax, but the same product in digital form can be considered a service by the tax authorities and attract a different rate of tax. It should be noted that EU recognises digitally delivered products such as software, digital music, digital books, etc. as services.
The existing VAT system applies to goods sold electronically and then delivered by traditional way. When a business, which was established in the EU, sells goods to a private citizen within the EU, the VAT rules for mail order apply. Some individuals and organisations are considered "non-taxable person" (private individuals, public bodies, charities, businesses with low turnover or wholly exempt activities).
The Internet is also a means of delivering a product itself (digitised product such as music, games, training material, software, books, etc.). In the EU Vat legislation such products are classified as supplying of services and also taxed as services. The EU mail order rules regarding turnover thresholds do not apply.
The current VAT rules for services do not adequately address the supply of services delivered on-line by digital means, especially these traded between EU and non-EU countries. Electronically delivered services originating in the EU are subject to VAT irrespective of the place of consumption. In the non-EU countries they are not subject to VAT even delivered within the EU. This situation may constitute a major distortion of competition and place EU service providers at a disadvantage in relation to non-EU ones.

The EU Commission has presented a proposal for a directive to modify the rules applying VAT to certain services supplied by electronically means, subscription-based and pay-per-view radio and television broadcasting. The goal of this initiative is to create a fair market for the taxation of digital e-commerce in accordance with the principle agreed at the 1998 OECD Ministerial Conference. A common rule in this proposal is that no new or additional taxes are needed for electronic commerce. Existing taxes should be adopted so that they can apply to e-commerce. The proposal will ensure that when electronic services (software, computer services, information and cultural, artistic, entertainment, etc. digital delivery by the Internet) are supplied for consumption within the EU, they are subject to VAT, but when they are supplied outside the EU they are exempt from VAT.

9.2 Direct Tax

E-commerce probably will not have any effect on direct taxation. Because Internet allows performing transaction on distance, it gives an opportunity to a business to reduce or avoid tax footprint outside the country where it is resident. Web sites and servers through which sales are made cannot be constitute a taxable presence in another country. A web site alone is not a fixed place of business and so does not create a taxable presence in another jurisdiction [2].

9.3 Withholding Tax

Many countries have withholding taxes on certain types of income originating within their borders. For a business, they are at best a cash flow but at worst a real cost if full credit for withheld taxes cannot be obtained against the business' home country tax liabilities. However, no country has yet introduced a withholding tax specifically on income generated by electronic means, so a company will not increase its exposure to withholding taxes by doing business on the Internet [2].

References

1. Baum M, Perrit H (1991) Electronic contracting, publishing and EDI law. New York
2. Baumgartner J, Schulze C (2000) Don't Panic! Do e-commerce. A beginner's guide to european law affecting e-commerce, The European Commission's Electronic Commerce Team
3. Bons R, Lee R, Wagenaar R (1994) Implementing international electronic trade using open-EDI. Working Report No. 94.12.01. the University of Erasmus, Rotterdam
4. Communication COM(2000)202 The organisation and management of the internet. International and European policy issues 1998-2000

5. Council Regulation (EC) no 44/2001 of 22 December 2000 on jurisdiction and the recognition and enforcement of judgements in civil and commercial matters
6. Directive 2000/31/EC of 8 June 2000 on certain legal aspects of information society services, in particular electronic commerce, in the Internal Market (Directive on electronic commerce)
7. Froomkin AM (1996) The essential role of trusted third parties in electronic commerce. 75 Oregon L. Rev. 49,
8. Ganzaroli A, Mitrakas A (1997) Trusted third parties in open electronic commerce: the phase of negotiations in the international trade transactions model, In: Global business in practice, 10th International Bled Electronic Commerce Conference, Bled, pp 242-256
9. Gisler M, Runge A, Zimmermann HD (1997) Realization of legal requirements on digital signatures in electronic commerce. In: Global business in practice. 10th International Bled Electronic Commerce Conference, Bled, pp 257-276
10. Grudziska-Kuna A, Ziemecka M (1999) Making secure and trustworthy environment for electronic commerce. In: BIS'99 3rd International Conference on Business Information Systems, Pozna, pp 107-116
11. International Trade Centre UNCTAD/WTO (2000) Secrets of electronic commerce. A guide for small and medium-sized exporters. Geneva
12. Lei L, Mitrakas A (1996) A multi-disciplinary perspective for electronic commerce. In: Electronic commerce for trade efficiency and effectiveness, 9th International Conference on EDI-IOS, Bled, pp 351-363
13. Liikanen E (2001) Regulatory reform in the information society – the European Commission's approach. In: Executive Briefing. e-Services for trade, investment and enterprise, Forum on Trading into the Future, Geneva, pp 73-74
14. Lynch E (1997) Protecting consumer in the cybermarket. The OECD Observer, Oct-Nov, pp 11-13
15. Marsh D (2000) The UN/CEFACT Electronic commerce interchange agreement. In: Business briefing. Global electronic commerce, Forum on EC for Transition Economies in the Digital Age, Geneva, pp 84-86
16. Organisation for Economic Co-operation and Development (1997) Electronic commerce: the challenges to tax authorities and taxpayers
17. Organisation for Economic Co-operation and Development (1999) Recommendation of the OECD Council concerning guidelines for consumer protection in the context of electronic commerce.
18. Organisation for Economic Co-operation and Development. Cryptography policy: the guidelines and the issues OCDE/GD(97)204
19. Poullet Y (2000) How to regulate the internet: New paradigms for internet governance. In: Business briefing. Global electronic commerce, Forum on EC for Transition Economies in the Digital Age, Geneva, pp 95-98
20. Proposal for a directive amending Directive 77/388/EEC as regards the value added tax arrangements applicable to certain services supplied by electronic mean, COM(2000) 349 final, Brussels
21. Proposal for a Regulation on administrative co-operation in the field of indirect taxation (VAT), COM(2000) 349 final, Brussels
22. Quirchmayr G (2001) Professional legal solutions – a prerequisite for successful electronic commerce. In: 14th Bled Electronic Commerce Conference, Bled, pp 11-16

23. Recommendation for a Council Decision for protection of privacy on the internet, COM (1999) 19 final, Brussels
24. Rigby A (2001) European regulations on e-commerce. In: Executive Briefing. e-Services for trade, investment and enterprise, Forum on Trading into the Future, Geneva, pp 86-88
25. Rodin RA, Vo-Verde D (2000) Domain name and regulation and cybersquatting. In: Business briefing. Global electronic commerce, Forum on EC for Transition Economies in the Digital Age, Geneva, pp 90-94
26. Scott C, Ross G (2000) e-Business and taxation: the business perspective. In: Business briefing. Global electronic commerce, Forum on EC for Transition Economies in the Digital Age, Geneva, pp 87-89
27. Visa International and MasterCard International (1997) Secure electronic transaction (SET) specification. Version 1.0
28. World Intellectual Property Organization (1999) Final report of the WIPO internet domain name process
29. World Intellectual Property Organization (2000) Primer on electronic commerce and intellectual property issues

Part 2 Neural Networks

Competitive Neural Networks for Customer Choice Models

Walter A. Kosters and Michiel C. van Wezel

Leiden Institute of Advanced Computer Science
Universiteit Leiden
P.O. Box 9512, 2300 RA Leiden, The Netherlands
Email: {kosters,michiel}@liacs.nl

Abstract. In this paper we propose and examine two different models for customer choices in for instance a wholesale department, given the actual sales. Both customers and products are modeled by points in a k-dimensional real vector space. Two possible strategies are discussed: in one model the customer buys the nearest option from categories of products, in the other he/she buys all products within a certain radius of his/her position. Now we deal with the following problem: given only the sales list, how can we retrieve the relative positions corresponding to customers and products? In particular we are interested in the dimension k of the space: we are looking for low dimensional solutions with a good "fit" to the real sales list. Theoretical complexity of these problems is addressed: they are very hard to solve exactly; special cases are shown to be NP-complete. We use competitive neural network techniques for both artificial and real life data, and report the results.

1 Introduction

Often shop owners know very little about their customers. We examine the situation where only sales slips are present, i.e., for every customer visiting the shop a list of his or her purchases is available. It is obvious that these data contain very valuable information, which could lead to interesting insights. The question we ask ourselves here is how many "underlying" dimensions do exist that influence the client in his/her decision when purchasing certain goods. Marketing literature suggests that such underlying dimensions indeed exist, see [11]. In the example of a wholesale department with an extensive catalogue of products, two such dimensions might be price and brand-quality.

We propose different models to analyse (and hopefully understand) the behaviour of the customers. In both models customers and products are modeled as points in a k-dimensional real vector space. These k dimensions are supposed to represent the underlying dimensions mentioned in the previous paragraph. Without using any interpretation of these dimensions, we try to find the number of relevant dimensions and the coordinates of customers and products. Contrary to many approaches (cf. [4]) our methods use only very partial information; instead of direct attributes like age or price, we only use the sales list. Notice that the identity of the customers is entirely hidden: only the sales slips are used; if a customer appears for the second time, he/she is even considered to be a new customer.

In the first model, the products are grouped into a small number of categories. Every customer has to buy a product from each category, choosing from the options (products) available in it. The customer chooses—from the different options within each category—the nearest one. In the second model every customer buys exactly those products that are within a certain distance, the so-called radius of the customer. Some notion of distance is required; we examined the Euclidean distance and some Manhattan-like distances.

Now the problem can be easily described. Given a list of sales slips, determine a dimension k such that the model generates those same purchases—up to a certain error. Here k should be as small as possible. Furthermore, we also want to find the coordinates of both customers and products. The models and the exact problem will be described in Section 2 and Section 3.

In Section 4 we will show (i.e., give a proof outline) that the problem is already NP-complete (see [5]) in special cases. This means that an exact solution is beyond reach, possibly for many years to come. This theoretical complexity justifies the use of approximating algorithms, such as neural networks (see [9,2]). In Section 5 we describe the neural networks that we have used in an attempt to find a satisfactory solution to this problem. They are related to simple competitive neural networks.

In Section 6 we provide some results of experiments on artificial data, using those neural networks. We pay special attention to the dimension of the space, and explain a method to find the "true" dimension k. Customer and product points in k-space were generated randomly, and sales were generated according to one of the models. Throwing away the original points, the problem was to retrieve their coordinates. Experiments show that this is feasible, especially in the case where every customer buys lots of products.

Exploratory experiments on real data are reported in Section 7. Real data offer more difficulties than artificial data. Motivated by the results on artificial data we restricted the experiments to those customers who bought at least 40 products. At first it seemed hard to improve upon the so-called naive error: the system that buys nothing at all has a relatively small error. Fortunately we had several runs that were promising. The experimental results can be analysed by, e.g., cluster analysis in order to obtain a better understanding of the coordinates—and the dimensions.

Finally, in Section 8, we discuss the techniques used, and we mention some practical applications. In order to use these techniques, it is only necessary to have the sales lists available. In case of the option model, a field expert has to divide the products into categories. The results have to be interpreted by experts, but can also be used directly.

Part of the work presented in this paper was published in [15] and [10]. More details on the NP-completeness issue can also be found in the second author's forthcoming PhD thesis.

2 The Models and the Data

Suppose we are given n different customers $x_1, x_2, \ldots, x_n$ and m different products $p_1, p_2, \ldots, p_m$. We assume that customers buy each product at most once. Customers buying exactly the same products are identified. We have to analyse the so-called sales list: for every customer we know exactly the products he or she bought. We now propose two models to understand the behaviour of the customers using embeddings in a real vector space.

In Fig. 1 we see a small example with $n = 2$ and $p = 6$. The embedding is realised in a 2-dimensional space.

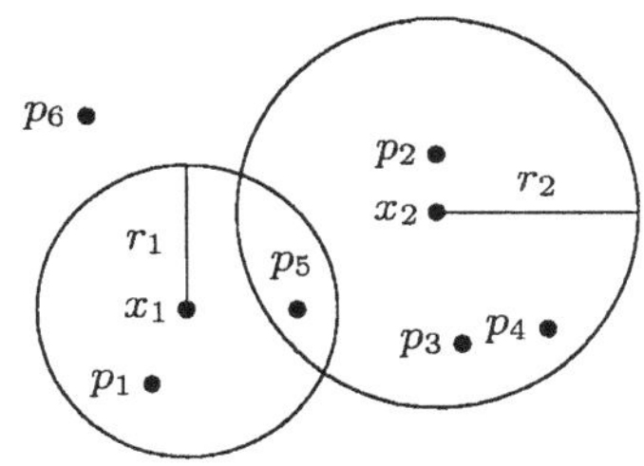

Fig. 1. Example of an embedding with 2 customers and 6 products. The spheres are only part of the product model.

2.1 The Option Model

The *option model* was introduced in [15]. In this model, the products are divided into c disjoint categories $C_1, C_2, \ldots, C_c$. In each category we have a number of products, say $c_\ell \geq 2$ in category C_ℓ ($\ell = 1, 2, \ldots, c$); these products are called the *options* or the *alternatives*, hence the name option model. Note that $\sum_{\ell=1}^{c} c_\ell = m$.

Every customer x_i has to choose exactly one product from every category. If both customers and products are represented by points in a k-dimensional vector space, the customer is supposed to choose (for every category) the option that is nearest to him/her. We assume that there always is exactly one option that is the nearest; if not, we slightly disturb the customers' coordinates. Here we need a certain metric on the space.

For the example in Fig. 1 we can imagine a situation where $c = 2$, and the first category consists of products p_1, p_2, p_3 and p_4, whereas the second category consists of products p_5 and p_6. Here customer x_1 will buy p_1 and p_5, and customer x_2 will buy p_2 and p_5.

It is also possible—but not obvious—to deal with the concept of non-buying in this model: an extra option could be added, corresponding to the situation where the customer does not want to choose from the original options. Finally, the division into categories is in principle done by the wholesale department.

2.2 The Product Model

Secondly, we describe the *product model.* It was introduced in [10]. Here, each customer x_i also has a *radius* r_i $(i = 1, 2, \ldots, n)$, proportional to the number of products he or she bought. Again, both customers and products are represented in our model by k-dimensional vectors. There is no subdivision of products into categories anymore. In this model a client buys all products within his/her own radius.

In Fig. 1 the radiuses r_1 and r_2 of the spheres are chosen in such a way that customer x_1 will buy p_1 and p_5 (as above), but customer x_2 will buy p_2, p_3, p_4 and p_5.

2.3 The Data

In our analyses the sales lists consisted of lines with numbers: each line represented one customer and each number represented one product.

Note that a sales list that is generated by customers behaving according to the option model is of a different type than one generated by customers behaving according to the product model, because in the latter case there is no subdivision into categories. This means that the type of sales lists we can analyse is different for both models. As an example, consider the following hypothetical supermarket sales list, where names have been added:

```
john      bananas    milk
mary      donuts     milk
harry     donuts     orange_juice
george    beer       orange_juice
```

If we assume that beverages form one category, this sales list cannot be generated by customers behaving according to the option model, because George buys two beverages, while in the option model the alternatives within one category exclude one another. Using the product model, this sales list could occur. Also note that in the option model every customer buys the same number of products.

3 Description of the Problem

Given an embedding of customers and products, the corresponding so-called virtual sales list can easily be constructed. To do so, we just have to determine the products that each customer will buy according to the model and the embedding. We can either use the option model or the product model as a model for the customer behaviour when constructing this virtual sales list. We denote the real sales list by RS, and the virtual sales list by VS. If customer x_i buys product p_j in sales list RS, we say that $(x_i, p_j) \in RS$; similarly, we can define $(x_i, p_j) \in VS$.

Now the problem is the following. Given RS, try to find an embedding such that VS resembles RS as much as possible, and such that the dimension k is as low as possible. In fact, it can be shown that if $k = m$ a zero error solution can be given. To do so for the option model, take the vector p_j ($j = 1, 2, \ldots, m$), corresponding to product j, to be $(0, \ldots, 0, 1, 0, \ldots, 0)$ (a one in coordinate j), and just add the vectors for the products bought in reality to produce the vector corresponding to customer i ($i = 1, 2, \ldots, n$). However, in order to hope for some real life interpretation we are interested in situations where k is in the order of magnitude 5 to 10 or even lower.

The two-sided error that is used for the evaluation of VS with respect to RS can be defined—for the moment—as the number of products/options bought by the model, but not by the customers (denoted by E_1), added to the number of products/options bought by the customers, but not by the model (denoted by E_2). More precisely, the total error E is

$$E = E_1 + E_2 = \sum_{i=1}^{n} \sum_{j=1}^{m} \{E_1(i,j) + E_2(i,j)\} ,$$

where

$$E_1(i,j) = \begin{cases} 1 \text{ if } (x_i, p_j) \in VS \text{ and } (x_i, p_j) \notin RS \\ 0 \text{ otherwise} \end{cases}$$

and

$$E_2(i,j) = \begin{cases} 1 \text{ if } (x_i, p_j) \in RS \text{ and } (x_i, p_j) \notin VS \\ 0 \text{ otherwise.} \end{cases}$$

So the naive error, where the system buys nothing at all, equals the total number of sales; in this case $E_1 = 0$.

4 Complexity of the Problem

In this section we shall examine a special case of the option model, and we shall prove that the corresponding decision problem is NP-complete in the sense of [5]. These problems are very difficult indeed; up to this moment nobody has been able to find efficient solutions to any of them. Often approximating or probabilistic algorithms are used, for instance neural networks. Since exact solutions are not feasible, one would be happy to accept near optimal ones. A famous example is the Traveling Salesman Problem, where a person is asked to visit a given number of cities using a route as short as possible. NP-complete problems are usually formulated as decision problems with a yes/no answer. The most common technique used to show NP-completeness is called reduction, where a known NP-complete problem is reduced—in a very precise way—to the problem at hand. For instance, in [5] a reduction is given from the Traveling Salesman Problem to the problem of finding a Hamiltonian circuit in a graph: a closed route connecting all nodes, visiting them once.

This section is meant for those who are interested in the theoretical background, and can be skipped on first reading. Instead of giving all details of proofs, we only provide some ideas underlying them. More details can be found in the second author's forthcoming PhD thesis. There the situation for the product model is also dealt with.

We first describe the special case of the option model we would like to address. We have n customers, who must choose from only $c = 2$ categories, with a total of m products. We identified customers who had bought exactly the same products. The customer choices are easily represented using a graph consisting of two horizontal rows of nodes, where the nodes in the first row correspond to the options from the first category, and the nodes in the second row to the options from the second category. The edges now correspond to the choices made: every customer corresponds to a unique edge. So the graph has m vertices and n edges; we call it a *sales graph*. We may assume that this graph is connected. An example, with $m = 6 + 5 = 11$ and $n = 10$, is shown in Fig. 2.

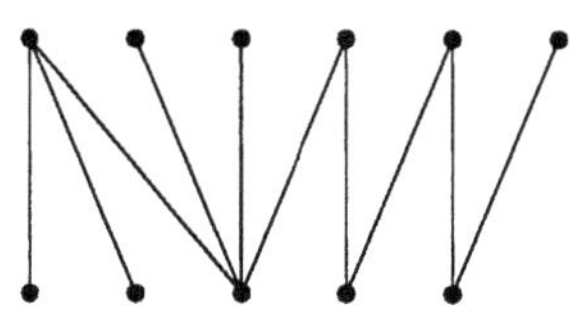

Fig. 2. Example of a sales graph with 10 customers and $6 + 5 = 11$ products.

A sales graph is *bipartite*: the nodes can be split into two nonempty disjoint sets, such that every edge is incident with a node from both sets. In fact, the partition corresponds to the categories. The converse also holds: every bipartite graph can be viewed as a sales graph.

Now we return to our original problem, and we consider the special case of dimension $k = 1$: e.g., "we only look at the price of the products". Is it possible to find an exact solution in this case? In other words, is it possible to attach real numbers to both customers and options (where customers choose the nearest option), in such a way that the graph represents the corresponding real sales? In dimension 1 we should divide the real axis for both categories into disjoint intervals, the product points lying in the centres of these intervals; in higher dimensions we get Voronoi cells here.

One can infer that the two subgraphs from Fig. 3 give rise to problems—and these are the only ones. If at least one of them occurs as a subgraph in the given graph, it is impossible to find the proper coordinates.

Fig. 3. Two forbidden subgraphs.

For instance, for the left hand side graph we have to cut the real axis into two parts—for both categories—in such a way that all four combinations have a nonempty intersection. This is impossible. In every way we choose the coordinates for customers and options, at least one customer will be treated incorrectly. In fact, if for the first category, with options A and B, we choose real numbers a and b with $a < b$, and for the second category, with options C and D, we choose real numbers c and d with $c < d$, then a customer corresponding to x chooses A if $x < (a+b)/2$ and B if $x > (a+b)/2$, and similarly for C and D. Now—given real a, b, c and d—it is not possible to find x_1 that buys both A and D, *and* x_2 that buys both B and C.

In general we see that cycles are forbidden, in other words: the sales graph should be acyclic, i.e., not contain any paths from a node to itself. It seems that in the example it could be possible to deal with this problem by allowing nondeterminism, for instance with x's precisely in the middle of a and b. However, first of all the model would become more complex, and secondly this would also fail in the case of cycles with more than four nodes.

Since crossing edges correspond to the fact that customers are treated correctly or not, they should be avoided. We can conclude that a sales graph can be realised in the way we want, if and only if it contains no cycles and no subgraphs isomorphic to the right hand side graph in Fig. 3—let us call it $\mathcal{H}$. The minimal number of edges that should be omitted in order to obtain a graph that meets the conditions, is exactly the minimal number of customers that is treated incorrectly.

So we are motivated to examine the following decision problem, called SG (Sales Graph). Given a bipartite graph $\mathcal{G}$; does $\mathcal{G}$ possess a spanning tree (a connected subgraph without cycles, containing every node) that does not have a subgraph isomorphic to $\mathcal{H}$? Stated otherwise, does $\mathcal{G}$ have a spanning tree that looks like a long "spine", to which several degree one nodes are attached?

We now arrive at the main result of this section:

Theorem SG *is* NP-*complete.*

The proof proceeds by reducing problem GT39 from [5] to SG. This problem is: given a bipartite graph $\mathcal{G}$; does $\mathcal{G}$ possess a Hamiltonian path, i.e., a path connecting all nodes without repeated visits to nodes?

Now that we know that SG is NP-complete, we can infer that given customers and their choices, it is not feasible to determine the minimal error that can be reached. If this were possible, the existence of a spanning tree without subgraphs isomorphic to $\mathcal{H}$ would be immanent. It is therefore appropriate to turn to approximating algorithms, such as neural networks.

5 The Neural Network Used

The neural networks we used in our experiments were inspired by simple competitive neural networks (see, e.g., [8,9]). In such neural networks, the weight vectors associated with the neurons are merely points in a k-dimensional real vector space if the input data for the network are k-dimensional real vectors. Each time a data vector is presented to a competitive neural network, a "winning unit" w is determined by calculating which unit has its weight vector closest to the presented pattern (in a Euclidean sense). Next, this units' weight vector is moved towards the presented pattern. This increases the chance of unit w being the winner if the same input pattern is presented again later on. This type of neural network is also known as a "winner-take-all-network" (see [9,6,7]). These networks perform a similar task as the classical k-means clustering methods (see [13]).

In our case, where we analyse sales lists, all customers and all products (or options within a category) are represented by a separate competitive unit. The weight-vectors of the units correspond to the points in a k-dimensional real vector space describing the customers and products (or options).

Of course, the learning process has to be modified in order to be able to work with sales lists. The aim of the learning process is to bring weight vectors of customers and weight vectors of the products bought sufficiently close to each other, whereas weight vectors of the products the customer has not bought should be at a sufficient distance.

The meaning of the word sufficient is crucial here, and it is determined by the model used. In the case where a customer buys everything within a certain radius of his or her own weight vector, sufficiently close means within this radius, and sufficiently distant means outside this radius. In the case where a customer buys the closest one of a number of options within a category, sufficiently close means closer than all the other options in the category, and sufficiently distant means at a greater distance than the option the customer *did* buy from the category.

5.1 Training Procedure for the Option Model

The training of our network in the case of the option model roughly proceeds as follows. First, the network weights are randomly initialized in the $[0;1]^k$ hypercube. Next, for a predetermined number of iterations the clients and the purchases they made are presented to the network once in random order. If client x_i chooses product p_j, the weight vectors of the units representing x_i and p_j were pulled together a little bit. This way, we hoped to increase the probability that the units representing the products that the customer has chosen, are the closest units within each product-category in the next iteration.

The parallel with a simple competitive neural network should be clear. In a simple competitive neural network the weight vectors of the units are pulled towards the input vectors. This way a Voronoi tessellation of the input space is created. In our case, we know in advance that the alternatives within one set divide the input space in a Voronoi tessellation. We also know which client should lie in which Voronoi cell for every product category in the choice process. By means of the "competitive learning" algorithm, we move the positions of the clients and the alternatives around, and we hope to reach a state where most of the clients lie in the correct Voronoi-cell for most of the product-categories in the choice-process.

Unfortunately, there is a problem associated with this learning-scheme. If we start with random initial weights, the average direction of the weight updates will be inward. This will cause the neural network to "implode". We can prevent this by re-normalising the weight vectors after each iteration.

There is another potential pitfall for our system. Typically, we have data on several thousands of customers, but there are only a few product categories, with a few alternatives within them. This causes the alternative coordinates to be updated much more frequently than the client coordinates. This problem can be solved by updating the weight vectors of the units representing the alternatives by a much smaller amount than the weight vectors of the units representing the customers.

5.2 Training Procedure for the Product Model

The training of our network in the case of the product model is very similar and roughly proceeds as follows. First, the network weights are randomly initialized in the $[0;1]^k$ hypercube. Next, the network is trained for a number of iterations (called cycles). In each iteration, a number (say 5000) of random customer/product pairs are examined. If the customer and the product are not sufficiently close, the weight vectors representing them are pulled towards each other in the k-dimensional hypercube. If they are not sufficiently far apart, they are pushed away from each other. The amount by which the weight vectors are altered is determined by a learning rate parameter. At the end of an iteration the coordinates are renormalised in order to make optimal use of the full unit cube. Iterating is stopped if the error (which is described below) has not decreased anymore for a sufficiently large number of iterations.

At the end of each run we in particular have three significant figures:

"Both bought": number of purchases that are correctly modeled.
"Only model bought": number of purchases only performed in the model, but not in reality; this is E_1.
"Only reality bought': number of purchases only performed in reality, but not in the model; this is E_2.

As we remarked before, the error E is defined as the sum of "only reality bought" and "only model bought": $E = E_1 + E_2$. Note that the sum of "both bought" and "only reality bought" always equals the total number of sales.

6 Results on Artificial Data

In this section we present the results we obtained in several experiments with artificial data. The artificial data were generated by randomly assigning values in the $[0;1]^k$ hypercube to the weight vectors representing a set of customers and a set of products. Subsequently, the product model or the option model was used to generate a sales list. Thus, these sales lists were generated by customers known to behave exactly as the model specifies. After generating these sales lists the customer and product embedding coordinates were thrown away, and it was attempted to recover them (or at least the relative coordinates) using the neural networks described in Section 5.

The experiments that were performed for the option model were aimed towards finding the best dimension for the embedding space (as reflected in the title of [15]). The results for the product model are more general.

6.1 Results on Artificial Data Using the Option Model

As stated above, the experiments with the option model neural networks were geared towards finding the "best" embedding dimension for a given sales list. We hope that the dimensions we find can be interpreted by a domain expert, revealing hidden motives underlying customer behaviour.

In Section 5 we explained how the neural networks could be used for finding embedding coordinates. During this discussion it was assumed that the correct embedding dimension k was given. However, in real situations k is unknown. How should we determine the best value for k?

This problem can be solved by making a "fit vs. number of dimensions"-plot. As fit measure for this plot we use the error function E from Section 3. Now we can construct a graph by running the neural network with dimension $D = 1, \ldots, N + 5$, where N is an educated guess about the true number of underlying dimensions. This "fit vs. number of dimensions"-plot will show an elbow at the right number of dimensions. An example of a "fit vs. number of dimensions"-plot clearly showing an elbow is given in Fig. 4.

A very similar procedure for obtaining the number of underlying dimensions is often used in Multidimensional Scaling (MDS; see, e.g., [3]) and Principal Component Analysis (PCA; see, e.g., [12]). In the context of the latter technique, the "fit vs. number of dimensions"-plot is often called "scree plot".

In total we performed experiments on eight datasets this way, where the underlying number of dimensions was varied from two to five. Four out of the eight datasets had 10 products, and 10 alternatives per product. The remaining four datasets had 15 products, and 5 alternatives per product. The number of customers was set to 150 in all datasets.

In Fig. 4 and Fig. 5 the resulting plots of fit vs. number of dimensions are shown. Elbows are clearly visible for each problem instance.

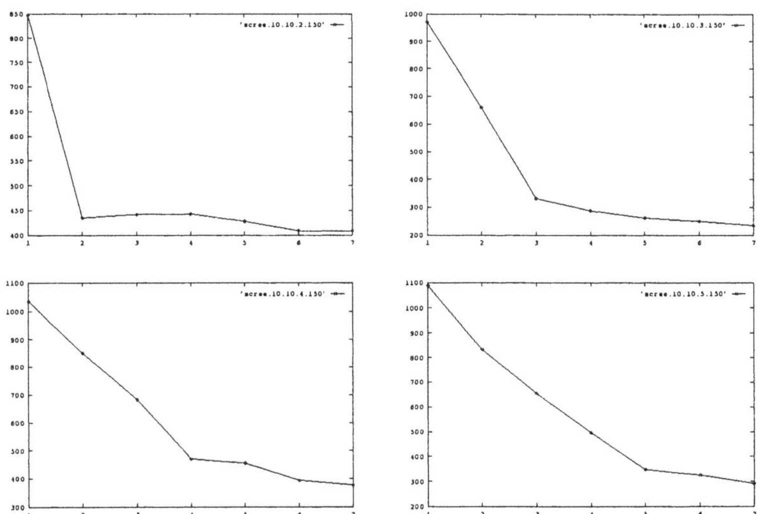

Fig. 4. The "fit vs. number of dimensions"-plots for the datasets with 10 product categories and 10 options per category.

We may conclude that the neural network is capable of discovering the dimension of the embedding space in the case of artificial data.

6.2 Results on Artificial Data Using the Product Model

In this subsection we shall describe several experiments that were performed on artificial data using the product model. We shall also draw some conclusions for the real situation. Let us now first restrict our attention to dimension $k = 2$ in the product model. In this case results can be easily visualised. We

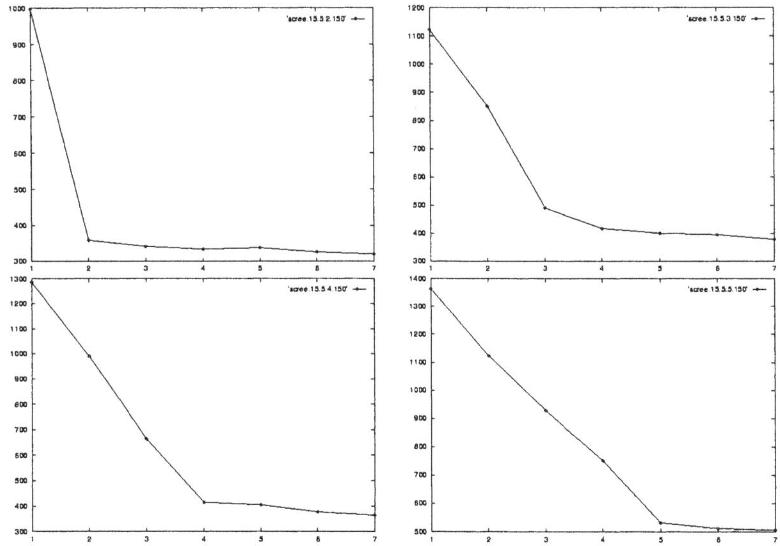

Fig. 5. The "fit vs. number of dimensions"-plots for the datasets with 15 product categories and 5 alternatives per category.

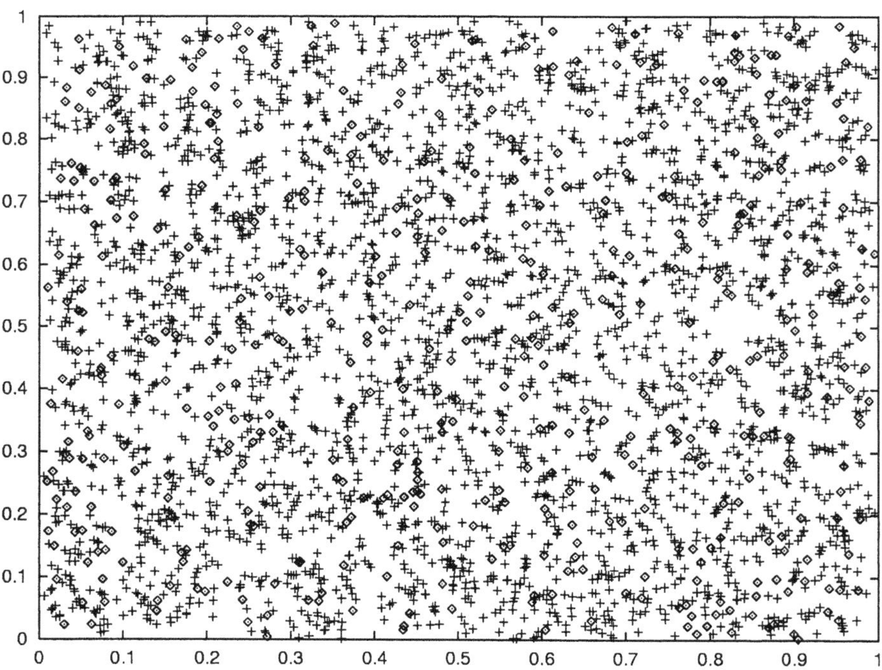

Fig. 6. Resulting customer and product coordinates of example run 1.

chose $n = 500$ customers and $m = 3,000$ products, so experiments took little time. As a good run we present example run 1: a situation where 116,638 products were sold, whereas the total error was a mere 8,928, with 7,122 "only model bought". In this case every customer bought at least about 200 products. Fig. 6 shows both customer and product coordinates; customers correspond to small squares, products to small +'s.

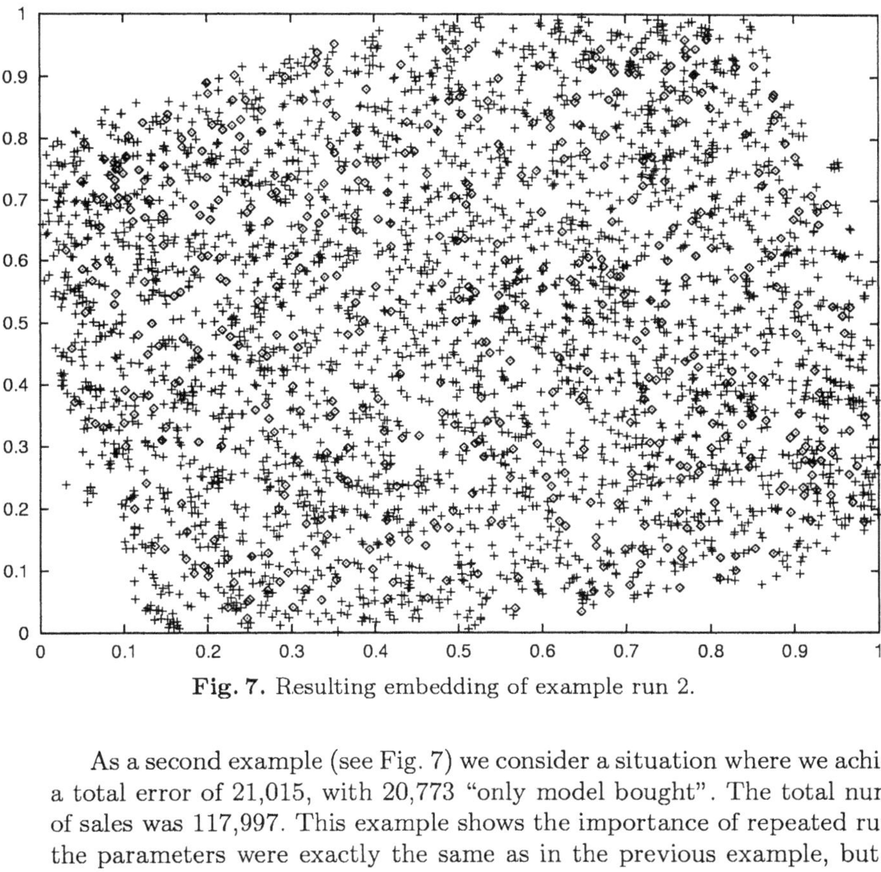

Fig. 7. Resulting embedding of example run 2.

As a second example (see Fig. 7) we consider a situation where we achieved a total error of 21,015, with 20,773 "only model bought". The total number of sales was 117,997. This example shows the importance of repeated runs—the parameters were exactly the same as in the previous example, but this time the unit square was only partially used. The result is not really bad, but if one fills the whole square, as in the previous example, a better result is possible. Note that the coordinates found are situated in a rectangular shape, suggesting that the regained coordinates have almost the same positions relative to each other as the original ones. This illustrates the fact that there are some degrees of freedom (i.e., rotations and scaling) in the behaviour of the model.

As a final example for dimension $k = 2$ we present example run 3. This was an experiment with few sales. In this case only 14,985 products were sold.

The total error was 24,094, with 20,850 "only model bought". Fig. 8 is representative for many experiments: the final error is large, whereas customers and products are not evenly distributed in space, contrary to the artificially generated ones.

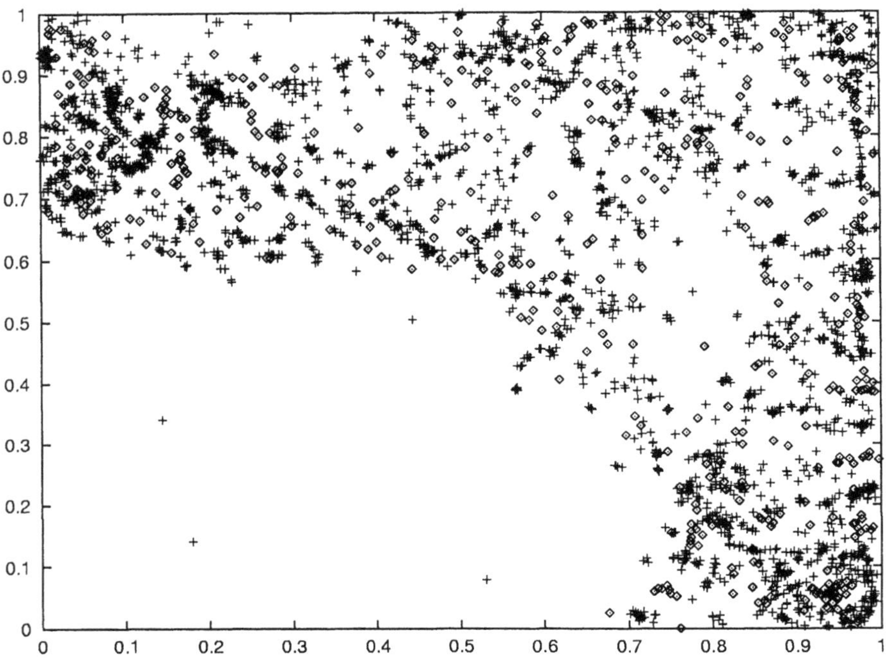

Fig. 8. Resulting embedding of example run 3.

From the experiments we concluded that the best results were obtained when customers bought very many products. Intuitively customers that buy only a few products are not representative, and from a marketing point of view, these customers are perhaps not the most interesting ones. In the sequel we therefore restrict our attention to customers buying at least 40 products.

In Table 1 we give some results in the case of artificial data for higher dimensions, where every customer bought about 50 products. The number of customers considered was near to 200. The experiments are labeled A through I. As an illustration the number of cycles is also tabulated. Here the experiments G, H and I had slightly different parameters. Some runs were almost perfect. Again we may conclude that the neural network is capable of fitting the coordinates in the case of artificial data.

In Table 2 we present some simple theoretical values. We denote by "k-wrong" a situation where the total number of products bought matches the

name	dimension	number of cycles	"both bought"	"only reality bought"	"only model bought"
A	4	2,820	6,868	493	83
B	5	2,460	12,323	1,294	267
C	6	2,400	12,348	1,768	331
D	7	2,000	13,422	1,648	345
E	8	2,060	12,072	356	207
F	9	1,480	10,956	338	91
G	10	1,680	6,695	25	12
H	10	1,760	6,115	38	17
I	10	1,320	24,426	4,259	1,042

Table 1. Results for some experiments on artificial data.

corresponding number from the sales list exactly, but precisely k products are replaced by incorrect ones. Of course, perfect is 0-wrong.

name	dimension	"both bought"	"only reality bought"	"only model bought"
naive	any	0	t	0
perfect	any	t	0	0
k-wrong	any	$t-k$	k	k

Table 2. Some theoretical values.

7 Results on Real Data

In this section we present some exploratory results from experiments on real data. Again, first the results are given for the option model and then the results for the product model. In the case of the option model the aim was to discover the most suitable dimension of the underlying space, whereas the aim in the case of the product model was merely minimization of the error, and studying the behaviour of the model.

7.1 Results on Real Data Using the Option Model

After a positive result was obtained with the option model on artificial data, we considered real data. The real data were obtained from a wholesale department. The subdivision of products into product categories was performed by domain experts from the wholesale department.

From each original dataset available we selected only the customers that actually bought a product from each product category, so we did not have to deal with the non-buying problem mentioned in Section 2. This left us with approximately 150 customers per dataset, about the same number as in the artificial datasets. The number of product categories was 11 for each dataset.

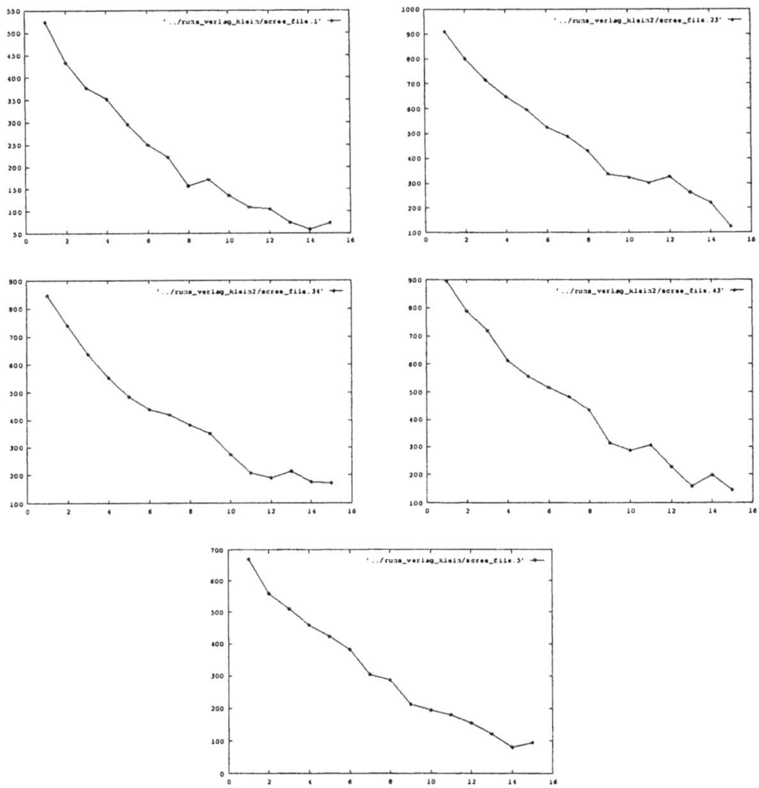

Fig. 9. The "fit vs. number of dimensions"-plots for the five real datasets — option model.

The "fit vs. number of dimensions"-plots resulting from these experiments are shown in Fig. 9. On first sight, it seems that the results of these experiments are not as good as the results with the artificial data. However, in some of the plots there is a vague elbow visible. An interpretation of the dimensions that were obtained by a domain expert could shed more light on these results. Furthermore, it may be the case that in other application areas more convincing results are obtained because customers in these other areas behave more similar to the model-customers, but this is speculative.

7.2 Results on Real Data Using the Product Model

We now turn our attention to the product model. As a running example we use a real sales list consisting of $n = 1,368$ customers, who bought 32,523 products. The number of different products was $m = 10,381$. We restricted our attention to customers buying at least 40 products. These $n = 228$ customers (17% of the total number of customers) bought $t = 11,769$ products (36% of the total number of products sold). As this example will show, reasonable results can be obtained.

In Table 3 we show results from interesting runs using real data. Note that "both bought" and "only reality bought" always add to $t = 11,769$. The error is a combination of the columns "only reality bought" and "only model bought". As an illustration two experiments, X and Y, in dimension 9 have

name	dimension	number of cycles	'both bought'	'only reality bought'	'only model bought'
X	9	2,340	6,468	5,301	1,211
Y	9	1,360	5,512	6,257	668
A	10	1,820	7,072	4,697	1,138
B	10	1,440	6,010	5,759	499
C	10	1,760	7,990	3,779	5,700

Table 3. Results for some experiments.

been added. The results arise from slightly different settings of parameters, and from repeated experiments with the same parameters. Experiment A shows a relatively good result. An average customer buys 52 products and the model correctly buys 31 of these, where instead of the remaining 21 it buys 5 incorrect products. For experiment B this last number is lowered to 2, but only 26 products are properly handled on average. In experiment C we see that on average even 35 products out of 52 are correctly predicted by the model; raising "both bought" seems only possible at the cost of raising "only model bought" too.

As a visualisation of experiment A we plot the error against the number of cycles. In Fig. 10 we show the "relative error": the sum of "only reality bought" and "only model bought" divided by "both bought".

From the experiments we noticed that the best results were achieved when using the Euclidean distance d, defined by $d(x,y) = \sqrt{\sum_{\ell=1}^{k}(x_\ell - y_\ell)^2}$ for vectors $x = (x_1, \ldots, x_k)$ and $y = (y_1, \ldots, y_k)$ in k-space. We also experimented with Manhattan-like distances (taking the sum of the absolute values of $x_\ell - y_\ell$), but results were not very promising in that case: the errors obtained were much larger.

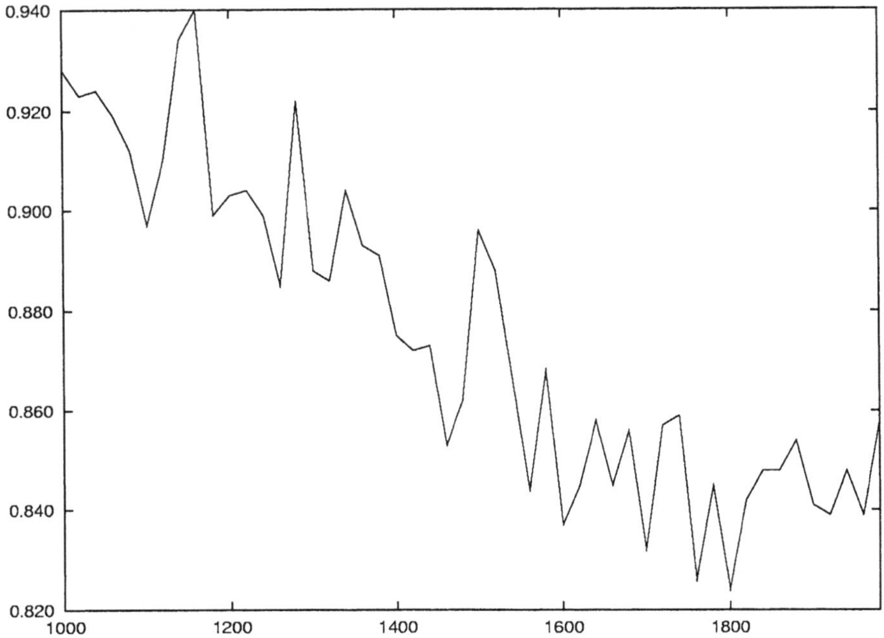

Fig. 10. Relative error vs. number of cycles.

As in the case of the option model, results are not as good as those for artificial data. We feel however that the results are promising, and may even be better for certain special application areas.

8 Summary and Conclusions

In this paper we described two models, the option model and the product model, to understand and analyse customer choices. The theoretical complexity of special cases of these models was addressed and the corresponding decision problems were shown to be NP-complete.

Using techniques from neural networks, we were able to obtain good results for artificial data using both the option model and the product model. For real data, the results were less convincing, but in the case of the product model where customers buy lots of products, the results were still reasonable.

At the moment it is not possible to conclude whether or not these models reflect real life customer choices. Of course, it would be unrealistic to expect customers to behave exactly as in a model, but we do hope to discover underlying trends. Feedback from domain experts may reveal the possible meaning of the dimensions.

Similar techniques have been used in the following situation. If one tries to understand customer behaviour in the case of different shops or products, 2-

dimensional plots showing their relative positions might be useful. These plots can be generated quite easily with the methods described above. In fact, once a notion of distance between shops/products has been introduced, the neural networks quickly discover reasonable embeddings in 2-space. The distance function is usually taken to be some sort of Hamming-distance, counting the number of absolute differences between vectors. In the shop case the vectors might consist of the week sales; in the product case the distances can be based on the number of times the products have been bought together. Note that the resulting networks resemble those using gravity from [14].

Finally, we would like to discuss the practical use of the methods discussed so far. One should not expect the answers to be precise and rigid. On the contrary, they rather give insights and ideas. One might think, for instance, that customers that are near to one another in k-space show similar behaviour. This is not necessarily true, but in many situations these customers do resemble each other. This property can be used in marketing situations. Not only is it possible to reveal interesting dimensions, also interesting customers or clusters of customers can be detected. Due to the randomness of the algorithms involved repeated runs might give somewhat or even totally different results. This does not mean that the methods are not sound, but it shows the difficulty of the problem at hand, reflected in the enormous number of solutions of acceptable quality.

References

1. Anderson, J.A., Rosenfeld, E. (Eds.) (1988): Neurocomputing: Foundations of Research. MIT Press, Cambridge
2. Bishop, C.M. (1995): Neural Networks for Pattern Recognition. Clarendon-Press, Oxford
3. Davison, M.L. (1983): Multidimensional Scaling. John Wiley and Sons, New York
4. Fayyad, U., Uthurusamy, R. (1996): Data Mining and Knowledge Discovery in Databases. Communications of the ACM 39, 24–27
5. Garey, M.R., Johnson, D.S. (1979): Computers and Intractability: A Guide to the Theory of NP-Completeness. W.H. Freeman and Company, New York
6. Grossberg, S. (1976): Adaptive Pattern Classifications and Universal Recording, I: Parallel Development and Coding of Neural Feature Detectors. Biological Cybernetics 23, 121–134
7. Grossberg, S. (1980): How Does a Brain Build a Cognitive Code? Psychological Review 87, 1–51; reprinted in [1]
8. Haykin, S. (1999): Neural Networks: A Comprehensive Foundation, 2nd edition. Prentice Hall, Upper Saddle River, New Jersey
9. Hertz, J., Krogh, A., Palmer, R.G. (1991): Introduction to the Theory of Neural Computation. Addison-Wesley, Reading, Massachusetts
10. Kosters, W.A., La Poutré, H., Wezel, M.C. van (1997): Understanding Customer Choice Processes Using Neural Networks. In: Arner Jr, H.F. (Ed.): Proceedings of the First International Conference on the Practical Application of Knowledge Discovery and Data Mining (PADD'97), London, 167–178

11. Kotler, P. (1999): Marketing Management: Analysis, Planning, Implementation and Control, 9th edition. Prentice Hall, Upper Saddle River, New Jersey
12. Krzanowski, W.J. (1988): Principles of Multivariate Analysis. Oxford Statistical Science Series, Oxford University Press, Oxford
13. Leeuw, J. de, Heiser, W. (1982): Theory of Multidimensional Scaling. In: Krishnaiah, P.R., Kanal, L.N. (Eds.): Handbook of Statistics 2: Classification, Pattern Recognition and Reduction of Dimensionality. North-Holland, Amsterdam, 285–316
14. Oyang, Y.-J., Chen, C.-Y., Yang, T.-W. (2001): A Study on the Hierarchical Data Clustering Algorithm Based on Gravity Theory. In: De Raedt, L., Siebes, A. (Eds.): Proceedings PKDD 2001 (Principles of Data Mining and Knowledge Discovery), Lecture Notes in Artificial Intelligence 2168, Springer, Berlin Heidelberg New York, 350–361
15. Wezel, M.C. van, Kok, J.N., Sere, K. (1996): Determining the Number of Dimensions Underlying Customer-Choices with a Competitive Neural Network. In: Proceedings of the IEEE International Conference on Neural Networks (ICNN'96), Washington D.C., 484–490

CRM in e-Business: a Client's Life Cycle Model Based on a Neural Network

Oscar Marbán[1], Ernestina Menasalvas[2], César Montes[3], John G. Rajakulendran[4] and Javier Segovia[2]

[1]Departamento de Informática, Universidad Carlos III de Madrid, Leganés, Madrid, Spain
[2]DLSIS, Facultad de Informatica, Universidad Politécnica, Madrid
[3]DIA, Facultad de Informatica, Universidad Politécnica, Madrid
[4]University of Newcasttle. United Kingdom

Abstract. The competitive environment in which organisations are moving together with the arrival of the web has made it necessary the application of intelligent methods both to gather and to analyse information. Information gathered in the web represents only the first step in the problem. Integrating that information with information supplied by external providers is a need if the users behaviour is to be studied. In this paper we present a new approach that will make it possible to build adaptive web sites. Firstly according to the user attributes and his/her behaviour the probability to acquire certain products is obtained, later the propensity through his/her life cycle to buy different products either of the same category or different is obtained with the help of a Neural Network. This will also allow us to conduct different online marketing campaigns of cross-selling and up-selling.

1 Introduction

The web is increasingly becoming a retailing channel of choice for million of users. Maybe we should better say that it is becoming one of the main communication channels for any kind of transaction, being obviously commerce one of its main uses. Communication is an extremely broad concept that covers many subtopics, which become more or less relevant depending on the specific domain for which it is conceived. In our case, e-commerce of any kind, communication may mean getting precise information, personal advice or even personalised care, just as it happens in ordinary commerce.

However, the traditional conception of web-based commerce systems fails to achieve many of the features that enable small businesses to develop a warm human relationship with customers. This must not be understood as if those features cannot be translated onto the web for thereby improving the shopping experience in Internet. Our point is just the opposite. It is crucial for any designer to understand that achieving proper customer relations is a very important aspect of all successful business.

The inability of e-business applications to establish good customer relationship by developing a mature understanding of their customers is the central motivating-force behind this paper. The failure of e-business, and therefor the need of seeking new friendlier communication procedures with users, is reflected in the colossal growth of electronic Personalisation and customisation tools developed by the worlds leading computer organisations, including IBM, ORACLE, Microsoft (Microsoft researches Data Mining and Exploration: DMX), Yahoo!, Lycos (its subsidiary Jubii launched a customer profiling project) - others include SPSS, CNET, DIGIMINE, WEBMINER, Macromedia, Accrue Software, Black Pearl Inc. etc. Some authors [9] also identify the two main purposes of 'customer-centric applications' as Personalisation and eCRM (electronic customer relationship management).

The wider recognition and valuation that data mining companies are experimenting are indicative of the current failure of e-Commerce in delivering eCRM or Personalisation, and the importance of both issues for e-Commerce. As Ansari et al. state [10]: "recently, a phase shift has occurred in the valuation of such companies (i.e. companies building data mining modelling tools), and recent acquisitions have given rise to valuations 10 to 100 times higher. KD1 was acquired by Net Perceptions for $116M, Rightpoint (previously DataMind) was acquired by E.piphany for $400M. DataSage was acquired by Vignette for $577M, and NeoVista was acquired by Accrue for $140M. The shift in valuations indicate a wider recognition of the value of data mining modelling techniques for e-commerce" .

Moreover, the growth of companies that promote electronic Personalisation indicates the failure of e-business in tackling the problems. "Accrue's solutions enable highly targeted campaigns to improve the profitability of customer interactions across multiple touch points. Accrue has over 600 customers, including industry leaders such as FedEx, Gateway, Dow Jones, Eastman Kodak Company, MTV, Macy's and Deutsche Telekom" [11].

Finally, the Internet customer has evolved leaving e-businesses behind. "Today's e-consumer is more savvy, more demanding and has more options than ever before. With the competition now just a click away, building lasting customer relationships has taken on a renewed importance" [12].

The reality is that the absence of physical contact minimises the personalised experience of shopping, and thus directly strikes at the heart of establishing a good one-to-one relationship. To the prior we should add to the fact that there is very little experience in creating fluent relationships with customers using e-commerce. Both aspects contribute to the lack of a close one-to-one relationship, which is a major drawback to shopping on the Internet.

However, the advantages of convenience, 'relative' speed and the cheapness of the products offered on the Web offset these disadvantages. A combination of these 'three killer factors' makes shopping on the Internet a must! On the other hand, some security issues plus the poorly conceived existing e-Business systems (many of them are just a ubiquitous extension onto the medium, instigated by fashion and mindless heard-instinct) are not contributing to its success. This paper will not discuss the nature of being a successful e-business, which entails a lot of different factors, among which good customer relation is but one. Is it not inherent to human nature to shop at places that are friendly, cost-competitive, convenient, and trustworthy and treat you as an individual?

The problems exemplified by not understanding your customer, which lead to a loss of close one-to-one relationship, are characterised by the following

- The inability to meet the customer's 'expected' need(s),
- The inability to retain the loyalty of the customer,
- The inability to improve and enhance products offered by the organisation,
- The inability to control the organisations contact with the customer and thereby erode the benefits of the contact,
- The inability to maximise the knowledge about the customer's preferences so as to offer products he/she likes, consequently missing opportunities to up-sell, or to cross-sell, or even to increase the sales to that customer,
- The inability to identify new customer or new marketing opportunities (i.e. Ineffective customer or market segmentation), which leads to unfocused marketing strategies that waste time and money,
- The inability to dynamically manage special offers and prevent from undertaking rapid-cycle offer testing,
- The inability to attract new customers,
- The inability to maximise the business performance of their web sites,
- The inability to maintain a competitive edge in a volatile marketplace,
- The inability to make intelligent, accurate decisions in a timely manner.

All these factors point directly to the generalised idea of increasing productivity, revenue and profitability while at the same time combating your competitors. "Marketers who recognise its vast commercial potential see data mining and web-based analysis as more than black and white. They also see green in the science's potential to create higher margins and inflate revenue." [13].

Most of the prior factors may be solved by developing a mature understanding of their customers, applying intelligent methods to data about them collected either from the web (web logs, questionnaires, ...) or from external sources (postal code data bases, statistics, ...). This paper will focus on understanding those problems, their effects on effective commercial relations and how to achieve a better understanding of and, therefor, relation with any user by means analysing its needs with a softcomputing method like a Neural Network

2 CRM in e-commerce

CRM indirectly/directly impacts on many aspects of business practices: logistics, pricing strategy, purchasing/production, etc. Among them, marketing is perhaps the main concern of CRM. CRM is interchangeable with the idea of 'fostering a mature one-to-one relationship' between business and its customers.

"As marketing guru Regis McKenna explains, 'it's about giving customers what they want, when, where, and how they want it'" [14]. "The theory of customer relationship management can be summed up in one phrase: targeting the right offer to the right customer at the right time for the right price" [15]. This assumes that an organisation 'understands' its customers well enough to offer them the right sort of product at the right price at the right time. This understanding makes it possible to overcome all the present failings, identified in the previous section.

'Personalised attention, on mass,' is the real aim of CRM, as it is too expensive for medium/large enterprises to have personalised management of all their customers, like they do for their more important ('big') customers. The process of market segmentation, where similar groups are identified within the whole, in order to understand better their domain specific behaviour, enables better modelling of their practices so as to perform what we can call 'targeted marketing'. The immediate consequence is that personalised relationships with customers, established via one-to-one marketing, customisation and sales force automation, are now possible.

This kind of close relations are data intensive in both directions. Companies need enough good quality data to perform them. But it is also true that the closer the relationship is, bigger is the amount of data available, therefor enabling better-informed decisions.

"Data mining will be essential for understanding customer behaviour on the Web and for helping the websites of the world create their personalised responses. In a sense, data mining recently 'got the order' to become one of the key ingredients of e-Commerce" [16]. This quotation highlights the two key advantages of good CRM: 'understanding the behaviour of customers' and allowing 'personalised responses' to that behaviour, both of which need of data mining techniques as the core tool for being successful.

Other general advantages are obtained by including good CRM methods: the discovery of potential new customers, the discovery of market niches, combating unseen commoditisation (the convergence in product identity), or overcoming the limitations of traditional marketing approaches (reduce money on ineffective an unfocused marketing) are just some of them. Moreover, appropriate CRM practices help to deal successfully with short life cycle products, which are typical in Internet-based commerce. Having a good knowledge about customers allows early identification of new or potential products. In the other hand, but not less important, knowing the needs of potential clients helps to choose better the products to include in the catalogue and the stock size for each of them. This ends in powerful defence against competitors, profit increase and better service, not to mention the increase of the loyalty of the customer to the e-business, which is a key aim of CRM.

In [17] Jeff Caplan identifies the benefits provided by good customer profiling to e-businesses, enabling them to:

- Intervene at the exact right time to gain, maintain or expand a customer's business
- Identify customers' seasonal preferences and positive or negative trends in their behaviour
- Gauge and act on customer inactivity – perhaps the most crucial indicator of waning loyalty
- Predict when a customer is about to take an action that will affect the company
- Dramatically improve the success rate of marketing messages
- Gain and deepen customer loyalty
- Reduce defections and lower attrition rates
- Gain more satisfied customers and maximise their profitability.

As a summary, "analysing and exploring regularities in Web log records can identify potential customers for electronic commerce, enhance the quality and delivery of Internet information services to the end user, and improve Web server system performance" [18]. The first two advantages, identifying customers and enhancing the delivery of service, are vital important for e-commerce. The latter is an important technical issue that will not be addressed by this investigation. Good CRM will overcome most of the problems identified in the introduction and transfer the advantages mentioned before to e-commerce organisations.

3 The Unconfident-Unable Dilemma: Reasons Why e-Commerce Has Failed to Establish Effective CRM

"Condemned by bad experiences". This can be an accurate qualifier for e-business, because how many cases have we heard of bad personal data use, or credit card frauds, or multiple billing for the same transaction, or even products bought that never arrive or arrive in bad conditions or were not what we expected? Of course, many of these problems have to do only with bad faith and are an exception, but other have to do with already commented poor relation procedures. What is clear is that users are not very confident about e-commerce, so many don't use it at all, or if they do, they prefer to remain anonymous, not even providing basic data about them.

This has a dramatic consequence on e-business. Not knowing about the customer means being unable to improve the relation and, therefor, the service provided. Then again, the visitor will not get enough satisfaction and the confidence will continue decreasing. This is a dangerous loop we call the Unconfident-Unable Dilemma. Unconfident users unable any improvement.

How can we break this dangerous loop? The answer is simple: understanding user's needs so as to provide a better personalised service. This seems a typical Data Mining domain in which data about the customers are collected and analysed to get useful segmentation that serve to create better relationships. The problem is that there are very few e-businesses with good and sufficient data concerning customers. Moreover, using these data when available normally needs the identity or some personal facts of the visitors, who, as commented before, are very reticent to provide them.

So now we know that we are dealing with unconfident customers and that we really know very little about them, but still we have to understand them so as to provide a better service. The only source of information left and the only moment in which we have direct contact, electronic but direct, with them is the session itself. So it seems clear that e-commerce has to learn to extract as much knowledge as possible about user's needs during it's visit, and to achieve so in an almost anonymous way, identifying users and user behaviours in terms of typologies. However, any solution is limited by the kind and the amount of information available about customers-business interactions. Until now, very little information concerning the behaviour of each single customer in a site was stored. Web-logs frequently consist on just the set of pages visited in a session, or not even that when pages contain applets or plug-ins. Even more, security issues and privacy laws also affect the kind and quality of the information stored about each visit to the site.

Taking all the prior into account, three major consequences can be derived:

- Any kind of e-business that wants to improve its relations with potential customers needs to know what kinds of behaviours can be expected, and which of them are profitable and which are not. Even more, it should be able to decide how to transform a session that potentially is not profitable in a beneficial one.
- In order to use that knowledge, a major concern must be to identify on the fly the kind of user that is visiting the site in a precise moment. Personal data will help, of course, but if the user prefers to remain anonymous then we are obliged to make some well-founded guess from the behaviour of the user in the site.
- Data Mining techniques are a must in all this decision-making process, and any available source of data must be considered. Deep data about customers are welcomed but many times web-logs plus additional behavioural information will be all we have to solve the problem. This illustrates the importance of why establishing the correct data set is so vital in electronic relations

4 Data Sources for e-CRM

By far the most effective method of gathering website visitors' information is via registration forms. The data generated from a website is only the starting point in the data mining process as its value increases when merged with datawarehouse and third party information. There are various optimal methods and sources for gathering information rather than asking for it directly. Asking too many questions can lead to intentionally incorrect information from visitors. Several external sources of information can be linked to a web site for additional insight into the identity, lifestyle and behaviour of your visitor. Thus additional information can assist a website to communicate, relate, and retain online customers.

"Analysing clickstream data is becoming the most important activity for e-businesses. Clickstream analysis can reveal usage patterns on the company's web site and give a highly improved understanding of customer behaviour. This understanding can then be utilised for improved customer satisfaction with the web site and the company in general, yielding a huge business advantage" [19].

The Web has the advantage of being able to track "nearly every gesture made by the individual when they are touring remote Websites" [16]. "One advantage of e-commerce is that not only the products bought by the customer but also the behaviour of the customer can be recorded and analysed" [20]. This is not possible in conventional business, and might even breach privacy legislation. Additionally the interactive nature of the Web enables customer-feedback and behaviour to be better quantified and measured. This level of 'interactiveness' is not present in conventional businesses. Consequently, the quality of the information captured by Web logs and their subsequent mining reach into the heart of the problem

Web logs are a means of capturing the clickstream of Web Users. Due to the lack of a globally accepted standard, the existence of multiple file formats and some synchronisation problems across the heterogeneous network connectivity, not all clikstream information is saved. Web logs hold data such as the domain name/IP address of the client, the time in which the request reached the server or information about the pages visited in a session to name a few. Nevertheless, there is a lack of quality information on web logs. We must not forget that they were conceived as a help for system administrators, not as a vital tool for marketing. Therefor, analysts had to add other tools for collecting data, such as applications logs, cookies, and the more conventional sources of user data: user registration forms, email responses, Web purchase data and data from external sources.

The sources of data for enabling customer profiling are (Figure 1):

- Information contained within the HTTP protocol (i.e. traditional Clickstream data via Web server/logs)
- Local company Web servers capturing user actions. (site's application server/logs)
- Cookies defined as "tiny text files that can be created on client machines to store information about who the user is and where they have travelled on a Web site." [21]
- Beacons or bugs, functions embedded in Web pages that can send access information directly to a database or Web application [21]
- Data from external sources (e.g. advertising agencies, specialist agencies holding large volumes of customer information, etc.);
- User registration forms
- E-mail inquiries or response data
- Web purchase data

The last four, identified by [22], are conventional sources, which require either voluntary responses or actions whereas the former four are more automated and are simply transparent for the user. Consequently the first four sources are more accurate and require no extra effort from the user. The most important sets of data are acquired from the session, application and click event levels [16]. In the next section we will discuss the problems that current systems find when mining such a wide, diverse, incomplete and unstructured source of data.

By far the most effective method of gathering website visitors' information is via registration forms. The data generated from a website is only the starting point in the data mining process as its value increases when merged with datawarehouse and third party information. There are various optimal methods and sources for gathering information rather than asking for it directly. Asking too many questions can lead to intentionally incorrect information from visitors. Several external sources of information can be linked to a web site for additional insight into the identity, lifestyle and behaviour of your visitor. Thus additional information can assist a website to communicate, relate, and retain online customers.

The merging of all this information can make any business more profitable as it presents the opportunity for not only after-the-fact analysis but also proactive "shopping time" customer interaction.

In traditional environments, data about customers and prospects is introduced into the data warehousing environment from transactional systems, synthesised, and made available for reporting and analysis. The after the fact nature of the data analysis added to the non automated business processes that are performed using the results typically results in a long business process cycle in which it is very difficult to react in "Internet time" [8].

The primary objectives of extended customer intelligence services are to decrease the elapsed time between the business and technical processes that use information in the data warehouse, to provide insight into customers' past behaviour as well as to guess likely future behaviours and to tailor interaction and dialogs so that they are likely to be more productive and profitable.

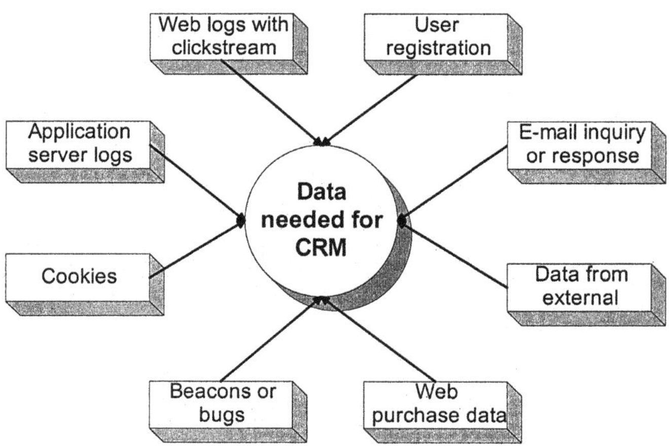

Fig. 1: Current Sources of User Data Enabling Customer Profiling

In the following sections we introduce an approach that makes possible to perform CRM in an on-line e-Commerce environment, accomplishing a good CRM strategy: targeting the right offer to the right customer at the right time for the right price. Using a neural network and taking as inputs the clickstream and purchase transactions collected at a web server of a virtual shop, we will produce a model of the clients. It will be based on their past behaviour and on their social and economic description, which will describe their tendency of purchasing different products during his/her life cycle. This model can be used to guide the interaction (including its content) with potential customers that visit the virtual shop.

5 Related Work

Many approaches have focused on applying intelligent techniques to provide personal advice and interaction. Collaborative filtering is one of the key techniques for providing customisation for e-commerce. Collaborative filtering is based on the assumption that finding similar users and examining their usage patterns leads to useful recommendations being made.

Automated methods are also needed to provide users information to efficiently locate and retrieve information. Personalised advice systems can be classified into two main categories: content-based, mostly used to retrieve relevant textual documents, and collaborative filtering. The task of collaborative filtering is to predict the preferences of a user, given a database of preferences usually expressed as numerical scores of other users' preferences. In this setting, the data set consists on a collection of pairs of objects where each pair consists of a person and an item (i.e. Web pages, products). In collaborative filtering the goal is to task we are interested in make predictions on how likely a person is to be interested in a particular item given information about its behaviour in the site and other user's historical behaviour or interests.

Memory-based collaborative filtering algorithms use a database of previous users' preferences and perform certain calculations on the database each time that a new prediction is needed [1]. The most common representatives are nearest neighbour-based algorithms where a subset of users that are as similar as possible to an active user is chosen and a weighted average of their scores is used to estimate preferences of the active user on other items [2], [3]. In contrast, model based algorithms first develop a description model from a database and use it to make predictions for a user. Systems of this type include Bayesian networks [1] and classification-based algorithms [4].

Neighbour based collaborative filtering algorithms are known to be superior to model based in terms of accuracy, but their high latency can be a drawback in systems with a large number of requests to be pre-processed in real time. Moreover, as the number of items evaluated for an active user decreases, the prediction accuracy on neighbour systems deteriorates dramatically. In [5] an alternative regression-based approach to collaborative filtering is proposed, which searches for relationships among items instead of looking for similarities among users and builds a collection of experts in the form of simple linear models that are combined to provide preference predictions. This method is two orders of magnitude faster than the neighbour based alternatives.

The majority of the approaches to the problem of collaborative filtering assume an attribute-value based kind of data representation for each object and focus on a single relationship between the objects. In [6], the authors examine a richer model that makes it possible to reason about many different relations between the objects. The authors also show how probabilistic relational models PRM can be applied to the task of collaborative filtering. PRM makes it possible to represent uncertainty about the existence of relationships in the model and allows the properties of an object to depend probabilistically both on the properties of that object and on properties of related objects. This is particularly important in the context of WWW where there is often more relational information than the simple person-item relationship. They also focus on model-based methods and review the two-side clustering model for collaborative filtering [7]. The two-side clustering method is based on the idea that for each person you have a hidden variable that represents the unknown cluster of that person and for each item a hidden variable that represents the cluster of that item. For each pair person-item you have a variable denoting the relation between this person and this item which depends on the cluster of the person and the cluster of the item, which is why it is called two-sided clustering. The authors describe how this model can be represented by a bayesian network (BN), and shows how this model can be represented as a probabilistic relational model (PRM) and how the PRM subsumes and extends the BN model.

6 A Client's Life Cycle Model Based on a Neural Network

6.1 Data Description

Clients' Clickstreams and purchase transactions were collected at a web server of a virtual shop, which sells legware and legcare products [25]. The web server logs customer transactions and clickstreams, assigning unique ids to sessions through the use of *jsp* pages.

The logged information was enriched adding demographic external data, following the principles described in section 5 (figure 3). The amount if available information was really vast. In order to keep our experiments small in size and easily manageable, we only worked with a small subset of the clients' attributes. This decision conditions the quality of the resulting models because the more complete description of the client is, the more accurate the models will be. However, the positive reading is that if we are able to obtain useful models with a small set of descriptors then we will assure the quality of the outputs when using the whole set. The used attributes and their possible values are described in Table 1. Variable called Brands indicates the brand of the acquired legware product.

Table 1: Attributes values and description

Attribute	Description	Values
Code	Unique ID for the session	Continuous
Age	Age of the customer	Continuous
Gender	Customer's gender	Female, Male
Occupation	Customer's occupation	Sales/service, professional/technical, self employed management, military, housewife, craftsman/blue collar, student, administrative/managerial, self employed prof/tech,retired, self employed sales/marketing, self employed, other, self employed blue collar, self employed clerical, self employed homemaker, clerical/white collar
Income	Customer's income	Ordered Under \$15;000, \$15;000-\$19;999, \$20;000-\$29;999, \$30;000-\$39;999, \$40;000-\$49;999, \$50;000-\$74;999, \$75;000-\$99;999, \$100;000-\$124;999, \$125;000 OR MORE
Brand	Brand of the bought product	NicoleMiller, Hanes, EllenTracy, Berkshire, AmericanEssentials

The data set consisted of 1575 purchasing records, with the following brand distribution: 138 NicoleMiller, 156 Hanes, 212 EllenTracy, 130 Berkshire, 387 AmericanEssentials, summing up a total of 1023, leaving 552 records for other products used as a "other brand" selection set.

6.2 The Client Model

The objective is to obtain a model of the Client's tendency of purchasing a particular brand of legware based on the available description of the client. The used description depends on 4 variables: gender, age, occupation and income of the client, and the purchased brand is described with a binary YES/NO variable.

Neural Networks such as a Multilayer Perceptron [23], have been extensively used to build categorizating models in which the inputs are descriptions of the category and the output indicates whether the description belongs or not to a category. Multilayer perceptrons implement a mathematical function f in the form of:

$$o = f(\vec{x})$$

where the components of the vector x_i are the description of the category and o is the output, indicating the category. The descriptors x_i are real numbers, so binary, integer or qualified data should be adapted to a desired continuous range, lets say [-1,+1].

In the case of qualified data, such as Occupation which has 17 values, the data must be expanded to the same number of binary inputs, each of them indicating if the current input record has that value or not. For example, Occupation must be expanded to 17 binary inputs, the first of them indicating whether the value is "Sales/service", the second whether it is "professional/technical", and so on. For a given input record, only one of the 17 binary inputs should be on. For instance, let's consider that the current record belongs to a Professional. The first binary input is then off, the second is on, the third off, and so on. Once we have all binary inputs, all of them are normalised to the continuous range, [-1,+1], with –1 indicating that the input is off, and +1 that is on.

Ordered qualified data, such as Income, can be translated to a continuous range if the distances between values can be calculated somehow. In the case of the variable Income, that distances can be calculated translating each value in various ways. One way is adopting the value of the arithmetic mean of each qualified range. For example, the value $20;000-$29;999 can be translated to 25000. Other way is to use one of the extremes, 20000 or 29999. In our experiments we adopted the later approach, selecting the upper extreme. For the problematic last value, $125;000 OR MORE, we used a compromised value of 175000.

In the case of the output, the process is reversed. The output is the result of the application of the function f to the input data. This function is a mathematical composition of functions called Activation Functions [23] which should be increasing, continuous and derivable functions in a specified range, such as [-1,+1], so the output o will stay within that range. Training the neural network consists on finding the right values for a set of constants that are used within the function f, so that the output o is producing +1 when the input data belongs to the category and –1 when it doesn't for all the training input set. But training a neural network is not a perfect process, and the outputs are few times +1 or –1 but rather a real number within (-1, +1). It is then needed a process for binarising the output.

To decide if a input record belongs or not to the category, the output o is binarised using the simple method of assigning a "yes" if the output is in the range of [0,+1] or "not" if it is within the range [-1, 0). That is the usual way of doing it, with some variations such as including an intermediate range like [-0.5, +0-5] to indicate "unknown" answers.

In our approach we decided not to interrupted the reversing process of binarise the output and just keep its continuous value, which can be interpreted as a "tendency" of belonging to a category. The closer it is to a value of +1 the greater the tendency is, and the opposite, the closer to a value of −1 the lesser the tendency is.

Summarising all the processing applied to the data, we have 1 input data for age, 1 for gender, 17 for occupation and 1 for income, making a total of 20 input variables within the range of [-1, +1]. In the case of the outputs, we treated separately each brand creating one different neural network model for each of them.

All Multiplayer Perceptron used as brand models have the same architecture [23]: 20 inputs, 8 hidden nodes and one output, and were trained with all the data set using the backpropagation learning procedure [23].

6.3 Applying the Neural Network Model to Build a Life Cycle Model

As stated in previous sections, a good CRM strategy must:

- Intervene at the exact right time to gain, maintain or expand a customer's business
- Identify customers' seasonal preferences and positive or negative trends in their behaviour
- Predict when a customer is about to take an action that will affect the company

And for doing so, any model made about clients' tendencies must take into account that the concept "client" is evolutionary; descriptors such as age or income change in time. The clear example is a teenager customer, a student, who remains loyal to a virtual shop during 10 more years while taking his first and probably second job. During this period he not only changed many of his preferences but also his purchasing capacity. Due to this, any useful model must cover a full customer's life cycle.

That is one of the goals of the neural network models described in the previous section. They output a model of purchasing tendencies for each brand and for each client description. How can these models be used to build Life Cycle based models? We say that a model is Life Cycle based when it is able to describe the variation of any descriptor, in our case purchasing tendencies, as the client's profile evolves, for example in age or income.

In the example, the models obtained using the training data set are able to react to inputs not present at training time. Therefor we can use those models to calculate tendencies with input combinations that describe possible Life Cycles of a person. The provided figures, show different but very related examples of the results obtained when applying the softcomputing approach to build these kind of models. The goal in this particular case is to analyse life cycles for customers with ages ranging from 20 to 80 years old and yearly incomes from 50,000$ up to 80,000$.

Figure 2 shows 4 different Life Cycle tendency models for a Woman with an occupation as a Professional. The figures show how these tendencies are affected by changes in age and income. For example, American Essentials seems to be the favourite brand for young professional woman, with low income. For high income, it seems that American Essentials enters in competence with Hanes. Berkshire is the preferred brand for middle age professional woman, with also low income, whilst Hanes is the favourite of adult and very young rich women.

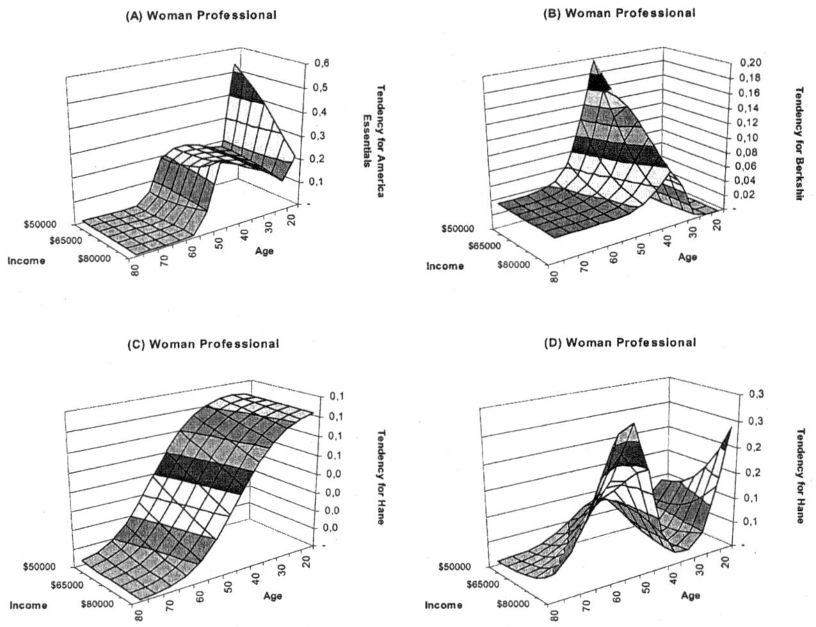

Fig. 2: 4 different Life Cycle models for 4 different brands of a woman professional.

Figure 3 shows clear differences in purchasing tendencies for the same branch depending on variables like occupation, and gender. A and B show the tendencies for the same brand, Ellen Tracy, showing notable differences depending on the occupation of the customer (professionals vs. housewives). In C, the same brand is analysed for men professionals. The results outline very low degrees of brand loyalty compared to the levels of women. In other words, there are only significant shopping levels at very precise and punctual customers profiles (middle age and low income) so the degree of loyalty is non-existent.

Figure 3.D shows another important result that can be achieved using this method. Common sense tells us that people with different incomes use to buy different products and even different brands of the same product. This is what companies normally call market segments. However, when we applied the neural approach to the data we came out with some results that show that the real tendencies were not exactly as expected. For most of the branches no clear shopping rate differentiation can be made taking into account customers incomes. Of course, there are slight variations for different income rates, but they are not as marked as expected. There is only a brand, EllenTracy, that is clearly segmented for people with rather high incomes.

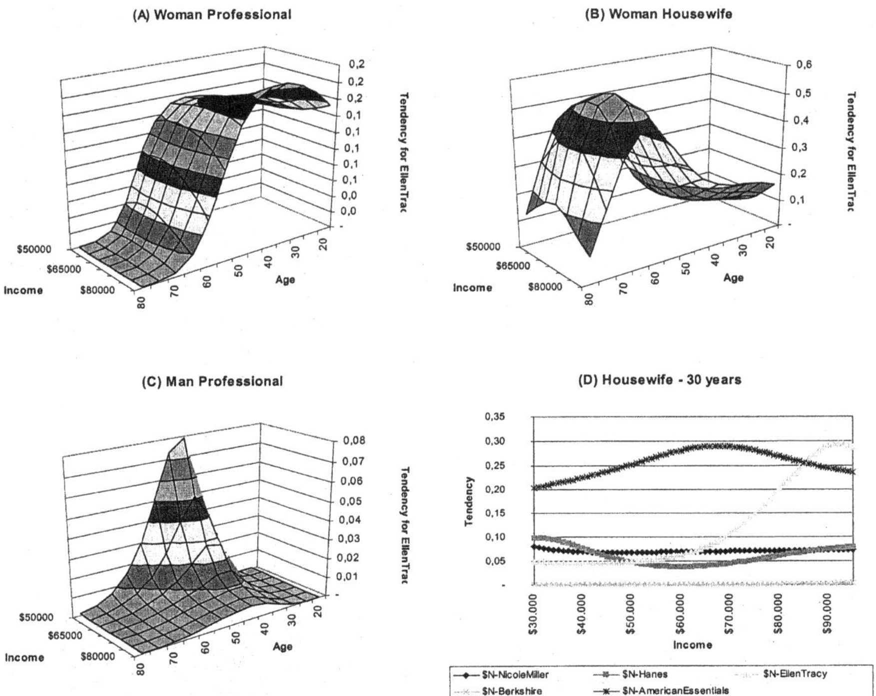

Fig 3: A, B and C show 3 different Life Cycle models for a unique brand, EllenTracy. D shows a combination of tendencies of a 30-year-old Housewife depending on the income.

7 Conclusions

There was a lot of hope placed on e-commerce systems and Internet services in general. But the truth is that, after some active years disappointment is the general sensation in this field. Users don't feel comfortable using these services and investors are no getting as much benefit as expected.

Day by day, there is a growing theory that says that the web is only a good channel for services or applications that meet any (or both) of the "Wyg Couple", Wyni and Wyli [24]. Wyni Wyg stands for "What you need is what you get" and Wyli Wyg for "What you like is what you get". Needs or pleasure are the two only reasons that move a person to a web site (for instance, in Spain one of the most visited places is the Tax Office Web Site). So any successful e-business must take these into account.

How can then e-commerce improve to meet any of the previous? Shopping is an obvious need, but people don't like shopping in those impersonal e-shops where

no help can be found and everybody is treated just in the same tedious way. Personalisation is the key concept, to offer the right thing in the right moment to the right customer.
Personalisation needs on-line detection plus prediction. Detection can be performed in any of the ways described in previous sections, whilst Life Cycle models can be used to anticipate to the behaviour and reactions of the clients during his/her life, therefor predicting their needs or tastes. Using models such as those shown in figures 4 or 5, the CRM manager is able to identify current or future trends in the purchasing tendencies of each individual client, being then ready to launch the appropriated marketing campaign or the personalised treatment.

Life Cycle models can be automated. When a tendency of a client is clearly dependent on a identified feature such as age or income, changes in that features can be detected automatically and an alert may be sent to the customer contact person while the personalised presentation of the virtual shop is adapted to the new client likeness.

References

1. John S. Breese, David Heckerman, and Carl Kadie. (1998) Empirical analysis of predictive algorithms for collaborative filtering. In Gregory F. Cooper and Serafín Moral, editors, Proceedings of the 14th Conference on Uncertainty in Artificial Intelligence (UAI-98), pages 43-52, San Francisco, July 24-26. Morgan Kaufmann.
2. Joseph A. Konstan, Bradley N. Miller, David Maltz, Jonathan L. Herlocker, Lee R. Gordon, and John Riedl. (1997) GroupLens: Applying collaborative filtering to Usenet news. Communications of the ACM, 40(3):77-87, March.
3. Upendra Shardanand and Patti Maes. (1995) Social information filtering: Algorithms for automating \word of mouth". In Proceedings of ACM CHI'95 Conference on Human Factors in Computing Systems, volume 1 of Papers: Using the Information of Others, pages 210-217.
4. Daniel Billsus and Michael J. Pazzani. (1998) Learning collaborative information filters. In Proc. 15th International Conf. on Machine Learning, pages 46-54. Morgan Kaufmann, San Francisco, CA.
5. Slodoban Vucetic and Zoran Obradovic. (2000) A regression based approach for scaling-up personalized recommeder systems in e-commerce. In The Sixth ACM SIGKDD International Conference on Knowledge Discovery and Data Mining (Workshop on Web Mining for E-Commerce - Challenges and Opportunities), August.
6. Lise Getoor and Mehran Sahami. Using probabiistic relational models for collaborative filtering.
7. Thomas Hofmann and Jan Puzicha. (1999) Latent class models for collaborative filtering. In Dean Thomas, editor, Proceedings of the 16th International Joint Conference on Artificial Intelligence (IJCAI-99-Vol2), pages 688-693, S.F., July 31-August 6. Morgan Kaufmann Publishers.

8. Simon, S. Shaffer 2001. Data Warehousing and Business Intelligence for e-commerce. Morgan.Kaufman 2001.
9. http://www.netmining.com/page.jsp?PadeID=152
10. Ansari S, Kohavi R, Mason L, Zheng Z, (2000). "Integrating E-Commerce and Data Mining: Archetecture and Challenges." WEBKDD 2000 Workshop: Web Mining for E-Commerce – Challenges and Opportunities. http://robotics.Stanford.EDU/~ronnyk/WEBKDD2000/index.html
11. http://www.acrue.com/Company/Press_Releases/pr_010625.html
12. Microsoft, Great Plains eEnterprise (2001). "Fully Integrated Customer Relationship Management Solutions." Microsoft Corporation, www.greatplains.com
13. http://www.acius.net/pdf/pdf_cID-24.pdf
14. Fingar P, Kumar H, & Sharma T, (2000). "Enterprise E-Commerce." Meghan-Kiffer Press. ISBN: 0929652118
15. Berry M.J.A & Linoff G. (2000). "Mastering Data Mining; The Art and Science of Customer Relationship Management." Wiley Computer Publishing. ISBN 0-471-33123-6
16. Kimball R, & Merz R, (2000). "The Data Webhouse Toolkit; Building The Web-Enabled Data Warehouse." Wiley Computer Publishing. ISBN 0-471-37680-9
17. DM Review "Business Intelligence: Enabling E-Business." Volume 10, Number 10, October 2000, p36-38
18. Han J, & Kamber M, (2001). "Data Mining Concepts and Techniques." Morgan Kaufmann Publishers. ISBN 1-55860-489-8
19. Andersen J, Giversen A, Jensen A, Larsen R.S, Pedersen T.B, & Skyt J, (2000). "Analysing Clickstreams Using Subsessions." ACM
20. Theusinger C, Huber KP, (2000). "Analysing the footsteps of your customers- A case study by ASK|net and SAS Institute GmbH." SAS Institute GmbH, Heidelberg, Germany
21. http://www.appiancorp.com/consulting/expertise/clickstreamanalysis.asp
22. Rudd O.P, (2001). "Data Mining Cookbook: Modelling Data for Marketing, Risk, and Customer Relationship Management." Wiley Computer Publishing. ISBN 0-471-38564-6
23. Hertz J, Krogh A, & Palmer R (1991). "Introduction to the theory of Neural Computation", Santa Fe Institute, Addison-Wesley.
24. Avatars Virtual Technologies (2001). "Strategies in Internet". White Paper. http://www.avatarsvt.com.
25. Ron Kohavi, Carla Brodley, Brian Frasca, Llew Mason, and Zijian Zheng. KDD-Cup 2000 organizers' report: Peeling the onion. SIGKDD Explorations, 2(2):86-98, 2000. http://www.ecn.purdue.edu/KDDCUP

Customer Relationship Management Systems: The Application of Fuzzy ART Neural Network

Sungjune Park[1] and Nallan C. Suresh[2]

[1] College of Business Administration, University of North Carolina at Charlotte, Charlotte, North Carolina 28223, USA, email: supark@email.uncc.edu
[2] School of Management, State University of New York at Buffalo, Buffalo, New York 14260, USA, email: ncsuresh@acsu.buffalo.edu

Abstract. An essential element of e-commerce customer relationship management (eCCRM) systems is the analytical subsystem, or model base for analyzing customer-related data. We present a neural network-based application for this data mining function for effective customer relationship management. We first list the various objectives of CRM, the essential elements and the requisite e-business architectures. Then we propose, and illustrate the application of Fuzzy ART neural network for customer grouping and buying pattern recognition, based on customer's purchasing history. Step-by-step procedures for implementing the algorithm, and contextual framework for real-world CRM system are presented.

1 Introduction

Faced with the new competitive pressures of e-commerce era, there has been a concerted effort in industry to integrate front-end business functions and customer interfaces in radically new ways. This has been pursued primarily through new managerial and marketing philosophies based on customer relationship management (CRM) and adoption of e-commerce CRM (eCCRM) systems and technologies.

The emergence of CRM systems is a direct result of many trends: increased customer expectations, increasing service levels provided by competing firms, globalization, cost of acquiring new customers, high customer turnover and, above all, the emergence of Internet and other information systems and technologies. These new information technologies have enabled new levels of sophistication in data access, storage, and communication with customers. CRM market value and growth estimates vary widely, but almost all estimates agree on a period of high growth rates during the next few years.

Going beyond mere integration and automation of marketing and sales functions, which are typically fragmented in most firms, CRM also seeks to provide a unified and multi-faceted view of the customer, and a consistent and responsive image of the company for the customers. As pointed out often, customers are unconcerned about how a company stores its information, and how it integrates data from many internal sources; customers merely require unique, personalized, meaningful interactions and service, and attention to their special needs. To accomplish these objectives, CRM systems also attempt to provide meaningful storage and use of data and information (data warehousing) and analytical (data mining) capabilities to probe and meet the strategic needs of businesses.

The technologies resident in eCCRM provide businesses with a wide array of tools to enhance customer relationships. Numerous software providers offer software solutions and services to improve sales and marketing performance and integrate multiple selling channels. Evolving from technologies that were originally designed to automate sales and service functions, eCCRM has now become a major means for aggregating customer information into data warehouses, analyzing the data, and managing collaboration proactively with customers through an expanding number of points of interaction.

An essential element of customer relationship management systems is an analytical subsystem, or model base for the analysis of customer-related data, often in real time, during interactions with the customer. Focusing on this data mining function, the primary objective of this paper is to dwell on requisite tools and techniques, especially various artificial neural networks (ANNs), for data mining for effective CRM. Compared to other application areas, neural network applications for data mining, and marketing applications in general, seem to be in an incipient stage.

The collection of consumer information in electronic form has improved considerably, but how to analyze data effectively is also of interest to marketers and researchers. Target marketing as well as direct marketing can be effective when a company is able to collect rich information about consumers. Marketers use the term *data mining* to describe the process of analyzing a company's internal data for customer profiling and targeting. Marketing databases often handle tens of millions of customer records, and in the case of direct marketing even small improvements in yield for a mailing can mean substantial profits. Thus, most direct marketers use modeling techniques to analyze and select names for a catalog or flyer and to predict the percentage response.

Popular data mining techniques available today are discriminant analysis, decision tree induction, and neural networks including multiple linear regression [14]. In this chapter, the use of Fuzzy ART neural network method is illustrated for mining customer data. Neural networks, which attempt to simulate biological intelligence of human neural system, have emerged as viable methods for a wide range of applications in many areas of management: stock price predictions and bank failure predictions in finance [16], cell formation and part family identification problems in manufacturing [15], and sales forecasting, target marketing and direct marketing [18] in marketing, etc.

The applicable areas of neural networks in marketing can be divided into three sectors: retail sales forecasting, direct marketing, and target marketing [18]. Sales forecasting is essential for efficient management of inventory while maintaining the ability to meet demand at multiple store location. Dependent variable is typically market demand for a specific product, and independent variables are consumers' income, size of population within the coverage of a store, price of the product, price of substitutes and price of complementary products. Supervised neural networks such as back propagation algorithm [19] have been proved to perform better than regression analysis that has been applied to sales forecasting for a long time.

Direct marketing involves selling products to customers without an intermediary action such as advertising and sales promotion [10]. Since the main objective for direct marketers is to identify prospective customers to whom they mail sales solicitations, supervised learning methods are generally accepted setting output variable as individual's likelihood of buying. Independent variables includes demographic variables, socio-economic variables, and other customer attributes such as housing type, purchase decisions, and household type.

Target marketing involves grouping a major market into segments so as to target one or more of these segments or to develop products and marketing programs tailored to each segment. [10] Market segmentation is, in some sense, based on individual customer's preference on certain types of products. In practice, demographic information, geographic location, purchase behavior information, consumption behavior information, attitude to product, etc. are the determinants of market segmentation. As opposed to sales forecasting or direct marketing, the division of market into distinct groups of customers can be made using unsupervised neural network algorithm such as self organizing feature map (SOFM) [9] or ART-based algorithms [2]. Although not easy to get immediate outputs, unsupervised learning methods can be used in direct marketing as an alternative by identifying similar customer groups first, then finding out if a certain customer group contains significant number of prospective customers.

The proposed model of finding target customers in this paper assumes that history of products purchased or services provided to a certain customer contains most knowledge about consumer attributes, and accordingly provide enough information to identify target customer groups. Thus, only customer's purchasing history is used as input value for grouping similar customers based on their past decisions on products or services.

The rationale behind this is that individual consumer's buying behavior is reflected in his/her choices of products and services, and the behavior can be uncovered by analyzing the products and services he/she purchases. An "if-and-only-if relationship" does not always hold true. For example, the statement, "If a person is a student, he or she needs a math textbook." does not imply "If a person needs the math textbook, he or she is a student." Teachers need math textbooks, too. However, we can conclude that the person is a student with some supporting evidence such as "That person also buys history book, science book, and so on." Thus, each individual's product purchasing history can be a powerful information source to identify a customer when many data points from other individuals interact together. Mining the product purchase history data has now become very convenient in the era of electronic commerce, and there is no reason not to take advantage of this kind of data.

2 The Integrative Framework of eCCRM

2.1 The Basic Features of eCCRM

E-commerce customer relationship management systems primarily attempt to create, nurture, and manage *relationships with customers*, driven by new approaches to customer service, marketing and business strategies, utilizing new information systems and technologies. The eCCRM system represents, or incorporates almost all major integration trends currently taking place within marketing and sales contexts of firms.

Besides the information technology aspects, the emergence of eCCRM also represents a major shift in marketing philosophy based on the tenets of *relationship marketing,* in the quest for competitive advantage. Many Marketing researchers view relationship marketing as a genuine paradigm shift of marketing, from an exchange, transactional focus to one in favor of a relationship between the supplier and its customer(s) [13]. Tzokas and Saren [17] define relationship marketing as "the process of planning, developing and nurturing a relationship climate that will promote a dialogue between a firm and its customers which aims to imbue an understanding, confidence and respect of each others' capabilities and concerns when enacting their role in the market place and the society". A basic premise is that one-to-one dialog between the firm and customers can bring a higher level of learning about each other. Not withstanding these dialectics, it may be safely stated that relationship marketing is becoming widely adopted as the prevailing marketing philosophy, through the implementation of CRM systems.

Originating from legacy systems, the evolution to full-fledged CRM systems may be represented as shown in Table 1. CRM systems may be seen to be relationship-centric, with high levels of functional integration, as reengineered business processes. CRM systems are also endowed with data warehousing and mining capabilities. It may thus be stated that CRM is a combination of business processes and technology that seek to understand a customer from a multi-faceted perspective, enabling, among other benefits, a focus on the “best” customers and their needs, creating new delivery channels to meet their needs, capturing a large volume of customer-related data, and tying them to create a unique experience.

CRM systems must fulfill three basic requirements. They should: 1) provide a consistent and unified view of a customer for every interaction; 2) enable a customer to have a complete view of the company regardless of the way the customer contacts it; and, 3) enable front-end staff perform sales, service, and marketing tasks more efficiently as a team, reducing costs and boosting efficiency.

Thus the core functionality of CRM is its ability to maintain a single, cohesive view of the customer for the customer-facing functions of sales, service, and marketing.

In addition, CRM software is also expected to have the ability to support sales processes, opportunity management, and pipeline management. It examines forecasting, territory management, and team-selling capability. CRM systems also provide sales productivity tools, including sales configuration and quote generation.

Likewise, Marketing performs two functions that require capability from CRM software: campaign management and prospect generation. CRM software must have the ability to run a customer-service or -support operation, including the capability to record interactions with the customer, as well as being able to provide differentiated service according to the terms of a contract.

The expected benefits from CRM systems include: 1) increased sales revenues; 2) increased win rates; 3) increased margins; 4) improved customer satisfaction ratings; and, 5) decreased general sales and marketing administrative costs. These benefits may arise due to a variety of reasons, including, better specification of target segment customers, knowing their needs better, more productive selling time and efforts, mailing information to the right customers and market segments, etc.

Table 1. Evolution of CRM (from Kalakota & Robinson [8])

	Legacy Application	**Evolving Legacy Applications**	**Data-centric Applications**	**Relationship-centric Applications**
Applications	No cross-channel Systems	Customer information	Limited functional integration	Functional Integration
Service & Support	No access to Customer information	Access to customer information	Access to Relationship Information	Integrated Sales & Service Information
Marketing	No marketing tools	Batch processes for Marketing	Customer Information File	Closed loop Integrated Marketing
Decision Support	No customer analysis	Limited Customer Analysis	Data Warehouse Applications	Data mining & Knowledge Discovery

2.2 Objectives of eCCRM

As an integrated sales, marketing, service and business strategy, the objectives of eCCRM are primarily to:

Create a comprehensive, unified and consistent view of the customer to maximize his / her relationship with the company. This presents opportunities for cross-selling and up-selling, and providing a pleasant and productive relationship for the customer, etc. Thus CRM provides opportunities to use existing relationships to augment revenues.

Create consistent, dependable and convenient interactions for customers in every encounter, and at different points of contact with the firm, through standardized and consistent sales processes.

Enable identification, attraction and retention of the "best" customers. This includes: a) targeting those customers who will purchase a particular product; b) discriminating between most profitable customers and customers who result in a loss; c) identifying customers who will remain loyal and ones who may switch to competing firms; d) cross-selling products to interested customers; and, f) taking a relationship view (consolidated view) to avoid departments working against each other.

Enable better customer retention programs that will maximize lifetime revenues; even a small magnitude of customer retention generally leads to a large increase in profitability.

Enable effective use of integrated information for quality service, saving time for customers, easing frustrations, obviating the need to repeat information to different departments, and delighting customers by revealing how well the firm knows them.

Create new value to products offered, in real time, instilling loyalty.

Enable implementation of proactive solution strategy, instead of reactive data collection and analysis.

2.3 Functional Capabilities and Elements of CRM

Encompassing both sales and marketing functions, with communication with prospects and customers taking place through fax, telephone, Internet and e-mail, etc., eCCRM systems must possess the capability of integrating a diverse range of sales and marketing functions, as shown in Figure 1. Specifically, eCCRM systems must provide the following eleven capabilities [5]:

1. Sales functionality: contact management profiles and history, account management activities including order entry and proposal generation
2. Sales management functionality: pipeline analysis (forecasting, sales cycle analysis, territory alignment and assignment, roll-up and drill-down reporting)
3. Telemarketing/telesales functionality: call list assembly, auto dialing, scripting, order taking
4. Time management functionality: single user and group calendar/scheduling
5. Customer service and support functionality: incident assignment, tracking, reporting, problem management, resolution, order management, promising, warranty, contract management
6. Marketing functionality: campaign management, opportunity management, web-based encyclopedia, configurator, market segmentation, lead generation
7. Executive information functionality: extensive and easy-to-use reporting
8. ERP integration functionality: legacy systems, the web, third-party external information

9. Data synchronization functionality: mobile synchronization with multiple field devices, enterprise synchronization with multiple databases and application servers
10. E-commerce functionality: through EDI link and web-server, B2B and B2C applications
11. Field service support functionality: work orders, dispatching, real time information transfer to field personnel via mobile technologies.

These functions may also be classified under three discrete, but interrelated functional categories:

Operational CRM: Customer-facing applications that integrate the front, back, and mobile offices, including sales-force automation, enterprise marketing automation, and customer service and support.

Analytical CRM: Applications that analyze customer data generated by operational tools for the purpose of business performance management. Analytical CRM is inextricably tied to a data warehouse.

Collaborative CRM: Collaborative services such as personalized publishing, E-mail, communities, conferencing, and Web-enabled customer interaction centers that facilitate interactions between customers and businesses. Collaborative CRM is used to establish the lifetime value of customers beyond the transaction by creating a partnering relationship.

As pointed above, the analytical elements of CRM rely on *data warehouses, data marts and data mining* as major elements, and they are defined in the next section.

2.4 Data Warehouses, Data Marts and Data Mining

Data warehouses and data marts are primarily repositories of data that facilitate proactive marketing and sales efforts. A *data warehouse* may be defined as an enterprise-level data repository that draws its contents from all critical operational systems and selected external data sources. It is built according to an enterprise data model that must be pre-designed, and resulting from a cross-functional effort. Creation of data warehouses requires considerable time and resource commitments: they may cost several millions of dollars and may take as long as three years to complete. A *data mart* is more narrow in scope, and may be defined as a functional, subject-area or departmental data repository that draws its contents from systems that are critical to the unit owning the data mart and from selected external sources.

Data mining may be defined as the automated discovery of non-obvious and non-trivial patterns hidden in a database having a high potential for contributions to the bottom line. Generally, the most useful non-trivial pattern is predictive. If a firm can predict customer behavior, like remaining loyal or purchasing in response to a campaign, then it can gain commercial advantage. Predictions can be made using data mining techniques and statistical models. Data mining may encompass computer-based machine-learning methods that may extract patterns or information from data while requiring only limited human involvement. These methods have evolved from artificial intelligence (AI) techniques such as neural networks, association rules, decision trees, and genetic algorithms. Using the terms precisely, data mining identifies patterns of behavior for some (but not all) of the data, while statistical modeling produces models that explain the different types of behavior of all the data.

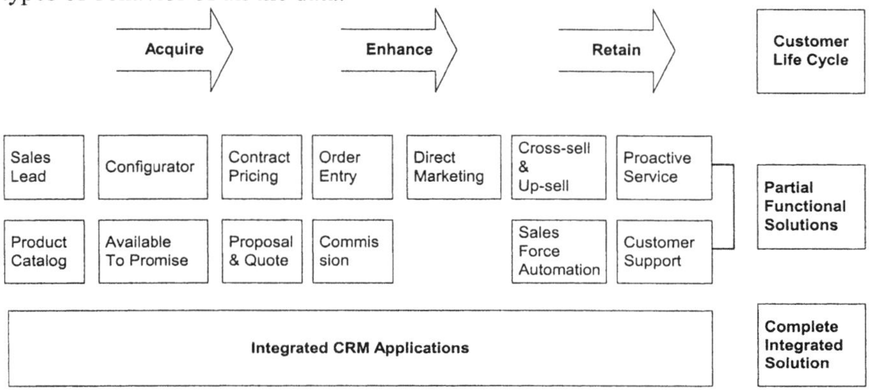

Fig. 1. Sales and Marketing Functions in the Order Life Cycle

The discovery of patterns implies looking for relationships that are not known beforehand. Discovery is akin to surfing, i.e., searching for interesting patterns and following the data trail wherever it leads. The discovery process often involves sifting through massive quantities of data: electronic point-of-sale transactions, inventory records, and online customer orders, which when matched with demographics, can require hundreds of gigabytes of data storage.

In a broader sense, data mining may encompasses "confirmation" or the testing of relationships revealed through the discovery process. Both classical and Bayesian statistical methods may be employed to formally assess hypotheses turned up at the discovery stage, or relationships may be searched for and confirmed to support the theories, models, and hypotheses formulated within the narrow scope of data mining. Prior to confirmation, beliefs are more akin to hunches. Within the broad scope, the data mining also encompasses simple queries and traditional investigative procedures, most of which have their roots in statistics. Examples of these procedures are exploratory data analysis, ordinary least squares regression, logistic regression, and discriminant analysis. There is also a greater involvement of the manager and analyst in structuring the investigation, identifying important variables prior to analysis, and attempting to ensure that the variables are in a form suitable for analysis.

Data mining may also be stated as one stage of *knowledge discovery in databases* (KDD). The stages of KDD are data preparation, data exploration, data mining, modeling, implementation and finally a report or white paper.

Current interest in data mining stems from advances in data storage and data processing technology, enabling the analysis of large amount of data; reductions in the cost of collecting and storing the customer data as well as operational data flowing from networks such as point-of-sale data from retail stores and Web users' click streams from companies' web sites. Artificial neural networks have come to be applied widely for this function and this paper describes the application of Fuzzy ART neural network for data mining.

2.5 Consumer Information and Electronic Commerce

Over the past five years, emergence of the World Wide Web, rapid growth of the Internet, e-mail as a common communication method, and other related technologies lead us to the success of electronic commerce. For example, emails begin to take significant portion of personal communications and people are spending more and more time sending and receiving emails through the Internet. Another remarkable change is totally automated process of purchasing goods and services on commercial Web sites. Customers can shop around a virtual store and buy products as they do in physical store. The information flow such as retailers' product information and consumer's purchasing history is stored in the database and readily available for analysis using database query. Moreover, advanced Web technology such as cookie enables the retailer to keep track of a certain customers purchasing activity over time.

The main theme of this paper is that clustering customers into groups can lead to better marketing practice. In view of direct marketing, with the easiness of disseminating advertisements through e-mails, one might think mass marketing through email is not costly. However, reduction in mailing cost does not mean mass marketing through email is effective in electronic commerce. There is trade-off between mass marketing and target marketing. The key problem of mass marketing via email is email user's lack of attention. Lack of attention to email advertising is unavoidable because customers tend to get tired of unsolicited emails. In order to maximize the response from email advertising, marketer should not send information that customers do not like. In doing so, customers will trust those companies and pay attention to emails from them expecting valuable information to themselves. Therefore, marketing cost can decrease not only because of reduced mailing list, but also because of efficient identification of prospect customers.

Hagel and Rayport [7] anticipated that collecting consumer information is going to be costly and complex. They explained that it was made possible for consumers to obtain much more comprehensive and accurate profiles of their own commercial activities than any individual vendor could hope to collect; for example, smart cards contains detailed information about product such as item, price, and location of store. Thus, through those technologies, consumers will be able to choose whether to release or withhold information about themselves. "Their decision will hinge, in large part, on what vendors offer them in return for the data." Releasing privacy-related information is also dependent on the consumers' expectation about benefit in return for privacy. In a survey study regarding the use of secondary information and privacy, consumers less concerned about privacy on catalogs and promotions from the same vendor from which they made a purchase whereas they consider using secondary information from third party a privacy invasion. [4] In this regard, the proposed customer grouping method, to identify target groups for marketing, can utilize company's internal data that are less costly and has few problems with consumers' privacy concern.

3 Neural Network Applications for CRM

3.1 Overview of ANNs

Many types of artificial neural network (ANN) models have been developed over the years. The taxonomy of ANNs proposed by Lippmann [11] is widely used in the literature. This classifies ANNs first into those that accept binary-valued inputs and those accepting continuous-valued inputs. Secondly, these are classified on the basis of whether they are based on supervised or unsupervised training. These are further refined into six basic types of classifiers. However, within ART networks, the recent emergence of Fuzzy ART, which accepts continuous values, and various other developments require revision of this taxonomy.

Among the many properties of ANNs, their pattern recognition capability is of foremost relevance in the context of data mining. Unlike traditional artificial intelligence (AI) methods, employing logic and rule-driven procedures for pattern recognition, ANNs are adaptive devices that recognize patterns more through experience. Neural networks also have the ability to learn complex patterns and to generalize the learned information faster. They have the ability to work with incomplete information. Compared to rule-driven expert systems, neural networks are applicable when [1]: 1) the rules underlying decisions are not well understood; 2) numerous examples of decisions are available; and, 3) a large number of attributes describe the inputs.

Based on the direction of signal flow, two types of neural networks can be identified. The first type of architecture is the *feedforward* network, in which there is unidirectional signal flow from the input layers, via intermediate layers, to an output stage. In the *feedback* network, signals may flow from the output of any neuron to the input of any neuron. Neural networks are also classified on the basis of the type of learning adopted. In *supervised learning*, the network is trained, so that the inputs, as well as information indicating correct outputs are presented to the network. The network is also "programmed" to know the procedure to be applied to adjust the weights. Thus, the network has the means to determine whether or not its output was correct and the means to apply the learning law to adjust its weights in response to the resulting errors. The weights are modified on the basis of the errors between desired and actual outputs in an iterative fashion.

In *unsupervised learning*, the network has no knowledge of what the correct outputs should be, since side information is not provided to convey the correct answers. Accordingly, unsupervised learning is typically applicable to grouping problems. As a series of input vectors are applied, the network clusters the input vectors into distinct classes depending on the similarities. An *exemplar vector* (representative vector) is used to represent each class. The exemplar vector, after being created, is also updated in response to a new input that has been found to be similar to the exemplar. As all inputs are fed to the network, several exemplars are created, each one representing one cluster of vectors. *Combined unsupervised-supervised learning* first uses unsupervised learning to form clusters. Labels are then assigned to the clusters identified and a supervised training follows.

3.2 Data Mining Tasks and Associated Neural Network Methods

There are at least five major data mining tasks that are applicable to CRM with traditional statistical techniques: *summarization, predictive modeling, classification, clustering and link analysis* [12].

Summarization refers to methods that condense large amounts of data into summary measures that provide general descriptions of variables and their relationships. In addition to summary measures such as mean, various kinds of charts that graphically visualize characteristics of data can also be classified into summarization task.

The objective of predictive modeling is to predict outcomes using one or more of independent variables. Outcomes are typically treated as dependent variables taking numeric values in order to apply statistical techniques. This task can be easily modeled with multiple regression analysis, which models a relationship between independent variables and dependent variables.

Classification involves the task of classifying an object into one of several groups. Classification can be considered as predictive modeling when the outcomes in predictive modeling are category variables. For example, we may be interested in the decision whether or not a customer is profitable whereas the expected profit of the customer can be output variable in the analysis.

Link analysis refers to a family of methods that is employed to correlate purchase patterns cross-sectionally or over time.

Clustering refers to the process of grouping objects based on information contained in the sets of variables that describe them. In marketing practice, grouping similar customers can produce market segments to which customized marketing programs are targeted. Market-basket analysis, which determines what combinations of products are purchased at a given time, is an example of link analysis. Among the five major data mining tasks, predictive modeling, clustering, and classification are the tasks that neural networks can replace conventional statistical methods with better performances. In this section we will briefly introduce those three data mining tasks using neural networks as well as statistical analysis in the context of CRM.

3.2.1 Clustering Problem in CRM Context

Clustering is used to identify occurrences in the database with similar characteristics, subsequently grouping them into clusters. Unlike classification, the analyst does not specify the groupings ahead of time, and the results of clustering may or may not be valuable. Hence, building and executing campaigns based on classification tasks that favorably impact the behavior of customers with high profit potential often follow clustering task, in which marketers identify market segments containing customers or prospects with high profit potential. The opportunities that clustering can offer in eCCRM context involve comprehensive analysis of web server's log of page activity and a profile database, since identifying market segments requires significant data about prospective customers and buying behaviors. Moreover, the recent ART-based neural networks are capable of processing such large amount of data as web click-streams and all the individual customer profiles without statistical sampling.

Suppose clustering resulted in four segments based on customers' potential contribution and current contribution, as shown in Figure 2. In order to have such easily interpretable customer segments, the variables should be made as compact as possible using principal component factor analysis. Factor analysis is a widely used data reduction technique with which a set of correlated variables are removed and represented with a smaller set of derived variables, or *factors*. Given that four customer segments are found, we may select different major campaigns for each segment, and then we may perform classification tasks described above within each segment to improve the efficiency and effectiveness of the campaigns.

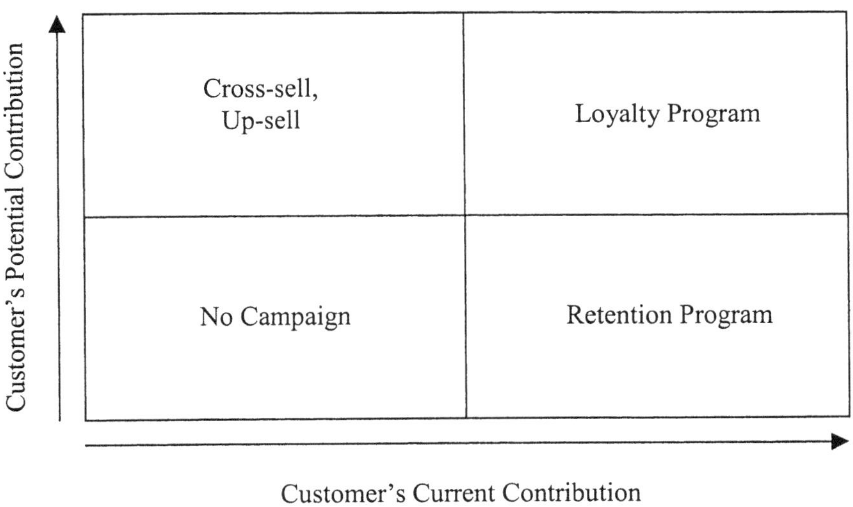

Fig. 2. Customer Segmentation by Profitability

There are two types of statistical tools to create groups of similar objects (customers in this context): hierarchical and iterative methods. The hierarchical method is based on a *similarity or proximity measure* between objects. Alternatively, we can deal with the *distance* between the pairs of objects, as complements of similarity. For example, with *single linkage method*, groups initially consisting of single objects are fused according to the distance between their nearest members, the groups with the smallest distance being fused. After the fusion, the distance between two clusters, C_K and C_L, is defined by: $D_{KL} = \min [\min \{d(x_i, x_j); j \in C_L\} ; j \in C_K]$, where $d(x_i, x_j)$ is the distance between observations or vectors x_i, x_j . The fusion continues until the number of clusters reaches a pre-determined number of clusters set by an analyst.

The most popular iterative method is *k*-means clustering method. This requires a number of groups, *k*, *a priori*. Initial seeds for those *k* groups are to be determined either randomly or by some other means. In the first step, each object is assigned to one of the *k* groups. Then, the cluster seeds are replaced by cluster means, and repeated until changes in cluster seeds become small or zero.

In contrast to traditional statistical clustering methods, ANNs offer a powerful clustering option, especially when [1]: 1) the input generating distribution is unknown and probably non-Gaussian; 2) estimating statistical parameters can be expensive and / or time consuming; 3) nonlinear relationships, and noise and outliers in the data may exist; and, 4) on-line decision making is required.

The advantages of ANNs over conventional statistical methods are as follows. First, neural networks are good at modeling non-linear relationships, while conventional statistical analysis in most cases assumes linear relationship between independent variables and dependent variables. Conventional statistical analysis may start with an assumed linear model such as causal relationship, but neural networks do not require *a priori* model. Neural networks build their own models with the help of learning process whether the relationships among variables are linear or not. Secondly, ANNs perform well with missing or incomplete data. Finally, ANNs do not require scale adjustment or statistical assumptions such as normality or independent error terms. Number of layers and weights between layers by design take care of scales of inputs, interdependency, etc. during the learning process.

ANNs for clustering purpose can be constructed using a feedforward network with back-propagation algorithm. However, the practical limitations and inflexibility of supervised, back-propagation systems have encouraged the development of numerous unsupervised methods, which take advantage of the natural groupings that may exist within a data set. Unsupervised methods do not require training and supervised prior learning, and they also have the capability of processing large amounts of input data. Current popular unsupervised neural networks include methods based on adaptive resonance theory (ART), including the recently developed Fuzzy ART network, and Kohonen's self-organizing feature maps (SOM). Both SOM and ART-based neural network utilize the *competitive learning model.*

Competitive learning models use a network consisting of two layers: an input layer and an output layer, which are fully connected as shown in Figure 3. First, the weight vectors are initialized using small random or uniform values. The input vector, $\boldsymbol{x}$, is a set of values characterizing the corresponding object. The output for each node in the output layer is computed as the weighted sum of the inputs and weight vectors in the customary manner.

The output node with the largest net input, j^* is selected as the winning node. In this "winner-take-all" approach, the weight vector associated with the winning node, $\boldsymbol{w}(j^*)$ is updated as: $\boldsymbol{w}'(j^*) = \boldsymbol{w}(j^*) + g\ \{ \boldsymbol{x} - \boldsymbol{w}(j^*)\}$, where g is a learning rate which assumes values between zero and one.

The competitive learning algorithm emulates the k-means clustering algorithm. This network is known to be very sensitive to the learning rate. Adaptive resonance theory (ART) networks developed later, extended competitive learning methods by introducing additional properties of stability and vigilance, as we see below. The SOM network uses a two-dimensional output layer (Kohonen layer). When a winning output node is selected, its weight vectors are updated as mentioned above. However, the weights of nearby nodes, within a specified neighborhood, are also updated using the learning rule. The size of the neighborhood is made to decrease progressively. Thus, eventually each output node has an associated topological relationship with other nodes in the neighborhood.

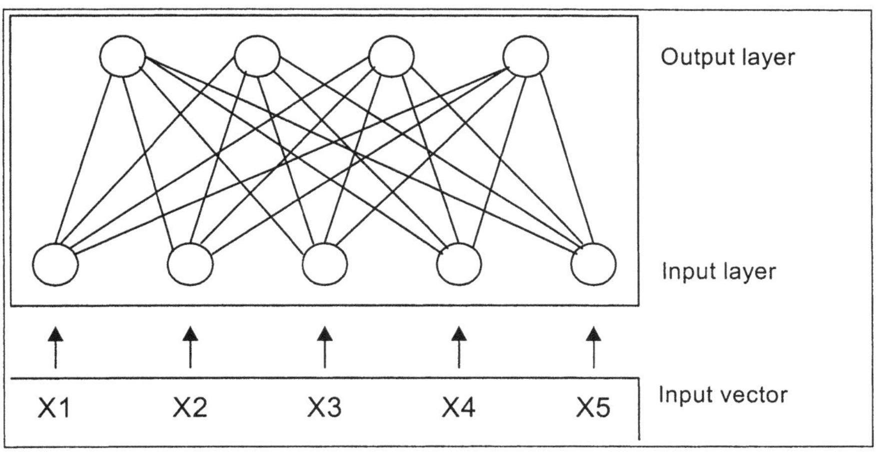

Fig. 3. Competitive learning model

Adaptive resonance theory (ART) represents an advancement over competitive learning and interactive activation models. This model uses the two-layer architecture, but introduces a vigilance measure and stability properties. This model implements a clustering algorithm that is similar to the *leader algorithm* (Lippmann, 1987).

ART has led to a series of networks for unsupervised learning and pattern recognition. Among these, ART1 [2] is the earliest development. The inputs for ART1 network are still the binary-valued pattern vectors. As the inputs are presented to the network, the model selects the first input as belonging to the first family. The first neuron in the output layer is made to represent this family. The weight vector associated with this neuron becomes the *exemplar* (representative vector) for the first family. If the next input is similar to this vector, within a specified *vigilance threshold* (ρ), then it is treated as a member of the first group. The weights connected to this group are also updated in light of the new input vector. If the new input is not similar to the exemplar, it becomes the exemplar for a new group, associated with the second neuron in the output layer. This process is repeated for all inputs. This same process is followed in all ART networks, including Fuzzy ART, the latest development in the series.

The Fuzzy ART network was introduced by Carpenter, Grossberg and Rosen [3]. It incorporates fuzzy logic and can handle both analog and binary-valued inputs. In addition, it uses a different learning law and permits a fast-commit-slow-recode option.

4 Fuzzy ART for Customer Group Identification

Like other ART networks, Fuzzy ART is also based on unsupervised learning. No training is performed initially to provide correct responses to the network. The network is operated as a leader algorithm. As each input vector is read, the network clusters each input into a distinct class. An *exemplar vector* (a representative vector) is created and maintained for each new class. If a new input is found to be similar (within a specified limit, referred to as vigilance threshold) to an existing exemplar, the input is classified under the category of that exemplar. The matching exemplar is also updated in the light of the new input. If a new input is not similar to any of the existing exemplars, it becomes a new exemplar. After all inputs are fed to the network, several exemplars are created, each representing one cluster.

The steps involved with Fuzzy ART are summarized in Table 1. The Fuzzy ART network consists of an input and an output layer. In step 1, all weight vectors, storing input patterns of output nodes, are initialized to values of one. The number of possible categories (output nodes) can be chosen arbitrarily large; the remaining output nodes are said to be uncommitted after feeding all inputs to the network. Fuzzy ART requires the specification of three parameters: choice parameter (α), learning parameter (β) and vigilance parameter (ρ). The choice parameter α is typically suggested to be close to 0. The learning parameter $\beta \in [0,1]$, defines the degree to which the weight vector $\mathbf{W}_j$ is updated (recoded) with respect to an input vector claimed by node j. The vigilance parameter $\rho \in [0,1]$, defines the required level of similarity between new inputs and existing exemplars (weights).

In the fast learning mode, Carpenter *et al.* (1991) suggest $\beta = 1$. In fast-commit slow-recode mode, they suggest $\beta = 1$ for first time committing an uncommitted node, and $\beta < 1$ (slow recode) for training a node that is already committed.

Step 2 involves reading each input. Each input **I** is represented by an M-dimensional vector, **I.** Each component in $\mathbf{I} \in [0,1]$ and M is the number of products. In our problem, scaling of product input is required in order to make each component in **I** less than or equal to 0. Scaling inputs can be done with the following procedure. Let $\mathbf{Q}^i$ be the quantity of the product purchased by customer i. Then scaled input $\mathbf{I}^i = (\mathrm{I}_1^i, \mathrm{I}_2^i, \mathrm{I}_3^i, \ldots, \mathrm{I}_\mathrm{M}^i)$ is determined by

$$\mathbf{I}_j^i = \frac{\mathbf{Q}_j^i - \min\limits_{1 \le l \le N}\{\mathbf{Q}_j^l\}}{\max\limits_{1 \le l \le N}\{\mathbf{Q}_j^l\} - \min\limits_{1 \le l \le N}\{\mathbf{Q}_j^l\}}$$

where N is the number inputs (customers).

Step 3 computes the choice function, $\mathbf{T}_j$, for each output node, j = 1 to U (expected maximum number of categories). From these, the output node j, with the largest $\mathbf{T}_j$ value, is selected in Step 4. However, it is necessary to check whether this 'best-match' meets the specified level of similarity (ρ). This is determined in Step 5.

The similarity measure computed in Step 5 is based on the 'fuzzy AND' operator. If this similarity level is greater than the specified ρ value, the part is classified under that class. The best-matching exemplar is also updated by modifying the associated weight vectors in Step 7. If it does not pass the similarity test, a new exemplar is created to reflect the new input. Thus, the process is repeated until all inputs are processed.

Table 2. Fuzzy ART for customer group identification

Step	Operation
1.	Initialize network weights and parameters: $\mathbf{W}_{jk}$, α, β, ρ. Set $\mathbf{W}_{jk} = 1, j = 1, 2, \ldots, \mathrm{U}, k = 1, 2, \ldots, \mathrm{M}$ Select values for parameters: $\alpha>0$, $\beta\in[0,1]$, and $\rho\in[0,1]$.
2.	Read scaled input **I.**
3.	For every output node j, compute: $T_j = \frac{\lvert \mathbf{I} \wedge \mathbf{W}_j \rvert}{\alpha + \lvert \mathbf{W}_j \rvert}$ for nodes j = 1, ..., U where '$\wedge$' is the fuzzy AND operator defined as $(\mathbf{X} \wedge \mathbf{Y})_i = \min(x_i, y_i)$ and the norm $\lvert\cdot\rvert$ is defined by $\lvert \mathbf{X} \rvert = \sum_i x_i, i = 1, \ldots, M$.
4.	Select output node whose exemplar matches with input best, Best matching exemplar: $\mathrm{T}_\theta = \max\{\mathrm{T}_\mathrm{j}\}$
5.	Check if this match is within specified similarity level: Resonance test (degree of similarity with best-matching exemplar) If similarity $= \frac{\lvert \mathbf{I} \wedge \mathbf{W}_j \rvert}{\lvert \mathbf{I} \rvert} \ge \rho$ go to Step 7; Else go to next Step 6.
6.	Enable selection of a new output node and exemplar for this input: Mismatch reset: Set $\mathbf{T}_\theta = -1$ and go to Step 4.
7.	Update best-matching exemplar (learning law): $\mathbf{W}_\theta^{(new)} = \beta(\mathbf{I} \wedge \mathbf{W}_\theta^{(old)}) + (1-\beta)\mathbf{W}_\theta^{(old)}$

5 Application of Fuzzy ART: An Illustrative Example

Consider an example situation where 5 customers made purchases among the choice of 6 products. For a given customer, the quantity of product purchased are known as below. First, we transform the raw data (**Q** vectors) to scaled inputs (**I** vectors) like the following:

$\mathbf{Q}^1 = [9\ 4\ 3\ 0\ 2\ 0] \Rightarrow \mathbf{I}^1 = [1\ .67\ \ 1\ \ 0\ \ 1\ \ 0]$
$\mathbf{Q}^2 = [2\ 6\ 0\ 1\ 0\ 1] \Rightarrow \mathbf{I}^2 = [.13\ 1\ \ 0\ \ 1\ \ 0\ .5]$
$\mathbf{Q}^3 = [1\ 3\ 0\ 0\ 0\ 1] \Rightarrow \mathbf{I}^3 = [0\ \ .5\ \ 0\ \ 0\ \ 0\ \ 1]$
$\mathbf{Q}^4 = [2\ 0\ 1\ 0\ 1\ 0] \Rightarrow \mathbf{I}^4 = [.13\ 0\ .33\ 0\ .5\ \ 0]$
$\mathbf{Q}^5 = [1\ 1\ 0\ 1\ 0\ 2] \Rightarrow \mathbf{I}^5 = [0\ .17\ \ 0\ \ 1\ \ 0\ \ 1]$

Initially, all nodes are uncommitted. All uncommitted nodes, i, have weight vectors, W_i = [111111]. Thus, initially only node 1 will be considered. Then, as node j becomes committed, node (j+1) represents all uncommitted weight vectors. For fast-commit slow-recode mode, initial $\beta = 1$; subsequent $\beta = .3$. We use .01 for the parameter α and .5 for ρ.

Processing of input 1: $\mathbf{I}^1 = [1\ .67\ \ 1\ \ 0\ \ 1\ \ 0]$
$\mathbf{T}_1 = 2.67/6.01$
Vigilance check: similarity = 2.67/2.67 = $1 > \rho$
Node 1 becomes committed. Since $\beta = 1$ initially, new $\mathbf{W}_1 = [1\ .67\ 1\ 0\ 1\ 0]$.

Processing of input 2: $\mathbf{I}^2 = [.13\ 1\ \ 0\ \ 1\ \ 0\ .5]$
$\mathbf{T}_1 = .8/2.68$
$\mathbf{T}_2 = 2.63/6.01$
Node 2 "wins" ($\mathbf{T}_2 > \mathbf{T}_1$).
Vigilance check: 2.63/2.63 = $1 > \rho$
Node 2 becomes committed. $\mathbf{W}_2 = [.13\ 1\ 0\ 1\ 0\ .5]$

Processing of input 3: $\mathbf{I}^3 = [0\ \ .5\ \ 0\ \ 0\ \ 0\ \ 1]$
$\mathbf{T}_1 = .5/2.68$
$\mathbf{T}_2 = 1/2.64$
$\mathbf{T}_3 = 1.5/6.01$
Node 2 "wins"
Vigilance check: 1/1.5 = $.67 > \rho$
Weight updates lead to new $\mathbf{W}_2 = [.09\ .85\ 0\ .7\ 0\ .5]$

Processing of input 4: $\mathbf{I}^4 = [.13\ 0\ .33\ 0\ .5\ \ 0]$
$\mathbf{T}_1 = .97/2.68$
$\mathbf{T}_2 = .09/2.15$
$\mathbf{T}_3 = .97/6.01$
Node 1 "wins"
Vigilance check: .97/.97 = $1 > \rho$
Weight updates lead to new $\mathbf{W}_1 = [.74\ .47\ .8\ 0\ .85\ 0]$

Processing of input 5: $\mathbf{I}^5 = [\,0\ \ .17\ \ 0\ \ 1\ \ 0\ \ 1\,]$

$\mathbf{T}_1 = .17/2.86$

$\mathbf{T}_2 = 1.37/2.15$

$\mathbf{T}_3 = 2.17/6$

Node 2 "wins"

Vigilance check: $1.37/2.17 = .64 > \rho$

Weight updates lead to new $\mathbf{W}_2 = [.06\ .65\ \ 0\ \ .7\ \ 0\ \ .5]$

Now, two customer groups have been identified with the algorithm: one group with customer 1 and 4 and the other with customer 2, 3, and 4. Note that if we have used high value of vigilance parameter, we could have end up with more groups.

As we can infer from the algorithm description and example, key advantage of using Fuzzy ART algorithm for customer group identification is that no matter how many products are processed in the network, sequential reading of inputs enables minimal storage requirement and less computation effort because computations required are in general proportional to the number of inputs. Test run on sample data set with 1,000 products, 1,000,000 customers took less than 30 minutes in Pentium II PC. However, in SOFM and any other clustering algorithm that requires similarity between inputs, face with storage and manipulation of large matrices which is time-consuming and requiring more memory space.

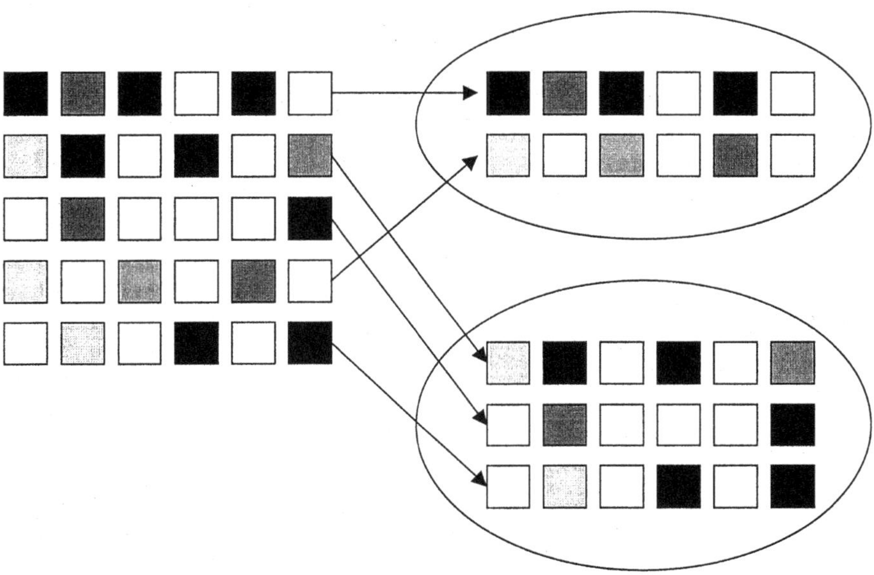

Fig. 4. Customer Grouping Example

Fuzzy ART can also accept non-binary inputs whereas ART1 network accepts only binary inputs into the network. Hence, product quantity is also considered in the algorithm. Unlike supervised neural network, Fuzzy ART algorithm does not require separate training session, but has the learning ability. As in most neural networks, high degree of interdependence between factors is taken care of in the network during learning process. The other advantage of using Fuzzy ART is that there is no need to process all inputs when new inputs are added. New inputs can be clustered into existing clusters or form a new cluster with trained weight vectors.

There are some limitations, however. Lack of formal methods to decide network parameters is a major limitation of neural networks in general. Depending on the data, different learning parameter as well as vigilance parameter produces significantly different result. Other limitation that also applies to most neural network approaches, is that the outputs obtained from analysis sometimes are not easy to understand due to the absence of assumed model based on theories.

In practice, data being used in the proposed Fuzzy ART application can be gathered without complex transformation in any retail stores in electronic commerce. In addition, Fuzzy ART does not require number of categories in advance. Limiting the number of categories can produce redundant categories and force dissimilar inputs to join together in one category. Because Fuzzy ART categorizes inputs based on similarity, it determines the number of cluster during the execution time, which seems more natural in some cases. Target marketing in itself gives more importance on homogeneity within segment, rather than number of market segments.

6 Application of Customer Group Identification System

In practice, data to be used in the proposed Fuzzy ART application can be gathered without complex transformation in any on-line retail stores in electronic commerce, or large brick-and-mortar retail chains having the capability of tracking each customer's purchasing history. Three major database systems are required for a successful use of the customer grouping outlined in the previous sections: product database, customer database, and marketing database. As seen in Fig. 5, customer database and product database will provide purchasing history to Customer Group Identification System (CGIS) and marketing database will determine a marketing campaign depending on the customer groups identified.

Considering current major trends in production, represented by short product life cycle and a wide variety of product choices due to varying functionality, product database should be equipped with the capability that can identify reasonable product classes. That is, two or more products may have the same functionality but may use different model numbers due to emerging new models that discontinue preceding models. Often, a new model does not add significant improvement, which should be classified as the same item provided that customers are not aware of small changes in design and function. So the ultimate inputs to

CGIS are to be product classifications that make the customer grouping more accurate. For example, a relationship that product 111, 112, 113 belongs to the same product class 110 is to be passed to CGIS. Most manufacturers do in fact use very similar and consistent numbering system for their products, thus it is not very challenging task to make product class from the product database.

Customer database passes customers' purchasing records to CGIS. At this time, it is recommended that only customers' data that contain significant amount of purchasing history be passed to CGIS. There are two major reasons why we need enough purchasing history. First, for customers who did not purchase many items, it is better to use quite different marketing campaign, for instance a promotional discount program revealing their purchasing patterns and needs which may not have been possible without promotions. Secondly, clustering performance of fuzzy ART will decrease if we allow non-significant and exceptional data. It is often the case that fuzzy ART will cluster those non-significant customers as single-item cluster.

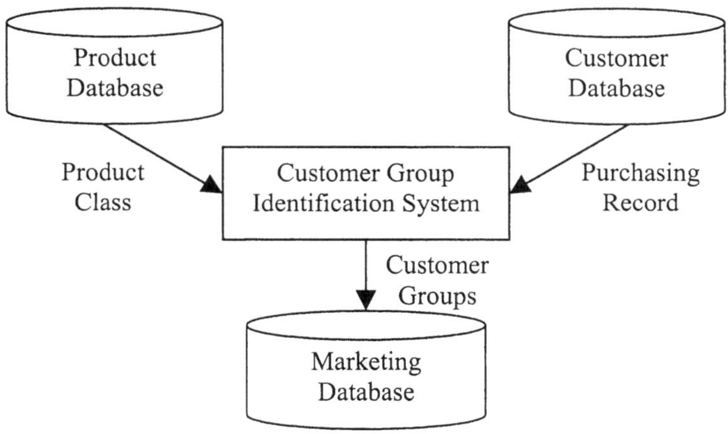

Fig. 5. Customer Group Identification System

In order to make CGIS successful should furnish with good marketing database which contains many marketing programs that are appropriate to different situations. Then, it is only a matter of applying those programs to groups identified customer groups. That is, the unit of analysis becomes the customer groups identified by CGIS. Fuzzy ART does not require number of categories in advance. Limiting the number of categories can produce redundant categories or force dissimilar inputs to join together in one category. Because Fuzzy ART categorizes inputs based on similarity, it determines the number of cluster during the execution time, which seems more natural in some cases. Target marketing in itself gives more importance on homogeneity within segment, rather than number of customer segments.

In general, an ideal firm to apply CGIS is Internet shopping mall or a large retail store with a high number of product items. Internet shopping mall carries various kinds of products and the customer transaction data across different product categories (e.g. clothes, computers, books, toys, etc.) is believed to provide valuable information with regards to direct and indirect relationships with consumer characteristics.

Customer grouping in electronic commerce also can make their Web site a valuable customer's resource and virtual store at the same time. Personalized Web services are now commonly seen in portal sites. To the retailers in electronic commerce, customized Web catalog based on customer grouping is another application that will have great impact in terms of marketing. Grouping customer will also provide better customer service, supposing customer service representatives (CSRs) are assigned based on the determined customer groups. Customers in each group will have similar products and similar consumer behavior, hence CSRs can learn the characteristics of customers and their product fast and process requested services efficiently and effectively.

Online communities may form in the process of supporting those groups of customers. According to a book by Hagel and Amstrong [6], vendors who learn to capitalize on the dynamics of online communities will have huge advantages over their competitors in terms of geographic reach, market information, customer loyalty, and the economics of increasing returns. They also argued that companies have to learn to champion their customers, and criticized companies with Web sites that don't allow their customers to interact. Therefore, better customer service is expected when customers are involved in interactive activities such as discussion about products and services and discover bargaining opportunities between the members of online communities. Amazon.com is a real-world example of this theory, with its book reviews, personalized recommendations, and e-mail notification.

To the retailers, forecasting demand of products is one of the major concerns. Based on the assumption that groups of customers are formed based on their buying patterns, retailers can take advantage of those groups of customers. For example, suppose a new product is being sold in a retail store and a significant increase in sales are detected. Then, a retailer can estimate how many potential buyers are in their customer profile and decide whether they need to change inventory level to prevent backorder. Inventory management is all the more critical to business success when products have short lifecycles and when competition is intense.

7 Conclusions

This chapter has addressed a marketing application in electronic commerce, namely, how to target customers based on a firm's sales data. To fulfill the current expectations for CRM systems, a proper analytical subsystem, or model base for analysis of customer-related data is a vital necessity. This analytical subsystem must be capable of operating in real time, during interactions with the customer. Focusing on this *data mining* function, or more broadly, the knowledge discovery function, the primary objective of this paper was to dwell on the requisite tools and techniques for data mining for effective customer relationship management.

The chapter focused on the role of artificial neural networks (ANNs) as an essential addition to the set of tools and techniques for data mining within the emerging eCCRM framework. Given conflicting, and expanding definitions of CRM proposed so far, we first listed the objectives of CRM, the various elements of CRM, and the required e-business architectures. After defining the eCCRM context, we focused on data mining issues for relationship management, and summarized the role of various artificial neural networks (ANNs) as a useful set of tools and techniques for data mining within eCCRM framework. Data mining and warehousing were defined, followed by a discussion of changing marketing applications and how well they are met by both traditional, statistical tools and neural networks.

The complementary roles of ANNs with conventional statistical techniques were also summarized. The Fuzzy ART network was described as a desirable ANN, due to its ability to handle large data sets, and due to less storage requirements and computational effort.

Even as CRM-related concepts are still being refined and redefined, much work still needs to be done on the role of traditional statistical methods, and the complementary role of neural networks for knowledge discovery applications. Many types of neural networks have been developed, especially those based on unsupervised learning. It appears however, that in the context of data mining, unsupervised networks such as Fuzzy ART and Kohonen's SOM are hardly ever mentioned. More than supervised networks, it is the unsupervised networks that are likely to play a meaningful role in discovery of customer behavior patterns. These networks have been extensively used in manufacturing applications such as group technology and cellular manufacturing and these methods are clearly transportable to the CRM application domain.

Thus, alongside much needed developments in ANNs and other data mining and knowledge discovery methods, marketing paradigms themselves are likely to undergo further changes as the e-commerce era unfolds. This chapter has attempted to set the stage for a fuller utilization of ANNs for this application.

References

1. Burke, L. I.. 1991. Introduction to Artificial Neural Systems for Pattern Recognition, *Computers Ops. Res.* 18(2): 211-220.
2. Carpenter, G. A., and Grossberg, S., 1987, A massively parallel architecture for a self-organizing neural pattern recognition machine, *Computer Vision, Graphics and Image Processing*, **37**, 54-115.

3. Carpenter, G. A., Grossberg, S. and Rosen, D. B., 1991, Fuzzy ART: Fast stable learning and categorization of analog patterns by an adaptive resonance system, *Neural Networks*, **4**, 759-771.
4. Culnan, M. J. "How did they get my name?": An exploratory investigation of consumer attitudes toward secondary information use. *MIS Quarterly*, 17(3): 341-363, 1993.
5. Goldenberg, B., 1999, Customer Relationship Management: What Is It All About? CRM Forum Resources, http://www.crm-forum.com/doclib/
6. Hagel, J. III and A. Armstrong. *Net Gain: Expanding Markets through Virtual Communities*, Boston, Harvard Business School Press, 1997.
7. Hagel, J. III and J. F. Rayport. The coming battle for customer information. *Harvard Business Review*, 75(1): 53-65, 1997.
8. Kalakota, R., and Robinson, M., 1999, e-Business: Roadmap for Success, Addison Wesley.
9. Kohonen, T., 1984, *Self-Organisation and Associative Memory*, Springer-Verlag, Berlin.
10. Kotler, P. *Marketing Management*. Englewood Cliff, NJ, Prentice-Hall, Inc., 1991.
11. Lippmann RP. An Introduction to Computing with Neural Networks. IEEE ASSP Magazine, 4-22, 1987.
12. Peacock, P. R. "Data Mining in Marketing: Part 1", *Marketing Management*, 6(4), 8-18 Winter 1998.
13. Sheth, J.N. and A. Parvatiyar, (1995), Relationship Marketing in Consumer Markets: Antecedents and Consequences, *Journal of the Academy of Marketing Science*, 23(4), 255-271.
14. Spangler, W. E., J. H. May, *et al.* Choosing data-mining methods for multiple classification: Representation and performance measurement implications for decision support. *Journal of Management Information Systems*, 16(1): 37-62, 1999.
15. Suresh, N.C., "Neural Network Applications for Group Technology in Design and Manufacturing", *Handbook of Computational Intelligence for Design and Manufacturing*, (Eds. J. Wang and A. Kusiak), CRC Press, Boca Raton, FL, 2000.
16. Tam, K. Y. and M. Y. Kiang. Managerial Applications of Neural Networks: The Case of Bank Failure Predictions. *Management Science*, 38(7): 926-947, 1992.
17. Tzokas, N. and M. Saren, (1997), Building Relationship Platforms In Consumer Markets: A Value Chain Approach, *Journal of Strategic Marketing*, 5 (2), 105-120.
18. Venugopal, V. and W. Baets. Neural networks & their applications in marketing management. *Journal of Systems Management*, 45(9): 16-21, 1994.
19. Werbos, P. Backpropagation: Past and future. *The IEEE International Conference on Neural Networks*, IEEE Press, 1988.

Characterizing and Segmenting the Online Customer Market Using Neural Networks

Alfredo Vellido[1]*, Paulo JG Lisboa[1], and Karon Meehan[2]

[1] Liverpool John Moores University. School of Computing and Mathematical Sciences. Byrom St. L3 3AF, Liverpool, U.K.

[2] Liverpool John Moores University. Business School. 98 Mount Pleasant. L3 5UZ, Liverpool, U.K.

* Currently at iSOCO (avellido@isoco.com)

Abstract. The proliferation of Business-to-Consumer (B2C) Internet companies that characterised the late '90s seems now under threat. A focus on customers' needs and expectations seems more justified than ever and, with it, the quantitative analysis of customer behavioural data. Neural networks, as quantitative analytical tools, have been proposed as a leading methodology for data mining. This chapter provides guidelines for the application of neural networks to the characterization and segmentation of the on-line customer market, in a way that we consider being best practice.

1 Introduction

The last few years of the past decade witnessed an unprecedented explosion of Internet business. A number of these were business-to-consumer outlets, often start-up companies without a brick-and-mortar counterpart. For a while, predictions of growth, supported by the exponential Internet adoption rate, portrayed a buoyant future for these new enterprises. In the wake of the high-tech stock crash, many of these companies have started to experience problems, or even gone out of business. The latter months of 2000 saw the likes of boo.com and boxman.com in Europe and e-Toys.com in the U.S.A. amongst the casualties, and this trend has not eased up in 2001.

In this fiercely competitive environment, survival will be more likely for those who do not lose sight of the end-customers, ensuring their loyalty by focusing on satisfying their needs and fulfilling their expectations. The exploration of these needs and expectations justifies a data-based analysis of the customers' shopping behaviour, in order to provide a sound empirical basis for managerial decision making. Neural networks have emerged in the last decade as a leading methodology for data mining (DM). Since then, they have been applied to the analysis of a wide variety of business-related problems including on-line marketing, an area in which they have been proposed as personalization tools. This chapter provides guidelines for the application of neural networks to the characterization and segmentation of the on-line customer market, in a way that we consider being best practice.

2 Business Applications of Neural Networks

Although neural networks originated in mathematical neurobiology, the rather simplified practical models currently in use have moved steadily towards the field of statistics, sacrificing neurological rigour for mathematical expediency. During the last decade, neural network methods have been applied across a wide range of business-related problems, with varying success, in the areas of management, marketing, decision-making, information systems and industrial production/engineering. Surveys covering the whole range of business applications of neural networks can be found in [24], [32], [37], and [38].

Some authors have also echoed the possibilities of these techniques in the field of e-commerce: Wallin [35] proposes the use of artificial neural networks for consumer's commercial behavior personalization or, in other words, for user modeling. From a different perspective, Scharl and Brandtweiner [26] discuss the use of neural networks in the context of intelligent mobile agents, which promise to "radically change inherent characteristics of electronic commerce". Ha and Park [9] develop Intranet data mart mining tools, including neural networks, in a very interesting real-world application. Finally, Changchien and Lu [5] discuss and develop a mining association rules procedure from a database to support online recommendation, using the unsupervised neural network SOM model.

3 Neural Networks for Prediction

A review of recent literature on business applications of neural networks [32] revealed that widespread beliefs regarding the limitations of neural networks are still causing concern among practitioners. In this section, we provide practical pointers to resolve these drawbacks, with recourse to theoretically principled frameworks, based on the application of Bayesian techniques for the training of neural networks.

3.1 Best Practice in DM Using Neural Networks for Prediction

Some of the limitations of the traditional supervised neural network models that have frequently been highlighted include, amongst others:

- The difficulty of finding out what a neural network has learnt by training, and expressing it in the form of simple rules and relative relevance of each variable (the "black-box syndrome").
- The existence of internal learning parameters that have to be tuned "off-line", due to the lack of consistent guidelines for their optimization.
- There lack of formal rules to select an optimal model (in terms, for instance, of the number of hidden nodes or hidden layers) from different options.

In this section, we describe a framework for the training of supervised neural networks within a Bayesian approach [17, 18]. Amongst its advantages [19], the Bayesian theory provides a unifying framework for data modeling and naturally embodies model selection. The probabilistic setting also forces us to make all the modeling assumptions explicit.

3.1.1 The Bayesian Approach to the Training of Neural Networks

The Bayesian approach to the training of a multi-layer perceptron (MLP) does not simply attempt to find a single set of weights (a point estimate, as in the case in the maximum-likelihood approach, in which the training consists merely in the optimization of an objective function). Instead, it is grounded on the definition of a probability distribution over the weights, which reflects the uncertainty resulting from the use of finite data sets. This results in the interpretation of the outputs of the neural network in a classification problem as posterior probabilities of class membership given the data and the weights,

$$P(C_i \mid \mathbf{x}, \mathbf{w}) = y(\mathbf{x}; \mathbf{w}) \tag{1}$$

where y is the network function, $\mathbf{x}$ is a vector of input data, $\mathbf{w}$ is the vector of the trained network parameters (weights and biases), and C_i is class i. The probability of membership of a specific class for an input vector with which the network has not been trained (test vector), is obtained by marginalizing (1) using the conditional distribution for the weights, to give

$$P(C_i \mid \mathbf{x}, D) = \int y(\mathbf{x}; \mathbf{w}) p(\mathbf{w} \mid D) d\mathbf{w} \tag{2}$$

where D are the target data for the training set. In regression problems, and given a Gaussian approximation for the posterior distribution of the weights $p(\mathbf{w}|D)$, Eq. 2 can be calculated and the variance of the resulting posterior distribution can be used to calculate error bars on the predicted test outputs. In classification problems, though, the network output involves a sigmoidal activation function, which cannot be approximated by a linear function of the weights, since

$$y = f(a) = \frac{1}{1+\exp(-a)} \tag{3}$$

where the activation a is the weighted linear sum of the hidden node responses which is fed into the output nodes. Nevertheless, reasonably good approximations can be provided for Eq. 2 [18].

The complexity of neural network models can be controlled by using a regularization term, typically of the form $\frac{1}{2}\alpha\sum_{i=1}^{W} w_i^2$, where $\{w_i\}_{,i=1...W}$ is the vector of network weights. Overly complex models should be avoided, because they over-fit the data and, as a result, generalize poorly. As part of a standard neural network model, this regularization term would have to be tuned "by hand" or by a systematic cross-validation procedure. Instead, within the Bayesian approach the regularization coefficient α can be automatically optimized, according to the demands of the own training data set, using the *evidence approximation* [17, 18].

The Bayesian framework can also be deployed beyond the selection of the model parameters, to involve the model selection itself. The probability of a neural network model M_i, given the data D, is

$$P(M_i|D) \propto P(D|M_i)P(M_i) \tag{4}$$

where $P(D| M_i)$ is called the *evidence* of model i. Assuming equal priors for all the models (and this is the case when there is no reason to assume that one model is to perform better than others for a given data set), these can be ranked according to their *evidence*, which can be calculated within the Bayesian framework.

3.1.2 Dispelling a Few Myths about Neural Networks

- *Data over-fitting*: As described above, the problem of over-fitting is tackled explicitly within the Bayesian framework for the training of the MLP: thanks to the automatic calculation of optimal levels of regularization, over-complex models are penalized, as they yield low probabilities for the target data given the regularization coefficients.
- *Feature selection*: Neural Networks are frequently considered as *black boxes* due, amongst other things, to their supposed incapacity to identify the relevance of independent variables in non-linear terms. This makes it difficult to automatically carry out input variable selection. Automatic Relevance Determination (ARD), for supervised Bayesian Neural Networks [19], is a model that tackles that shortcoming. Within the basic Bayesian approach, the single weight decay or regularization term is interpreted as a Gaussian prior distribution over the network parameters (weights and biases), of the form

$$p(\mathbf{w}) = A\exp\left(-\sum_{i=1}^{W} w_i^2/2\right) \tag{5}$$

where $\mathbf{w}=\{w_i\}$ is the vector of network parameters, W is the total number of network parameters, and A is a normalization factor and is constant. In ARD, individual regularization terms are associated with each group of network parameters. The fan-out weights from each input to the hidden layer are grouped separately, and the remaining weights form two additional groups, namely bias to the hidden nodes and weights plus bias to the output. The prior distribution of the weights now becomes

$$p(\mathbf{w}) = A\exp\left(-\sum_{c}^{C}\alpha_c \sum_{i}^{n_{w(c)}} w_i^2/2\right) \tag{6}$$

where C = (number of inputs + 2) is the number of weight groups, and $n_{w(c)}$ is the number of parameters in group c, so that $\sum_{c}^{C} n_{w(c)} = N_w$. As a result of the network training, the hyperparameters α_c associated with irrelevant inputs will be inferred to be large, and the corresponding weights will be set to small values. Therefore, ARD is performing soft feature selection, and a direct inspection of the final $\{\alpha_c\}$ values indicates the relative relevance of each variable. ARD has shown itself to be a useful feature selection method for classification problems [23].

- *Model selection*: How to select the best neural network model? It could be argued that the best model is that with best generalization properties. But, what is the best number of hidden nodes or hidden layers? What is the best performing training algorithm? As explained in the previous section, the Bayesian approach provides a principled methodology for the selection of the best model, as a ranking can be produced according to the *evidence*, i.e., the posterior probability of the data, given the model.
- *Class-unbalanced data sets*: A common problem in the application of supervised neural networks for classification to real-world problems is that of class-unbalanced data sets. For example, the problem faced by a bank in which the credit-worthiness of potential customers has to be assessed with respect to a limited amount of information, on a yes-no basis. The data set available to create any classification model will usually contain a much lower proportion of the class of former customers who turned out to, say, default with their credit payments. A possible solution would entail to sample the bigger class in order to create a class-balanced training set. The drawback is that lots of valuable information would have to be discarded. An alternative would entail the use of all the available data, but transforming the outputs to compensate for the different priors of both classes C_A and C_B [28]. As part of the Bayesian approach to the training of neural networks, this type of compensation can be implemented online, so that the different prior probabilities are accounted for in the error function itself, during training [16]. This change entails that, instead of the standard cross-entropy error function for classification problems:

$$LL = -\sum_{N}\left[t\log(y) + (1-t)\log(1-y)\right] \tag{7}$$

where y is the network output, t the data targets, and N the number of data observations, the following modified expression is to be used:

$$LL = -\sum_{N}\left[t\log(y)\left(\frac{1}{2P(C_A)}\right) + (1-t)\log(1-y)\left(\frac{1}{2(1-P(C_A))}\right)\right] \tag{8}$$

where the prior probability $P(C_B) = 1 - P(C_A)$.

3.2. Predicting the Propensity to Buy On-Line Using Neural Networks

3.2.1 Factors Influencing Purchasing Behaviour: Definition and Selection

This section provides an example of the application of a MLP, trained within the Bayesian approach as described in the previous section, to the prediction of the propensity to buy online. The analysis focuses on a survey-based data set containing a large number of Internet user behaviour-related variables, plus information on whether the user has or has not ever purchased online. The complete survey questionnaires are publicly available from the *9th GVU's WWW Users Survey*, produced by the Graphics, Visualization & Usability Center [14].

We are interested in reducing the high dimensionality of this original data set. There are two main approaches to accomplish this: either the selection of a subset of the original, observable variables, or the generation of a group of new variables, non-observable or latent, as a combination of the original ones [10]. Factor analysis, our technique of choice, follows the latter approach. The factor analysis of the data can be further justified on the basis of the following arguments [8]:

- It can help to overcome some of the limitations associated with survey data: presence of noise, poorly measured variables, inadequate selection of survey items in terms of balance across studied constructs.
- The resulting factor structure can be interpreted in terms which are not explicit in the observable data, whilst more operative in the business context.

Table 1. Descriptive summary of the factor structure.

FACTOR	DESCRIPTION	ATTRIBUTES
1	Shopping experience: Compatibility	Control and convenience
2	Consumer risk perception / Environmental control	Trust and security
3	Customer service	Responsiveness and empathy/ Information richness
4	Affordability	--
5	Shopping experience: Effort	Ease of use
6	Product perception	Variety: Information richness
7	Customer service / Consumer risk	Assurance and reliability / Performance risk
8	Consumer risk: Image risk	Elitism
9	Shopping experience / Customer service	Effort / Responsiveness and empathy

The application of factor analysis to the original data results in a set of factors, shown in table 1, that form the basis to assemble characteristic profiles of Internet users. Each factor is interpreted using the factor loadings onto the survey-questionnaire items and the concepts proposed in previous studies concerning the analysis of online shopping behavior [12, 13].

The scores associated to these factors, together with demographic, socio-economic, and Web usage information, also from the original survey, are now used to construct a global predictive model of the propensity to buy online. The Bayesian Neural Network model proposed as best practice is utilized for this purpose, implemented using ARD for variable selection.

For the sake of brevity, the results of the ARD procedure and the predictive performance of the neural networks will just be summarized. A subset of 5 factors, namely: Consumer risk perception /Environmental control, Shopping experience: Compatibility, Shopping experience /Customer service, Affordability, and Shopping experience: Effort, are shown to be the most relevant. None of the extra variables: Age, Household Income, Hours-per-week Online, and Years of Internet Experience, turns out to be a good predictor. The income variable, in particular, reveals almost null discriminatory power. This is consistent with other published results [2, 12]. Furthermore, the 5-factor subset predicts the propensity to buy online for test data with comparable, if not higher, accuracy than the full 9-factor set. The rate of successful classification for the test sample lies in the region of 80%. More detailed results can be found in [30, 31]

4. Neural Networks for Market Segmentation

4.1. The Segmentation Problem

In the context of Internet retailing, the identification of clusters of customer types has been stated as the most important use of DM. Market segmentation techniques, grounded on the benefits sought by the customers, can give the marketer a leading edge: the identification of such segments can be the basis for effective targeting, enabling the redirection of personalized content towards the customer.

4.2. Segmenting the On-Line Customer Market

The application of neural networks-based models to market segmentation is a new and promising research area. Nevertheless, neural networks have seldom been evaluated with respect to market response applications. Even though unsupervised neural networks would appear to suit the clustering strategies better, they have only rarely been used. Market segmentation techniques frequently combine quantitative and qualitative methods, but it has been recognized that their design and deployment can be more clearly grounded in a sound statistical framework. In this section, one such a model is presented.

4.2.1 The GTM Model

We introduce the Generative Topographic Mapping (GTM), a non-linear latent variable model for data clustering and visualization that is based in a solid statistical framework. It can be seen as a probabilistic alternative to the well-known Self-Organizing Map (SOM).

Why the GTM and Not, Say, K-means?

There is a plethora of clustering methods available to the online market researcher interested in the problem of segmentation, some of them part of off-the-shelve software packages. There are some features of the GTM (mostly in common with the SOM) that make it particularly attractive for online DM, namely: it provides a principled mapping between a multi-dimensional data space and a low-dimensional (usually 1-, 2- or 3-D) representation space. It does so preserving the original topology of the data, i.e., data points that are close together are represented as neighbors. As a result, even complex multi-dimensional data are extremely easy to visualize and the segmentation results are readily interpretable [33] in terms of the original variables. Furthermore, the GTM provides an adequate framework to make micro- and macro-segmentation results compatible.

Why the GTM and not the SOM?

The main advantage of the GTM over the more widely used SOM model is that the former generates a density distribution in data space so that the model can be described and developed within a principled probabilistic framework in which all the modeling assumptions are made explicit. The GTM also provides the well-defined objective function; its maximization, using either standard techniques for non-linear optimization or the EM-algorithm, has been proved to converge. As part of this process, the calculation of the optimum GTM *learning parameters* is automated, avoiding cumbersome, and often unreliable, procedures of cross-validation. One of the main limitations of the SOM model is the impossibility to define such an objective function. Most importantly, the GTM provides a posterior probability of segment membership, something beyond the reach of the SOM model. Finally, the local levels of distortion in the mapping from the latent space to the data space (the *magnification factor*, see [3]) can be properly calculated as a continuous function of the latent variables, avoiding the discrete approximation to which the SOM is limited.

Matlab and C implementations of the SOM are publicly available from http://www.cis.hut.fi/research/software.shtml. A Matlab implementation of the GTM is publicly available from http://www.ncrg.aston.ac.uk/GTM/

A Brief Description of the GTM

The Generative Topographic Mapping (GTM) [27] is a non-linear latent variable model that generates a probability density in the multi-dimensional data space, using a set of latent variables of smaller dimension. This non-linear mapping is described by the generalized linear regression model

$$\mathbf{y} = \mathbf{W}\phi(\mathbf{u}) \tag{9}$$

where $\mathbf{u}$ is an L-dimensional vector of latent variables, $\mathbf{W}$ is the matrix that generates the explicit mapping from latent space to an L-dimensional manifold embedded in data space, and ϕ is a set of R basis functions which, in this study, are chosen to be Gaussians. For the non-linear mapping to remain analytically and computationally tractable, and also to elaborate a principled alternative to the SOM, the prior distribution of $\mathbf{u}$ in latent space is defined as a discrete grid, similar in spirit to the grid of the SOM

$$p(\mathbf{u}) = \frac{1}{M}\sum_{i=1}^{M}\delta(\mathbf{u} - \mathbf{u}_i) \tag{10}$$

where M is the number of its nodes. Since the data do not necessarily lie in an L-dimensional space, it is necessary to make use of a noise model for the distribution of the data points $\mathbf{x}$. The integration of this data distribution over the latent space distribution, gives

$$p(\mathbf{x} \mid \mathbf{W}, \beta) = \int p(\mathbf{x} \mid \mathbf{u}, \mathbf{W}, \beta)p(\mathbf{u})d\mathbf{u} = \tag{11}$$
$$\frac{1}{M}\sum_{i=1}^{M}\left(\frac{\beta}{2\pi}\right)^{\frac{D}{2}} \exp\left\{-\frac{\beta}{2}\left\|\mathbf{m}_i - \mathbf{x}\right\|^2\right\}$$

where D is the dimensionality of the input space, and $\mathbf{m}_i = \mathbf{W}\phi(\mathbf{u}_i)$ for the discrete node representation in Eq. 10, according to Eq. 9. Using the SOM terminology, $\mathbf{m}_i$ can be considered as *reference vectors*, each of them the centre of an isotropic Gaussian distribution in data space [4]. A log-likelihood can now be defined as

$$L(\mathbf{W}, \beta) = \sum_{n=1}^{N} \ln p(\mathbf{x}^n \mid \mathbf{W}, \beta) \tag{12}$$

for the whole input data set $\{\mathbf{x}^n\}$.

The distribution described by Eq. 11 corresponds to a constrained Gaussian mixture model [11], hence its parameters, $\mathbf{W}$ and β, can be determined using the Expectation-Maximization (EM) algorithm [6], details of which can be found in [27]. As part of the Expectation step, the mapping from latent space to data space, defined by Eq. 9, can be inverted using Bayes' theorem so that the posterior probability of a GTM node *i*, given a data-space point, is defined as

$$R_i^n \equiv p(\mathbf{u}_i | \mathbf{x}^n) = \frac{\exp\left[-\frac{\beta}{2}\left\|\mathbf{m}_i - \mathbf{x}^n\right\|^2\right]}{\sum_{i'}^{M} \exp\left[-\frac{\beta}{2}\left\|\mathbf{m}_{i'} - \mathbf{x}^n\right\|^2\right]} \tag{13}$$

This is known as the *responsibility* taken by each node *i* for each point *n* in the data space. It will prove itself extremely useful, given a 2-dimensional latent space, for data visualization and also for cluster analysis in the context of market segmentation.

The complexity of the mapping generated by the GTM model is mainly controlled by the number and form of the basis functions. Further control of this effective complexity can be achieved with the addition of a regularization term to the objective function in Eq. 12, in such a way that the training of the GTM would consist of the maximization of a *penalized* log-likelihood

$$L_{PEN}(\mathbf{W},\beta)=\sum_{n=1}^{N}\ln p(\mathbf{x}_n\mid\mathbf{W},\beta)+\frac{1}{2}\alpha\|\mathbf{w}\|^2 \tag{14}$$

where **w** is a vector shaped by concatenation of the different column vectors of the weight matrix **W**. This regularization term is effectively preventing the GTM to fit the noise in the data and is used under the assumption that there exists an underlying data generator, which is a combination of the density functions for each of the segments.

The optimum values for all these complexity-controlling parameters should ideally be evaluated in a continuous space of solutions. Given that the GTM is formulated within a probabilistic framework, this can be accomplished using the Bayesian formalism and, more specifically, the evidence approximation [17]. The application of this methodology [4] produces update formulae for the regularization coefficient α and for the inverse variance of the noise model β.

Once the parameters α and β have been adaptively optimized, the best GTM model (in the sense that it reaches the best compromise between fitting the data and representing the underlying distribution from which the data were generated) can be obtained by experimenting with different combinations of the number of Gaussian basis functions and its width, σ. The number of basis functions can also be optimized as part of the Bayesian approach, but details of this are beyond the scope of this chapter.

In simple terms, the GTM is trying to "re-create" the original data from a discrete representation, in the form of "nodes", of a low dimensional space. If we select this space to be 2-dimensional, all the data will be visualized in a (possibly square) grid of nodes. Individual data observations will be attributed to individual nodes according to proximity to the corresponding reference vectors $\mathbf{m}_i$.

From Micro-segments to Macro-segments

Depending on the goals set up for the market segmentation, the analyst might consider the definition of segments at different levels of detail. As stated in [36, p.328]: "for different strategic goals, different segments may need to be identified in the same population". Each of the units of the GTM can be itself considered as a cluster/segment [25]. Therefore, higher levels of segment detail will be achieved by increasing the number of units of the model, for a fixed number of data observations. These individual units can then be grouped to form bigger market segments following some of the procedures outlined below. It remains to be seen whether the benefits derived from augmented consumer response can outstrip the costs of online content personalization that are implicit in a more detailed segmentation strategy. This conflict between personalization and aggregate (macro) segmentation is nicely worded in [15] within a product-based perspective:

"...high product customization requires extensive profiling and customization tools to identify and target individual customers ... When product customization is low, one would still need tools that can broadly cluster customers for target marketing."

The problem of going from micro- to macro-segments can now be addressed. We might take advantage of the topology-preserving properties of the GTM by defining a contiguity-constrained agglomerative procedure similar to that proposed [22] for the SOM. This simple algorithm proceeds as follows:

1. Each unit i of the map is initialized as a cluster/segment with its center at $\mathbf{m}_i$, and is uniquely labeled.
2. At every step of the algorithm, the two closest (in terms of a defined distance) neighboring clusters are merged. This merger entails substituting the previous centers with their mean.
3. Repeat step 2 until the cluster partition reaches a predefined number of clusters

Variants of this method are described in [34]. Alternatively, the units of the GTM can undergo this "second level" of clustering using K-means, a method already proposed in [1] to address the problem of brand choice data segmentation. The design of a hierarchical model, with a "second-level" GTM cluster the "first-level" GTM results, could also be considered.

An important question remains to be answered: what is the appropriate number of clusters/segments in the data. Are there any methods that allow the automatic calculation of this magic number? A survey of such methods can be found in [21], and an evaluation in [7]. A very interesting procedure, valid for any type of clustering, that has recently been described is the GAP statistic [29]. It compares the change in within cluster dispersion to that expected under an appropriate reference null distribution. Among its advantages, it can also be used as a criterion to decide whether segmentation is appropriate at all for a given data set. Another measure, entropy-related, has been defined for the case in which class-membership information is available [31]: in this case class-discrimination and cluster-separation are optimized simultaneously. The GTM results can also be used on their own as an approximate guidance to obtain the optimal number of clusters/segments. For that purpose, the *Magnification Factor* [3] and the *Cumulative Responsibility* [31] can be utilized. Both of them replace the u-matrix heuristic that is commonly applied to the SOM.

Some Segmentation Results

Let us recall the behavioral data, concerning Internet users, that was used in Sect. 3.2 to illustrate the problem of the prediction of the propensity to buy online using supervised neural networks. We want to use the 5 best predictors of that propensity, summarized in that section, to segment the data set using the GTM model. Figure 1 provides the visualization of a very detailed partition, comprising 225 nodes or micro-segments. It has been color-coded to display class-membership information. Although this information was not used to train the unsupervised model, Fig. 1 clearly reflects that the class-discrimination capabilities of the 5 factors are retained in the 2-dimensional display provided by the GTM.

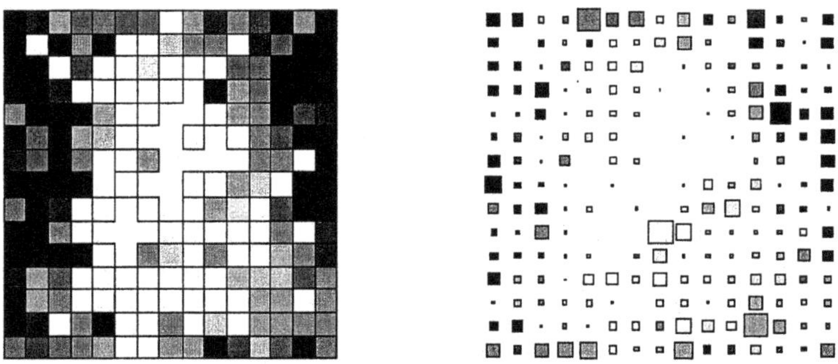

Fig. 1. GTM class-membership maps. All the individuals in the training sample are mapped onto the nodes in the latent visualization space: left) Each individual has been shaded according to its class-membership: white for *purchasers*, black for *non-purchasers*. Nodes with more than one pattern mapped onto them are depicted in shades of grey, corresponding to the class-membership proportion. Right) The same representation but, this time, the relative size of the squares representing the nodes corresponds to the number of individuals mapped onto them.

Nevertheless, the data are unlikely to be naturally divided into so many segments. Macro-segments can be obtained using the methods described in the previous section. An example of the application of those methods is displayed in Fig. 2. We can now make a sensible interpretation of these segments in terms of the 5 factors, using the reference vectors shown in Fig. 3. These are just a simple visualization of the elements of $\mathbf{m}_i$, or, in other words, the way the GTM has "reconstructed" each of the factors as seen in the 2-dimensional visualization space. The interpretation and labeling of the segments is summarized in table 2.

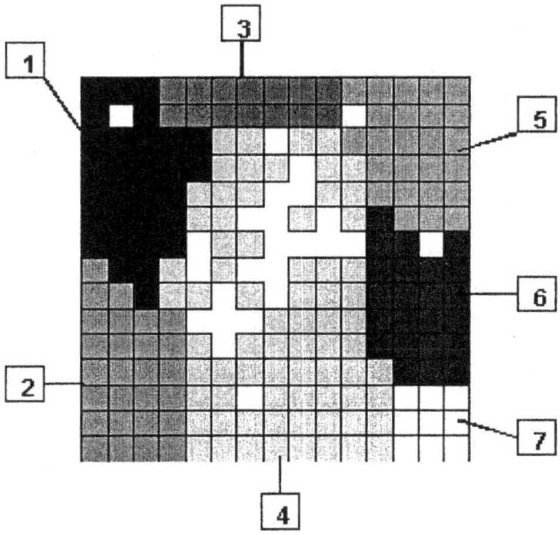

Fig. 2. A 7-segment solution obtained following the procedures described in the text.

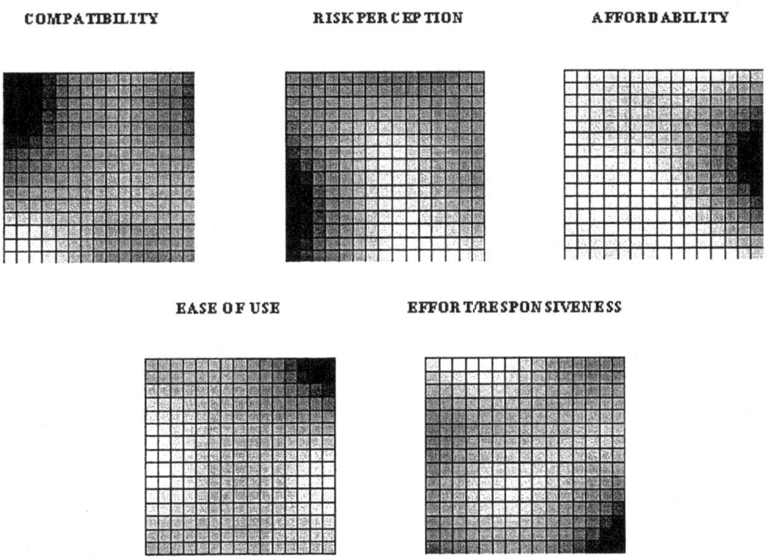

Fig. 3. Reference maps of the trained GTM. They are associated with each of the factors in the 5-factor selection, in a pseudo-color representation. Light shades of grey correspond to high values of the elements of the reference vectors, whereas dark colors correspond to low values.

Table 2. Description of the segments corresponding to Fig.2

	SEGMENT DESCRIPTION	LABEL and SIZE (%)
1	Reference maps: All factors present medium-to-high values. The values of Perception of risk, Affordability and Effort/Responsiveness are especially high..(91.0% purchasers – 9.0% non-purchasers)	Convinced (22.7%)
2	Reference maps: Most factors present medium values except Affordability, which is very low. (27.7% purchasers – 72.3% non-purchasers)	Cost conscious (16.7%)
3	Reference maps: High values of Affordability and Perception of risk, but rather low values of Effort/responsiveness. (71.2% purchasers – 28.8% non-purchasers)	Security and cost confident (9.4%)
4	Reference maps: Low Compatibility and very low Ease of use. Medium to high Affordability. (19.6% purchasers – 80.4% non-purchasers)	Complexity avoiders (5.9%)
5	Reference maps: Similar to the segment 7 but scoring higher in the factor of Compatibility. (58.7% purchasers – 41.3% non-purchasers)	Undecided (9.6%)
6	Reference maps: This small group scores very low in Effort/responsiveness, but medium-to-high in the rest of factors. (45.4% purchasers – 54.6% non-purchasers)	Customer service wary (5.6%)
7	Reference maps: Very low on Compatibility and rather low on Perception of risk, although rather high on Affordability. (14.5% purchasers – 85.5% non-purchasers)	Unconvinced (8.9%)
8	Reference maps: High Compatibility compounded with low values of Perception of risk. (31.7% purchasers – 68.3% non-purchasers)	Security conscious (5.3%)
9	Reference maps: High on Affordability and Ease of Use, but low in all the risk related factors. (36.3% purchasers – 63.7% non-purchasers)	Risk avoiders (15.9%)

Segments are numbered, according to the labels in Fig.2, in the first column of the table, and described in the second column according to the *reference maps* of Fig.3. This column also includes the percentages of *purchasers* and *non-purchasers* present in each segment. The relative size of the segments is included in the third column together with their proposed labels.

Profiling the Segments

There are several criteria that define the feasibility of a business strategy based on a market segmentation analysis: amongst others, the *substantiality* and *actionability* of the segments. Another two criteria, the *identifiability* and *accessibility* might sometimes depend on the availability of further information such as demographic and socio-economic data that allow us to create neat customer profiles. This type of information, though, has been shown to be neither the most effective in developing segments nor a good predictor of the propensity to buy on-line. Nevertheless, it might be useful to explore profiling methodologies such as, for instance, the psychographics-based iVALS, from the SRI institute, which was specifically developed for the Internet market context.

Let us now profile the segment solution described in table 2, using some variables that were not readily available during the segmentation process, namely: *age, household income, years of Internet experience, average of hours a week of Internet usage* and *gender.* This selection is by no means exhaustive. Bearing in mind that this is just an illustration of a procedure that ultimately depends on the availability of secondary information, and for the sake of brevity, the profiling, summarized in table 3, will be limited to the aforementioned variables.

A few conclusions can be drawn from these results. Firstly, segment 4 (*Convinced*), mainly composed of *online purchasers*, can be characterized as mostly male in their late twenties to early forties, with high-band income and Internet-savvy. Most of the segments with a majority of *non-purchasers* tend to be dominated by females, especially the core non-purchaser segment 1, the *Unconvinced.* It reveals women, at the time of the survey, as the type of customers that find buying online incompatible with their life and shopping styles.

The division of segment 5, the *Complexity Avoiders*, into 3 sub-segments seems strongly justified by their very different profiles. Sub-segment 5a is the top-left part of segment 5 and is close to segment 3, the *Undecided*, which makes it a somehow "softer" target for potential marketing campaigns. Its profile is most interesting: quite older than the rest of segment 5, more Internet-savvy and with very high average income level. It is also more male-dominated. Sub-segment 5c, in the top-right corner of the map is the hard core of the segment, with a profile that is extremely young, barely Internet experienced and with the lowest average income in the map. Sub-segment 5b is halfway between the other two sub-segments and presents a strongly female profile.

Segment 6, the *Cost Conscious*, add rather lower incomes (which is consistent with the low values of the *affordability* factor that the individuals in this segment present) to lack of Internet experience. Segment 3 (*Undecided*) is similar to the *Cost Conscious*, with a young profile and average-to-low Internet usage and experience. Their main difference lies in the higher income distribution of the *Undecided*, which makes this segment highly attractive to marketers. Segment 7 (*Customer Service Wary*) is almost a variant on the *Unconvinced*, only younger and with lower Internet usage. Another interesting fact made apparent by the profiles is that, generally speaking, the levels of Internet usage and experience seem to be related to the membership of segments dominated by *purchasers*.

Table 3. Segment profiles

		Whole	Sg.1	Sg.2	Sg.3	Sg.4
	A ≤ 25	26.1	27.5	25.5	35.3	19.8
Age	25 <A ≤35	25.2	22.0	26.5	30.9	29.3
(A)	35 <A ≤45	23.4	17.4	25.5	19.1	24.2
	A > 45	25.3	33.1	22.5	14.7	26.7
	H ≤ 10	34.1	31.2	44.1	38.2	22.7
Hours	10 <H ≤20	31.9	35.8	30.4	35.3	28.9
(H)	H > 20	34.0	33.0	25.5	26.5	48.4
	Y ≤ 1	18.2	23.8	22.5	13.2	6.6
Years	1 <Y ≤3	38.2	35.8	37.2	42.6	35.5
(Y)	3 <Y ≤5	22.4	21.1	24.5	26.5	26.0
	Y > 5	21.2	19.3	15.8	17.7	31.9
	I ≤ 30K	26.1	30.3	24.5	27.9	20.1
Income	30K<I ≤50K	28.1	23.8	36.3	25.0	23.1
(I)	50K<I ≤70K	18.8	22.0	16.7	16.2	23.8
	I > 70K	27.0	23.9	22.5	30.9	33.0
Gender	Male	51.6	42.2	47.1	47.1	64.5
(G)	Female	48.4	57.8	52.9	52.9	35.5
Segment	Absolute size	778	109	102	68	272
	%	100	14.0	13.1	8.7	35.0

Table 3.(cont.)

	Sg.5a	S.5b	Sg.5c	Sg.6	Sg.7
	16.0	24.6	52.4	32.1	34.4
Age	12.0	16.9	4.8	26.2	25.0
(A) *	48.0	23.1	28.6	19.1	28.1
	24.0	35.4	14.2	22.6	12.5
	48.0	49.2	52.4	35.7	43.7
Hours	40.0	29.2	23.8	38.1	28.1
(H) **	12.0	21.6	23.8	26.2	28.2
	20.0	36.9	42.9	23.8	25.0
Years	32.0	43.1	38.1	46.4	34.4
(Y) **	28.0	13.8	4.8	16.7	21.9
	20.0	6.2	14.2	13.1	18.7
	4.0	32.3	52.4	33.3	31.2
Income	28.0	29.2	23.8	40.5	34.4
(I) *	28.0	12.3	9.5	10.7	12.5
	40.0	26.2	14.3	15.5	21.9
Gender	60.0	40.0	47.6	42.9	40.6
(G) **	40.0	60.0	52.4	57.1	59.4
Segment	25	65	21	84	32
%	3.2	8.4	2.7	10.8	4.1

Age, average of hours a week of Internet usage, years of Internet experience, household income and gender are represented in the table as *Age, Hours, Years, Income* (in US $) and *Gender*. All figures (but absolute size) are percentages.

5 Commercial Neural Network Tools

In this chapter, we have laid a few best practice guidelines for the use of supervised and unsupervised neural network techniques in the analysis of e-commerce market data. In a real-world context, though, an online marketer might have to resort to off-the-shelve software tools. In this section we review, by no means exhaustively, some of the neural network-based packages available for DM.

Several companies have developed products that use neural network techniques for data analysis in the area of electronic commerce. Amongst them: WebHouse™ for Orchestrate™ from Torrent, Decider e-Commerce™ from Neural Technologies, eFalcon™, and Mindwave™ from HNC, and OptiMatch™ from Neural Inc.

Generic DM tools with neural network-based components include Virdix™ from Trajecta, 4Thought™ from Cognos, and NGO™ from BioComp System. More comprehensive DM suites that also include neural networks feature SPSS' Clementine™, SAS' Enterprise Miner™ Quadstone's DecisionHouse™, Urban Sciences' GainSmarts™, and IBM's Intelligent Miner™. For a comparative analysis of some of these tools see, for instance, [20].

6 Summary

The mining of online data is likely to involve the combination of different analytical tools. As stated in [20], "The mining of website transactional data with artificial intelligence-based tools is an attempt to recognize, anticipate, and learn the buying habits and preferences of customers in this new evolutionary business environment". In this chapter we have introduced two neural network-based tools for the mining of e-commerce information, emphasizing what we consider is best practice for their design and deployment.

A supervised neural network, trained within a Bayesian framework, has been described and applied to the prediction of the propensity to buy online. Publicly available behavioral data have been utilized to illustrate this application. Further uses of the model within the online context would include product-specific purchase prediction, amount of sales estimation, and the prediction of the propensity to respond to offers and click-through rates.

An unsupervised neural network-related model, the GTM, has been presented as a statistically principled alternative to the widely used SOM. The GTM is a powerful tool for exploratory data visualization and market segmentation, and its use has been illustrated with the data mentioned above. Further applications of the GTM would include the segmentation of website visitors according to link-browsing or shopping-cart use behaviors, and these results could then be combined, for instance, with purchasing predictions. It could also be used for the analysis of transaction records to support personalized recommendation strategies (See [5]).

Again quoting [20], "the Web is an ideal marketing environment where every transaction can be captured, stored, and subsequently mined for strategic advantage". In the e-commerce highly competitive and information-driven arena, only the coming together of traditional business practices and business intelligence, obtained through the use of sophisticated and scalable DM tools, will guarantee the online marketer the necessary leading edge.

References

1. Balakrishnan PVS, Cooper MC, Jacob VS, Lewis PA (1996) Comparative performance of the FSCL neural net and K-means algorithm for market segmentation. European Journal of Operational Research, 93: 346357
2. Bellman S, Lohse GL, Johnson EJ (1999) Predictors of online buying behaviour, Communications of the ACM, 42(12): 3238
3. Bishop CM, Svensén M, Williams, CKI (1997) Magnification factors for the GTM algorithm. In Proceedings IEE Fifth International Conference on Artificial Neural Networks, Cambridge, pp 6469
4. Bishop CM, Svensén M, Williams, CKI (1998) Developments of the Generative Topographic Mapping. Neurocomputing 21(1-3): 203224
5. Changchien SW, Lu, T-C (2001) Mining association rules procedure to support on-line recommendation by customers and product fragmentation. Expert Systems with Applications 20: 325-335
6. Dempster AP, Laird NM, Rubin DB (1977) Maximum likelihood from incomplete data via the EM algorithm. Journal of the Royal Statistical Society, B, 39(1): 138
7. Gordon A (1999) Classification. Chapman and Hall / CRC Press, London
8. Green PE, Krieger, AM (1995) Alternative approaches to cluster-based market segmentation. Journal of the Market Reseach Society, 37(3): 221239
9. Ha SH, Park SC (1998) Application of data mining tools to hotel data mart on the Intranet for database marketing. Expert Systems With Applications 15: 131
10. Hand DJ (1997) Construction and Assessment of Classification Rules. John Wiley & Sons, Chichester
11. Hinton GE, Williams CKI, Revow MD (1992) Adaptive elastic models for hand-printed character recognition. In Moody JE, Hanson SJ, Lippmann RP (eds) Advances in Neural Information Processing Systems vol 4, Morgan Kauffmann, pp 512519
12. Hoffman DL, Novak TP, Peralta MA (1999) Information privacy in the marketspace: implications for the commercial uses of anonymity on the Web. The Information Society, 15(2): 129139
13. Jarvenpaa SL, Todd PA (1996/1997) Consumer reactions to electronic shopping on the WWW. International Journal of Electronic Commerce 1(2): 5988
14. Kehoe C, Pitkow J, Rogers JD (1998) 9th GVU's WWW User Survey URL: http://www.gvu.gatech.edu/user_surveys/survey-1998-04/
15. Kiang MY, Raghu TS, Shang KH-M (2000) Marketing on the Internet-who can benefit from an online marketing approach. Decision Support Systems 27: 383393
16. Lisboa PJG, Vellido A, Wong H (2000) Bias reduction in skewed binary classification with Bayesian neural networks. Neural Networks 13: 407410

17. Mackay DJC (1992a) A practical Bayesian framework for back-propagation networks. Neural Computation 4(3): 448472
18. Mackay DJC (1992b) The evidence framework applied to classification networks. Neural Computation 4(5): 698714
19. Mackay DJC (1995) Probable networks and plausible predictions a review of practical Bayesian methods for supervised neural networks. Network: Computation in Neural Systems 6: 469505
20. Mena J (1999) Data Mining Your Website. Butterworth-Heinemann / Digital Press, Woburn, MA
21. Milligan GW, Cooper MC (1985) An examination of procedures for determining the number of clusters in a data set. Psychometrika, 50: 159179
22. Murtagh F (1995) Interpreting the Kohonen self-organizing feature map using contiguity-constrained clustering. Pattern Recognition Letters 16(4): 399408
23. Penny WD, Roberts SJ (1999) Bayesian neural networks for classification: how useful is the evidence framework? Neural Networks 12: 877892
24. Refenes A, Burgess AN, Bentz Y (1997) Neural networks in financial engineering: A study in methodology. IEEE Transactions on Neural Networks 8(6): 12221267
25. Ripley B (1996) Pattern Recognition and Neural Networks. Cambridge University Press, Cambridge
26. Scharl A, Brandtweiner R (1998) A conceptual research framework for analyzing the evolution of electronic markets. Electronic Markets Newsletter 8(2): 16
27. Svensén M (1998) GTM: The Generative Topographic Mapping. PhD thesis. Aston University, UK
28. Tarassenko L (1998) A Guide to Neural Computing Applications. Arnold, London
29. Tibshirani R, Walther G, Hastie T (2000) Estimating the number of clusters in a data set via the Gap statistic. Technical Report, Stanford University, California
30. Vellido A, Lisboa PJG, Meehan K (2000a) Quantitative characterization and prediction of on-line purchasing behaviour: a latent variable approach. International Journal of Electronic Commerce 4(4): 83104
31. Vellido A, Lisboa PJG, Meehan K (2000b) The Generative Topographic Mapping as a principled model for data visualization and market segmentation: an electronic commerce case study. International Journal of Computers, Systems and Signals 1(2): 119-138
32. Vellido A, Lisboa PJG, Vaughan J (1999) Neural networks in business: a survey of applications (1992-1998). Expert Systems with Applications 17(1): 5170
33. Vesanto J (1999) SOM-based data visualization. Intelligent Data Analysis 3(2): 111126
34. Vesanto J, Alhoniemi E (2000) Clustering of the Self-Organizing Map. IEEE Transactions on Neural Networks 11(3) 586600
35. Wallin EO (1999) Consumer personalization technologies for e-commerce on the Internet: a taxonomy. In Roger, J-Y, Standford-Smith B, Kidd, PT (eds) Proceedings of the European Multimedia, Microprocessor Systems and Electronic Commerce (EMMSEC'99). IOS Press, Amsterdam
36. Wedel M, Kamakura WA (1998) Market Segmentation. Conceptual and Methodological Foundations. Kluwer, Massachusetts
37. Wong BK, Bodnovich TA, Selvi Y (1997) Neural network applications in business: A review and analysis of the literature (1988-95). Decision Support Systems 19: 301320
38. Zhang G, Patuwo BE, Hu, MY (1998) Forecasting with artificial neural networks: The state of the art. International Journal of Forecasting 14(1): 3562

Data Mining for Diverse E-Commerce Applications

Amar Gupta, Sanjeev Vadhavkar, Jason Yeung

Massachusetts Institute of Technology, Room E60-309, Cambridge, MA 02139

Abstract. In their effort to incorporate electronic commerce capabilities, many organizations have established comprehensive data warehouses to integrate operational data with customers, suppliers, and other channel partners. Emerging data mining techniques enable organizations to prioritize and structure information from these warehouses. Through its discovery of changes, associations, rules, anomalies, and patterns, data mining can lead to significant business benefits when combined with current information systems. This chapter illustrates the pivotal role that data mining plays in an electronic commerce environment by highlighting two case studies in which neural network-based data mining techniques were used for inventory optimization. Issues such as automated identification of input-output lags, data augmentation, and optimal neural network architectures are discussed.

1 Introduction

Over the last two decades, electronic format has become the dominant medium for information storage. With an increasing number of organizations embracing electronic commerce, this trend will continue to grow. Currently, the amount of information in the world is estimated to double every 20 months, while the size and number of databases are increasing at a still faster rate. As a result of this escalating volume of data, human domain experts are no longer adequate for making timely and accurate data analysis. New data mining technique offer far superior capabilities in discovering hidden knowledge, interesting patterns, and new business rules within repositories of electronic data. This data mining paradigm encompasses theoretical perspectives from the fields of statistics, machine learning, and artificial intelligence and relies on advances in data modeling, data warehousing, and information retrieval. The most important challenge lies in organizing business practices around the knowledge discovery activity. As the economy becomes more web-oriented, organizations will rely on data mining techniques in the electronic marketplace.

Data mining focuses on the semi-automatic discovery of patterns, changes, associations, anomalies, rules, and statistically significant structures in data.

Unlike traditional statistics, which is assumption-driven by forming a hypothesis and validating it against data, data mining is discovery-driven. Patterns and hypothesis are automatically extracted from large data sets. In addition, data mining extracts qualitative models that can easily be translated into business patterns, logical rules, or visual representations. The results may be in the forms of patterns, insights, rules, or models, and they are difficult for even the best human domain experts to derive without the use of the nascent technology.

In various environments, data mining have succeeded in accomplishing the following tasks:

- Anticipating inventory demands,
- Mapping market developments,
- Identifying new clients,
- Calibrating customer loyalty,
- Predicting customer buying habits,
- Finding perpetrators of fraud, and
- Implementing efficient supply chains.

In the electronic commerce domain, data mining techniques offer companies competitive advantages by optimizing their use of information. Potential benefits include the following:

- To manage customer relationships by analyzing customer segments, target marketing and promotion effectiveness, customer profitability, customer lifetime value, customer loyalty and retention, and customer acquisition effectiveness.
- To enable financial management through analytical fraud detection, claims reduction, detection of high cost to serve orders or customers, risk scoring, credit scoring, audit targeting and enforcement targeting.
- To position products by product affinity analysis that shows opportunities for cross-selling, up-selling and strategic product bundling.
- To develop efficient and optimized inventory management system based on Web customer demand predictions.

2 Data Mining Techniques

Commonly used data mining techniques include the following:

- Artificial Neural Networks (ANNs) are non-linear predictive models that learn through training, and they resemble biological neural networks in structure. They contain developing mathematical structures that has the ability to learn from historical information. Neural networks exhibit remarkable ability to derive meaning from complicated or imprecise data. They can be used to extract patterns and detect trends that are too complex to be detected by human experts and many other computer techniques (the case study discussed above utilized artificial neural networks).

- Genetic algorithms are optimization techniques that use genetic combination, mutation, natural selection, and other concepts of natural evolution.
- Decision trees are knowledge representation schemes based on tree-shaped structures that represent sets of decisions. These decision sets generate rules for the classification of a data set. Specific decision tree methods include Classification and Regression Trees (CART) and Chi Square Automatic Interaction Detection (CHAID). CART and CHAID are decision tree techniques used for classification of a data set. They provide a set of rules that one can apply to a new (unclassified) data set to predict which records will yield a given outcome.
- Nearest neighbor method is a technique that classifies each record in a data set based on a combination of the classes most similar to it within a historical data set.
- Rule induction techniques involve the extraction of useful if-then rules from data based on statistical significance.

The phrase "business patterns" often comes up during discussions of data mining. For most problems, a business pattern is a set of measurable characteristics that can be correlated with some other set of characteristics. For example, a pattern resulting from data mining could be something like this: "if you are a Massachusetts male aged between 25 and 45 suffering from chronic asthma, then in 95% of the cases, you fill your weekly medical prescription over the Web." What this pattern does not say is everyone matching this pattern must fill his or her medical prescription over the Web. Usually a pattern is associated with an "accuracy," which specifies the percentage of pattern matches where the correlated characteristic is likely to be correct. As can be expected, the business patterns discovered by data mining have validity only within a particular business context. Outside this context, the difference between pattern and raw data fades away.

3 Case Study: *Medicorp*

Large organizations, especially geographically dispersed organizations, are usually obliged to carry large inventories of products ready for delivery on customer demand. Inventory optimization focuses on the appropriate amount of products that should be kept in the inventory at each store and each warehouse. Lack of supply would turn customers toward competitors, while excess supply would lead to additional costs. In addition, products with short expiration periods and shelf life need to be replaced periodically. The best way to manage an inventory is through the development of better techniques for predicting customer demands and managing stock inventories accordingly. In this way, the size and the constitution of the inventory can be optimized with respect to changing demands.

"*Medicorp*" is a large retail distribution company, with hundreds of chains stores and revenues of several billion dollars per annum. The company's revenues, from over 4100 stores in 25 states in the United States, exceeded $15 billion. *Medicorp* dispenses approximately 12% of all retail prescriptions in the United States. To maintain its market-leading position, *Medicorp* keeps a large standing inventory of products to deliver on customer demand. As a result, the company faces similar problems of large organizations described above.

Medicorp has generally maintained an inventory of approximately a billion dollars on a continuing basis, using traditional regression models to determine inventory levels for each drug item. The corporate policy of *Medicorp* is governed by two competing principles: to minimize total inventory and to achieve highest level of customer satisfaction. On the latter issue, *Medicorp* strives to achieve a 95% fulfillment level. If a random customer walks into a random store on a random day for a random drug, the probability for the availability of the particular item must be 95%. This figure is based on the type of goods that *Medicorp* carries, and the service levels offered by competitors of *Medicorp* for the same items. The company maintains a corporate wide data warehouse system to keep track of what was sold, at what price, and to whom at each store.

After reviewing various options, and using conventional inventory optimization techniques, *Medicorp* adopted a "three-weeks of supply" approach. Through regression study of historical data, the company computed a seasonally adjusted estimate of the forecasted demand for the next three-week period. This estimated demand becomes the inventory level that *Medicorp* keeps on a continuing basis. Each store within the chain orders replenishments on a weekly basis and receives the ordered items two to three days later from a regional data warehouse. Historically, this model has yielded the 95% target for customer satisfaction.

In order to determine the best solution for this inventory problem, we analyzed data maintained within the data warehouse at *Medicorp*. This data warehouse contains data of several gigabytes in size. In the modeling phase, we extracted a portion of the recent data fields from this vast data warehouse, which provided adequate raw data for a preliminary analysis:

1. Date field – Date of the drug transaction
2. NDC number – Drug identification (equivalent to a drug name)
3. Customer number – Customer identification (useful in tracking repeat customers)
4. Quantity number – Amount of the drug purchased
5. Sex field – Sex of the customer
6. Days of Supply -- Duration of that particular drug
7. Cost Unit Price – Per unit cost to *Medicorp*

8. Sold Unit Price – Per unit cost to the customer

Before adopting artificial neural network (ANN) based data mining techniques, preliminary data analysis helped in searching for seasonal trends, correlation between field variables and significance of variables, etc. Our preliminary data provided evidence for the following patterns:

- Most sales of drug items showed minimal correlation to seasonal changes.
- Women are more careful about consuming medication than men, indicating that women customers were more likely to complete the prescription fully than men.
- Drug sales are heaviest on Thursdays and Fridays, indicating that inventory replenishment would be best ordered on Monday.
- Drug sales (in terms of quantity of drug sold) show differing degrees of variability:
- *Maintenance type drugs* (for chronic ailments) show low degrees of sales variability.
- *Acute type drugs* (for temporary ailments) show high degrees of sales variability.

No general theory dictates the type of neural network, number of layers, number of nodes (at various layers), or learning algorithm for a given problem. As a result, data mining analysts must experiment with a large number of neural networks before converging upon the appropriate one for the problem in hand. In order to evaluate the relative performance of each neural network, we applied statistical techniques to measure the error values in predictions. We tested most major neural network architectures and major learning algorithms, using sample data patterns from *Medicorp*. Multi Layer Perceptron (MLP) models and Time Delay Neural Network (TDNN) models yielded promising results and were studied in greater detail.

Modeling short time-interval predictions is difficult, as it requires a greater number of forecast points, shows greater sales demand variability, and exhibits lesser dependence on previous sales history. Using MLP architectures and sales data for one class of products, we initially attempted to forecast sales demand on a daily basis. The results were unsatisfactory, as the networks produced predictions with low correlation (generally below 20%) and high absolute error values (generally above 80%). Therefore, we designed our subsequent modeling with larger time intervals.

As expected, forecasting accuracy increased as the time interval became larger. Indeed, when predicting aggregate annual sales demand, we obtained average error values of only 2%. Keeping a weekly prediction interval provided the best compromise between the accuracy of prediction and the usefulness of the predicted information for *Medicorp*. The weekly forecasts are helpful in designing inventory management systems for individual *Medicorp* stores, while the yearly forecasts are useful for determining the performance of a particular item in a market and the overall financial performance of the organization.

The neural network was trained with historic sales data using two methods: the standard method and the rolling method. The difference between these two methods is best explained with an example. Assume that weekly sales data (in units sold) were 10, 20, 30, 40, 50, 60, 70, 80, 90, 100, etc. In the standard method, we would present the data: "10, 20, 30" and ask the network to predict the fourth value: "40". Then, we would present the network with "40, 50, 60" and ask it to predict the next value: "70". We would continue this process until all training data were exhausted. On the other hand, using the rolling method, we would present historic data as "10, 20, 30" and ask the network to predict the fourth value: "40"; then, we would present the network with "20, 30, 40" and ask it to predict the fifth value: "50". We would continue using the rolling method until all the training data were exhausted.

The rolling method has an advantage over the standard method in that it produces a greater quantity of training examples from the same data sample, but at the expense of training data quality. For example, the rolling method can confuse the neural network because of the close similarity between training samples. Under the previous example, the rolling method would produce "10, 20, 30"; "20, 30, 40"; "30, 40, 50". Each of these training samples differs from another data set by a single number only. This minuscule difference may reduce the neural network's ability to understand the underlying pattern in the data.

At *Medicorp*, some items sell infrequently. In fact, some of the specialized drugs may sell only twice or thrice a year at a particular store. This lack of sales data presents a major problem in training neural networks. To solve it, we used other methods for transformation, reuse, and aggregation of data. The one we found most effective involved changing future data sets with some known fraction of past data sets. If $X[i]'$ represents the ith changed data set, $X[i]$ represents the ith initial data set, $X[i-1]$ represents the initial $(i-1)^{th}$ initial data set and μ is some numerical factor, then the new time series can be computed as $X[i]' = X[i] + \mu * X[i-1]$, $X[0]' = X[0]$. The modified time series thus has data elements that retain a fraction of the information of past elements. By modifying the actual time series with the proposed scheme, the memory of non-zero sales items is retained for a longer period of time, making it easier to train the neural networks with the modified time series.

As mentioned earlier, the policies at *Medicorp* are governed by two competing principles: minimize drug inventories and enhance customer satisfaction via high availability of items in stock. As such, we calibrated the different inventory models using two parameters: "undershoot" and "days of supply". The number of "undershoots" denotes the number of times a customer would be turned away if a particular inventory model was used over the "test" period. The "days-of-supply" statistic represents the number of days the particular item is expected to last. By using the latter parameter, one reduces the complexity and allows for equitable comparisons across different categories of items. For example, items in the inventory are measured in different ways: by weight, volume, or number. If one talked in terms of raw amount, one would need to take into account different units of measure. However, the "days-of-supply" parameter allows all items to be specified in terms of one unit: days. The level of popularity of the item gets factored into the "days-of-supply" parameter. For slow-moving or established drugs, the MLP model is considerably better than the Flat model (for example, in Table 1, file numbers #78, #82, #1235). While maintaining a 95% probability of customer satisfaction (that is, *Medicorp* is able to fill the prescription), the MLP model reduces days-of-supply for established drugs in the inventory by 66%. Since established drugs constitute the majority of the drugs in the total drug inventory, a reduction in the days-of-supply offers a major benefit. The neural network model seems to work best in terms of undershoots and days-of-supply.

			Flat Sales		MLP Model	
File #	Average	Std Dev	Undershoots	Days of Supply	Undershoots	Days of Supply
78	68	99	1	84	1	25
79	134	145	2	28	2	26
80	1224	729	5	18	10	20
81	9	37	0	12	0	7
82	138	170	0	80	2	24
360	582	133	3	19	5	14
441	487	233	0	32	3	13
446	398	152	1	26	5	14
1118	520	182	1	21	4	15
1119	381	136	0	21	4	13
1120	381	136	0	21	4	11
1121	381	136	0	21	2	22
1122	158	79	1	21	7	15
1234	137	133	1	60	1	19
1235	17	51	1	186	1	41
1236	1318	928	3	23	3	16
1237	115	113	2	37	1	38
1238	53	107	3	31	1	23
1255	11831	7136	2	21	8	19

Table 1: Comparison of results for acute type drug #ABCDEF

Our models suggested that, as compared to the "three-weeks of supply" thumb rule, the level of inventory needs to be "reduced" for popular items and "increased" for less popular or unpopular items. This inference appears counter-intuitive at first glance. However, since fast moving items are already carried in large amounts and can be replenished at weekly intervals, one can reduce the inventory level without adversely impacting the likelihood of availability when needed. This factor permits significant reduction in the size of the total inventory, and has been highlighted by a number of observers in the popular press.

In summary, we developed a neural network based data mining model for reducing the inventory at *Medicorp* from over a billion dollars worth of drugs to about one-half billion dollars (reduction by 50%), while maintaining the original customer satisfaction level (95% availability level).

4 Case Study: *Steelcorp*

Artificial Neural Networks (ANNs) described in the previous case have also been used in industrial applications for tasks such as modeling and predicting complex industrial processes. For the most part, ANNs have been used for their ability to capture arbitrary non-linear and highly complex relationships between the inputs and outputs of processes. In addition, neural networks are becoming increasingly attractive in data mining of large corporate databases because they require no prior domain knowledge and because they are computationally efficient.

This case study presents preliminary results from the use of Artificial Neural Networks (ANNs) as a mean of modeling complex inter-variable relationships. The research is based on three months of operational data collected from the blast furnace of *"Steelcorp." Steelcorp* is one of Asia's largest manufacturers of iron and steel, and the company has multiple blast furnaces operating in tandem at multiple locations. Most of the blast furnaces are state-of-the-art and automatically collect and store data at periodic intervals on a number of input and output parameters for future analysis.

At the blast furnace, inputs such as coke, iron ore and sinter are combined in a complex chemical process to yield liquid pig iron, the pre-cursor of steel. The hot metal temperature (HMT) is an important indicator on the internal state of a blast furnace as well as of the quality of the pig iron being produced. Hence, steel-makers and blast furnace operators would like to predict these quality parameters based on current and past conditions of the furnace and on the levels of the various input chemicals used. This analysis would provide them with information regarding the quality of the steel produced, and would allow them to take corrective action if future HMT predictions indicate sub-optimal operating conditions.

Unfortunately, researchers have not been able to find a precise function mapping these input variables to HMT. The production of pig iron involves complicated heat and mass transfers and introduces complex relationships between the various chemicals used. These relationships are often non-linear and therefore cannot be accurately estimated by standard statistical techniques or mass-transfer equations. Therefore, researchers have turned to ANNs to model these complex inter-variable relationships. Attempts have been made by researchers to use ANNs to predict the silicon content of pig iron produced from a blast furnace. Due to the success of this previous work, and the fact that silicon content is directly related to HMT, it seems natural to use ANNs in order to predict HMT.

During the predictive modeling phase of the domain for the ANNs, it became clear that multiple ANN configurations would need to be developed and the ensuing results tested under real-life constraints, before the final choice of the network could be made. To automate the ANN configuration steps, NNRUN, an artificial neural network training suite was conceived and developed. NNRUN provides a menu-driven interface to perform customized data cleansing and manipulation. Given a set of training and testing data, it can automate the search for the optimal neural network.

Raw furnace data must be transformed into a more useful form before it can be presented as learning examples to the neural network. These techniques try to overcome the problems of missing, scaling and lack of data. The initial data set from *Steelcorp* consisted of approximately 30,100 data points, measured at 1-minute intervals. After consulting the domain experts at the blast furnace, it was suggested that we use hourly data to perform training. Thus type of hourly averaging can suppress some of the measurement noise that is present in the 1-minute data. However, averaging every contiguous group of 12 data points would leave only 30100/60 ≈ 501 data points to be split between testing and training. Therefore, moving window averaging was adopted to perform hourly averaging. Every contiguous set of 10 data points is first averaged to create dataset of 3010 data points at 10-minute intervals. The first m 10-minute interval data points are averaged into one hourly data point. Next, this window is shifted down by one 10-minute data point, and the next m data points are averaged. If the initial 10-minute data set has N number of rows, using a window of size m the results in an averaged data set of size $N - m + 1$. Therefore, each new data point contains ten minutes, rather than one minute, of new information. At the same time, potential measurement errors at the 10-minute level are being suppressed by averaging the "new" 10-minute point with $m-1$ other 10-minute data points. Since the goal was to obtain hourly data, m=6 and the number of data points in the new dataset was 3100 – (6 – 1) = 3095, a significant improvement over the 501 data points mentioned earlier.

In order to find the best performing neural network for a given set of data, it is necessary to find the optimal MLP hidden-node configuration, defined to be the network whose predictions on the validation sample exhibit the lowest mean square error (MSE). NNRUN provides the user a choice, through menus, to select the number of hidden layers that the network should have, as well as a minimum and maximum number of nodes for each hidden-layer that should be considered. Therefore, if one wants to find the best two-hidden layer network, and consider number of hidden nodes in the range for the first layer and nodes in the range in the second layer, the total number of network configurations trained will be 10 * 5 = 50.

Typically, the initial dataset is divided into a training set, which comprises 80% of the data, and a testing or validation set, which makes up the other 20%. In the event the number of data points in the testing set is small, if performance of various neural nets is compared using only one particular partition of data, the best performing network will necessarily be the one that is best fit to describe the particular data subset, and not necessarily one that best describes the overall mapping. To alleviate this problem, NNRUN allows the user to set the number of random runs. This parameter allows the user to train the neural networks on a large number (up to the number of data points) of different testing/training partitions of the original data set. This results in the selection of the ANN hidden layer/node configuration with the best mean performance over different partitions. The best configuration is then ensured to reflect the general properties of the mapping and not a particular choice of data partition. If the number of runs chosen is *m*, then choose the best node configuration such that: $(MSE_1 + MSE_2 +\ldots\ldots + MSE_m) / m$ is minimized, where MSE_n is the mean square error over the nth randomized testing data set.

The user can also specify whether the different partitions are selected randomly or sequentially from the main data set. Once the best network configuration is identified, it is retrained on the default training set in order to produce the "best mean" network. Based on the results of running NNRUN with different numbers of runs, it was confirmed that the ANN exhibiting the lowest error on the default data partition rarely provides the best mean-performance ANN. Further, it was observed that, for the best mean network, the mean square error (MSE) indicators of performance are significantly higher for the default partition than the MSE for randomized train/test selections. It is probable that this discrepancy is the result of fundamental changes in the properties of the mapping in the time period covering the train/test partition.

There are three main measures that were used to evaluate network performance and have been cited in many articles. These include the Pearson correlation coefficient, the average error (AE) and the Normalized Mean Square Error (NMSE). The Pearson coefficient measures how well the model predicts *trends* in the output variable. A coefficient of 1 indicates that the model is predicting trends with the highest possible accuracy, while a value of –1 means the model is not predicting trends at all. The average error is just the average difference (in degrees C) between the actual HMT and that predicted by the network. NMSE compares the accuracy of the model's predictions versus predicting the mean. An NMSE value less than 1 indicates that the model performs better than the mean, while a value greater than 1 means that the model performs worse than the mean.

The performance of all trained models was evaluated on the last 20% of the entire dataset, which is the default validation data set.

For *Steelcorp* data, the Pearson coefficient values for the best overall performing networks range from 0.986 for 1-hour prediction to 0.837 for 8-hour prediction. NMSE ranges from 0.0284 for the 1-hour network to 0.306 for the 8-hour network. Average error ranges from 2.92 to 6.95 degrees Celsius. Thus, although the prediction accuracy deteriorates with increasing time horizon, the overall prediction remains favorable. The fact that the Pearson coefficient does not fall below 0.837 indicates that each network has significant ability to predict the trends of HMT. Below are three figures that illustrate the performance of networks used to predict HMT 2 hours, 4 hours and 8 hours into the future.

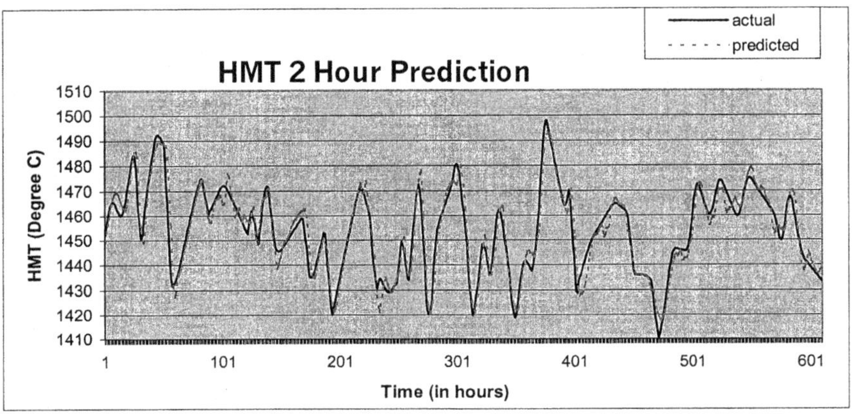

Figure 1: 2-hour HMT results. Configuration: 1 hidden layer with 12 nodes. NMSE: .0986 Correlation: 0.984

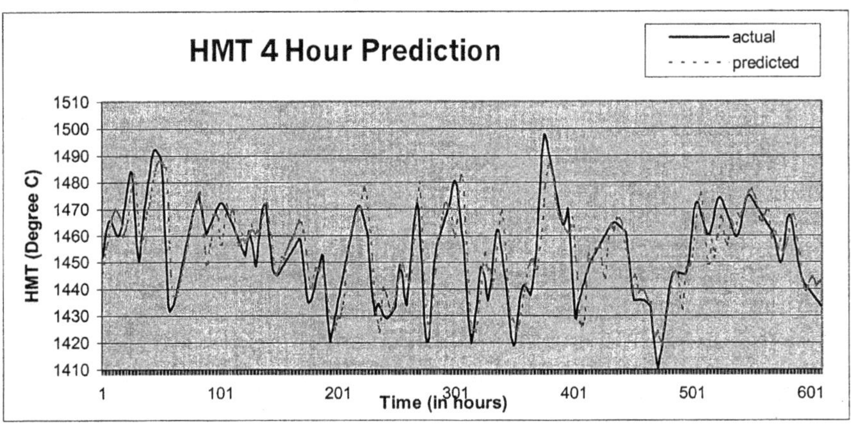

Figure 2: 4-hour HMT results. Configuration: 1 hidden layer with 15 nodes. NMSE: .241 Correlation: 0.878

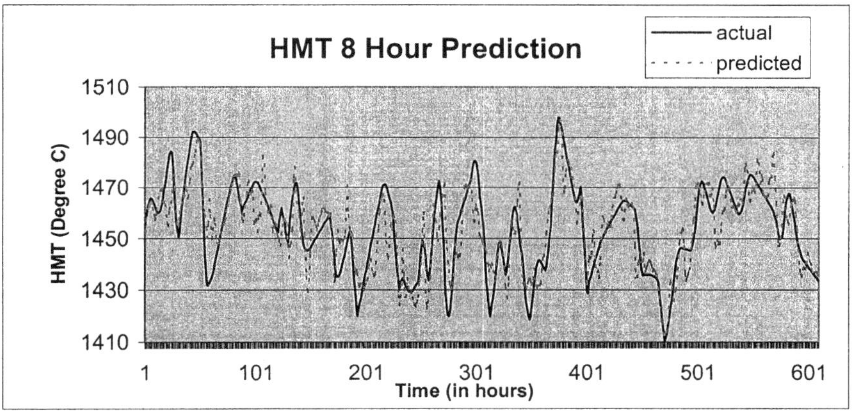

Figure 3: 8-hour HMT results. Configuration: 1 hidden layer with 15 nodes. NMSE: .301 Correlation: 0.839

While the 2 hour and 4 hour predictions are much smoother and more accurate, the 8 hour predictions appear to be more jagged and not as close to the actual values. Nevertheless, the trends of the HMT can still be predicted at a high precision. For the blast furnace operator, knowing the trends of future HMT offers important insights when deciding upon what actions to take.

The complexity of the neural network configuration that performs best over all random partitions is generally higher than the node configuration that performs best only on the default dataset. For example, for 4-hour prediction, the best mean configuration has 15 hidden nodes, while the best default configuration contains only 7 hidden nodes. One reason for this finding could be that the best mean network configuration requires increased generalization to perform well over test data, sampled from many different regions of the overall dataset.

To summarize, this case presents a design and implementation of a multi layer perceptron ANN model used to predict HMT data in blast furnaces. The predicted results were a good indicator of the trends and had strong (high amplitude) predictions. This case also highlights some of the benefits of developing an automated system for testing multiple neural network configurations. NNRUN highlighted in this chapter provides a menu-driven interface to perform customized data cleansing and manipulation, as well as a means to automate the search for the optimal neural network, given a set of training and testing data.

5 Data Mining Functions

The above cases highlighted one type of relationship or classification that the data miners were striving to achieve. From a theoretical perspective, data mining methods can be classified by the function or by the class of application, as enumerated below:

Associations

For a collection of items and a set of records, each of which contain some number of items from the given collection, an *association* function is an operation against this set of records which return affinities or patterns that exist among the collection of items. These patterns can be expressed by rules such as "90% of the time that a specific antibiotic is sold, the patient also buys a bottle of vitamins at the same time."

Sequential/Temporal Patterns

Sequential/temporal pattern functions analyze a collection of records over a period of time for example to identify trends. If the identity of a customer is known, an analysis can be made of the collection of related records of the same structure. The records are related by the identity of the customer who made repeated purchases. Such a situation is typical in electronic commerce settings where a catalogue merchant possesses the information, by customer, of the sets of products that the customer buys in successive purchase orders. A *sequential* pattern function will analyze such collections of related records and will detect frequently occurring patterns of products bought over time. *Sequential* pattern mining functions are quite powerful in electronic commerce settings and can be used to detect the set of customers associated with particular frequent buying patterns. For example, "all buyers of cold medication also buy headache medicine after two weeks."

Clustering/Segmentation

Clustering and *segmentation* are processes for creating a partition so that all the members of each set of the partition are similar, based on some metric. A cluster is a set of objects grouped together because of their similarity or proximity. Objects are often decomposed into an exhaustive and/or mutually exclusive set of clusters. Clustering translates some intuitive measure of similarity into a quantitative measure. There are a number of approaches for forming clusters. One approach is to form rules that dictate membership in the same group based on the level of similarity between members. For example, "offer a 10% discount to all repeat customers of chronic asthma drug from the Massachusetts area."

6 Checklist for Potential Beneficiaries

Based on our experience with data mining projects, we offer the following suggestions:

- *Determine whether data mining is the proper solution technology.* With plenty of hype, data mining is sometimes viewed as the solution for all business problems. While it might be tempting to use data mining to solve every business-related issue, some problems are simply unsuited to data mining. For example, a question such as "What were my sales from Web customers in New York last month?" can be best answered with a database query or on-line analytical processing tool. Data mining, on the other hand, should be used to answer questions such as: "What are the characteristics of my most profitable Web customers from New York?" or "How do I optimize my inventory for the next month?" Above all, data mining directs technology toward a strategic objective: competitive intelligence. In the electronic commerce space, data mining can be used effectively to increase market share by learning about your most valuable customers, studying their features, and then using that profile to either retain them or target new, similar customers.
- *Involve business division(s) in the endeavor from the beginning.* Data mining is gradually evolving from a technology-driven concept to a business solution-driven concept. In the past, information technology users employed data mining technologies without much regard to its incumbent business processes and organizational disciplines. Now, business divisions, rather than technology divisions, in organizations are leading the data mining efforts in major corporations. This allows for further tapping into the full potential of the nascent technology.
- *Realize that data mining is still an art, not (at least, not yet) a science.* For the *Medicorp* study described earlier in this paper, the sponsor organization asked us to look at ways for predicting the time of sale on a slow-moving drug. The results were borderline. However, in the process, we were able to address a much larger problem and outline the strategy for reducing aggregate inventory levels by 50 per cent. With any art, experience is indeed the major distinguishing characteristic. As such, make sure you have experienced data miners in your endeavor to retrieve the hidden treasures.
- *Understand and deliver the fundamentals.* The data mining effort must incorporate the fundamentals of business process. No amount of technology firepower can replace it. For example, data miners need to consider that Web customers are different from non-Web customers; therefore, any data mining results derived from analyzing an entire customer base may not be applicable to a web-customer base. In fact, data mining tools can be used to model the differences in the two types of customer bases, thereby creating a more effective experience for the customer.
- *Engage your technology personnel in the process.* Software vendors are responding to the technology-to-business migration by emphasizing on one-

button data mining products. Vendors can repackage data mining tools, enhance their graphical user interface and automate some of their more esoteric aspects. However, analysts still need to acquire, clean, and feed data to the software; create dynamic selection of appropriate algorithms; validate and assimilate the results of the data mining runs; and generate business rules from the patterns in the data. Most of the operational complexity, time consumption and potential benefits of data mining lie in performing these steps and performing them well.

7 Acknowledgements

The authors would like to thank past and present research members of the Data Mining research group at the Sloan School of Management for their help in testing various ANN models. Proactive support from *Medicorp* and *Steelcorp* throughout the work is greatly appreciated.

References

For Further Reading

1. Fayyad, U.M., Piatetsky-Shapiro, G., Smyth, P. and Uthurusamy, R. (Eds.), *Advances in Knowledge Discovery and Data Mining*, MIT Press, 1996.
2. Soulie, F, *Artificial Neural Networks*, Vol. 1, 605-615, 1991.
3. Dhar, V. & R. Stein, Seven Methods for transforming Corporate data into Business intelligence, Prentice Hall, 1997.
4. Hamilton, J.D., *Time Series Analysis*. Princeton University Press, 1994.
5. Prokhorov, D., Saadm E., Wunsch, D. "Comparative Study of Stock Trend Prediction Using Time Delay, Recurrent and Probabilistic Neural Networks," in IEEE Transactions on Neural Networks, Vol. 9 No. 6 Nov. 1998.
6. Penny, W., Frost, D. "Neural Networks in Clinical Medicine," in Medical Decision Making: an International Journal of the Society for Medical Decision Making. Vol.16, No. 4, 1996.
7. Rumelhart, D.E., G.E. Hinton and R.J. Williams. "Learning representation by back-propagating error," in Nature 323 (1986) 533-536.
8. Biswas A.K., Principles of Blast Furnace Ironmaking, SBA Publications, 1984.
9. Ullmann's Encyclopedia of Industrial Chemistry, 5th complete revised edition. VCH 1985. Vol. A 14. P 517-540.
10. Bulsari, A. and Saxen, H. and Saxen B. "Time-series prediction of silicon in pig iron using neural networks," in International Conference on Engineering Applications of Neural Networks (EANN '92).

11.Bhat, N and McAvoy, T.J. "Use of Neural Nets For Dynamic Modeling and Control of Chemical Process Systems," in Computers in Chemical Engineering, Vol. 14, No. 4/5, pp 573-583. 1990.
12.Smith, M. Neural Networks for Statistical Modeling. pp 111-133. Van Nostrand Reinhold, 1993.
13.Weigend, A.S. and Gershenfeld, N.A. "Results of the time series prediction competition at the Santa Fe Institute," in IEEE International Conference on Neural Networks, pp 1786-1793. IEEE Press, Piscataway, NJ, 1993.
14.Osamu, L., Ushijima, Y. and Toshiro, S. "Application of AI techniques to blast furnace operations," in Iron and Steel Engineer, October 1992.
15.Knoblock, C., ed. "Neural networks in real-world applications," in IEEE Expert. August 1996, pp 4-10.
16.Bhattacharjee, D., Dash S.K., Das, A.K. "Application of Artificial Intelligence in Tata Steel," in Tata Search 1999, 1999.
17.Hertz, J., Krogh, A., Palmer, R.G. Introduction to the Theory of Neural Computation. Addision_Wesley, 1991.

Other Papers from the Research Group

18.Bansal, K., Gupta, A., Vadhavkar, S. "Neural Networks Based Forecasting Techniques for Inventory Control Applications," in Data Mining and Knowledge Discovery, Vol. 2, 1998.
19.Bansal, K., Vadhavkar, S. and Gupta, A "Neural Networks Based Data Mining Applications for Medical Inventory Problems", in International Journal of Agile Manufacturing, Volume 1 Issue 2, 1998, pp. 187-200, Urvashi Press, India.
20.Reyes, Carlos, Ganguly, A, Lemus, G and Gupta, A. "A hybrid model based on dynamic programming, neural networks, and surrogate value for inventory optimization applications," in Journal of the Operational Research Society, Vol. 49, 1998, pp. 1-10.
21.Banks, Bradley. "Neural Network Based Modeling and Data Mining of Blast Furnace Operations." MIT M.Eng Thesis, Sept. 1999.
22.Dhond, A., Gupta, V., Vadhavkar, S., "Data Mining Techniques for Optimizing Inventories for Electronic Commerce," in Proceedings of ACM SIGKDD International Conference on Knowledge Discovery and Data Mining, August 2000.

Extreme Sample Classification and Credit Card Fraud Detection

José R. Dorronsoro, Ana M. González and Carlos Santa Cruz *

Department of Computer Engineering and
Instituto de Ingeniería del Conocimiento
Universidad Autónoma de Madrid
28049 Madrid, Spain

Abstract. Credit card fraud detection is an obviously difficult problem. There are two reasons for that. The first one is the overwhelming majority of good operations over fraudulent ones. The second one is the similarity of many bad operations to legal ones. In other words, to catch a fraudulent operation is akin to find needles in a haystack, only that some needles are in fact hay! In this type of problems (that we term below as Extreme Sample problems) well established methods for classifier construction, such as Multilayer Perceptrons (MLPs), may fail. Non Linear Discriminant Analysis, an alternative method, is described here and some issues pertaining to its practical use, such as fast convergence and architecture selection, are also discussed. Its performance is also compared with that of MLPs over Extreme Sample problems, and it is shown that it gives better results both over synthetic data and on credit card fraud.

1 Introduction

Credit cards are probably the most widely used payment system, with hundreds, if not thousands, of millions of operations taking place worldwide any given day. These huge operation numbers move still more huge amounts of money and any type of fraud, no matter how modest, may result in large benefits for its perpetrators and, accordingly, large losses for credit card owners, merchants and issuers. There are several risk aspects in the credit card industry. First, the credit worthiness of the card holder has to be carefully evaluted by the issuing institution when deciding whether to grant a card. Also, this credit worthiness may change with time, or simply a large accumulation of credit card debt may cast doubts on the repayment ability of the card holder. These aspects are not far away from similar situations a credit institution has to consider when granting standard loans or mortgages. However, there is another possibility, different from the preceding ones: the fraudulent operation of a given credit card or credit card number. By this we mean the use of a lost, stolen or falsified card by a third person against the will of the card's true owner. We shall concentrate in the following in this concrete aspect of credit card fraud.

* With partial support from Spain's CICyT, grant TIC 98–247.

From a scientific point of view, card fraud can be seen more or less straightforwardly as a pattern recognition problem. In this general setting, a pool of individuals is to be classified as belonging to one of a number of classes. When actually assigning a concrete pattern to its class, a number of features are measured, and classification is made upon them. In any case, credit card fraud has two distinct characteristics that make it a rather difficult problem. The first one is the presence in overall card traffic of an overwhelming majority of "good" patterns against a small number of fraudulent cases. This is certainly to be expected, for if not, the underlying card issuer would be soon out of business. A second factor is the presence of a sizeable number of fraud transactions that have operating characteristics quite similar to those of legal ones. Notice that a straightforward way to lengthen the "operating life" of a stolen or forged card is to use it in transactions with otherwise "normal" characteristics. From a higher point of view, these factors are also to be expected in other classification problems in the following ways:

- Unbalanced class sample sizes will appear if the prior probabilities of patterns in some classes are much smaller than those of others.
- Large class overlapping are to be found when the mean error probability of the optimal Bayes classifier is relatively large.

Let us precise these points. Assume that a given pattern ω comes from one of C classes indexed as $1, \ldots, C$, and let δ be any classifier, that is, a function $\delta : R^D \to \{1, \ldots, C\}$ that assigns a D–dimensional pattern ω to one of the C classes. The rule δ acts upon a "feature vector" $X = X(\omega)$, that can be seen as a set of measurements made on ω. Let π_c, $c = 1, \ldots, C$, be the c class prior probabilities, and $f(X|c)$ each class' a priori density. In this setting, Bayes formula

$$P(c|X) = \frac{\pi_c f(X|c)}{\sum_1^C \pi_{c'} f(X|c')}$$

gives the conditional a posteriori probabilities. Now, unbalanced class samples are to be expected if for some class c, $\pi_c << \pi_{c'}$, for one or several other classes c'. Next, the Bayes rule

$$\delta_B(X) = \arg\max_c P(c|X) = \arg\max_c \pi_k f(X|c)$$

defines the optimal decision rule with respect to a 0–1 loss function i.e., a wrong class assignment is assumed to have a cost of 1, while a right one has zero cost. With $E_c = \{X : \delta(X) = c\}$ and $f(X) = \sum_1^C \pi_c f(X|c)$ the overall density, the Mean Error Probability of δ is defined as

$$MEP(\delta) = \sum_1^C \int_{E_c} (1 - P(c|X)) f(X) dX.$$

and it is clear from the above definition that $MEP(\delta) \geq MEP(\delta_B)$. Thus, $MEP(\delta_B)$ gives another measure of the difficulty of a classification problem.

We can term classification problems with the above characteristics as "extreme", in the sense that the presence of the above factors can make them very difficult to solve. Notice that a large $MEP(\delta_B^X)$ of the original features X implies that no matter what extraction procedure is used, the $MEP(\delta_B^{X'})$ of the new features X' will still be larger. If, moreover, class samples are unbalanced, the construction of the extraction procedure may fail (we shall illustrate this situation over a synthetical problem). Of course, there are other possible circumstances, such as for instance, large input dimensions, that may give a high degree of difficulty to a concrete problem, but in what follows we shall concentrate in the two previous ones. Going back to our credit card discusion, there usually will be an overwhelming majority of "good" patterns against a small number of fraudulent cases. Thus, the prior probability of legitimate operations is much larger than that of fraudulent ones and, therefore, highly unbalanced sample sizes are unavoidable. Moreover, the presence of a sizeable number of fraud transactions that have operating characteristics quite similar to those of legal ones is to be expected. This will imply that the MEP of the hypothetical Bayes rule for this problem should be quite large.

A natural consequence is that in such an extreme problem, clear cut, crisp classification decisions will be very difficult, if not impossible, to make. This places such problems as a natural ground for soft computing methods, that may be able to combine feature extraction procedures derived from neural networks, machine learning algorithms or evolutionary methods with flexible decision rules derived through fuzzy logic or probabilistic reasoning. Of course, as stated, this would be result in a large and ambitious program. We shall concentrate here in a more modest solution, where we will construct a feature extraction procedure using a Multilayer Perceptron (MLP)–like architecture but where the criterion function whose minimization yields the procedure's optimal weights will not be the usual, "crisp" target based square error. More precisely, the features looked for will be derived using a Fisher discriminant analysis type criterion function. In other words, we will not try to attach clear cut, a priori defined targets to patterns that come from different classes but have similar features. We will strive, instead, to concentrate the new features of same class patterns around their class means while trying to keep these means apart. A decision rule is still to be defined upon the new features and we can follow various paths. In any case, a fixed, rule based decision is not likely to be applied in a credit card setting, where many of the alerts that any system emits may be due to slightly off main stream operations of otherwise perfectly good clients. A more nuanced decision path is needed, for which complementary information of the concrete transaction to be qualified may be used. To help in this direction, a desirable output of a classifier is a sort of "probability" that the transaction under consideration is fraudulent. A possible probability–like assignment will be discused later.

The rest of the paper is organised as follows. The next section will briefly discuss MLPs as classification tools, pointing out some dificulties in an extreme problem in the above sense. Non Linear Discriminant Analysis (NLDA) is introduced in the third section as an alternative feature extraction procedure. NLDA network training is discussed there and also some ideas on how to define optimal NLDA architectures. Sections 4 and 5 contain some experiments. In section 4 a synthetic problem is used to illustrate extreme sample classification, while credit card fraud detection is discussed in section 5. Both sections contain comparisons between MLP and NLDA feature based classification. The paper closes with a short conclusions section.

2 Multilayer Perceptron Classification

Multilayer Perceptrons (MLPs) are the neural tools of choice in classification problems and have given excellent results in a large number of situations. As it is well known, they define a transfer function $Y = F(X, W)$ that receives a certain input feature vector X, processes it through a series of so called hidden units after which it produces an output Y. Typically, the connections between the input and first hidden layer and between these are non linear, and the outputs $O^h = (o_1, \ldots, o_{M_h})^t$ of layer h are derived from the O^{h-1} outputs of the previous layer as $o_m = f((W^h_m)^t O^{h-1})$ (in what follows, A^t denotes the transpose of a matrix A). Here W^h denote the $M_{h-1} \times M_h$ weight matrix connecting the M_{h-1} unit layer $h-1$ to the M_h unit layer h, and W^O the $M_H \times C-1$ weight matrix connecting the M_H unit last hidden layer to the network's $C-1$ dimensional output. Moreover, f denotes the sigmoid function $\sigma(x) = 1/(1+e^{-x})$ or the hyperbolic tangent $tanh(x) = (1-e^{-x})/(1+e^{-x}) = 2\sigma(x)-1$. The connections between the last hidden layer and the ouputs may be either sigmoidal or simply linear. In this last case the final network outputs Y are obtained from the outputs O^H at the last hidden layer by $Y = (W^O)^t O^H$, with W^O the connecting weights. We shall denote by $\mathcal{W} = (W^1, \ldots, W^H)$ the hidden weight set and the full weight set as $W = (W^O, \mathcal{W})$. Network training is done using for each input X a concrete teaching target $T = T^X$ and an optimal weigth set W^* is sought by the minimization of an error function $E(W)$ that measures the global discrepancy between network outputs $Y = F(X, W)$ and targets T^X. Generally the squared error

$$E(W) = E[||Y - T||^2] = \int ||F(X, W) - T^X||^2 f(X) dX,$$

with $f(X)$ the density of the X in sample space, is used.

When aplied in a C class classification problem, C–dimensional targets $e^c = (0, \ldots, 1, \ldots, 0)^t$, whose coordinates are all 0 except the c–th one, which is 1, are customarily employed. The main reason for this is that the optimal weights W^* that minimize the overall error function

$$E(W) = \sum_{c=1}^{C} \int (F_c(X,W) - T_c^X)^2 f(X) dX$$

also minimize [19] the square distance

$$\epsilon(W) = \sum_{c} \int (F_c(X,W) - P(c|X))^2 f(X) dX$$

between the network's transfer function outputs $F(X,W)$ and the a posteriori class membership probabilities $P(c|X)$. Viewing the outputs $Y = F(X,W)$ as a new feature set, a standard decision rule for MLPs is defined by

$$\delta_{MLP}(X) = \arg\ \max_c \{F_c(X,W^*)\}.$$

Notice that if the approximation $P(c|X) \approx F_c(X,W^*)$ holds, we would have [11,19,22]

$$\delta_{MLP}(X) = \arg\ \max_i \Phi_i(X,W^*) \simeq \arg\ \max_i P(i|X) = \delta_B(X).$$

Therefore, the classifying performance of the MLP decision rule should be close to that of the optimal Bayes rule. MLPs, however, are not trained with the error function $E(W)$ but with the sample square error

$$e(W) = \frac{1}{N} \sum_{j=1}^{N} ||F(X_j,W) - T^{X_j}||^2.$$

This and other facts may result in a failure of the approximation $\delta_{MLP}(X) \simeq \delta_B(X)$ and, subsequently, poor classification performance. This has been observed when classes are unequally represented in the training set (one of our "extreme sample" properties), resulting in a bias towards the sample dominant classes [3,4] and in an inaccurate a posteriori probability estimation [5].

Webb and Lowe [24] have given a reason for this. They show that the weights W^* minimizing $e(W)$ at the output also minimize at the last hidden layer what they call the "network discriminant function" $\mathrm{tr}((\hat{S}_T^O)^{-1}\hat{S}_B^O)$. Here

$$\hat{S}_T^O = \frac{1}{N} \sum_{1}^{N} (O^i - \overline{O})(O^i - \overline{O})^t,$$

with N denoting the total number of patterns, is the total sample covariance of the outputs O at that layer, and

$$\hat{S}_B^O = \sum_{c} \left(\frac{N_c}{N}\right)^2 (\overline{O}_c - \overline{O})(\overline{O}_c - \overline{O})^t,$$

with N_c the sample patterns in class c, is a weighted version (notice the squared factors) of the standard between class sample covariance (see below) at the same layer. If all the N_c/N are approximately equal, $\tilde{S}_B^O$ is just a multiple of the true between class covariance. If, however, they are not so, as it would be the case in an extreme sample problem, $\tilde{S}_B^O$ may favor heavily classes with larger N_c/N, to the point that they may overwhelm the smaller sample classes. Several techniques have been proposed in order alleviate this situation. For instance, in [24] it is suggested that the e_i targets be changed by $e_i' = (0, \ldots, 1/\sqrt{N_i}, \ldots, 0)^t$, where N_i denotes the number of sample patterns in class i. This is an example of what we may term "equalising" techniques, that attempt some kind of class size balance before training, such as for instance by subsampling in the larger classes [21]. As an alternative, several types of "scaling" techniques have also been suggested to remedy this situation, such as multiply all weight updates associated to patterns of a given class by a factor depending on the a priori probabilities [13]. Other techniques may involve probabilistic sampling [26], where patterns from each class are selected randomly with probabilities that balance the unequal priors. Finally, another technique is the post–scaling of network outputs according to the prior class probability values [19].

As the results in [24] show, the reason for the above problems may be traced to the target based nature of MLP training, suggesting the interest of getting rid of targets while retaining the very useful transformation properties of the MLP architecture. Non Linear Discriminant Analysis (NLDA), to be discussed next, is a way to achieve this.

3 Non Linear Discriminant Analysis

A Non Linear Discriminant Analysis (NLDA) network has the same architecture and, hence, transfer function F than an MLP. More precisely, in a C class problem with D dimensional patterns, an NLDA network will have D input units, $C-1$ output units (as it is the case in Fisher's linear discriminants for C classes), and a certain number of hidden layers. The NLDA network transfer function is the same than for MLPs, as described in the previous section. The difference lies in the selection of the optimal weights $W_* = (W_*^O, \mathcal{W}_*)$, obtained by minimizing any of the criterion functions customarily used in Fisher's analysis instead of the MLP's square error. A convenient choice that simplifies further computations is [9,10] the trace quotient criterion $J(W) = \frac{tr(s_T)}{tr(s_B)}$ or its determinant based counterpart $J(W) = \frac{det(s_T)}{det(s_B)}$. Here

$$s_T = E[(Y - \overline{Y})(Y - \overline{Y})^t]$$

is the total covariance of the outputs Y and

$$s_B = \sum_c \pi_c(\overline{Y}_c - \overline{Y})(\overline{Y}_c - \overline{Y})^t$$

is their between class covariance. By $\overline{Y} = E[Y]$ we denote the overall output mean, $\overline{Y}_c = E[Y|c]$ denotes the output class conditional means and π_c are the class prior probabilities. As it is well known, the Fisher weights are unique up to dilations, and we shall normalize them to unit norm in what follows.

These considerations show that in some sense, the hidden layer weights determine the values of the W^O weights: in fact, they establish for each input X the values o_h of the last hidden layer outputs that, in turn, determine the Fisher weights. More precisely, if the last hidden layer has M_H units, the $M_H \times (C-1)$ matrix W^O is made up of the $C-1$ largest eigenvectors of the $M_h \times M_H$ matrix $(S_T)^{-1} S_B$, with

$$S_T = E[(O - \overline{O})(O - \overline{O})^t]$$

the total covariance of the last hidden layer outputs O and

$$S_B = \sum_c \pi_c (\overline{O}_c - \overline{O})(\overline{O}_c - \overline{O})^t$$

their between class covariance. In other words, the input sample and the current hidden weight set completely determine the last hidden layer outputs, that in turn also determine the Fisher weights W^O. This suggests the following general setting for weight update in NLDA networks: starting with a given hidden weight set $\mathcal{W}_t = (W_t^1, \ldots, W_t^H)$ at time t, we update it to $\mathcal{W}_{t+1} = (W_{t+1}^1, \ldots, W_{t+1}^H)$ as follows:

1. Compute the hidden output O values and then the associated Fisher weights W_{t+1}^O by the previous procedure.
2. Compute the new weights $\mathcal{W}_{t+1}$ as $\mathcal{W}_{t+1} = \mathcal{W}_t - \Delta_t \mathcal{W}$.

The step t increment $\Delta_t \mathcal{W}$ can be derived following a variety of numerical procedures. For instance, notice that NLDA learning is a "batch" process, in the sense that a full sample is needed to compute the second order information required. We could therefore use a global minimization procedure such as Conjugate Gradients or Quasi Newton methods [18] to update $\mathcal{W}$. On the other hand, we can opt for a much simpler gradient descent procedure, in which the update is given by $\Delta_t \mathcal{W} = \eta_t \nabla_{\mathcal{W}} J_t^H(\mathcal{W}_t)$. Here $J_t^H(\mathcal{W})$ denotes the value of the criterion function $J(W_t^O, \mathcal{W})$ where the Fisher weights W_t^O are clamped down to a fixed value and η_t is an appropriately chosen learning rate. Both approaches have opposite pros and cons: the higher computational complexity of a Conjugate Gradient or Quasi Newton method is alleviated by a convergence presumably faster than that of a computationally simpler gradient descent.

We shall consider later an intermediate training procedure, but in any case, all these minimization procedures rely on the computation of the gradient of J, something that we shall do next. For simplicity we shall concentrate on the $C = 2$ case; the network has then a single dimensional output y and, therefore, the matrices s_T and s_B being just scalars, the trace and determinant criterion functions just coincide. We then have

$$\frac{\partial J}{\partial w_{kl}} = \frac{1}{s_B}\left(\frac{\partial s_T}{\partial w_{kl}} - J\frac{\partial s_B}{\partial w_{kl}}\right),$$

and since $s_T = E[(y-\overline{y})^2]$, it follows that

$$\frac{\partial s_T}{\partial w_{kl}} = 2E\left[(y-\overline{y})\left(\frac{\partial y}{\partial w_{kl}} - \frac{\partial \overline{y}}{\partial w_{kl}}\right)\right]$$

Recall that we have $a_l = \sum_k w_{kl} o_k$ and $o_l = f(a_l)$, with f the network's activation function. Using the a_l as intermediate coordinates, we have

$$\frac{\partial y}{\partial w_{kl}} = \frac{\partial y}{\partial o_l}\frac{\partial o_l}{\partial a_l}\frac{\partial a_l}{\partial w_{kl}} = d_l f'(a_l) o_k$$

where $d_l = \partial y/\partial o_l$. Observe that if the unit l is at the last hidden layer and $W_O = (w_1, \ldots w_H)^t$, $y = \sum w_l o_l$, and hence $d_l = w_l$. If the unit l is at another layer and w_{lp} is the weight connecting this unit with the p unit at the next layer, we have

$$d_l = \frac{\partial y}{\partial o_l} = \sum_p \frac{\partial y}{\partial o_p}\frac{\partial o_p}{\partial a_p}\frac{\partial a_p}{\partial o_l} = \sum_p d_p f'(a_p) w_{lp}.$$

In other words, and similarly to what happens in standard backpropagation, the d_l at a given layer can be computed in terms of the values d_p of the preceding layer. It now follows that

$$\begin{aligned}\frac{\partial s_T}{\partial w_{kl}} &= 2E\left[(y-\overline{y})\;(d_l f'(a_l)o_k - E[d_l f'(a_l)o_k])\right] \\ &= 2\left(E\left[y d_l f'(a_l)o_k\right] - \overline{y}E\left[d_l f'(a_l)o_k\right],\right).\end{aligned}$$

Similarly, $(s_B) = \sum_c \pi_c(\overline{y}^c - \overline{y})^2$, where $\overline{y}^c = E_c[y]$ and we recall that $E_c[z] = E[z|c]$ denotes class conditional expectation. As a consequence

$$\begin{aligned}\frac{\partial s_B}{\partial w_{kl}} &= 2\sum_c \pi_c\left(\overline{y}^c - \overline{y}\right)\left(E_c\left[d_l f'(a_l)o_k\right] - E\left[d_l f'(a_l)o_k\right]\right) \\ &= 2\sum_c \pi_c\left(\overline{y}^c E_c\left[d_l f'(a_l)o_k\right] - \overline{y}E\left[d_l f'(a_l)o_k\right]\right).\end{aligned}$$

Putting all together, we have finally get the gradient of the NLDA criterion function

$$\frac{\partial J}{\partial w_{kl}} = \frac{2}{s_B}\left(E\left[yd_l f'(a_l)o_k\right] - \overline{y}E\left[d_l f'(a_l)o_k\right]\right) - \frac{2J}{s_B}\sum_c \pi_c \left(\overline{y}^c E_c\left[d_l f'(a_l)o_k\right] - \overline{y}E\left[d_l f'(a_l)o_k\right]\right). \tag{1}$$

4 Learning and Architecture Selection in NLDA Networks

If we define $\Psi = (\Psi_{kl})$ as

$$\Psi_{kl}(X,W) = \frac{2}{s_B}yd_l f'(a_l)o_k - \frac{2}{s_B}\overline{y}E\left[d_l f'(a_l)o_k\right] - \frac{2J}{s_B}\sum_c \pi_c \left(\overline{y}^c E_c\left[d_l f'(a_l)o_k\right] - \overline{y}E\left[d_l f'(a_l)o_k\right]\right) \tag{2}$$

$$= z_{kl} - \lambda_{kl} \tag{3}$$

where the nonrandom term $\lambda_{kl}(W)$ is given by

$$\lambda_{kl}(W) = \frac{2w_l}{s_B}\overline{y}E\left[d_l f'(a_l)o_k\right] + \frac{2w_l}{s_B}J\sum_c \pi_c \left(\overline{y}^c E_c\left[d_l f'(a_l)o_k\right] - \overline{y}E\left[d_l f'(a_l)o_k\right]\right),$$

(1) shows that the gradient of J can be written as the expectation of the Ψ_{kl}:

$$\frac{\partial J}{\partial w_{kl}}(W) = E[\Psi_{kl}(X,W)] = E[z_{kl}] - \lambda_{kl}.$$

In particular, the covariance matrix $\mathcal{I}$ of the Ψ_{kl} is given by

$$\mathcal{I}_{(kl)(mn)} = \mathcal{I}_{(kl)(mn)}(W) = E[(\Psi_{kl} - \overline{\Psi}_{kl})(\Psi_{mn} - \overline{\Psi}_{mn}] = E[(z_{kl} - \overline{z}_{kl})(z_{mn} - \overline{z}_{mn})], \tag{4}$$

and therefore $(\mathcal{I})_{(kl)(mn)} = cov(z_{kl}z_{mn})$.

There is a formal similitude between the $\mathcal{I}$ matrix and the well known Fisher information matrix of mathematical statistics. This is more clear if we consider what happens with the gradient of a standard MLP. When used, for instance, in regression problems, that is, when the MLP tries to establish a relationship between an input X and output y for each pattern $Z = (X, y)$, a probability model $p(Z; W) = p(X, y; W)$ can be defined in pattern space so that the on line MLP error function $e(Z, W) = e(X, y, W) =$

$(y - F(X;W))^2/2$ is seen as the log–likelihood $e(Z,W) = \log p(Z;W)$ of $p(Z;W)$; here $F(X,W)$ denotes the MLP transfer function. Moreover, the MLP square error function $E(W)$ is then given by

$$E(W) = \frac{1}{2}E\left[(y - F(X;W))^2\right] = \frac{1}{2}E\left[\log p(Z;W)\right]$$

and its gradient,

$$\frac{\partial E}{\partial W} = E\left[\frac{\partial \log p(Z;W)}{\partial W}\right]$$

is then the expectation of the random variable $\Psi(Z,W) = \frac{\partial \log p(Z;W)}{\partial W}$. This allows one to recast network learning as the likelihood estimation of a certain semi–parametric probability density $p(X,y,W)$. In this setting, there is [1,16] a natural Riemannian metric on the space $\{p(X,y;W) : W\}$ of these densities, determined by a metric tensor given by the matrix

$$\begin{aligned} G(W) &= E\left[(\nabla_W \log p)(\nabla_W \log p)^t\right] \\ &= \int\int \frac{\partial \log p}{\partial W}\left(\frac{\partial \log p}{\partial W}\right)^t p(X,y;W)dX dy. \end{aligned}$$

$G(W)$ is also known as the Fisher Information matrix, as it gives the variance of the Cramr–Rao bound for the optimal parameter estimator. Notice that G is also the covariance at the optimal weights of the gradient of the MLP criterion function The existence of the underlying G metric suggests [17,2] to use the "natural" gradient in this Riemannian setting, that is, $G(W)^{-1}\nabla_W e(X,y;W)$, instead of the ordinary euclidean gradient $\nabla_W e(X,y;W)$. This approach has received recently considerable attention in the literature for MLPs in regression and classification problems, and in other settings such as Independent Component Analysis and Systems Space [17]. Among other results, it has been experimentally checked that the natural gradient can noticeably speed up the convergence of on line MLP training, in the sense that many less training epochs (i.e., presentations of individual patterns) are needed.

Going back to NLDA networks, a "natural gradient" in the previous sense could be defined in terms of the NLDA equivalent of the Fisher Information matrix, that is, the matrix $\mathcal{I}$ of (4). The corresponding "natural gradient" descent weight update would then be given by

$$W_{t+1}^H = W_t^H - \eta_t \mathcal{I}^{-1}\nabla_W J_t(W_t^H). \tag{5}$$

This is the situation studied in [7], where preliminary experiments show that natural gradient descent requires far less iterations to converge than it is the case with ordinary descent. A possible draw back would be larger computational costs needed by natural gradient. In fact, it is easily seen from (1) that for a network with D dimensional inputs, a single layer of H units and an N pattern sample, the computation of ∇J requires $O(NDH)$ time. If natural gradient is used, the D^2H^2 components of $\mathcal{I}$ have to be computed, each with a cost of $O(N)$, and the D^3H^3 cost of inverting $\mathcal{I}$ has to be added. Since in practice $N >> DH$ is to be expected, the cost of natural gradient descent is thus $O(ND^2H^2)$, that is, about DH times bigger than that of ordinary gradient descent. A simple way to alleviate this is to work just with the diagonal of $\mathcal{I}$, that is, to replace (5) by

$$w_{kl}^{t+1} = w_{kl}^t - \eta_t \frac{1}{\mathcal{I}_{(kl)(kl)}} \frac{\partial J_t}{\partial w_{kl}}(W_t^H), \tag{6}$$

with a cost of $O(NDH)$, as only the DH diagonal terms of $\mathcal{I}$ are needed. The experimental results of [7] show that (6), although requiring more iterations than the full natural descent, is still much faster the ordinary descent. Moreover, there may be other advantages to the use of natural descent. For instance, it seems that the minima obtained this way are rather good in other senses. For instance, when experiments over synthetic data are conducted, the optimal J values obtained are quite close to the theoretical minimum. Moreover, convergence is quite consistent, in the sense that the optimal W obtained from different initializations are more or less the same, modulo sign and unit permutation changes. Finally, the structure of the Fisher matrices $\mathcal{I}(W^*)$ that correspond to optimal weights W^* is often block diagonal with respect to the hidden unit index. By this we mean that $\mathcal{I}_{(kl)(mn)} = 0$ if $l \neq n$. In other words, making the standard approximation

$$\mathcal{H}_{(kl)(mn)} = E\left[\frac{\partial^2 J}{\partial w_{kl} \partial w_{mn}}\right] \simeq E\left[\frac{\partial J}{\partial w_{kl}} \frac{\partial J}{\partial w_{mn}}\right]$$

to the Hessian $\mathcal{H}$ of J, it follows that around a minimum W^* we have a much simpler "block diagonal" second order Taylor approximation instead of a full expansion. All these advantages of natural gradient descent are currently under research.

Another consequence of the expression (1) for the NLDA gradient is the possibility of deriving architecture selection criteria for these networks. In our setting we have to decide on the number of hidden layers and the number of units on each layer. Also, if the relevance of the original features is to be discussed, the number of input units cannot be taken to be fixed in advance, and may have to be lowered. Architecture selection is a long studied question for MLPs, and many approaches, such as bootstrapping, pruning, regularization, stopped training or information criteria have been proposed (see [12,21,25] for an overview of these approaches). The situation is somewhat different in the case of the last hidden layer. NLDA performs classical Fisher analysis on them and, therefore, its outputs can be seen as input features upon which a classical linear discriminant acts. We can thus use classical results to determine the relevance of input features for linear discriminants. For instance, and assuming again a two class problem, it can be shown [20,15] that if the inputs come from two d–dimensional multinormal distributions with a common covariance, the statistic

$$R_h = \frac{(N-d-1)c^2 w_h^2}{(N-2)T_{hh}(N-2+c^2D^2)}, \tag{7}$$

with $c^2 = N_1 N_2/N$, N_i the number of sample patterns in class i and $N = N_1 + N_2$, follows an $F_{1,N-2}$ distribution under the null hypothesis $w_h = 0$. In our context, the values of the last hidden outputs would be taken as the inputs of a classical Fisher transformation. Of course, the preceding common multinormal distribution assumption may not be true for these hidden layer outputs and, therefore, tests for significance at a given level may not be strictly applicable. However, a value of the statistic that would warrant the rejection of the null hypothesis could be taken as an indicator of that weight's relevance. On the other hand, a value of the statistic compatible with the acceptance of the null hypothesis should indicate the convenience of that weight removal.

The situation is, of course different, for NLDA inputs and other hidden units, for which asymptotic weight distribution results can be derived. Let us denote again by Ψ the function defined in (3), whose covariance we recall is given by the Fisher matrix $\mathcal{I}$ and let

$$\mathcal{H} = \mathcal{H}(W) = \nabla^2 J(W) = E[\nabla_W \Psi(X,W)]$$

be the Hessian of J. At an isolated minimum W^* of J, $\mathcal{H}$ is definite positive, and it can be shown [14] that if X_n is a sequence of i.i.d. random vectors distributed as X, the equation $\sum_1^N \Psi(X_n, W) = 0$ or, equivalently,

$$\frac{1}{N}\sum_{j=1}^{n}\left(y^j d_l^j x_k^j - \lambda_{kl}(W)\right) = 0,$$

has a solution sequence $\widetilde{W}_n$ converging in probability to W^* and such that $\sqrt{N}(\widetilde{W}_n - W^*)$ converges in distribution to a multivariate normal with 0 mean and variance $\mathcal{C}^* = \mathcal{C}(W^*) = (\mathcal{H}^*)^{-1}\mathcal{I}^*(\mathcal{H}^*)^{-1}$.

Now, if S is a 0–1 selection vector with a given number K of 1's, then, under the null hypothesis $H_0 : SW^* = 0$, it follows that $\sqrt{N}S\widetilde{W}_N \to N(0, S^t\mathcal{C}^*S)$ in distribution. The radom variable $\zeta_N = \sqrt{N}(S^t\mathcal{C}^*S)^{-1/2}S\widetilde{W}_N$ coverges thus to a K dimensional $N(0,I)$ and

$$||\zeta_N||^2 = N(S\widetilde{W}_N)^t(S^t\mathcal{C}S)^{-1}(S\widetilde{W}_N)$$

converges in distribution to a chi–square χ_K^2 with K degrees of freedom.

We can apply this result to test the relevance of a unit d. That relevance can be defined in terms of a subset of weights related to that unit. Obvious choices are the subsets of either input or output weights. However, notice that

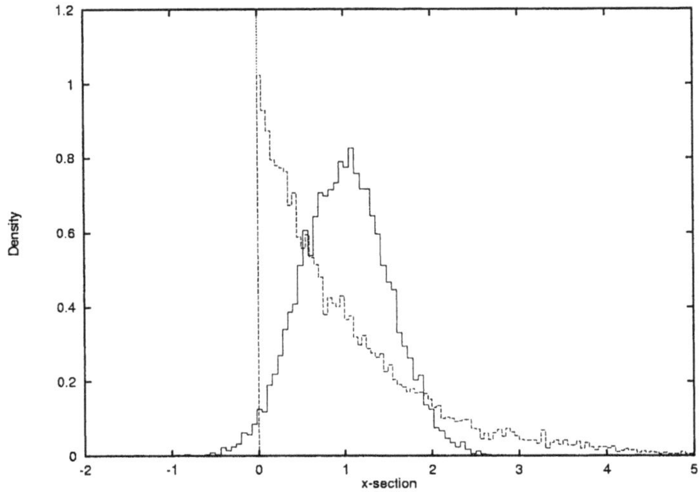

Fig. 1. Histograms of the x–sections of a bidimensional sample of 1.000 normal (solid line) and exponential (dashed line) data.

if all the weights w_{kl} starting at a given hidden unit k are zero, the weights w_{hk} leading to that unit can take any value without affecting network outputs. We shall thus consider what we could term "output unit" relevance, that is, the joint relevance of the weights leaving it. To measure it for unit d we can just take as the selection vector S one such that $S = (s_{(pq)})$, where $s_{(dq)} = 1$ and all the others are zero. Setting

$$R_d = N(S\widehat{W}_N)^t(S\hat{C}S)^{-1}(S\widehat{W}_N) \simeq N \sum_h \frac{(\hat{w}^*_{dh})^2}{(\hat{\mathcal{H}}^{-1}\hat{\mathcal{I}}\hat{\mathcal{H}}^{-1})_{(dh)(dh)}},$$

R_d should approximately follow a χ^2_H distribution with H degrees of freedom when computed on the value $R(d)$. We can thus decide to keep or remove the unit d according to a chosen confidence level α depending on whether R_d is larger or smaller than the value v_α for which $P(\{\chi^2_H > v_\alpha\}) = \alpha$.

5 A Synthetic Extreme Sample Problem

We will first compare the performance of MLP and NLDA networks upon a synthetic example, in which samples are randomly drawn from explicitly known probability distributions. Obviously they do not represent models for problems to be encountered in real world applications. However, they provide an easily controlled environment upon which various scenarios for extreme sample situations can be defined. In this section we will work with a two class problem. The density function of the first class will be given by a normal family with mean $(1, \ldots, 1)^t$ and covariance matrix $\Sigma = 0.25 I_D$, I_D being the

Dimension	2	4	6	8	10
$MEP(\delta_B)$	0.263	0.202	0.160	0.130	0.108

Table 1. MEP values of the optimal Bayes classifier for the exponential and normal samples in different dimensions.

$D \times D$ identity matrix. The second class will be defined in terms of the negative exponential density function $e^{-(x_1+\ldots+x_D)}$, with support in the positive quadrant $Q = \{X : x_i \geq 0\}$. Notice that a rather large class overlapping will take place around the common mean vector $(1, \ldots, 1)^t$ for both classes. For instance, figure 1 shows the histograms of the x–values of a sample of 1.000 bidimensional patterns from each class. This picture clearly implies that the corresponding classification problems should be fairly difficult, something that is also made clear when the MEPs for different dimensions are computed. They are shown in Table 1 to go from a value of 0.263 in the two dimensional case, to one of 0.108 in dimension 10 (these MEP values are experimental approximations to the true ones). Notice that as the dimension D increases, the Bayes MEP values decrease, meaning that the corresponding classification problems become somewhat easier. This is a consequence of the fact that we keep the exponential class confined to the first quadrant, whereas the normal patterns are distributed among the 2^D quadrants existing in D dimensions. We will take equal priors of 0.5 for both classes. No matter what classifier is used, it is clear that its performance will not be good upon patterns coming from the regions where class overlapping is large (around the common mean in our case). However, a good classifier should make correct class assignments when patterns come from regions where both distributions are markedly different. For instance, in our case, they should handle correctly those patterns coming from the distribution tails. Notice that in figure 1 the normal density dominates when $x < 0$, while the exponential one does so for x large and also when x is near 0.

We will measure the performance of a given classifier δ in terms of its $MEP(\delta)$. For MLP classification, we shall use the rule δ_{MLP} previously defined. In the case of NLDA networks, if $Y = F(X)$ are the new features and $\overline{Y}_{c'}$ is the mean of $\{Y = F(X) = F(X(\omega)) : \omega \in c'\}$, we simply can assign a new ω to class c with c given as

$$\delta_{NLDA}(X) = \arg\max_{c'} \left\{ ||Y - \overline{Y}_{c'}|| \right\} = \arg\max_{c'} \left\{ ||F(X) - \overline{Y}_{c'}|| \right\}.$$

We will compute the δ_{NLDA} and δ_{MLP} MEP values numerically, taking advantage of our perfect knowledge of the underlying distributions and generating large and equal numbers of random samples of each class and computing the confusion matrices after each MLP and NLDA classifier is applied. For instance, if in a 2 class problem we denote by r_{ij} the rate of patterns of class

Sample Ratios	D = 2 MLP	D = 2 NLDA	D = 4 MLP	D = 4 NLDA	D = 8 MLP	D = 8 NLDA
1	0.283	0.270	0.206	0.209	0.128	0.132
6	0.320	0.276	0.265	0.199	0.175	0.130
12	0.373	0.292	0.302	0.215	0.231	0.134
18	0.375	0.288	0.301	0.221	0.280	0.139
21	0.381	0.293	0.317	0.229	0.282	0.147
24	0.395	0.298	0.337	0.237	0.308	0.150

Table 2. MEP values of the MLP and NLDA classifiers built upon samples for which the ratio of the normal to exponential sample sizes are given at the leftmost column. Normal base sizes are 2.000, 8.500 and 45.000 for dimensions 2, 4 and 8, respectively.

i assigned to class j, $0 \leq i, j \leq 1$, the average of the error rates r_{01} and r_{10}

$$\widehat{MEP}_\delta = \pi_0 r_{01} + \pi_1 r_{10}$$

is then a good approximation to MEP_δ. As our examples will show, even in these large overlapping situations, both classifiers provide good results when the number of sample patterns is relatively large and evenly distributed among the different classes. This goodness means that for each dimension D the MEP values of the MLP and NLDA classifiers will be near those $MEP(\delta_B^D)$ of the D–dimensional Bayes optimal classifier.

Our examples have a rather large $MEP(\delta_B^D)$ and clearly satisfy the first of our two "extreme" problem conditions. To simulate the other, we shall fix the number of patterns from one class and decrease that of the other. One class will thus overwhelm the other and could make the constructed classifier to "forget" the class less present in the sample. As pointed out before, credit card fraud can be considered to follow this scenario, We will consider progressively unbalanced sample sizes, for which the ratio $|\mathcal{S}_N|/|\mathcal{S}_E|$ of the sizes of the normal $\mathcal{S}_N$ and exponential $\mathcal{S}_E$ samples will go from a value of 1 (when 50% of the patterns belong to each class) to 24 (when 96% belong to the normal class). If in the limit a classifier constructed with only normal class patterns would assign every test pattern to the normal class, and its MEP should then be 0.5, for it would correctly classify half the number of patterns (i.e., the normal ones) and would err on the other half (the exponential ones).

The dimensions considered have been 2, 4 and 8, and for each of them we have kept fixed the number of normal patterns, and have reduced the exponential sample sizes according to the above ratios. In order to maintain the "sample density" across the different dimensions, the number n_D of sample patterns at dimension D should be scaled according to the formula $n_D = (n_2)^{D/2}$. However, this would lead to enormously large values for n_8 We have used instead the scaling $n_D = (n_2)^{\sqrt[4]{D/2}}$, which for $n_2 = 2.000$ gives the approximate sample sizes $n_4 = 8.500$ and $n_8 = 45.000$. Table 2 contains MEP values obtained for MLP and NLDA classifiers. As it can be seen, initial MEP values are nearly equal for both classifiers when sample sizes are relatively balanced, but as the exponential sample size decreases, the MEP of the MLP classifier starts to degrade faster than that of the NLDA classifier. Thus, in this concrete extreme sample problem, the performance of NLDA networks is better than that of MLPs.

6 Credit Card Fraud Detection as an Extreme Sample problem

As mentioned in the introduction, credit card fraud detection is a clear cut example of an extreme sample problem. Classifier construction is thus rather difficult, but we must point out that other difficult previous issues must be dealt with before that construction may start. We will not address them here, but we will simply point out that feature selection is a crucial question. Moreover, the degree of unbalancement among classes is way much higher than in the previous synthetic example. Some kind of segmentation has to be performed to reduce those ratios to more manageable ranges. Of course, this segmentation will be done at the expense of excluding from system analysis a large number of operations, among them, of course bad ones. Segmentation is thus another key issue, that must guarantee that, although certain fraud will pass through the system, it won't signify a too large reduction of the system prevention capabilities. Observe also that, even after segmentation, large sample overlapping is bound to appear. as there will be fraudulent operations rather similar to many legal ones. Manual database removal of these operations is very costly (if at all possible), so classifier construction should be robust enough to cope with them. Of course, discrimination of the relatively few bad borderline operations won't be made possible by the larger number of good ones. This fact, however, should not "muddle" the resulting classifiers, that should still be able to discriminate operations with more salient characteristics.

Once these difficulties have been dealt with, the construction of fraud detection modules may begin along a familiar path, starting with the selection of training and test sets. This selection can be easily done in credit card fraud detection, as the definition of training and test sets can be made very naturally in terms of the traffic time periods considered. We can simply fix a concrete date and use traffic prior to that date for the training sets, and traffic processed after it for test purposes (of course, factors such as seasonal influences in card traffic have to be taken into account). In any case, once such a date is set, the simulation of test traffic from actual traffic logs is very easy; furthermore, it gives a highly realistic way of evaluating the effectiveness of a classifier on real data.

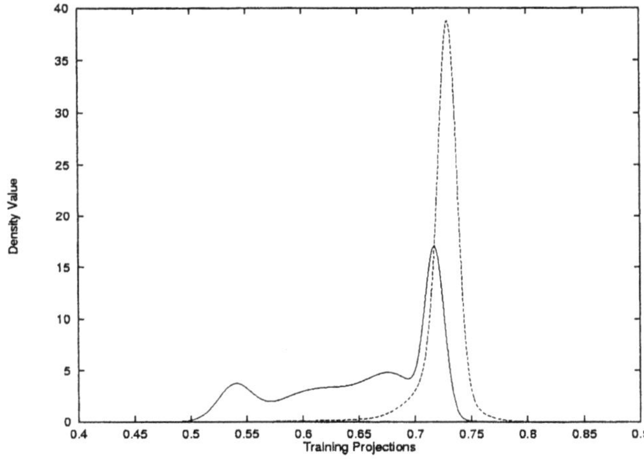

Fig. 2. Normal mixture approximation to credit card training traffic features extracted by a NLDA network.

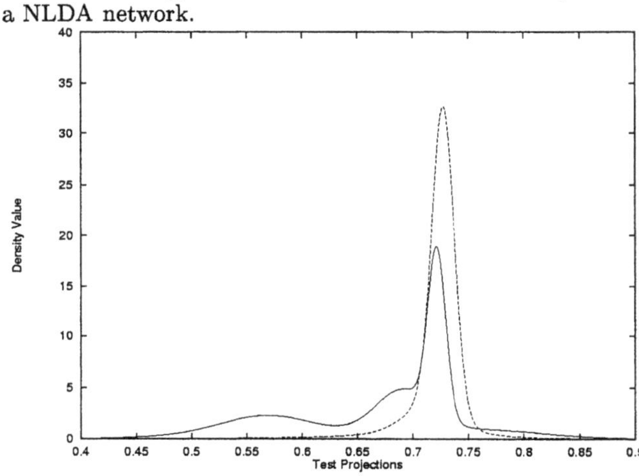

Fig. 3. Normal mixture approximation to credit card test traffic features extracted by a NLDA network.

Although certainly possible, a crisp classifier will not result in a workable executive tool for fraud prevention. A softer but more sensible idea is to compute numerical operation profiles and to derive from them some kind of density distribution and, therefore, assign to each operation a "fraud probability". Figure 2 (taken from [6]) shows an approximation to the NLDA training profile histogram by a density mixture of 5 gaussians. Notice the overlapping between good and bad operation network outputs, but also that the NLDA network is capable of finding a sizeable subset of bad operations with specific features. Figure 3 shows the same approximation for network test outputs. Notice that the densities of the training and test legal oper-

	85% Fraud detected				65% Fraud detected			
	MLP		NLDA		MLP		NLDA	
Class	0	1	0	1	0	1	0	1
0	6.407	93.523	6.508	93.422	44.491	55.439	42.845	57.085
1	39	266	39	266	110	195	110	195
	50% Fraud detected				40% Fraud detected			
	MLP		NLDA		MLP		NLDA	
Class	0	1	0	1	0	1	0	1
0	53.446	46.484	79.680	20.250	73.814	26.116	94.040	5.890
1	153	152	153	152	180	125	180	125

Table 3. Confusion matrices for the MLP and NLDA classifiers in the credit card fraud detection example.

ations are fairly similar, which suggests the stability of the legal traffic on the time periods considered in both cases. However, this is not the case for the fraudulent traffic, and there is a larger overlapping of the test legal and fraudulent traffics, which must produce worse test results.

Actuation thresholds can be defined on these "probability valued" network outputs. At a given threshold several measures of classifier performance can be used, such as the percentage of the total fraud stopped at that level, the coverage of the system (i.e., how much future fraud has been prevented with respect to the card's remaining credit) or the number of alarms per day. We shall concentrate here with another measure, the ratio of false to positive operations (RFP), that is, the number of false alarms generated from each fraudulent operation.

Consider the results of table 3 for MLP and NLDA classifiers. They have been obtained at four different threshold settings that allow to stop 40 %, 50%, 65% and 85% of fraudulent operations. The exploitation scenarios associated to those settings go from a very active one, with 266 fraudulent operations detected out of 305 (85%) to a more selective one (at 40%). Notice that at the 85% level, both NLDA and MLP classifiers have very similar (and poor!) results, for to stop the 266 bad operations, both classifiers would require us to act on about 93.000 good operations. The ratio of false to positive (RFP) alarms would then be an intolerably high 351. On the other hand, at the 40% level, the MLP classifier would generate more than 26.000 alarms, with a RFP value of 208, still too high. However, the RFP at this level of the NLDA classifier is about 47, nearly 5 times less than for the MLP. At the intermediate levels, the RFP for both classifiers is nearly equal at the 65% level, but the MLP RFP is already twice than that of the NLDA at the 50% level. The interpretation of these values is again quite clear. There is a sizeable overlapping between operations of both classes, which is shown by the 85% level values. This overlapping leads MLP training not to distinguish many fraudulent operations, something shown by the 26.000 good operations that it classifies as bad at the 40% decision level. We can consider NLDA training, on the other hand, to be more robust, as it misclassifies at the 40% level just about 5% of the legal operations, in marked contrast with the 25% misclassified by the MLP.

7 Conclusions

The main subject of this work is what we have termed "Extreme Sample Classification", by which we mean pattern recognition problems with large class overlapping (as given by the optimum mean error probability of the underlying distributions), a basic difficulty that may be compounded with unbalanced samples. The resulting problems are bound to be quite difficult, but may also arise in situations of considerable practical interest. We have shown on synthetic and application examples how Multilayer Perceptrons, a widely used neuronal technique with good results in many applications, may not give too satisfactory results upon these extreme problems. We have also introduced a new technique, Non Linear Discriminant Analysis (NLDA), as a potentially successful MLP alternative for these problems, something that is supported by its results in synthetic and application examples. The key to this better behaviour is partially due to the supervised but "target free" nature of NLDA. Given the practical relevance of classification problems very likely to be extreme in the previous sense, further exploration of these methods and even the introduction of new ones is a research area where new efforts are, in our opinion, well justified and can be very fruitful.

References

1. Amari S (1985) Differential Geometric Methods in Statistics. Lecture Notes in Statistics 28, Springer–Verlag.
2. Amari S (1998) Natural Gradient Works Efficiently in Learning. Neural Computation 10: 251–276.
3. Bernard E, Botha EC (1993) Backpropagation uses prior information efficiently. IEEE Trans. in Neural Networks 4: 794–802.
4. Bernard E, Casasent D (1989) A comparison between criterion functions with an application to neural nets. IEEE Trans. in Systems, Man and Cybernetics 19: 1030–1041.
5. Bourlard HA, Morgan N (1994) Connectionist Speech Recognition. Kluwer.
6. Dorronsoro J, Ginel F, Sánchez C, Santa Cruz C (1997) Neural Fraud Detection in Credit Card Operations. IEEE Trans. in Neural Networks 8: 827–834.
7. Dorronsoro J, Gonzlez A, Santa Cruz C (2001) Natural gradient learning in NLDA networks. In: Proceedings of the 2001 IWANN Conference, Lecture Notes in Computer Science 2084. Springer Verlag, pp 427–434.
8. Dorronsoro J, Gonzlez A, Santa Cruz C (2001) Arquitecture selection in NLDA networks. In: Proceedings of the 2001 Internationa Conference on Artifical Neural Networks, Lecture Notes in Computer Science 2130. Springer Verlag, pp 27–32.

9. Duda R, Hart P (1973) Pattern classification and scene analysis. Wiley.
10. Fukunaga K (1972) Introduction to Statistical Pattern Recognition. Academic Press.
11. Geman S, Bienenstock E, Doursat R ((1992) Neural networks and the bias/variance dilemma. Neural Computation 4: 1–58.
12. Golden R (1996). Mathematical Models for Neural Network Analysis and Design. MIT Press.
13. Lawrence S, Burns I, Back A, Tsoi A, Giles C (1998). Neural network classification and prior class probabilities. In: Lecture Notes in Computer Science State–of–the–Art Surveys. Springer, pp 299–314.
14. Manoukian E (1986) Modern Concepts and Theorems of Mathematical Statistics. Springer.
15. Mardia K, Kent J, Bibby J (1979) Multivariate Analysis. Academic Press.
16. Murray M, Rice J (1993) Differential Geometry and Statistics. Chapman & Hall.
17. Park H, Amari S, Fukumizu K (2000) Adaptive Natural Gradient Learning Algorithms for Various Stochastic Models. Neural Networks 13: 755–764.
18. Press W, Flannery B, Teukolski S, Vetterling W (1992) Numerical Recipes in C. Cambridge U. Press.
19. Richard M, Lippmann R (1991), Neural network classifiers estimate Bayesian a posteriori probabilities. Neural Computation 3: 461–483.
20. Rao C (1973) Linear Statistical Inference and its Applications. Wiley.
21. Ripley B (1996) Pattern Recognition and Neural Networks. Cambridge University Press.
22. Ruck D, Rogers S, Kabrisky K, Oxley M, Suter B (1990) The multilayer perceptron as an approximation to an optimal Bayes estimator. IEEE Trans. in Neural Networks 1: 296–298.
23. Santa Cruz C, Dorronsoro J (1998) A non-linear discriminant algorithm for data projection and feature extraction. IEEE Trans. in Neural Networks 9: 1370–1376.
24. Webb A, Lowe D (1990) The optimised internal representation of multilayer classifier networks performs non-linear discriminant analysis. Neural Networks 3: 367–375.
25. White H (1989) Learning in artificial neural networks: a statistical perspective, Neural Computation 1: 425–464.
26. Yaeger L, Lyon R, Webb B (1997) Effective training of a neural network character classifier for word recognition. In: Advances in Neural Information Processing Systems 9. MIT Press.

Part 3 Evolutionary Programming

A Review of Evolutionary Algorithms for E-Commerce

Alex A. Freitas

PUC-PR
PPGIA-CCET
R. Imaculada Conceicao, 1155
Curitiba – PR. 80215-901. Brazil
alex@ppgia.pucpr.br
http://www.ppgia.pucpr.br/~alex

Abstract. Evolutionary Algorithms (EAs) are adaptive algorithms based on the Darwinian principle of natural selection. Intuitively, their adaptive nature makes them suitable for highly dynamic environments, which is often the case in e-commerce applications. This chapter presents a review of EAs for e-commerce. It starts by discussing the main characteristics of EAs in general. Then it discusses several EAs developed for e-commerce applications, focusing on three kinds of e-commerce related tasks, namely: information retrieval on the web, discovery of negotiation strategies and improvement of web-page presentation.

1 Introduction

E-commerce is a relatively new, interdisciplinary field, consisting of the integration of commercial activities with several areas of computer science, such as the world wide web, database systems, metadata and ontologies, agent-based systems, multimedia and visualization, information security and privacy, etc.. It should be noted that sometimes the terms e-commerce and e-business are used with different meanings, with the latter being used as a more general term, which includes the former. In this chapter we use the terms e-commerce and e-business interchangeably, following [25]'s chap. 16. To quote from the page 259 of that reference:

"As far as we are concerned, e-commerce can be considered to be broad such as putting up a web page or listening to music on the web or conducting transactions on the web."

This means that we are using the term e-commerce to refer not only to the process of carrying out commercial transactions on the web but also to activities that give support to this process, such as learning, training and entertainment on the web, displaying information on web pages in such a way that the web page is as nice as possible for the user, retrieving relevant information from the web, etc.

E-commerce is an interesting research topic, not only due to its strategic economic value [1], but also to its potential for research in advanced areas of computer science, such as data mining [14] and artificial intelligence (AI) in general.

In this chapter we explore the use of a paradigm of artificial intelligence (AI) techniques, called evolutionary algorithms (EAs), for e-commerce applications. The basic motivation, as usual in the case of an AI paradigm, is to increase the degree of computational "intelligence" of a system, making it more autonomous and more adaptive to changes in its environment.

The potential of e-commerce for AI research stems mainly from two facts. First, e-commerce systems are already automated. This means that many of the hurdles associated with system building (such as data collection, integration with other automated systems of the organization, etc.) are significantly lower in e-commerce, by comparison with the process of automating a manual commercial system from scratch. Second, e-commerce systems tend to be very dynamic. This is due to several reasons. For instance, the contents of the web changes very fast. In addition, in e-commerce customers who are currently visiting a given company's web site can switch to the web site of a competitor in a few seconds, which would be much more difficult in a physical commerce environment.

Hence, the application of EAs techniques in e-commerce seems a promising research direction. EAs are robust, adaptive techniques, which – at least in principle – have a good potential for coping with dynamic environments.

In this chapter we discuss evolutionary algorithms for three kinds of e-commerce tasks:

(a) information retrieval in the web;

(b) discovering negotiation strategies;

(c) improving the presentation of web pages.

Out of these three tasks, the second one – discovering negotiation strategies – seems the most related to the central activity of e-commerce, namely carrying out commercial transactions on the web. Indeed, people like to negotiate prices at e-stores [16]. The other two tasks are less related to this central goal, but they are important tasks to support the broader process of e-commerce. Indeed, an attempt to retrieve relevant information from the web (among the huge amount of information stored in the web), say relevant information about a given kind of product, is often one of the first steps performed by a customer interested in buying something on the web. In addition, the layout and other graphical aspects of a web page can have a significant impact on the decision of a customer to buy or not a product announced in a given web page.

This chapter is organized as follows. Section 2 presents a brief review of EAs. Section 3 discusses the application of EAs to the three above-mentioned tasks of e-commerce. Finally, section 4 presents a summary and some conclusions drawn from the discussion of section 3.

2 A Review of Evolutionary Algorithms (EAs)

Evolutionary Algorithms (EAs) is essentially the name given to a large class of computational problem-solving algorithms inspired by the principle of natural selection. The basic idea is that at each generation the fittest (the best) individuals of the current population survive and produce offspring resembling them, so that the population gradually contains fitter and fitter individuals.

This idea is used, at a high level of abstraction, as a basis for designing computational EAs, as follows. Each "individual" of an evolving population represents a candidate solution to a given problem. Each individual is evaluated by a fitness function, which measures the quality of its corresponding solution. Then these individuals evolve towards better and better individuals via operators based on natural selection, i.e. survival and reproduction of the fittest, and genetics, e.g. crossover and mutation operators.

There are several kinds of evolutionary algorithms (EA) proposed in the literature. For a comprehensive review of several kinds of EA the reader is referred to [3]. In this chapter we are mainly interested in genetic algorithms (GA) and genetic programming (GP), which seem to be the kinds of EA that have been the most used in e-commerce-related tasks. In particular, most EAs discussed in this chapter will be GAs, but two GPs will also be discussed here.

Hence, in the remainder of this section and in the next two subsections we present a brief introduction to GAs and GP, to make this chapter self-contained. As will be seen in the next subsections, GAs and GP differ mainly with respect to the representation of an individual, which in turn leads to some differences in genetic operators. However, both kinds of EA are still based on the same principle of natural selection and genetics. Indeed, at a high level of abstraction, both GAs and GP perform essentially the same sequence of steps, as shown in the generic pseudocode of Algorithm 1.

```
create initial population of individuals;
compute fitness of each individual;
REPEAT
   select individuals based on fitness;
   apply genetic operators to selected
     individuals, creating offspring;
   compute fitness of each offspring individual;
   update the current population;
UNTIL (stopping criterion)
```

Algorithm 1: Generic, abstract pseudocode for GA and GP

As shown in this pseudocode, the first step is to create a population of individuals. The initial population can be generated at random or by using some problem-dependent heuristic. Then the individuals of the initial population are evaluated according to a fitness function, and the algorithm starts the REPEAT-UNTIL loop.

An important step of this loop is the selection of individuals based on fitness. In general the better the fitness of an individual (i.e., the better the quality of its candidate solution) the higher the probability of an individual being selected. There are several different selection methods that can be used to implement this basic idea. Here we mention just one, tournament selection [5], which is both simple and effective. For a more comprehensive discussion of selection methods the reader is referred to [3]. In tournament selection the EA randomly chooses k individuals from the current population, where k is a parameter called the tournament size. Then the k individuals "play a tournament" to decide which of them will be selected to produce offspring. The winner of the tournament can be chosen either in a deterministic manner or in a probabilistic manner. In the former case the winner is simply the individual with the best fitness among the k individuals playing the tournament, whereas in the latter case each of the k individuals can be chosen as the winner with a probability proportional to its fitness. Deterministic tournament seems more common in practice.

Once individuals are selected, the next step of Algorithm 1 is to apply genetic operators to the selected individuals (parents), in order to produce new individuals (offspring) that, hopefully, will inherit good genetic material from their parents. This step will be discussed in sections 2.1 and 2.2 separately for GA and GP, since these two kinds of EA usually require different genetic operators – due to their different individual representations.

Then the fitness of each of the new individuals is computed, and another iteration of the REPEAT-UNTIL loop is started. This process is repeated until a given stopping criterion is satisfied. Typical stopping criteria are a fixed number of iterations (generations) or the generation of an individual representing a very good solution.

It is worthwhile to mention that EAs perform a *global* search in the space of candidate solutions, by contrast with the local search performed by hill climbing-like, greedy search algorithms [11]. In particular, EAs work with a population of candidate solutions, rather than working with a single candidate solution at a time. This, together with the fact they they use stochastic operators to perform their search (as will be seen below), tend to reduce the probability that they will get stuck in local maxima, and increase the probability that they will find the global maximum in the space of candidate solutions.

2.1 Genetic Algorithms

Recall that an individual corresponds to a candidate solution to a given problem. In GAs an individual is usually a linear string of "symbols", often called "genes". A gene can be any kind of symbol, depending on the kind of candidate solution being represented. For instance, in GAs for information retrieval (to be discussed in section 3.1) a gene can be a word found in a text, or a pair composed by a word and its importance weight.

In general the main genetic operator of GAs is the crossover operator. It essentially consists of swapping genes between (usually two) individuals [13], [18]. Figure 1 illustrates a simple kind of crossover, called one-point crossover. Figure 1(a) shows two individuals, called the parents, before crossover. A crossover point is randomly chosen, represented in the figure by the symbol "|" between the second and third genes. Then the genes to the right of the crossover point are swapped between the two parents, yielding the new individuals shown in Figure 1(b).

X1 X2	X3 X4 X5	X1 X2	Y3 Y4 Y5
Y1 Y2	Y3 Y4 Y5	Y1 Y2	X3 X4 X5

(a) Before crossover (b) After crossover

Figure 1: Example of one-point crossover

X1	X2 X3	X4 X5	X1	Y2 Y3	X4 X5
Y1	Y2 Y3	Y4 Y5	Y1	X2 X3	Y4 Y5

(a) Before crossover (b) After crossover

Figure 2: Example of two-point crossover

Figure 2 illustrates another kind of crossover, called two-point crossover. Now a pair of crossover points is randomly selected in each of two parent individuals. In each parent the genes lying between the pair of crossover points are considered a block to be swapped, as a whole, by the crossover operator.

In addition to crossover, which is the main genetic operator in GAs, it is also common to use mutation. In essence mutation replaces the value of a gene with a new randomly-generated value (among the values that are valid for the gene in question). Note that mutation can yield gene values that are not present in the current population, unlike crossover, which swaps existing gene values between individuals.

Both crossover and mutation are stochastic operators, applied with user-defined probabilities. In GAs the probability of mutation is usually much lower than that of crossover, in part due to an analogy with natural selection and genetics, where mutations are rare and usually harmful for the organism.

2.2 Genetic Programming

As mentioned above, the main difference between GAs and GP is in the individual representation used by each kind of EA, which in turn leads to some differences in the genetic operators used by each of them.

First of all, most GP algorithms use a tree-based individual representation, and this will be the only kind of GP representation discussed in this chapter. For a discussion of other kinds of GP representation the reader is referred to [4]. Each individual is represented by a tree consisting of two kinds of nodes: internal nodes, containing functions, and terminal (leaf) nodes, containing variables of the problem being solved or constants.

It should be noted that an individual's tree can vary a lot in both size and shape, unlike the linear strings of "conventional" GAs, which usually have a fixed length (although there are several exceptions, where the length of the string is variable). Most important, in GP an individual (candidate solution) consists not only of problem-specific variables and/or their values (data) but also functions (operators applied to the variables/values) – unlike GAs, where an individual's candidate solution usually consists only of variables/values. Hence, a GP individual is often called a "program", even though in many cases this term should be interpreted in a loose sense. In any case, the distinction between GA and GP is blurring as there is a growing tendency towards the unification of the field of EAs [9].

The set of all functions (or operators) available to be used in internal tree nodes is called the function set, whereas the set of all variables and/or variable values available to be used in leaf nodes is called the terminal set.

In general the function set of a GP algorithm must satisfy at least two properties, namely sufficiency and closure [15]. Sufficiency means that the function set's expressive power is good enough to be able to represent a correct solution (or at least a very good solution) to the target problem. Closure means that each function of the function set should be able to accept, as input, any output produced by any function in the function set.

GP crossover essentially swaps two subtrees between two parent individuals. In each parent the subtree to be swapped is usually chosen at random. This kind of subtree crossover is illustrated in Figure 3, where the "crossover point" is indicated by a tilted line and the subtrees swapped by crossover are shown in bold.

In addition to crossover, mutation is also often used in GP. There are several kinds of GP mutation operator. We briefly mention here only two kinds, namely point mutation and subtree mutation. A more comprehensive discussion on several kinds of GP mutation operators can be found in [4] (pp. 240-243), [6].

Point mutation is the simplest form of mutation. It replaces a single node in a tree with another randomly-generated node of the same kind. By "same kind" we mean that an internal node is replaced by another internal node (with another function) and a terminal node is replaced by another terminal node (with another variable or value). Subtree mutation randomly selects an internal node in the tree, and then it replaces the subtree rooted at that node with a new randomly-generated subtree. The new randomly-generated subtree should be created subject to some restrictions of depth and/or size, to avoid the generation of a too large subtree.

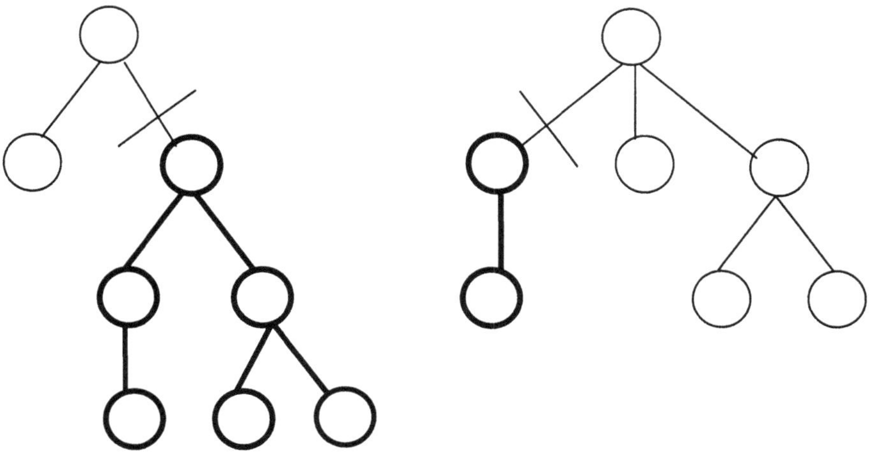

(a) Two parents before crossover

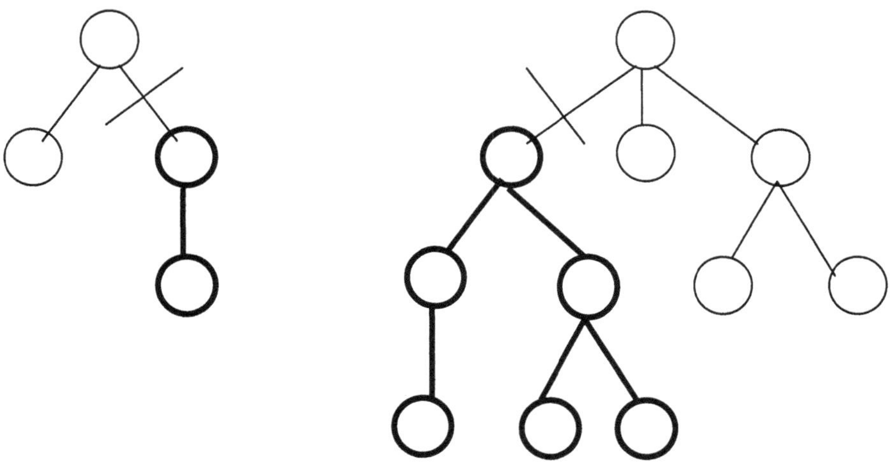

(b) Two children (offspring) produced by crossover

Figure 3: Conventional tree crossover in genetic programming

2.3 Co-Evolution

Co-evolution means the complementary evolution of two or more populations [21]. In nature a typical example is the co-evolution of predators and preys, where new features developed by predators trigger an evolutionary response in the preys.

In the context of EAs, the basic idea is that the individuals of each population evolve to be adapted to the individuals of the other population(s). Co-evolution involves a dynamic fitness function, where the fitness of an individual in a given population is determined by how adapted that individual is to individuals in other population(s). Hence, the same individual can have a high value of fitness in one generation but a low value of fitness in another generation, depending on the current contents of the other population(s).

This basic concept of co-evolution will be particularly useful to understand the application of EAs to the problem of evolving negotiation strategies in an e-commerce framework, as will be seen in section 3.2.

2.4 Interactive Evolutionary Algorithms

In some problems the quality of the candidate solution represented by an individual is inherently subjective, and it would be very difficult to design a good fitness function specified by a well-defined, objective mathematical formula. In such cases it is natural to use an interactive fitness function. The basic idea is that the fitness of an individual is directly evaluated by a human user, based on his/her own subjective preferences.

Two applications of interactive fitness function are briefly mentioned here. One involves an image-enhancement application [22], where the user drives GP by deciding which individual should be the winner in tournament selection. The other application involves attribute selection for the well-known classification task of data mining. In this application each individual of a GA represents a candidate attribute subset [24]. In order to evaluate an individual its candidate attribute set is given to an algorithm that discover classification rules, and the quality (fitness) of these rules are interactively and subjectively evaluated by the user.

In the context of e-commerce an interactive fitness function can be naturally used, for instance, to allow a user to subjectively evaluate how "nice" a given web page is. An example of this application will be discussed in section 3.3. Another example of the use of interactive fitness function will be discussed in section 3.1, in information retrieval.

3 Applying Evolutionary Algorithms (EAs) to E-Commerce

This section is divided into three subsections, according to the kind of e-commerce-related problem for which the EA was designed. Subsection 3.1 discusses EAs for information retrieval in the web. Subsection 3.2 discusses EAs for negotiation strategies. Subsection 3.3 discusses EAs for improving the presentation of web pages.

3.1 Information Retrieval in the Web

In this section we discuss evolutionary algorithms (EAs) designed for retrieving information in the web. In general the EAs discussed in this section are genetic algorithms (GAs).

Before we proceed, we present a brief introduction to information retrieval. The basic idea is as follows. Given a query, representing the interest of the user, and a set of documents, the system must select the documents most relevant to the user's query. The query can take different forms, from a small set of keywords to an entire text. In any case the contents of the query is compared with the contents of each document in the document base, and a similarity measure is computed for each document. The documents most similar (most relevant) to the query are returned to the user, in decreasing order of similarity. In the context of this section, each web page can be considered a document.

One important point in information retrieval is how to represent the contents of a document. A popular form of representation of documents is the vectorial model [23]. In this model each document is represented by a multi-dimensional vector, where each dimension corresponds to a term (usually a single word). For each document, the value of each dimension of its vector typically depends on the frequency of occurrence of the corresponding term in the document (the term frequency) or some related measure. Hence, the similarity between the query and each document can be naturally measured by the angle formed by the respective two vectors – i.e., the smaller the angle formed by a query vector and a document vector, the more similar the query and the document are.

3.1.1 GAs Without Focus on Web Page Structure

In this subsection we discuss two GAs for information retrieval in the web with two different individual representations. However, both GAs have in common the fact that they do *not* focus on the use of information about web-page structure. By contrast, in subsection 3.1.2 we will discuss a GA that focus on the use of information about web-page structure.

In [2] an individual represents the profile of a user's interest, consisting of a set of terms and their corresponding weights. Hence, the GA tries to find the best possible combination of terms (words) and term weights that allow the retrieval of documents relevant for the user.

More precisely, an individual consists of a variable-length list of genes. Each gene is a term-weight pair, i.e. a term and its associated weight. This structure is illustrated in Figure 4. This representation also includes an intuitive semantic-integrity constraint, namely the fact that a given term can occur at most once in the genome of a given individual. We will call this a term-uniqueness constraint.

$term_1$	$weight_1$	. . . . .	$term_m$	$weight_m$

Figure 4: Genome consisting of term-weight pairs for information retrieval

In GAs constraints can be handled in at least three ways: (a) penalizing the fitness of "invalid" individuals, i.e., individuals that violate the constraint; (b) using special repair operators that transform an invalid individual into a valid one; or (c) avoiding the creation of an invalid individual altogether, by not applying a genetic operator when it would produce an invalid individual. The third approach (c) seems to be the one used in [2]. Crossover and mutation are performed only if they produce valid offspring, respecting the term-uniqueness constraint.

The crossover operator is based on the idea of two-point crossover, as discussed in section 2.1.

There are two kinds of mutation operator, weight mutation and term mutation. Weight mutation randomly modifies the value of the weight in a gene. Term mutation randomly modifies both the term and its weight value in a gene.

We now turn to the work of [20]. In this work an individual also represents a kind of profile of a user's interest, like in [2]. In both systems an individual essentially represents a query, but there are two important differences between these systems, as follows.

1) In the former an individual consists of only a set of terms of a query, whereas in the latter an individual consists of a set of terms and their corresponding weights, as discussed above.

2) The GA proposed by Morgan & Kilgour was designed to support on-line information retrieval in a dynamic environment where user interests are continuously changing, whereas the GA proposed by Atsumi seems to cope with a somewhat less dynamic environment.

Let us discuss each of these points in turn. First, Morgan & Kilgour's GA use an individual representation consisting of a set of query terms, such as {"philosophy", "science", "induction"}. Note that this representation does not include term weights. Each individual is represented by a fixed-length list of terms (genes), but some genes can contain a special symbol denoting an "empty" gene, with no associated term. Therefore, each individual effectively represents a variable number of terms. For instance, the above-mentioned individual, containing a set of three terms, might be internally represented by a 5-gene genome such as {" philosophy", "science", "induction", [], []}, where the symbol

"[]" denotes an empty gene. (The number of genes per individual suggested by the authors is 10.)

Second, in Morgan & Kilgour's GA the fitness of an individual (query) is evaluated by the user's subjective judgement, which is based on the usefulness of the information retrieved by the query. Note that this is quite different from the more objective rates of recall and precision used by most information retrieval systems, including the above-described system proposed by [2]. To reduce the amount of time that the user spends evaluating query results the system works with a small population of 10 individuals.

The system is an interactive GA (section 2.4) that continuously interacts with the user, as follows. Since the GA is run on-line, the user can submit new queries to the database of texts during the GA run. Whenever the user submits a new query, that query is added to the current population of system-created queries maintained by the GA. The new individual (query) is assigned a maximum value of fitness, based on the assumption that user-created queries are the most important kind of information for building a profile of a user's interest.

Both user-created queries and system-created queries are used to produce the next population of (system-created) queries via the conventional process of selection, crossover and mutation. An one-point crossover operator (section 2.1) recombines the terms of two parents to produce two offspring.

There are two kinds of mutation, namely random mutation and synonym mutation. The former replaces terms by randomly-chosen words from the UNIX spell dictionary. The latter replaces terms by one of their synonyms from the WordNet synonym dictionary [10]. The system uses high rates of mutation – on the order of 50%. Hence, in this system mutation is a major operator to explore the search space – unlike conventional GAs, where mutation is usually a minor search operator.

3.1.2 A GA with Focus on Web Page Structure

In the previous subsection we have discussed two projects which proposed GAs for information retrieval in the web. However, in both projects the use of information about web page structure was limited. We now discuss a GA for information retrieval on the web with considerable more focus on the use of web page structure [7].

The basic idea is to take into account not only the frequency of terms in web pages, but also information about the relative importance of each term as indicated by the web page structure. More precisely, for each term the GA takes into count the kind of HTML tag in which that term occurs. Cutler et al. grouped HTML tags into six classes, namely: Plain Text, Strong, List, Header, Anchor and Title. Intuitively, the relative importance of a term, for information retrieval purposes, depends on the class of tag in which that term occurs. For instance, a term occurring in a Title tag tends to be more important than a term occurring in a Plain Text tag. The question is how to quantify the importance of each tag class. This is essentially the task addressed by the GA.

Each individual of the GA represents a vector of six weights, called a class importance vector (CIV). Each position i (i=1,...,6) of this vector, corresponding to a gene, contains the importance weight assigned to the i-th tag class. Hence, the GA tries to find the best possible combination of tag-class importance weights.

In order to evaluate the fitness of an individual, the information in its CIV has to be combined with information about term frequencies in web pages. This is done as follows. For each term and for each web page in which that term occurs the system computes a term frequency vector (TFV). Each position i (i=1,...,6) of this vector contains the frequency of occurrence of the term in the i-th tag class. When an information retrieval query is submitted, the system computes the weight of terms in web pages according to the formulas:

$$w = tf \,.\, idf,$$

where idf is the well-known inverse document frequency [23] and tf (term frequency), which represents the importance of a given term to a given document, is given by tf = TFV . CIV, where "." denotes the inner product of the two vectors TFV and CIV.

Hence, the better the CIV represented by an individual, the better the results of the information retrieval query will be. The fitness of an individual is computed by an information retrieval metric based on recall and precision. Hence, the fitness measure is objective, like in [2] but unlike in [20].

Computational experiments showed that the terms in the Strong and Anchor classes had the highest weights in the best CIV evolved by the GA. Hence, these two classes of tags were found to be the most useful ones for improving the effectiveness of information retrieval in the performed experiments.

3.2 Co-Evolving Negotiation Strategies

In this section we discuss two evolutionary algorithms for evolving negotiation strategies. Both algorithms are based on the use of co-evolution, as discussed in section 2.3.

[8] studied the co-evolution of agents representing bargaining strategies. Their study involved a simple, artificial game problem consisting of three agents which competitively negotiate to form a two-agent coalition. The agents bargain with each other to decide which two-agent coalition will be formed and how the points constituting the coalition's value will be divided between the two agents forming the coalition. The agent who is excluded from the coalition receives zero.

For instance, in a given game the value v of each of the three possible coalitions are as follows: v(AB) = 18, v(AC) = 24, v(BC) = 30, where A, B, C denote the three agents and v(X,Y) denotes the value of the coalition formed by agents X,Y $\in$ {A, B, C}. If, say, A proposes to form a coalition with B, A makes an offer to B. Such an offer specifies how the 18 points of the coalition are to be divided between A and B.

Hence, a game proceeds as follows. An agent (the initiator) makes an offer to another agent (the responder). If the responder accepts the offer the game ends, and each of those two agents receives a part of the coalition points, as specified in the offer, while the third agent receives zero. If the responder does not accept the offer then it becomes the initiator and makes an offer to either of the two other agents. The game proceeds in this fashion until an offer is accepted or a maximum number of offers has been rejected – in which case all three agents receive zero.

Each agent consists of a set of alternative strategies for playing the above-described game. Each agent's strategies are represented by a population of 50 genetic programming (GP) individuals. In essence, each individual (strategy) is an IF-THEN-ELSE statement of the form:

IF {*condition*} THEN {*action-1*} ELSE {*action-2*}.

The *condition* part of the strategy is a triple of the form {*Player*, *LB*, *UP*}, which evaluates to true if, in the current received offer, the amount of points assigned to *Player* is between the values *LB (Lower Bound)* and *(Upper Bound)*, inclusive. Otherwise the condition evaluates to false. *Action-1* and *action-2* can be one of the following three statements: (a) the *ACCEPT* symbol, indicating that the offer is accepted and the game ends; (b) an offer; or (c) another IF-THEN-ELSE statement – so that complex strategies can be specified by nesting IF-THEN-ELSE statements. An offer is a pair of the form {*Player*, *V*}, meaning that the current agent offers to *Player* (another agent) *V* points.

For instance, suppose that agent B is responding to an offer with the strategy IF {B 4 9} THEN {ACCEPT} ELSE {A 10}. If the amount of points assigned to B in the received offer is between 4 and 9 (inclusive) then B accepts the offer. Otherwise it offers A 10 points.

Recall that an agent (player) is represent by a population of 50 individuals (strategies). In order to compute the fitness of an individual, its strategy plays against a number of combinations of strategies of the two other agents (players). In other words, the fitness of a given individual in a given population is determined by how adapted that individual is to the individuals in the other two populations (representing other players' strategies), characterizing a co-evolution scheme – see section 2.3.

It should be noted that, although the above-described coalition game simulates an environment with competing bargaining strategies found in e-commerce applications, the simulation is still oversimplified, for several reasons, including the following ones.

First, the number of points assigned to an agent is a single scalar value. In reality agents are likely to be interested in maximizing the value of several different, possibly-conflicting aspects (or issues) of a commercial agreement. Such aspects may include the price of a product, its quality, time to delivery, etc. Second, it ignores important factors of real-world commercial agreements, such as the length of time available for an agent to reach an agreement.

We now discuss a project where the problem being solved is a less simplified, more realistic model of e-commerce applications. In this project [17] each agent has a negotiation strategy that takes into account the values of several different issues. More precisely, each agent a has a scoring function $V_{a,j}$ for each issue j. This function determines the score (in the interval [0,1]) that agent a assigns to the value x of issue j specified in a given offer. An offer consists essentially of a vector of values, one value for each issue. When an agent receives an offer, it rates it by using a utility function $V_a(\boldsymbol{x})$ that is a linear combination of the values of the issues specified in the offer, i.e.:

$$V_a(\boldsymbol{x}) = \sum_j w_{aj} V_{aj}(x_j),$$

where w_{aj} is the importance (weight) of issue j for agent a. If the value of this utility function for the received offer is greater than the corresponding value of the counter offer that the agent would send at this point, then the offer is accepted. Otherwise a counter offer is submitted – unless the deadline assigned for negotiation has been reached.

The question is how to generate an offer or a counter offer. In essence, (counter) offers are generated by linear combinations of functions called tactics. Each tactic generates a value for a single negotiation issue based on a single criterion. There are 3 basic criteria used by tactics, namely the time remaining for reaching an agreement, the amount of resources remaining and the behavior of the opponent (which is determined by its tactics). In general as the deadline for reaching an agreement approaches and the quantity of resources is reduced an agent becomes progressively more likely to concede. Behavior-dependent tactics are variations of tic-for-tat that differ with respect to which aspect of the opponent's behavior they imitate and to what extent.

Each tactic is assigned an importance weight. For each negotiation issue, its value in an offer is specified by a linear, weighted combination of tactics. In other words, an agent can use a different weighted combination of tactics for each negotiation issue. Finally, each agent is associated with a strategy which, over time, varies the weights of the different tactics for each of the negotiation issues in order to adapt to changing environmental conditions – such as the observed behavior of the opponent.

This is where a GA comes in. The GA evolves a population of individuals, where each individual represents an agent. The genetic material of an individual represents the parameters of the negotiation tactics and their importance weights.

The fitness of an individual (agent) is determined by how well that individual performs with respect to other individuals. More precisely, there are two kinds of agents, buyers and sellers. To compute an agent's fitness the system performs a round-robin tournament where each buyer negotiates with each seller, following the basic idea of co-evolution discussed in section 2.3.

3.3 EAs for Improving the Presentation of Web Pages

In this section we discuss two GAs developed for improving the presentation of web pages. The first one is an interactive GA for generating HTML style sheets that are as nice as possible from the (subjective) viewpoint of a user, whereas the second one is a GA for improving the layout of a web page in more objective terms. Both systems assume that the contents of a web page has already been determined. What the systems try to find is the best visual presentation of that contents.

Let us start with the GA for generating HTML style sheets proposed by [19]. Each individual of the GA population represents an HTML style sheet. The genetic material of an individual consists of 26 characteristics determining the look of a web site. Each characteristic is represented by a gene. These characteristics can be divided into two broad groups, namely:

(a) 5 global characteristics of an HTML page: the background, color of links, rules, bullets and arrows ("back", "next", "home"); and

(b) 21 characteristics determining the appearance of the text and paragraphs – these include, for instance, the font and color of text in title and paragraph tags.

The main question is how to compute the fitness of an individual – i.e., how to evaluate the "quality" of a style sheet. The author's proposed solution for this problem is to use an interactive GA. The motivation for this is that the quality of a style sheet strongly depends on subjective preferences of the user, which could hardly be mathematically defined. Hence, an individual's fitness is computed by presenting its style sheet to the user in a graphical way and letting the user explicitly select the style sheets that (s)he favors.

In order to facilitate the comparison of individuals (style sheets) by the user the system displays the whole population of individuals simultaneously. Of course, this severely limits the number of individuals in the population. In order to solve this problem the authors use a non-standard GA which uses a vector of probabilities to model an infinite population.

The basic idea is that the GA explicitly manages the probability of occurrence of each gene value. Let L be the number of genes of an individual. As discussed above, $L = 26$. Let k_i, i=1,...L, be the number of possible values of the i-th gene, and let $p(V_{ij})$ be the probability that the i-th gene has its j-th value, i=1,...L and j=1,...,k_i. The GA initializes the probability values so that, for each gene, all its values are equally likely to occur. Mathematically, $p(V_{ij}) = 1 / k_i, \forall i,j$. Then 12 individuals are generated, and their style sheets are applied to the web pages provided by the user, producing 12 pages that are simultaneously shown to the user. Next, the user selects the individuals corresponding to the style sheets that (s)he likes the most. (The user may also directly modify the genes of an individual in order to improve its style sheet. Such modifications are considered mutations.) The set of individuals selected by the user, which are supposed to contain the best gene values (characteristics of style sheets), are then used to update the probability values $p(V_{ij})$. This is done in such a way that the probability values $p(V_{ij})$ for the gene values occurring in the selected individuals is increased. Once the new values of $p(V_{ij})$ have been computed the next generation of individuals is generated. This new generation includes all individuals selected by the user in the previous generation, without modification, and the remaining individuals are generated based on the updated probability values $p(V_{ij})$. This iterative process is repeated until the user is satisfied with the style sheets proposed by the GA.

Let us now discuss the GP to automate the layout of web pages proposed by [12]. The system was designed to optimize the layout of web pages consisting mainly of pictures in the form of rectangles. The problem is to arrange $n \geq 1$ rectangles (pictures) $r_1,...,r_n$ on a larger rectangle (web page) R in such a way that some layout-quality criterion (discussed later) is optimized.

A layout for the web page is obtained by subdividing it into n rectangles using a recursive binary-partition method. Hence, a layout is represented by a binary tree with n leaves, each of them representing a rectangle r_i. A simple example is shown in Figure 5, involving three rectangles r_1, r_2, r_3. Figure 5(a) shows a possible layout arranging those three rectangles on the larger rectangle, and Figure 5(b) shows a high-level view of the GP individual – in the form of a binary tree – representing the solution shown in Figure 5(a). The root node indicates that the rectangle R is horizontally partitioned, at coordinate h_1, into two subrectangles. The first of these subrectangles is simply r_3, as indicated by the root's left child (a leaf node). The root's right child is an internal node, indicating that the second subrectangle is vertically partitioned, at coordinate v_1, into two subrectangles. These subrectangles are simply r_1 and r_2, since both children of this internal node are leaf nodes.

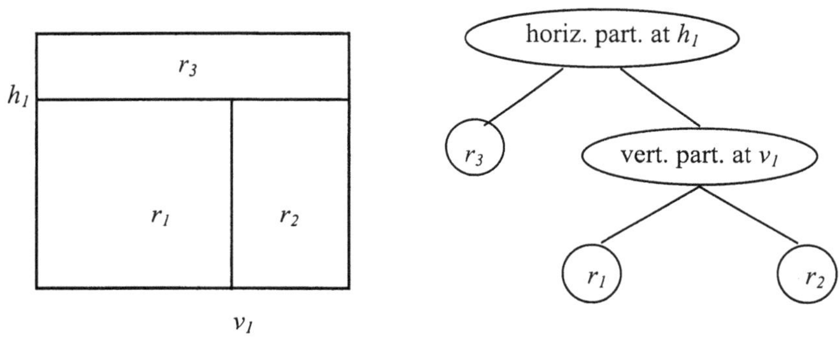

(a) A candidate layout (b) GP individual representing layout in (a)

Figure 5: Arranging three rectangles on a larger rectangle via GP

In order to put a rectangle r_i into a given subrectangle produced by a GP individual it might be necessary to scale down r_i - i.e. to reduce its width and length in order for it to fit into the corresponding subrectangle. As pointed out by Fuchs, in the context of web pages such scaling down is possible and sensible, as long as the amount of scaling down is not excessive.

The question is how to determine the fitness function for this layout-optimization problem. The basic idea is that the fitness function must take into account two kinds of factor, namely the amount of left-over blank space in the layout (i.e. space in the web page that is not used by any picture) and the amount of scaling down used to fit the pictures into the web page. Both factors are to be minimized – i.e. the smaller their values, the better the corresponding candidate layout.

4 Summary and Discussion

In this section we summarize the main characteristics of the EAs reviewed in the previous section and provide a comparative analysis of those algorithms.

Table 1 summarizes the main characteristics of the above-discussed EAs. This table contains seven rows, one for each of those algorithms. The table contains five columns. The first column simply mentions the bibliographical reference for the corresponding EA. The algorithms are listed in the table in the same order as they were discussed in section 3.

Table 1: Summary of EAs for E-Commerce-related tasks

Reference	EA	Task	Individual representation	Fitness
[2]	GA	information retrieval	a set of term-weight pairs	objective, static
[20]	GA	information retrieval	a set of terms	subjective, interactive, dynamic
[7]	GA	information retrieval	a set of tag-class weights	objective, static
[8]	GP	negotiation	a negotiation strategy	competitive, dynamic
[17]	GA	negotiation	parameters of negotiation tactics	competitive, dynamic
[19]	GA*	web page presentation	an HTML style sheet	subjective, interactive, dynamic
[12]	GP	web page presentation	the layout of a web page	objective, static

* non-standard GA, using a vector of probabilities to model a population

The second column specifies the kind of EA, either a GA or GP. As can be observed in the table, most systems are GAs, but there are also two GP systems. We emphasize that the categorizations used in the cells of Table 1 are not absolute. They serve as rough approximations of their corresponding characteristics, for pedagogical purposes. For instance, as mentioned above, the distinction between GA and GP is blurring. In addition, the GA used in [19] is a non-standard, different kind of GA, since it uses a vector of probabilities to model a population. In any case, we believe the contents of Table 1 – particularly the fourth and fifth columns – are useful to draw some conclusions about trends and important issues in the application of EAs to the e-commerce-related tasks studied in this chapter.

The third column of Table 1 specifies the task being performed by the corresponding EA, which is either information retrieval in the web (subsection 3.1), or evolving negotiation strategies (subsection 3.2), or improving web page presentation (subsection 3.3).

The fourth column indicates the individual representation used by the corresponding EA. Of course, the individual representation depends on the kind of task being performed, and even within the same kind of task there are significant differences between the representations of different algorithms. Two interesting remarks can be made about the contents of this column. First, out of the three GAs for information retrieval in the web mentioned in the table, only the one proposed by [7]) focus on the use of information about web-page structure. More precisely, this system identifies six classes of tags found in web pages: Plain Text, Strong, List, Header, Anchor and Title. The system takes into account the class of tag in which each term (word) occurs, and explicitly searches for an optimum vector of importance weights for the tag classes. Second, the two EAs for evolving negotiation strategies use quite different individual representations, although their target task is quite similar. One of these EAs is a GP system, where a negotiation strategy is a (possibly nested, complex) list of IF-THEN-ELSE statements; whereas the other EA is a relatively simple GA, where only parameters of negotiation tactics (rather than the structure of a negotiation strategy itself) are evolved. On the other hand, the problem being solved by the GA seems to a more "realistic" model (although still just a model) of an e-commerce environment. The problem being solved by the GP seems to be "oversimplified", ignoring several important issues of a real-world e-commerce environment. In the future it would be interesting to see the use of GP to search for negotiation strategies in a more realistic e-commerce model.

Finally, the fifth column of Table 1 indicates the kind of fitness function used by the corresponding EA. There are three possible values for the cells of this column: an objective, static fitness function; a subjective, interactive, dynamic one; or a competitive, dynamic one. It is interesting to note that, out of the seven EAs, only three use an objective, static fitness function. The term "static" is used here to indicate that the fitness of an individual has the same value regardless of the time (generation number) in which it is computed and regardless of the other individuals in the population(s). By contrast, the value of a dynamic fitness function for an individual can change depending on the time in which it is computed and/or on the other individuals in the population(s). Four out of the seven EAs – i.e. the majority of them – use some kind of dynamic fitness function, more precisely either a competitive fitness function (in a co-evolution framework) or a subjective, interactive fitness function (whose value is explicitly determined by the user). Note that in the co-evolution frameworks studied here the fitness function is naturally dynamic, since the fitness of an individual (a negotiation strategy or parameters of a negotiation tactic) is determined by how adapted that individual is to individuals in the other population. Similarly, a subjective, interactive fitness function is naturally a dynamic one, since a user's interests and evaluations are continuously changing – and can even be inconsistent from one generation to another or among a group of individuals of a given generation.

To summarize this important conclusion: dynamic fitness functions – either competitive ones in a co-evolution framework or interactive ones – tend to have an important role in several e-commerce applications, due to the inherently dynamic nature of this kind of application. In particular, co-evolution seems naturally useful for evolving negotiation strategies, and subjective, interactive fitness functions are intuitively useful in tasks such as improving web-page presentation.

As a final remark, the potential of EA for e-commerce applications goes considerably beyond what has been discussed in this chapter. The area of "evolutionary e-commerce systems" is still in its infancy, and it is likely that significant progress will be made in the next few years, motivated by at least two factors: (a) a growing interest in both e-commerce and evolutionary algorithms – from both academia and industry; (b) the need for robust, adaptive AI techniques (such as EA) that can significantly increase the degree of automation and computational "intelligence" of e-commerce systems, making them better prepared for effectively coping with the dynamic environments typically found in e-commerce applications.

References

1. Akkermans H. (2001) Intelligent E-Business: from technology to value. *Guest Editor's Introduction. IEEE Intelligent Systems, July/August 2001*, pp 8-10.
2. Atsumi M. (1997) Extraction of user's interests from web pages based on genetic algorithm. *English version of the original Japanese paper published in IPSJ SIG Notes (Information Processing Society of Japan, The Special Interest Groups Notes)*, 97(51), pp 13-18.
3. Back T, Fogel DB and Michalewicz T. (Eds) (2000) *Evolutionary Computation 1: Basic Algorithms and Operators*. Institute of Physics Publishing, Bristol.
4. Banzhaf W, Nordin P, Keller RE, and Francone FD. (1998) *Genetic Programming ~ an Introduction: On the Automatic Evolution of Computer Programs and Its Applications.* Morgan Kaufmann, San Mateo, CA.
5. Blickle T. Tournament selection. (2000) In: Back T, Fogel DB and Michalewicz T. (Eds) *Evolutionary Computation 1: Basic Algorithms and Operators*, pp 181-186. Institute of Physics Publishing, Bristol.
6. Cavaretta MJ and Chellapilla K. (1999) Data mining using genetic programming: the implications of parsimony on generalization error. *Proc.*

1999 Congress on Evolutionary Computation (CEC-99), pp 1330-1337. IEEE Press, Piscataway, NJ.

7. Cutler M, Deng H, Maniccam SS and Meng W. (1999) A new study on using HTML structures to improve retrieval. *Proc. 11th IEEE Int. Conf. on Tools with Artificial Intelligence*, pp 406-409. IEEE Press, Piscataway, NJ.
8. Dworman G, Kimbrough SO and Laing JD. (1996) Bargaining by artificial agents in two coalition games: a study in genetic programming for electronic commerce. *Genetic Programming 1996: Proc. 1st Annual Conf. (GP-96).* Morgan Kaufmann, San Mateo, CA.
9. De Jong K. (2000) Evolutionary computation: an unified overview. *2000 Genetic and Evolutionary Computation Conf. Tutorial Program*, pp 471-479. Las Vegas, NV.
10. Fellbaum C. (Ed) (2000) *WordNet: an Electronic Lexical Database.* MIT Press, Cambridge, MA.
11. Freitas AA. (2001) Understanding the crucial role of attribute interaction in data mining. *Artificial Intelligence Review*, 16(3), pp 177-199, Nov 2001.
12. Fuchs MM. (2000) An evolutionary approach to support web page design. *Proc. 2000 Congress on Evolutionary Computation (CEC-2000)*, pp 1312-1319. IEEE Press, Piscataway, NJ.
13. Goldberg DE. (1989) *Genetic Algorithms in Search, Optimization and Machine Learning.* Addison-Wesley, Reading, MA.
14. Kohavi R. and Provost F. (Eds) (2001) Special Issue on Applications of data mining to electronic commerce. *Data Mining and Knowledge Discovery 5(1/2)*, pp 5-10. 20. Jan/Apr 2001.
15. Koza JR. (1992) *Genetic Programming: on the programming of computers by means of natural selection.* MIT Press, Cambridge, MA.
16. Lina F-R and Chang K-Y. (2001) A multiagent framework for automated online bargaining. *IEEE Intelligent Systems,* pp 41-47, *July/August 2001.*
17. Matos N, Sierra C, Jennings NR. (1998) Determining successful negotiation strategies: an evolutionary approach. *Proc. 1998 Int. Conf. on Multi-Agent Systems (ICMAS-98)*, pp 182-189.
18. Michalewicz Z. (1996) *Genetic Algorithms + Data Structures = Evolution Programs.* 3rd Ed. Springer-Verlag, Berlin.
19. Monmarche N, Nocent G, Slimane M, Venturini G and Santini P. (1999) Imagine: a tool for generating HTML style sheets with an interactive genetic algorithm based on genes frequencies. *Proc. 1999 IEEE Int. Conf. on Systems, Man and Cybernetics (SMC'99)*, pp 640-645. IEEE Press, Piscataway, NJ.
20. Morgan JJ and Kilgour AC. (1996) Personalising on-line information retrieval support with a genetic algorithm. In: Moscardini AO & Smith P. (Eds.) *Proc. of PolyModel 16: applications of artificial intelligence*, pp 142-149.
21. Paredis J. (2000) Co-evolutionary algorithms. In: Back T, Fogel DB and Michalewicz Z. (Eds) *Evolutionary computation 2: Advanced Algorithms and Operators*, pp 224-238. Institute of Physics Publishing, Bristol.
22. Poli R and Cagnoni S. (1997) Genetic programming with user-driven selection: experiments on the evolution of algorithms for image enhancement.

Genetic Programming 1997: Proc. 2nd Annual Conf., pp 269-277. Morgan Kaufmann, San Mateo, CA.

23. Salton G and Buckley C. (1998) Term-weighting approaches in automatic text retrieval. *Information Processing and Management 24*, 513-523. Reprinted in: Sparck Jones K and Willet P. (Eds.) *Readings in Information Retrieval*, pp 323-328. Morgan Kaufmann, San Mateo, CA.
24. Terano T and Ishino Y. (1998) Interactive genetic algorithm based feature selection and its application to marketing data analysis. In: Liu H and Motoda H. (Eds) *Feature Extraction, Construction and Selection*, pp 393-406. Kluwer, Boston.
25. Thuraisingham B. (2000) *Web Data Management and Electronic Commerce.* CRC Press.

Artificial Adaptive Market Traders Based in Genetic Algorithms for a Stock Market Simulator

Pedro Isasi and Manuel Velasco

Computer Science Department, Universidad Carlos III de Madrid
Avda. Universidad 30, 28911, Leganés, Spain
e mail: isasi@ia.uc3m.es, velasco@ia.uc3m.es
telephone: +34916249455

Abstract. Some aspects of classical stock market economic theories are unrealistic and do not fulfill the expectations of market traders. Other paradigms can help to overcome the shortcomings of these theories. In this paper, a paradigm based on learning conception is presented. A simulator has been developed to research the stock market. Some aspects like dynamic prices, investment strategies, market statistics have been considered. Also, an artificial adapted market trader based on genetic algorithms has been implemented. Some experimental work has been done to observe the behavior of these automatic market traders in different situations.

1 Introduction

Traders usually see the stock market as something that provides speculative opportunities. Many of them think that technical commerce is profitable and that there is a market psychology that cause bubbles and crashes. Sometimes the market is described as having its own mood and personality, and it is often described as nervous, wavy or anxious. So, the market can be seen as psychologically organic and imperfectly efficient.

From this point of view, classical economic theories are unrealistic and not borne out by the perception of market traders. Therefore, there are other paradigms, like for instance, artificial intelligence, that can support the understanding of the stock market process. These paradigms are focused on the concept of learning; that is, the possibility of modifying the modus operandi as the market changes. A system of this type has to be able to relate the information that defines the market at earlier times to all the events that could have some influence in the future. These relations are very complex and could change very quickly. However, they are often related to previous events in the market.

Learning systems have a disadvantage: they start from scratch, i. e. from imprecise knowledge, and they have to learn from experience. So, the system has to deal with and learn from the other traders. A market simulator has been designed to perform this task. This simulator can investigate dynamic prices, investment strategies, market statistics, all performed by carefully controlled experiments. This simulator has also been used to study the accuracy of some automatic market traders. These market traders have been implemented as software agents applying some well-known artificial intelligent techniques. These techniques are mainly related to genetic algorithms and rule-based systems.

In section 2, some issues about genetic algorithms used in the implementation of the agents are presented. In section 3, the relation between genetic algorithms and the stock market is outlined to give an overview of related work. This is followed by a description of the simulator, the implemented agents, the experimentation, and the conclusions.

2 Genetic Algorithms

Genetic Algorithms (GA) are blind, stochastic and near-optimal heuristic search methods. GAs do not work directly with the problem solutions. On the contrary, they use a codification (usually binary) of the solutions, called a chromosome.

GAs imitate the process of evolution by means of Natural Selection to solve optimization problems. This is a Darwinian approach to the idea of the survival of the fittest. However, individuals have to fight in order to overcome the survival chances of others in a natural process of selection. Computationally, this has to be measured in terms of an evaluation function, called fitness function. This function produces a fitness value for each individual, which is used for the selection process. After selecting the parents, new solutions are created by applying functions to the parents. These functions are called genetic operators: selection, mutation and crossover. These operators create new designs, in the hope that the new designs achieved will improve features of the old ones. New individuals replace the ones from the old population to create a new population for the next generation.

The components of a GA are:

- Individuals: Each partial solution to a problem is codified as a string. Each string is called an individual.
- Population: A set of individuals is called a population. The GA method involves generating new populations of individuals in such a way that better individuals could be generated in newer populations.
- Genetic Operators: GOs are functions applied to populations to generate new populations.

- Fitness Function: FF is a measure of the goodness of an individual, in terms of the ability of this individual to solve the problem. This measure is used as a parameter for the GO and guides the generation of new and better populations.

The search process is based on the fitness function and the genetic operators. More specifically, the fitness function is a numerical value that measures how successfully the codified solution solves the problem. In these terms, the GA works with set of solutions (populations), in which the individuals gradually become more accurate [5] [7], as the genetic operators are applied to successive populations.

Evolution can be viewed, from a simplified perspective, as a process of genetic information transference between individuals [12]. This transference can be summarized in three rules:

- Selection of the more accurate individuals for reproduction.
- Genetic recombination of the selected individuals and generation of new individuals containing this information.
- Generation of new genetic information by randomly altering some old information in the chromosomes.

GAs use very little domain information about problems to guide the search process. This feature makes GAs a good method for many different kinds of problems, especially, in domains where there is little information about how to reach the goal or where the domain could change in time.

Some applications of GAs have proved more efficient when more information about the domain has been included. This information is often easily included by designing new genetic operators "ad hoc" for a specific problem. Even in these cases, the specific operators designed have proved to be useful in different domains.

A simple, or canonical GA, could be described as a 7-tuple, AG = (P^0, λ, I, s, ω, f, t) where:

- $P_0 = (a^0_1, \dots, a^0_\lambda)$ is the initial population
- λ is the size of the population
- I is the size of each individual's representation
- s: $P^i \rightarrow P^j$, where $P^j \subset P^i$, is the selection operator
- $\omega = \{w_1, w_2, \dots\}$ is the set of genetic operators that create new individuals
- f: $a^j_i \rightarrow \Re$ is the fitness function
- t: $P^i \rightarrow$ {Yes, No} is the convergence criterion.

2.1 Genetic Operators

There are three main genetic operators used to guide the search procedure:

Selection

This is an implementation of Darwin's Natural Selection of the fittest. It involves selecting the best individuals in the population to generate an intermediate population, named mating pool. The mating pool is of the same size as the population and is generated selecting individuals from the population at random, proportionally to their fitness value. This means that, in terms of fitness, there would be more copies of better individuals in the mating pool.

Crossover

Individuals in the mating pool are crossed-over to generate new individuals that share some genetic material from one parent and some from the other. These new individuals are included in the newly generated population.

$i_1 \rightarrow$ {11101]001000
$i_2 \rightarrow$ 00001{010101}

They generate

$ni_1 \rightarrow$ 11101010101 (first 5 bits of i1 with last 6 bits of i2)
$ni_2 \rightarrow$ 00001001000 (first 5 bits of i2 with last 6 bits of i1)

Mutation

This operator randomly changes the value of a bit of an individual. This operator is useful for increasing the genetic diversity of populations, avoiding the biases that could exist in the initial population. Another important effect is to make the search process more exploratory. There is a mutation probability that is applied to all the bits in the population. The higher this probability is, the more exploratory the process will become. The mutation probability has some short fixed value, but some papers [6] [9] have proved that an adaptive mutation probability is beneficial.

2.2 Working Procedure

A generation in a GA can be described as follows:

1. Generate a population of n individuals randomly in generation 0.
2. Generate a mating pool of n individuals, selecting individuals from the population using the selection genetic operator.
3. Select two individuals from the mating pool at random and remove these individuals from the mating pool. These two individuals are then crossed-over and the two new offspring generated are included in a new population.
4. If the mating pool is not empty, go to (3).
5. Apply the mutation operator to all the elements of the new one population.
6. Substitute the old population with the new one generated in (3-5).
7. If the convergence criteria have not been reached yet, go to (2).

Genetic algorithm-based methods are a natural approach when the best (or, at least, a very good) solution to a problem from a really wide range of possibilities is to be found. Genetic algorithms are also a way of doing a guided search through the space of tri-dimensional vectors (a, b, m) in natural numbers, which, if well designed, is much better than exhaustive searching.

3 Using Genetic Algorithms to Analyze Technical Estimators

In this section, the relation between stock market techniques and genetic algorithms is introduced. Adaptive stock market agents are the result of the combination of both ideas.

3.1 Combining Estimators

Decisions about operations have to be made in the stock market. When making decisions, analysts usually do not found their selection on only one technical estimator. The selection is usually made by combining several technical estimators. It depends on different factors, like the experience of the analysts, their skill, their ability, even fads or personal preferences that are difficult to formalize [2].

Therefore, if, at the end of a session or working day, an analyst fails to take into account a specific technical estimator, which has lately proved to be more profitable, the analyst can be said, with some reserve, to have made a mistake when selecting which technical estimator to use.

Imagine a system where 10 estimators are considered. Each estimator gives a purchase ($\text{Estimator}_i(t) = 1$) or sale signal ($\text{Estimator}_i(t) = -1$) at some time t. An integrated estimator can be built as follows:

$$\text{Estimator}(t) = \alpha_1 * \text{Estimator}_1(t) + \alpha_2 * \text{Estimator}_2(t) + \ldots + \alpha_{10} * \text{Estimator}_{10}(t)$$

where α_1, α_2, ..., α_{10} are numbers that represent the liability degree of the estimator at earlier times in the process.

Then the problem is to determine the combination of values (α_1, α_2, ..., α_{10}) that would have maximized the profits in the past and later use this combination to make future decisions.

Also all the estimators depend on some internal parameters that can influence their forecasting ability. It is not an easy task to tune all the parameters of an estimator in order to improve its accuracy. It is also important to take into account that the right parameters are not always the same, they could change in time as the market evolves. In these terms, a more general expression will be:

$$\text{Estimator}(t) = \alpha_1 * \text{Estimator}_1(t, \theta_1) + \ldots + \alpha_{10} * \text{Estimator}_{10}(t, \theta_{10})$$

where α_i has the same meaning as above and θ_i is a vector of parameters for each estimator. In this sense, the goal is to characterize the values α and θ for a future maximal profit.

3.2 Genetic Algorithms and Adaptive Market Agents

The above goal can be achieved by designing an agent (computer independent program) able to determine, for each market and period of time, the values of the parameters of the estimators for maximizing the profits.

Agents can be of several types: random, intelligent with no learning, and intelligent with learning. For our purpose, we have studied the last type, which is presented below.

A given rule is composed of three parts: condition, action, and previous success. The condition determines whether or not the rule is fulfilled. The action defines whether the agent should purchase or sell. And, finally, previous success is an estimator based on the results achieved, if the rule has been used [8].

The condition is a set of zeros, ones, and an undetermined character represented by the symbol *. The condition structure depends on the information represented, since conditions based on the RSI (Relative Strength Indicator) technical estimator [10], for instance, are not performed in the same way as the Williams technical estimator [11].

The action is codified in a bit that indicates which operation it is to carry out. For instance, we can define the value 1 as "assets purchase", and the value 0 as "assets sale". Previous success is a way to evaluate the application of the rule in the past.

The estimators, on which our agents are based, are calculated for each market cycle. These indicators include moving average, RSI, etc. This information is codified in a string of zeros and ones as a text string, and it is called state string. Thus, a characteristic text string is built for each state. The conditions of the rules of the agents are as long as the state string.

A rule is fulfilled if each bit in the rule coincides with the bit in the same position in the state string. If the bit in the string is an undetermined symbol (*), the value of the bit in the state string is insignificant.

When a new cycle starts, the agent determines which rules are to be fulfilled. The agent examines every bit in the condition of the rule, by comparing it with the respective bit in the state string (ignoring the positions marked as *). One of the rules that are fulfilled and have a value over 0 for the "success" variable is selected at random but with a probability proportional to the success achieved in past uses.

The selected operation (sell or buy) will be carried out. When the whole cycle ends, all the values for success in the rules that are fulfilled will be calculated again according to the equation below:

$$\text{Success}(t) = (1-c) * \text{Success}(t-1) + c * a_i * [\, p(t) - (1+r) * p(t-1) + d(t) \,]$$

where:

- a_i is the action (1 for buy, -1 for sell),
- r is the interest rate,
- c is a constant whose usual value is 0.01 (Palmer 94),
- p(t) is the price of the asset at time t
- d(t) is the earnings at time t

It is essential to establish lower and upper bounds for the success variable.

A genetic algorithm works every time t with the rules in the agent so that only specific rules that have highest values for the variable success are selected for the next process. Besides, each time t_p (whose value can change), all the rules with very negative success are selected to change their action and transform the success into positive values. Also, each time t_q, the rules that have never been selected are subjected to mutations.

The equation $t_p \ll t_q$ has to be true, since, otherwise, mutations could affect some rules that just have been generated by the genetic algorithm, that is, rules that have never been selected, although this does not necessarily imply that these rules are not effective.

4 Theoretical Foundations of the Market Simulator

The stock market simulator for pricing assets is presented [3] [4] in this section. This market simulator only works with a specific asset and some agents that perform its market operations (sell, buy, or idle). Each sale or purchase order works on one and only one specific package of assets [1].

At time t, the market opens and the asset has a determined price. Each agent knows the values for the estimators it needs to carry out its selection. According to these estimators, the agent will decide to buy assets, to sell assets or to remain idle. When the market closes the price of the asset is updated after the session according to the agent sales and purchases. Once the price of the asset is updated, each agent determines how much profit it has made, how much money the agent has left, how many assets it has, etc. And then another market cycle starts.

The sales and purchases of the agents are made using the opening price. Once the operation takes place the capital for each agent is updated according to this price, the operation performed (sale or purchase) and in proportion to the number of agents that sold or bought.

4.1 Working Aspects

The working aspects of the implemented market simulator are explained in more detail below:

- Market cycles are represented by t, where a past cycle is t-1 and a future cycle is t+1.
- There is only one fixed market value in the market, but there are n agents, labelled as i=1, 2, 3, ..., n.
- Each agent has a number of asset packages at market value. This number is represented by h, so that $h_i(t)$ represents the number of asset packages that the agent i has at time t. Also, $h_i(t-1)$ indicates the number of asset packages that the agent had at time t-1, i. e. in the previous cycle.
- The money the agent has is represented by M, so $M_i(t)$ is the money the agent i has in the cycle t and $M_i(t-1)$ indicates the money the agent had in the previous cycle.
- Each agent can sell or buy at any time. Functions $o_i(t)$ and $b_i(t)$ have been used to represent these market operations.
- $o_i(t)$ represents the sale order of agent i. It takes value 1 if agent i has made a sale order, and value 0 if it did not make a sale order.
- $b_i(t)$ represents the purchase order of agent i. It takes value 1 if agent i has made a purchase order, and value 0 if it did not make a purchase order.

- O(t) is defined as the total number of assets sold on the market in the current cycle and B(t) as the total number of assets bought.

$$O(t) = \sum_{i=1}^{n} o_i(t) \qquad B(t) = \sum_{i=1}^{n} b_i(t)$$

- Volume is defined as the minimum value for total number of sales and purchases:

$$V(t) = \min \{B(t), O(t)\}$$

- Price is the value of the asset at the current time and is represented by p(t).
- When a market company makes profit, it can decide to share out part of the profit among the investors. This part of the distributed profit is called earnings. The earnings of the assets are represented in the system as j(t), which, as above, means the earnings in the current cycle.

4.2 Updating the Agents

The wealth, the value, of an agent depends on the money and the assets it has plus the price of the asset. So, if $R_i(t)$ represents the wealth of the agent i, its value can be stated as:

$$R_i(t) = M_i + h_i(t) * p(t)$$

The wealth of an agent just starting a new cycle is, therefore:

$$R_i(t) = (1+r) * M_i(t-1) + h_i(t-1) * p(t) + j(t)$$

where r is a constant that represents the interest type by period. Part of the wealth comes from the interests generated by the money the agent has. Another part is produced by the change in the price of the assets and, finally, another part is generated by the profit obtained by the earnings of the assets.

The total number of assets in the market is a fixed and constant value, represented by H. Therefore, the following equation has to hold for every cycle t:

$$H = \sum_{i=1}^{n} h_i(t)$$

If, at the end of a cycle, all the purchase and sale orders have been satisfied, the new number of assets for each agent is:

$$h_i(t) = h_i(t-1) + b_i(t) - o_i(t)$$

If there were more purchase than sale orders, i. e. B(t) > O(t), then the asset package offered is distributed among the buyer agents. The new number of assets for each agent is:

$$h_i(t) = h_i(t-1) + \frac{O(t)}{B(t)} * b_i(t) - o_i(t)$$

A similar thing happens when there are more sale orders than purchase orders:

$$h_i(t) = h_i(t-1) + b_i(t) - \frac{B(t)}{O(t)} * o_i(t)$$

Another equation can be defined to calculate the total number of assets of each agent related to volume:

$$h_i(t) = h_i(t-1) + \frac{V(t)}{B(t)} * b_i(t) - \frac{V(t)}{O(t)} * o_i(t)$$

V(t) was defined previously as the minimum value between total sale and total purchase orders. When an agent decides to buy as the same time as another agents, the asset package is distributed and the money for the agent changes its value as:

$$M_i(t) = M_i(t-1) - \frac{O(t-1) * p(t-1)}{B(t-1)}$$

and, similarly, the seller agent changes its money as:

$$M_i(t) = M_i(t-1) - \frac{B(t-1) * p(t-1)}{O(t-1)}$$

4.3 Updating Assets

The earnings of each asset are updated as defined by the equation below:

$$j = \bar{j} + \rho\,(j(t-1) - \bar{j}) + \xi(t)$$

where $\xi(t)$ is a Gaussian noise factor, $\bar{j}$ is the average earnings and ρ is a constant with value 0.99.

The price for each asset is updated according to supply and demand in the cycle using the equation below:

$$p(t) = p(t)\ \{1 + \eta\ [B(t) - O(t)]\}$$

Parameter η takes a very small value, thus $\eta\ [B(t) - O(t)] << 1$.

5 Stock Market Agents

Several behaviors have been programmed and introduced into the system to check the behavior of the simulator and to prove the accuracy of each stockbroker. Each behavior is related to a software agent. Five different types of agents have been included:

- Random Agent (66%).
- Random Agent (100%).
- Rules Based Agent.
- Rules and Previous Success Based Agent.
- Adaptive Agent.

Below, we detail how these agents work.

5.1 Random Agent (66%)

The operations performed by this agent are based on random aspects. This agent determines its operation in the stock market (sell, buy, remain idle) by generating random numbers. It works as follows:

1. The agent generates a random number between 0 and 99.
2. The agent applies module 3 to the number generated in step 1.
3. If the result is 0, then it sells, if it is 1, then it buys and, finally, if it is 2 then it remains idle.

Therefore, the agent is active in the stock market with probability of 0.66, since it will remain idle in only 33% of cycles.

5.2 Random Agent (100%)

It is very similar to the above agent, but this agent is always active in the market. It works as follows:

1. The agent generates a random number between 0 and 99.
2. The agent applies module 2 to the number generated in step 1.
3. If the result is 0, then it sells, if it is 1, then it buys.

5.3 Rule-Based Agent

The work of this agent is based on implemented rules. When a new market cycle ends, the market server recalculates the technical estimators, the new price for the asset, and the other parameters. When market values have been updated, the system codifies the state string. This string is a binary codification of each one of the technical estimators used in the system.

The rule-based agent has a rules database in which each rule has the following structure: a condition and an operation to perform if the condition is fulfilled. The condition is codified in the same way as the state string, except that the value 2 can appear in some positions. The operation is a bit that indicates what the agent will do if the condition is satisfied. It can only take two values: 1, buy assets, and 2, sell assets.

For every rule in the agent the condition is compared to the state string, except the positions with value 2. One of the satisfied rules is selected randomly, and its operation will decide the action the agent will take.

5.4 Rule- and Previous Success-Based Agent

The behavior of this agent is similar to the Rule-Based Agent, except as regards the selection of the rule from the set of the rules that satisfied the "condition-state string" comparison. The selection is made based on the possible success of the rules in previous cycles.

Therefore, for each rule, a variable is added (success variable), which will determine how successful the rule was in previous cycles. The rule is updated in each cycle as:

$$\text{Success}(t) = (1-c) * \text{Success}(t-1) + c * a_i * [\, p(t) - (1+r) * p(t-1) + d(t) \,]$$

This is only for rules that satisfied the condition.

5.5 Adaptive Agent

Its works like the above agent, but also has the following features:

1. Every time t_1, a filtering algorithm is run on all the rules, performing the following functions:

- All the rules with negative success are modified to positive success and the operation is inverted (sell for buy, buy for sell).
- The rules that are never fulfilled are mutated in a random number of bits.

2. Every time t_2, a genetic algorithm is run on the rules database trying to maximize the success for the rules. This means that only the best rules remain for the next cycle, and the rules database of the agent can be purged, thus providing learning capability and adaptation to the stock market.

5.6 Internal Considerations about the Agents Implemented in the System

In our system, each agent can have up to 50 rules, each one codified with 55 bits. The state string and the condition need 54 bits for codification. They have the following structure:

- Bits 0-8: Codification of the estimator

$$\frac{Moving\ Average\ 100}{Moving\ Average\ 50}$$

where bits 0-1 indicate the integer and bits 2-8 represent the decimal.

- Bits 9-16: RSI Oscillator, applied to 10 previous cycles.

- Bits 18-26: Williams Oscillator, applied to 10 previous cycles.

- Bits 27-35: Momentum applied to 5 previous cycles, where bit 27 indicates the sign (0 positive, 1 negative), and bits 28-35 represent the absolute value.

- Bits 36-44: Codification of the estimator

$$\frac{Exponential\ Average_t}{1{,}1 * Exponential\ Average_{t-1}}$$

where bits 36-37 indicate the integer and bits 38-44 represent the decimal.

- Bits 45-53: Price rate

$$\frac{Current\ Price}{Previous\ Price}$$

where bits 45-46 indicate the integer and bits 47-53 represent the decimal.

6 Experimentation

Two series of 32 experiments were run to test the efficiency of each agent (all 5 agents were considered) and to study the general behavior of the market. For every experiment, the initial configuration of the market had the following requirements:

- Initial price for the asset: 100 units
- Initial earnings with value 0 units
- Interest rate 0%
- 100 market cycles

The agent profit is calculated from the interests, the earnings, and the results of purchases and sales. Taking values 0 for earnings and interest, the profit is mainly based on purchases and sales, i. e. based on the interaction of the agent with the market within purchases and sales.

The experiments were analyzed according to different parameters. The results for each phase are presented below:

- Phase 1: Final profits
- Phase 2: General behavior
- Phase 3: Experiments with positive profits
- Phase 4: Number of assets
- Phase 5: Agent activity
- Phase 6: Total money.

6.1 Final Profits

The final profits have been studied. The mean and standard deviation are also presented for each agent. The following table shows these results. The order of success is: Rule-Based (RB), Rule-Based and Previous Success (RBPS), Adaptive (Ad), Random 100% (R100), and Random 66% (R66), but the difference between the first three is not significant.

Table 1: Final Profits					
	Ad	R66	R100	RB	RBPS
Total	13368952	257937	5662738	14542811	14701327
Mean	417780	8061	176961	454463	459416
Standard Deviation	1452773	39641	716513	1462004	1477634

When one agent has negative profits, the other agents usually have negative profits too. The reason is that when the price of the asset goes down, it is very difficult to sell the assets, because the agent can also offer a single package of assets.

6.2 General Behavior

This phase studied penalties for each agent. These penalties are assigned to each agent according to the behavior of other agents, considering the following rules:

- If the agent is the winner or, at least, the least loser, the penalty is 1.
- If the agent is the least winner, or the loser, the penalty is 5.
- The others are penalized, ordered by profit from 2 to 4.

Table 2 presents the mean for each agent.

Table 2: Penalties					
	Ad	R66	R100	RB	RBPS
Mean	3.1875	2.1875	3	3.34375	3.25

The best agent is the Random 66% agent, with the adaptive agent in third position, as in the previous phase.

6.3 Experiments with Positive Profits

The penalties observed only in experiments with positive profit for at least one agent have been studied in this phase. The adaptive agent is also third in this phase, and the best agent is the Rule-Based with Previous Success agent.

Table 3: Penalties with Positive Profit					
	Ad	R66	R100	RB	RBPS
Mean	3.1111	4	3.5555	2.3333	1.8888

6.4 Assets

In this phase, the total number of assets of asset packages by agent is studied, calculating the mean to establish a general criterion. The adaptive agent is the winner in this phase, and there are clear differences in some cases, mainly compared with the winner agents in other phases.

Table 4: Assets					
	Ad	R66	R100	RB	RBPS
Total	2702	910	2193	295	1274
Mean	84	28	69	9	40
Standard Deviation	114	73	89	25	82

6.5 Activity

This phase examines sale and purchase orders and agent idleness generally. Three means (sale, purchase and idleness) are presented for each agent. The idle periods can be explained as follows:

- The agent issues a purchase order, but it has no money to buy a package.
- The agent issues a sale order, but does not have a complete asset package.
- If the condition is not satisfied for the non-random agents.

Table 5: Activity					
	Ad	R66	R100	RB	RBPS
Sales	98	115	329	252	250
Purchases	89	112	340	295	292
Idleness	813	773	331	453	458

The idleness for the adaptive agent is due to the fact that the rules database gets very exhaustive during the cycles. Both rule-based agents are less idle than the random 66% agent.

6.6 Total Money

The total money that each agent has at the end of each experiment is considered in this phase. The mean and standard deviation are presented as well. The adaptive agent is again the best agent.

Table 6: Total Money

	Ad	R66	R100	RB	RBPS
Total	27349318	5048474	20603437	8163011	23654959
Mean	854666	157765	664627	255094	823592
Standard Deviation	1683696	393380	1128640	701302	1454653

7 Conclusions

The simulator provides a new tool to study the stock market. The evolution of the price of the assets according to the sales and purchases the stock market agents is coherent with the real world. The environment is also dynamic, which means that new agents that have their own rule database and personalized internal operation can be added.

In this paper, five types of stock market agents simulation are studied. One agent, the adaptive agent, has a solid theoretical basis inspired in genetic algorithms that provide knowledgeability. This agent has obtained the best results considering the whole set of experimental phases, although partial results have been disadvantageous. Anyway, it can be further optimized with a few changes.

There are some issues for future research:

- Study of the stock market state string. It would be interesting to define an independent state string for each agent, so the agent is able to determine the estimators on which to base its selection. Also, the distribution of the string, the number of bits by estimator, etc., could be considered.

- The simulator has a constraint concerning the uniqueness of the asset package. The agent could decide how many assets to sell or buy, even indicating the price.
- A bigger stock market, adding more, different types of assets, to allow the agent to operate with all the assets in the same cycle.

References

1. Andreoni, J., Miller, J. (1995) Auctions with Adaptive Artificial Agents, Journal of Games and Economic Behavior, vol 10, 39-64.
2. Arthur W. (1995) Complexity in Economics and Financial markets. Complexity 1:20-25
3. Caldarelli G., Marsili M., Zhang Y. (1997) A Prototype Model of Stock Exchange. Europhysics Letters, 40(5): 479-484
4. Dacorogna M (1993) The Main Ingredients of Simple Trading Models for use in Genetic Algorithm Optimization. Internal Document MMD-03-22, Olsen & Associates
5. Goldberg D. E. (1989) Genetic Algorithms in Search, Optimization, and Machine Learning, Addison-Wesley, Massachusetts
6. Maley C. (1995) The co-evolution of mutation rates, in Advances in Artificial Life, Springer-Verlag, 234-245
7. Mitchell M. (1996) An Introduction to Genetic Algorithms, MIT Press
8. Palmer R. G., Arthur W., Holland J., LeBaron B., Tyler P. (1994) Artificial Economic Life: a Simple Model of a Stockmarket, Physica D, vol 75, 264-274
9. Schmidt L. A., Farshi B. (1977) Optimum Design of Laminate Fiber Composite Plates. International Journal for Numerical Methods in Engineering, 11(1): 623-640
10. Wilder J. (1978) New Concepts in Technical Trading Systems. Greensboro, NC: Trend Research
11. Williams L. (1984) The Ultimate Oscillator. Technical Analysis of Stocks and Commodities, vol 3(4), 140-141
12. Wilson S. W. (1985) Knowledge Growth in an Artificial Animal. In Greffenstette, ed. 1st International Conference on Genetic Algorithms and Their Applications, Pittsburgh, July 1985

Data Mining in Marketing Using Bayesian Networks and Evolutionary Programming

Geng Cui[1] and Man Leung Wong[2]

[1]Department of Marketing and International Business, Lingnan University, Hong Kong, China
[2]Department of Information Systems, Lingnan University, Hong Kong, China

Abstract. Give the explosive growth of customer data collected electronically from current electronic business environment, data mining can potentially discover new knowledge to improve managerial decision making in marketing. This study proposes an innovative approach to data mining using Bayesian Networks and evolutionary programming and applies the methods to marketing data. The results suggest that this approach to knowledge discovery can generate superior results than the conventional method of logistic regression. Future research in this area should devote more attention to applying this and other data mining methods to solving complex problems facing today's electronic businesses.

1 Introduction

Conventional marketing research is a process in which data are analyzed manually to explore the relationships among various factors defined by the researcher. Even with powerful computers and versatile statistical software, many hidden and potentially useful relationships may not be recognized by the analyst. Nowadays, such problems are more acute as many businesses are capable of generating and collecting a huge amount of data in a relatively short period. The explosive growth of data requires a more efficient way to extract useful knowledge. Thus, marketing is a major area for applying data mining that aims at discovering novel, interesting and useful knowledge from databases. Through data mining, marketing researchers can discover complex relationships among various factors and extract meaningful knowledge to improve the efficiency and quality of managerial decision making.

In order for data mining for marketing managers, several issues have to be addressed. First, the process needs to adopt a method and produce results that can represent the structure of knowledge of the specific domain and specify the relationships among the variables. Secondly, the process should search the space for the best solution among all eligible candidates. Thirdly, the results of the data mining process should allow for comparison with existing methods using some common evaluation criteria to assist managerial decision making. Given these problems, we propose a novel approach to data mining in marketing using Bayesian networks and evolutionary programming. First, we introduce the background literature on data mining and the research problems. Secondly, we delineate the Bayesian network learning process and evolutionary programming for data mining purposes. Thirdly, we apply these methods to two datasets of direct marketing and compare the results with those of logistic regression models. Finally, we explore the implications for data mining in marketing and directions for further research.

2 An Innovative Approach to Knowledge Discovery

The increasing use of computers results in an explosion of information for businesses. Data can be best used if the hidden knowledge can be uncovered, thus making data mining an important research topic. Narrowly defined, data mining is the automated discovery of "interesting" non-obvious patterns hidden in a database that have a high potential for contributing to the bottom line [19]. Within the broad-scope definition, data mining encompasses "confirmation" or the testing of relationships revealed through the discovery process. Data mining is the core of the knowledge discovery in database (KDD) process. Thus, the two terms are often used interchangeably [26]. Research in this area can be useful for many real-world problems

With computerization of marketing operations, a huge amount of customer and transactional data can be collected. Thus, there is a need for a way to automatically discover knowledge from data [26]. Data mining is increasingly used by many companies to improve marketing efficiency. Data mining has many potential uses in marketing, including customer acquisition, customer retention, customer abandonment and market basket analysis. In addition to query tools, descriptive statistics, visualization tools, regression-type models, association rules, decision tree analysis, and case-based reasoning, recent development in artificial intelligence and machine learning has presented more powerful data mining techniques and analytical tools, such as artificial neural networks (ANN) and evolutionary computation methods such as genetic algorithms [19].

Despite the promises of data mining, practical analytical tools that can assist managerial decision making need to be developed. One of the promising methods of evolutionary computation for solving marketing problems is genetic algorithms (GA). GA was originally developed in the field of computer science. Management researchers have adopted its principles and methods to solve business problems. Genetic algorithms operate through procedures modeled upon the evolutionary biological processes of selection, reproduction, mutation, and survival of the fittest to search for good solutions to prediction and classification problems [19]. They are particularly effective for solving poorly understood, poor structured problems because they attempt to find many solutions simultaneously, whereas a linear regression model, for example, focuses on a single best solution. Another strength of GA is that they can explicitly model any decision criterion in the "fitness function," an objective system used to assess a GA's performance [9] [19].

Recently, methods based on the evolutionary theory such as genetic algorithms have been applied to marketing problems such as product design [1], inventory control and product assortment management [24], brand competition [17], and marketing mix elasticity [11], direct marketing response modeling [2] [16]. For instance, to solve the problem of optimal product design using conjoint analysis, Balakrishnan and Jacob [1] used Genetic Algorithms (GA) as an alliterative procedure for generating "good" solutions for product design. Midgley, Marks and Cooper [17] adopted genetic algorithms to study how strategies may evolve in oligopolistic markets characterized by asymmetric competition. Subsequent simulations of repeated interactions using scanner data of brand actions show that the artificial agents bred in this environment outperform the historical actions of brand managers in the real market.

Recent research and studies in marketing focus on how to apply GA techniques to specific marketing problems and how the results compare to other conventional methods. Other major applications of GA include rule finding, pattern matching, and optimization. However, a major benefit of GA relative to other procedures is knowledge discovery in that they can produce novel solutions and discover relationships not defined by the researchers. They may discover combinations of predictor variables that no one would have expected to be predictive beforehand [19]. Such beneficial features can be helpful for knowledge discovery in marketing and need to be explored.

As in other fields, data mining for marketing faces several significant challenges. First, conventional research emphasizes hypothesis testing based on *a priori* model with a limited number of variables selected by the researcher. Data mining, however, discovers the relationships and presents a *posterior* structure. Thus, the process needs to adopt a method and produce results that can represent the structure of knowledge of the specific domain and specify the relationships among the variables. Secondly, in the same vein, unlike conventional research that focuses on confirming an *a prior* model, data mining by definition should search the space for all possible alternative representations of the knowledge and then determine the best possible solution among all eligible candidates based on a fitness criterion. Thirdly, since data mining often adopts a method that is dissimilar to conventional statistical methods, the results of the data mining process should allow for comparison with those generated by other methods based on some common evaluation criteria so that they can assist managerial decision making. Against this backdrop, we propose a novel approach to data mining in marketing.

2.1 The Knowledge Discovery Process

Data mining experts have developed various knowledge discovery systems to extract knowledge from databases. To apply data mining to marketing problems and to address the above issues, we propose a novel approach to knowledge discovery in marketing using Bayesian Network (BnW) model and evolutionary programming. In the following section, we delineate the novel approach to data mining and describe the learning process using the Bayesian Networks approach and evolutionary programming (EP).

First, we adapt the data mining process developed by Ngan et al. [18] and briefly describe its five steps in the process. Initially, a selection is made to extract a relevant or a target data set from the database. Then, preprocessing is performed to remove noise and to handle missing data fields. Transformation is performed to reduce the number of variables under consideration. The third and fourth steps induce knowledge from the preprocessed data. A suitable data mining algorithm is applied to the prepared data. The causality and structure analysis learns the overall relationships among the variables. In the fifth step, the discovered knowledge is verified and evaluated by the domain experts, who may discover and correct mistakes in the discovered knowledge. The discovered knowledge can be used to refine the existing domain knowledge or incorporated into an expert system for decision making. If the discovered knowledge is not satisfactory, these five steps will be reiterated [26].

In this study, we focus on the third and fourth steps. For causality and structural analysis, we use Bayesian Network models to represent the knowledge structure. To learn a plausible Bayesian Network model, we adopt evolutionary programming (EP) for the learning process. In the following sections, we describe the Bayesian Network models and evolutionary programming including the criteria for model evaluation and methods for the learning process.

2.2 Bayesian Network Learning

Although the underlying theory of Bayesian probability has been around for a long time, building and executing realistic Bayesian Network models has only been made possible because of recent algorithms and software tools that implement them [10] [20]. Bayesian network is a method for formal knowledge representation based on the well-developed Bayesian probability theory. Bayesian networks have made tremendous progress and have been widely adopted by researchers in many fields. Several authors have given excellent introductions of Bayesian Networks and detailed comparisons with other methods [4] [6] [7] [8] [15].

The key feature of Bayesian networks is the fact they provide a method for decomposing a probability distribution into a set of local distributions. The independence semantics associated with the network topology specifies how to combine these local distributions to obtain the complete joint-probability over all the random variables represented by the nodes in the network [7]. The Bayesian network method has been successfully applied to solve many real-world problems including software engineering, space navigation, and medical diagnosis.

The most common computation performed using Bayesian Networks is determination of the posterior probability of some random variables in the network. Because of the symmetric nature of conditional probability, this computation can be used to perform both diagnosis and prediction [7]. In essence, a Bayesian Network captures the conditional probabilities between variables and can be used to perform reasoning under uncertainty. In practice, a Bayesian network is a directed acyclic graph (DAG). Each node represents a domain variable, and each edge represents a dependency between two nodes. An edge from node A to node B can represent a causality, with A being the cause and B being the effect. The value of each variable should be discrete. Each node is associated with a set of parameters. Thus, let N_i denotes a node and Π_{N_i} denotes the set of parents of N_i. And the parameters of N_i are conditional probability distributions in the form of $P(N_i \mid \Pi_{N_i})$ with one distribution for each possible instance of Π_{N_i}. Figure 1 is an example of Bayesian network structure. This network shows the relationships between whether the familiy is out of the house (fo), whether the outdoor light is turned on (lo), whether the dog has bowel problem (bp), whehter the dog is in the backyard (do), and whether the dog barking is heard (hb).

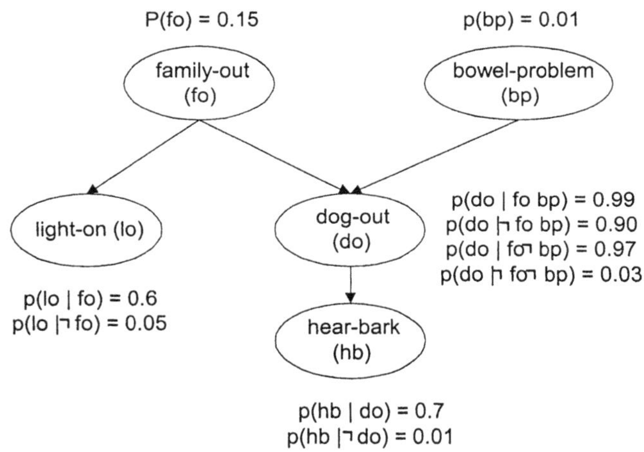

Fig. 1. An Example of Bayesian Network Structure

The main task of learning Bayesian networks from data is to automatically find directed edges between the nodes so that the network can best describe the causalities. Once the network structure is constructed, the conditional probabilities are calculated based on the data. The problem of Bayesian network learning is computationally intractable. However, Bayesian network learning can be implemented by imposing limitations and assumptions. For instance, the algorithms of Rebane and Pearl [21] can learn networks with tree structures, while the algorithms of Cooper and Herskovits [3] require the variables to have a total ordering. More general algorithms include those by Heckerman, Geiger and Chickering [8] and Spirtes, Glymour and Scheines [23]. More recently, Larranaga et al [15] proposed algorithms for learning Bayesian networks using GA.

The success of Bayesian networks lies largely in the fact that the formalism introduces structure into probabilistic modeling and cleanly separates the quantitative structure of a model from the quantitative aspect [7]. Although the formal definition of a Bayesian network is based on conditional independence, in practice a Bayesian network typically is constructed using notions of cause and effect, making it powerful for identifying and analyzing the structural relationships among variables [8]. In addition, the Bayesian networks method offers several other benefits for marketing research. Like logistic regression, the Bayesian networks approach is free from the normality assumption thus it can handle all types of data, binary, ordinal and continuous. Bayesian networks also test for independence among variables so that spurious relationships can be identified and avoided. Based on the generated model, Bayesian networks method also calculates a probability score for each case, which is useful for predicting consumer responses to marketing activities.

2.3 Evolutionary Computation

Evolutionary computation is a general term to describe computational methods that simulate the natural evolution based on the Darwinian principle of evolution to perform function optimization and machine learning. The algorithms maintain a group of individuals to explore the search space. A potential solution to the problem is encoded as an individual. An evolutionary algorithm maintains a group of individuals, called the population, to explore the search space. A fitness function evaluates the performance of each individual, a Bayesian network model in this case, to measure how close it is to the solution. The search space is explored by evolving new individuals. Based on the Darwinian principle of evolution through natural selection, the fitter individual has a higher chance of survival, and tends to pass on its favorable traits to its offspring. A "good" parent is assumed able to produce "good" or even better offspring. Thus, an individual with a higher score in the fitness function has a higher chance of undergoing evolution. Evolution is performed by changing the existing individuals. New individuals are generated by applying genetic operators that alter the underlying structure of individuals. It is a general, domain independent method that does not require any domain-specific heuristic to guide the search.

Examples of algorithms in evolutionary computation include genetic algorithms (GA), genetic programming (GP), evolutionary programming (EP), and evolution strategy. They mainly differ in the evolution models assumed, the evolutionary operators employed, the selection methods, and the fitness functions used. GA uses a fixed-length binary bit string as an individual. Three genetic operators are used to search for better individuals. Reproduction operator copies the unchanged individual. Crossover operator exchanges bits between two parents. Mutation operator randomly changes individual bits. Meanwhile, GP extends GA by using a tree structure as the individual. But EP emphasizes on the behavioral linkage between parents and their offspring. Mutation is the only genetic operator in EP. There is no constraint on the representation in EP. In contrast, ES focuses on the individual, i.e. the phenotype, to be the object to be optimized. A genetic change in the individual is within a narrow band of the mutation step size, which has self-adaptations. Since evolutionary computation is a robust and parallel search algorithm, it can be used in data mining to find interesting knowledge in noisy environment. Data mining can be considered as a search problem, which tries to find the most accurate knowledge from all possible hypotheses.

Evolutionary Programming

Again, Evolutionary Programming (EP) emphasizes on the behavioral linkage between parents and their offspring, rather than seeking to emulate specific genetic operators as observed in nature [5]. Different from GA, EP does not require any specific genotype in the individual. Thus, EP employs a model of evolution at a higher abstraction. Mutation is the only operator used for evolution. In a typical process of EP (Table 1), a set of individuals is randomly created to make up the initial population. Each individual is evaluated by the fitness function. Then each individual produces an offspring by mutation. There is a distribution of different types of mutation, ranging from minor to extreme. Minor modifications in the behavior of the offspring occur more frequently and substantial modifications occur less. The offspring is also evaluated by fitness function. Then tournaments are performed to select the individuals for the next generation. For each individual, a number of rivals are selected among the parents and offspring. The tournament score of the individual is the number of rivals with lower fitness scores than itself. Then, individuals with higher tournament scores are selected as the population of next generation. There is no requirement that the population size is held constant. The process is iterated until the termination criterion is satisfied.

Table 1. The Algorithm of Evolutionary Programming

```
Initialize the generation, t, to be 0.
Initialize a population of individual, Pop(t)
Evaluate the fitness of all individual in Pop(t)
While the termination criteria is not satisfied
        Produce one or more offspring from each individual by mutation
        Evaluate the fitness of each offspring
        Perform a tournament for each individual
        Put the individuals with high tournament scores into Pop(t+1)
        Increase the generation t by 1
Return the individual with the highest fitness value
```

EP has two distinctive advantages. First, there are no constraints on the representation. Mutation operator does not demand a particular genotype. The representation can follow from the problem. Second, mutations in EP attempt to preserve behavioral similarity between offspring and their parents. An offspring is generally similar to its parent at the behavioral level with slight variations. EP assumes that the distribution of potential offspring is under a normal distribution around the parent's behavior. Thus, the severity of mutations is according to a statistical distribution. The flexibility and freedom from constraints of EP make it an ideal tool as the search mechanism for data mining.

2.4 Structure Analysis

In the proposed knowledge discovery process, structure analysis induces a Bayesian network from the data. The learning approach is based on the works of Lam [12] and Lam and Bacchus [13] to evaluate a Bayesian network by applying the Minimum Description Length (MDL) principle, which minimizes error terms while improving the accuracy of the model. EP is employed to optimize this metric in order to search for the best network structure.

The MDL Metric

The MDL metric measures the total description length $D_t(B)$ of a network structure B. A better network has a smaller value on this metric. Let $N = \{N_1, \ldots N_n\}$ denotes the set of nodes in the network (and thus the set of variables, since each node represents a variable), and Π_{N_i} denotes the set of parents of node N_i. The total description length of a network is the sum of description lengths of each node:

$$D_t(B) = \sum_{N_i \in N} D_t(N_i, \Pi_{N_i}) \tag{2.1}$$

This length is based on two components, the network description length D_n and the data description length D_d:

$$D_t(N_i, \Pi_{N_i}) = D_n(N_i, \Pi_{N_i}) + D_d(N_i, \Pi_{N_i}) \tag{2.2}$$

The formula for the network description length is:

$$D_n(N_i, \Pi_{N_i}) = k_i \log_2(n) + d(s_i - 1) \prod_{j \in \Pi_{N_i}} s_j \tag{2.3}$$

where k_i is the number of parents of variable N_i, S_i is the number of values N_i can take on, S_j is the number of values a particular variable in Π_{N_i} can take on, and d is the number of bits required to store a numerical value. This is the description length for encoding the network structure. The first part in the addition is the length for encoding the parents, while the second part is the length for encoding the probability parameters. This length measured the simplicity of the network.

The formula for the data description length is:

$$D_d(N_i, \Pi_{N_i}) = \sum_{N_i \in \Pi_{N_i}} M(N_i, \Pi_{N_i}) \log_2 \frac{M(\Pi_{N_i})}{M(N_i, \Pi_{N_i})} \tag{2.4}$$

As for the description length for encoding the data, a Huffman code is used to encode the data using the probability measure defined by the network. This length measured the accuracy of the network.

Combining MDL and EP

As suggested by Lam et al. [14] and Wong, Lam and Leung [25], we combine the MDL metric and EP for Bayesian network learning. Each individual represents a network structure, which is a directed acyclic graph (DAG). A set of individuals is randomly created to make up the initial population. Each graph is evaluated by the MDL metric described above. Then, each individual produces an offspring by performing a number of mutations. The offspring also evaluated by the MDL metric. The next generation of population is selected among the parents and offsprings by tournaments. Each DAG B is compared with q other randomly selected DAGs. The tournament score of B equals to the number of rivals that B can win, that is, the number of DAGs among those selected that have higher MDL scores than B. In our setting, $q = 5$. One half of DAGs with the highest tournament scores are retained for the next generation. The process is repeated until the maximum number of generations is reached. The number of the maximum number of generations depends on the complexity of the network structure. If we expect a simple network, the maximum number of generations can be set to a lower value. The network with the lowest MDL score is output as the result. The process is illustrated in the flowchart in Figure 2.

Genetic Operators

Mutation, the only genetic operator used in EP, is an asexual operation. An offspring in EP is produced by using a specific number of mutations. The probabilities of using 1,2,3,4,5 or 6 mutations are set to 0.2,0.2,0.2,0.2,0.1 and 0.1 respectively. The mutation operators modify the edges of the DAG. If a cyclic graph is formed after the mutation, edges in the cycles are removed to keep it acyclic. Our approach uses four mutation operators, with the same probabilities of being used:

1. Simple mutation randomly adds an edge between two nodes or randomly deletes an existing edge from the parent.
2. Reversion mutation randomly selects an existing edge and reverses its direction.
3. Move mutation randomly selects an existing edge. It moves the parent of the edge to another node, or moves the child of the edge to another node.
4. Knowledge-guided mutation is similar to simple mutation, however, the MDL scores of the edges guide the selection of the edge to be added or removed. The MDL metric of all possible edges in the network is computed before the learning algorithm starts. This mutation operator stochastically adds an edge with a small MDL metric to the parental network or deletes an existing edge with a large MDL metric.

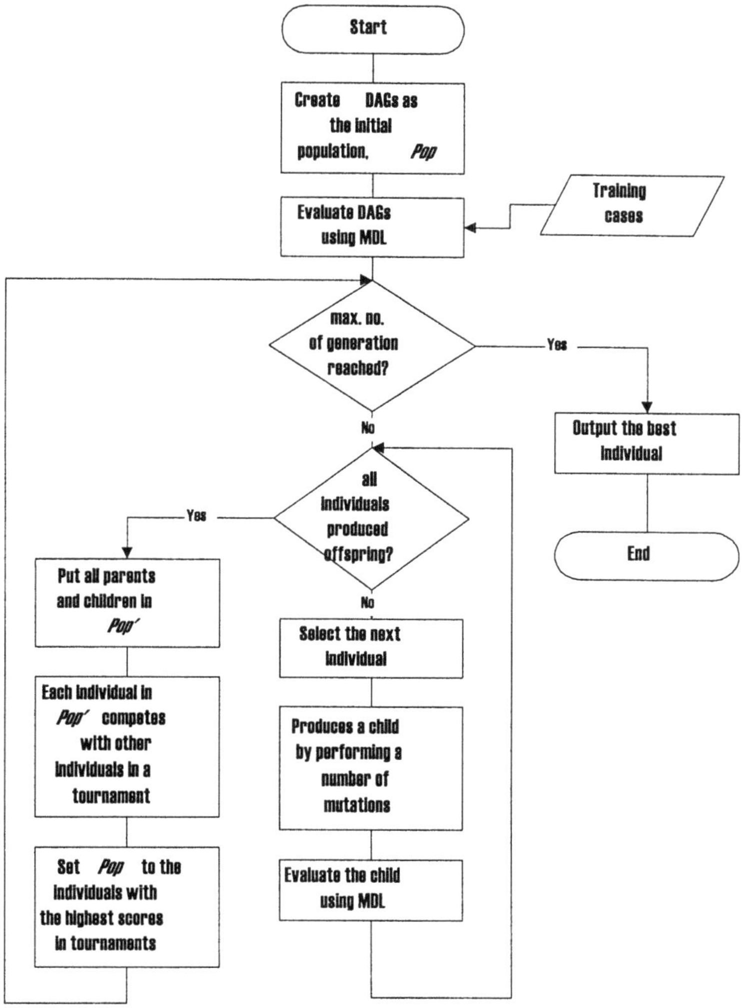

Fig. 2. The flowchart of the Bayesian network learning process

3 Method

The first data set for this study comes from a direct mail promotion program from the credit card division of a major U.S. bank. The database contains the data of 308,857 people who received an "invitation to apply" direct mail promotion from the bank. The data include over 2,000 variables, including consumer demographics and financial information as well as response data of the consumers to credit card promotions from a recent twelve-month period. The number of responders to the promotion was 1,623, representing a response rate of 0.53%, which is close to the industry average.

First, we sampled 3,785 records or 1.2% from the database, including 100% of the responders (1,623) and 0.7% non-responders (2,162). Following the industry practice, over-sampling of the responders is performed to ensure nearly symmetric distribution of responders and nonresponders in the training set and testing set for the logistic regression model. Since the Bayesian network also calculate the distribution of probabilities, the same concerns are also relevant. Thus, Bayesian network learning uses the same sample for direct comparisons with the results of logistic regression.

The second dataset comes from a U.S. based catalog direct marketing company. The particular database stores records of 106,284 consumers' purchase information from 12 catalog promotions over a twelve year period, including demographic information appended from the 1995 Census data and credit information from a commercial vendor. Each case contains over 300 variables. In this study, we focus on a specific catalog promotion with a 5.4% response rate. To facilitate the data mining process as well as model evaluation and comparison, the research team includes a marketing domain expert and a data mining expert.

4 Results

For both datasets, we split the sample into two sets, a training set and a testing set. For the first data set on credit card promotion, we developed a logistic regression using forward selection with the training set and validated with the testing set. Total 12 variables, considered important for mail operations by the bank's research department, were selected for model building. The 12 variables include the following information: response, household income, marital status, number of people, number of children, owner occupied housing, number of vehicles, vehicle value, number of bank cards, number of direct marketing mails received, number of pre-screened offers received in the last twelve months.

The logistic regression model has a Cox and Snell R-square of 0.101 and correctly classifies 64.5% of the cases. In addition, the Hosmer and Lemeshow test has an insignificant chi-square of 15.41 (DF=8, sig.=0.052), suggesting that the results predicted by the model is not significantly different the one that is observed. Thus, the logistic regression model has a good fit of the data. Then, we generated the empirical results -- decile analysis of cumulative lift -- a standard measure by the direct marketing industry (Table 2). The gains table indicates the first two deciles have cumulative lifts of 274 and 218 respectively, suggesting that by mailing to the top two deciles alone, logistic regression model generates over twice as many respondents as a random mailing without a model. The logistic regression model is used as the baseline model for comparison with the Bayesian network models. However, the lift in the fourth declines sharply to 78, which is lower than the next three deciles (94. 82, 81), suggesting instability in the model.

Decile	Records	% of File	Prob. of Active	% Active	Cum. % Active	no. of Actives	% of Total Actives	Cum. no. of Actives	Cum. % of Tot Actives	Lift	Cum. Lift
0	30833	10%	0.64	1.44	1.44	445	27.42	445	27.41	274	274
1	30794	20%	0.54	0.85	1.15	264	16.27	709	43.68	163	218
2	30721	30%	0.48	0.62	0.97	191	11.77	900	55.45	118	185
3	30798	40%	0.45	0.40	0.83	126	7.76	1026	63.21	78	158
4	30825	50%	0.42	0.49	0.77	153	9.42	1179	72.64	94	145
5	30805	60%	0.39	0.43	0.71	133	8.19	1312	80.84	82	135
6	30803	70%	0.34	0.42	0.67	131	8.07	1443	88.91	81	127
7	30768	80%	0.29	0.31	0.62	96	5.91	1539	94.82	59	119
8	30725	90%	0.22	0.17	0.57	53	3.26	1592	98.09	33	109
9	30845	100%	0.11	0.10	0.53	31	1.91	1623	100.00	19	100
Total	307917					1623	100				

Then, the Bayesian networks method using the same set of variables was performed, first with the training set and then validated with the same testing set so that the results compared with those of the logistic regression model (Table 3). Comparing to the cumulative lift of 274 in the top decile of the logistic regression model, the Bayesian network model has only a cumulative lift of 261 in the top decile, even though its lift of 167 in the second decile is slightly higher than that of 163 in the logistic regression. Overall, the results of the Bayesian network model fall slightly short of the logistic regression model. The Bayesian network model repeats the drop of lift in the third decile (91) that appeared in the logistic regression, again suggesting instability in the model (Table 3).

Table 3. Gains Table for Bayesian Network Model of Credit Card Promotion

Decile	Records	% of File	Prob. of Active	% Active	Cum. % Active	no. of Actives	% of Total Actives	Cum. no. of Actives	Cum. % of Tot Actives	Lift	Cum. Lift
0	30833	10%	0.64	1.37	1.37	420	25.88	420	25.88	261	261
1	30794	20%	0.55	0.88	1.12	271	16.70	691	42.58	167	214
2	30721	30%	0.50	0.48	0.91	146	9.00	837	51.58	91	173
3	30798	40%	0.47	0.53	0.82	164	10.11	1001	61.68	102	155
4	30825	50%	0.45	0.53	0.76	162	9.98	1163	71.67	100	144
5	30805	60%	0.41	0.56	0.72	171	10.54	1334	82.20	106	138
6	30803	70%	0.37	0.34	0.67	104	6.41	1438	88.61	65	127
7	30768	80%	0.32	0.28	0.62	85	5.24	1523	93.85	53	118
8	30725	90%	0.24	0.18	0.57	56	3.45	1579	97.30	35	109
9	30845	100%	0.12	0.13	0.53	44	2.71	1623	100.01	26	100
Total	307917					1623	100				

Furthermore, we generated the DAG for the Bayesian network learning using all 12 variables. The relationship structure among the variables discovered by the Bayesian networks appears to be much more complex than that of the logistic regression model. Most of the relationships discovered by the Bayesian network learning are meaningful and easy to understand based on the interpretation by the marketing domain expert. For instance, dwelling size and marital status are directly related. The number of children and the number of adults are also related, which in turn determine the number of people in the household. In the logistic regression, they would simply be treated as separate endogenous variables.

For the catalog promotion data set, we split the data set into two parts, one for training the response model and the other one for testing. The training set contains 2,870 respondents and 5,740 non-respondents. The testing set contains 2,870 respondents and 94,804 non-respondents. Nine variables were selected for model building: cash payment, total promotion orders, frequency of purchase in the last 36 months, money used in the last 36 months, use of house credit card, lifetime orders, average order size, telephone order, recency (number of months since the last order). The logistic regression model have cumulative lifts of 350 and 259 in the top two deciles, which are not exceptionally high given a response rate 5.4% response rate. The results show a gradual decline of lifts from the top deciles to the lower deciles (Table 4).

Decile	Records	% of File	Prob. of Active	% Active	Cum. % Active	no. of Actives	% of Total Actives	Cum. no. of Actives	Cum. % of Tot Actives	Lift	Cum. Lift
0	9768	10%	0.57	10.30	10.30	1006	35.05	1006	35.05	350	350
1	9768	20%	0.50	4.93	7.62	482	16.79	1488	51.85	167	259
2	9768	30%	0.47	4.39	6.54	429	14.95	1917	66.79	149	222
3	9768	40%	0.43	2.50	5.53	244	8.50	2161	75.30	85	188
4	9768	50%	0.38	1.98	4.82	193	6.72	2354	82.02	67	164
5	9768	60%	0.32	1.55	4.27	151	5.26	2505	87.28	52	145
6	9768	70%	0.26	1.26	3.84	123	4.29	2628	91.57	42	130
7	9768	80%	0.19	0.94	3.48	92	3.21	2720	94.77	32	118
8	9768	90%	0.14	0.84	3.19	82	2.86	2802	97.63	28	108
9	9762	100%	0.08	0.70	2.94	68	2.37	2870	100.00	23	100
Total	97,674					2870	100				

The same training and testing datasets were also used for Bayesian network learning. The results in Table 5 show that the Bayesian network model has a cumulative lift of 396 in the top decile and 290 in the second decile, significantly higher than those of the logistic regression model. In fact, all cumulative lifts in the first seven deciles are higher than those of the logistic regression model. We attribute this difference to the fact that the catalog data set is much bigger and has a much higher response rate than the credit card data, thus making the Bayesian network learning process more plausible and efficient. Overall, the Bayesian network model performs significantly better than the logistic regression model in terms of predicting consumer response to direct mail promotions.

To make a further comparison concerning the robustness of the response models, we have employed a 10-fold cross-validation for performance estimation. From the experimental results, the Bayesian network model predicts more accurately than the logistic regression model. Moreover, it provides a better cumulative lift in the first few deciles.

Table 5. Gains Table for Bayesian Network Model of Catalog Promotion

Decile	Records	% of File	Prob. of Active	% Active	Cum. % Active	no. of Actives	% of Total Actives	Cum. no. of Actives	Cum. % of Tot Actives	Lift	Cum. Lift
0	9768	10%	0.98	11.65	11.65	1138	39.65	1138	39.65	396	396
1	9768	20%	0.62	5.44	8.54	531	18.50	1669	58.15	185	290
2	9768	30%	0.38	3.71	6.93	362	12.61	2031	70.77	126	235
3	9768	40%	0.29	1.74	5.63	170	5.92	2201	76.69	59	191
4	9768	50%	0.22	1.96	4.90	191	6.66	2392	83.34	66	166
5	9768	60%	0.15	1.27	4.29	124	4.32	2516	87.67	43	146
6	9768	70%	0.10	1.26	3.86	123	4.29	2639	91.95	42	131
7	9768	80%	0.07	0.92	3.49	90	3.14	2729	95.09	31	118
8	9768	90%	0.05	0.76	3.19	74	2.58	2803	97.67	25	108
9	9762	100%	0.02	0.69	2.94	67	2.33	2870	100.00	23	100
Total	97,674					2870	100				

5 Discussion

5.1 Conclusions

Logistic regression has been widely adopted by researchers in direct marketing to select potential respondents. Most direct mail promotions only target the top two deciles. Comparing the empirical results of the logistic regression model, the Bayesian network model captures a larger percentage of buyers in the top two deciles and can potentially help improve sales and profitability of direct marketing programs. Although the results of the Bayesian networks method fall slightly short of the logistic regression with a small dataset, the Bayesian networks approach generates superior results with a larger sample, suggesting that the Bayesian network model furnishes a significant better representation of the structure of data. Meanwhile, the proposed data mining methods also have several pending problems. First, the Bayesian networks approach with evolutionary programming appears to be sensitive to sample size. With a small sample size, evolutionary programming may not have ample opportunities to learn the structure of data in order to extract more accurate representations. Secondly, results generated by the Bayesian networks method may be difficult to interpret and need the input from the domain expert to evaluate the validity of the discovered knowledge. Despite these problems, our study shows that the Bayesian networks approach with evolutionary programming can potentially become a powerful and efficient data mining tool for marketing professionals.

5.2 Implications

The explosive growth of data collected electronically is one of the most significant challenges facing marketing managers in current electronic business environment. The methods proposed in this study, i.e., Bayesian network models and evolutionary programming, provide useful tools for marketing managers to mine useful knowledge from data warehouses to assist their decision making. The proposed methods have two significant advantages. First, Bayesian network models can offer superior representation of the structure of data over the traditional methods such as logistic regression. The Bayesian networks method is flexible, assumption free, and more importantly, it considers the interrelationships among various factors. Secondly, given the large amount of data, evolutionary programming presents a robust and efficient tool to search and discover the best possible Bayesian network model. In essence, the combination of Bayesian network models and evolutionary programming lends a more powerful tool for data mining than if either method is applied alone.

In light of explosive growth of data, marketing researchers and database experts have devised various methods of data mining to discover new knowledge to assist managerial decision making. The conventional method in marketing research, like many social sciences studies, is often theory driven in that the researcher tests the hypotheses about the relationships among the interested variables. The current environment demands more problem-oriented research and efficient methods to explore the vast quantities of disaggregated data [22]. The explosive growth of marketing data requires efficient data mining tools in order to help managers uncover useful knowledge for decision making and improve sales and profitability.

5.3 Suggestions for Future Research

Wider applications of Bayesian networks and evolutionary programming to direct marketing response modeling face several significant challenges. First, EP procedures are computationally demanding and perform more slowly than mathematical optimization techniques. Despite the declining cost of computing power, model building and validation using evolutionary computation methods are still time-consuming for large data sets with a greater number of variables. More research is needed to improve the computing efficiency of the evolutionary algorithms so that computing time can be dramatically reduced. Secondly, a more efficient method is needed to automate or semi-automate the process of selecting meaningful variables for subsequent analyses and model building. Although researchers can always exercise their judgment in a trial-and-error selection process, the increasing variety and number of variables would make an automated or semi-automated process more desirable. Thirdly, in comparison to regression models, EP solutions are usually difficult to interpret since they do not have standard interpretative statistical measures that enable the user to understand why the procedure arrives at a particular solution. Sample size and proportion of buyers in the sample affect the performance of the method as they do with regression analysis. Finally, while evolutionary programming is a powerful tool for searching and optimizing decision problems, such methods need to be made user-friendlier to marketing researchers and more flexible to handle a greater variety of variables and marketing problems.

Acknowledgements

This research was partially supported by the RGC Earmarked Grant LU 3012/01E and the Lingnan University direct research grant (RES-021/200).

References

1. Balakrishnan, P.V. & Jacob, V.S. "Genetic algorithms for product design," *Management Science*, 1996, 42(8), 1105-1118.
2. Bhattacharyva, S. “Evolutionary algorithm in data mining: multi-objective performance modeling for direct marketing,” In *Proceedings of the Sixth ACM SIGKDD International Conference on Knowledge Discovery and Data Mining*, 2000, 465-473.
3. Cooper, G. & Herskovits, E.A. “A Bayesian Method for the Induction of Probabilistic Networks from Data,” *Machine Learning*, 1992, 9, 309-347.
4. D'Ambrosio, B. “Inference in Bayesian Networks,” *AI Magazine*, 1999, 20(2), 21-36.
5. Fogel, D.B. “An introduction to simulated evolutionary optimization.” *IEEE Transactions on Neural Network*, 1994, 5(1), 3-14.
6. Geiger, D. & Heckerman, D. “Knowledge representation and inference in similarity networks and Bayesian multinets,” *Artificial Intelligence*, 1996, 82(1-2), 45-74.
7. Haddawy, P. “An overview of some recent developments in Bayesian problem-solving techniques,” *AI Magazine*, 1999, 20(2), 11-19.
8. Heckerman, D. & Wellman, M.P. “Bayesian Networks,” *Communications of the ACM*, 1995, 38(3), 27-30.

9. Hurley, S., Moutinho, L. & Stephens, N.M. "Solving marketing optimization problems using genetic algorithms," *European Journal of Marketing*, 1995, 29(4), 39-56.
10. Jensen, F.V. *An Introduction to Bayesian Networks*, UCL Press, 1996.
11. Klemz, B.R. "Using genetic algorithms to assess the impact of pricing activity timing," *Omega*, 1999, 27(3), 363-372.
12. Lam, W. "Bayesian network refinement via machine learning approach," *IEEE Transactions on Pattern anal Machine Intelligence*, 1998, 20(3), 240-252 .
13. Lam, W. & Bacchus, F. (1994), Learning Bayesian Belief Networks -- an approach based on the MDL principle," *Computational Intelligence*, 1994, 10(3), 269-293.
14. Lam, W., Wong, M.L., Leung, M.S. & Ngan, P.S., "Discovering probabilistic knowledge from databases using evolutionary computation and Minimum Description Length principle," In *Genetic Programming: Proceedings of the Third Annual Conference*, 1998, 786-794.
15. Larranaga, P., Poza, M., Yurramendi, Y., Murga, R. & Kuijpers, C. (1996), "Structure learning of Bayesian Network by Genetic Algorithms: A performance analysis of control parameters," *IEEE Transactions on Pattern anal Machine Intelligence*, 1996, 18(9), 912-926.
16. Levin, N. & Zahavi, J. "Predictive modeling using segmentation," *Journal of Interactive Marketing*, 2001, 15(2), 2-22.
17. Midgley, D.F., Marks, R.E. & Cooper, L.G., "Breeding competitive strategies," *Management Science*, 1997, 43(3), 257-275.
18. Ngan, P.S., Wong, M.L., Lam, W., Leung, K.S. & Cheng, J.C.Y. (1999), "Medical data mining using evolutionary computation," *Artificial Intelligence in Medicine*, 16(1), 73-96.
19. Peacock, P.R. "Data mining in marketing: Part 1," *Marketing Management*, 1998, 6(4), 8-18.
20. Pearl, J. Probabilistic Reasoning in Intelligent Systems: Networks of Plausible Inference. Morgan Kaufmann, San Mateo, 1988.
21. Rebane, G. & Pearl, J. "The recovery of causal poly-trees from statistical data," In *Proceedings of the Conference on Uncertainty in Artificial Intelligence*, 1987, 222-228.
22. Silk, A.J. "Marketing science in a changing environment," *Journal of Marketing Research*, 1993, 30(4), 401-404.
23. Spirtes, P., Glymour, C. & Scheines, R. *Causation, Prediction and Search, Second Edition*, MIT Press, MA, 2000.
24. Urban, T. L. "An inventory-theoretic approach to product assortment and shelf-space allocation," *Journal of Retailing*, 1998, 74(1), 15-35.
25. Wong, M.L., Lam, W. & Leung, K.S. "Using Evolutionary Computation and Minimum Description Length principle for data mining of probabilistic knowledge," *IEEE Transactions: Pattern, Analysis, and Machine Intelligence,* 1999, 21(2), 174-178.
26. Wong, M.L., Lam, W., Leung, K.S., Ngan, P.S. & Cheng, J.C.Y. "Discovering knowledge from medical databases using evolutionary algorithms," *IEEE Engineering in Medicine and Biology*, 2000, 19(4), 45-55.

Improving User Profiles for E-Commerce by Genetic Algorithms*

Yi-Shin Chen and Cyrus Shahabi

Integrated Media Systems Center and Computer Science Department
University of Southern California, Los Angeles, CA 90089-2564

E-mail: [*shahabi, yishinc*]@*usc.edu*

Abstract. Recommendation systems are widely adopted in e-commerce businesses for helping customers locate products they would like to purchase. The major challenge for these systems is bridging the gap between the physical characteristics of data with the users' perceptions. In order to address this challenge, employing user profiles to improve accuracy becomes essential. However, the system performance may degrade due to inaccuracy of user profiles. Therefore, an effective system should offer learning mechanisms to correct erroneous user inputs. In this paper, we extend an existing recommendation system, Yoda, to improve the profiles automatically by utilizing users' relevance feedback with genetic algorithms (GA). Our experimental results indicate that the retrieval accuracy is significantly increased by using the GA-based learning mechanism.

Keywords: e-commerce, recommendation systems, fuzzy logic, soft query, clustering, genetic algorithm, relevance feedback

1 Introduction

As the amount of available products in e-commerce businesses is burgeoning, searching for desired products among enormous offerings is becoming increasingly difficult. As a result, e-commerce users frequently suffer from information overload. To alleviate this problem, recommendation systems are being widely adopted to help customers locate products they would like to purchase. In essence, these systems apply data analysis techniques to provide a list of recommended products for each online customer. The most famous example in e-commerce businesses is the "*Customers who bought*" feature used in Amazon.com™, which is basically applied to every product page on its websites. With the help of this feature, Amazon.com™'s system recommends similar products to the current buyer based on the purchase histories of previous customers who bought the same product.

* This research has been funded in part by NSF grants EEC-9529152 (IMSC ERC) and ITR-0082826, NIH-NLM R01-LM07061, DARPA and USAF under agreement nr. F30602-99-1-0524, and unrestricted cash/equipment gifts from NCR, IBM, Intel and SUN.

Systems such as Amazon.com^{TM} employ filtering techniques which fall into two classes: *content-based filtering* and *collaborative filtering*. Both types of systems have inherent strengths and weaknesses, where content-based approaches directly exploit the product information, and the collaboration filtering approaches utilize specific user rating information.

The content-based filtering approach generates recommendation lists based on comparisons between the feature vectors of products (e.g., artist, style) in the database with those in the user's profile. Hence, the accuracy of the user's profile is very important. To keep the user profile accurate, various learning techniques, such as *Bayesian classifiers*, *neural networks*, and *genetic algorithms* (GA), are utilized for revising user profiles [14–16,2].

Despite these improvements, this approach has several other weaknesses. One is *content limitation*, i.e., lexical fragment methods can only be applied to text content. The other is *over-specialization*, i.e., users can only obtain the information indicated in their profiles and have no chance of exploring new information they might desire. Moreover, because of the complexity of user profiles, the learning processes are always computationally costly and unable to adapt to frequently changing user preferences.

On the other hand, the collaborative filtering (CF) approach, does not use any information regarding the actual content of the products. The approach is based on the assumption that people having similar interests will possibly like the same objects. Typically, CF-based recommendation systems utilize users' rating of products to generate recommendation lists. Therefore, the over-specialization problem is avoided since a user could explore new items listed in other users' profiles.

The nearest-neighbor algorithm is the earliest CF-based technique used in recommendation systems [12]. With this algorithm, the similarity between users is evaluated based on their ratings of products, and the recommendation is generated considering the items visited by nearest neighbors of the user. In its original form, CF-based recommendations suffer from the problems of, **scalability**, **sparsity**, and **synonymy** (i.e., latent association between items is not considered for recommendations.)

In order to alleviate or even eliminate these problems, more recently, researchers introduced a variety of different techniques into collaborative filtering systems, such as *content analysis* [11] for avoiding the synonymy and sparsity problems; *categorization* [13] to alleviate the synonymy and sparsity problems; *Bayesian network* [9,8] for lightening the scalability problems; *clustering* [9] to lessen sparsity and scalability problems; and Singular Value Decomposition (SVD) [10,7] to ease all three problems. However, all these techniques have limitation and do not work well in all general cases.

In an earlier work [1], we introduced a hybrid recommendation system - *Yoda*, which simultaneously utilizes the advantages of *clustering*, *content analysis*, and *collaborate filtering* (CF) approaches. Basically, Yoda is a two-step approach recommendation system. Basically, during the offline process,

Yoda maintains numerous recommendation lists obtained from human experts, clusters of user evaluations, and web navigation patterns analyzed by clustering and content analysis techniques. During the online process, the confidence values of an active user to the experts are estimated and kept in the user profile. By utilizing the user profile and experts' recommendations, Yoda finally generates customized recommendations for the user. As a result, we reduce the time complexity through model based and clustering approaches, alleviate the synonymy problem with content analysis, and address the sparsity problem by implicit identification of the users interests [5,6].

Since Yoda relies on user profiles to recommend products, the accuracy of recommendation results will decline if the user profiles are inaccurate. In practice, obtaining user profiles by explicit acquisitions has been challenging. We utilized the users' relevance feedback and improved the profiles automatically using GA [4]. To the best of our knowledge, only a few studies [3,2] incorporate GA for improving the user profiles. In these studies, users are directly involved in the evolution processes. Because users have to enter data for each product inquiry, they are often frustrated with this method. On the contrary, in our design, users are not required to offer additional data to improve the confidence values. These confidence values are corrected by the GA-based learning mechanisms using users' future navigation behaviors. That is, Yoda assumes positive feedback from a user when the user actually navigates through Yoda's recommended items. Our experimental results indicate a significant increase in the accuracy of recommendation results due to the integration of the proposed learning mechanism.

The remainder of this paper is organized as follows. Section 2 describes the concept of genetic algorithms. In Section 3, we provide an overview on the functionality of Yoda. In Section 4, we discuss the detailed design of Yoda and the learning mechanism. The results of our evaluations as well as the details of the system implementation and our benchmarking method are described in Section 5. Section 6 concludes the paper.

2 Genetic Algorithms

Genetic algorithms (GAs), which were introduced by Holland [4], are iterative search techniques based on the spirit of natural evolution. By emulating biological selection and reproduction, GAs can efficiently search through the solution space of complex problems. Basically, a GA operates on a population of candidate solutions called *chromosomes*. A chromosome, which is composed of numerous genes, represents an encoding of the problem and associates it with a fitness value evaluated by the fitness function. This fitness value determines the goodness and the survival ability of the chromosome.

Generally, GA starts by initializing the population and evaluating its corresponding fitness values. Before it terminates, GA produces newer generations iteratively. At each generation, a portion of the chromosomes is selected according to the survival ability for reproducing offspring. The offspring are generated through crossover and mutation processes and are used for replacing some chromosomes in the population with a probability consistent with their fitness values. In other words, with the help of the fitness function to point out the correct direction, GA could construct better and better chromosomes from the best partial genes of past samplings. Please see reference [17] for mathematical foundations.

In summary, GA is composed of a fitness function, a population of chromosomes and three operators - selection, crossover and mutation. The parameter settings of the operators can be chosen depending on the applications or remain unchanged even when the applications are varied. However, the fitness function and the coding method are required to be specially designed for each problem. The design of fitness function and encoding method for Yoda will be described in Section 4.3.

3 Overview

The primary objective of a web-based recommendation system can be stated as follows:

Problem 1. Suppose the *item-set* $I = \{i | i$ is an item presented in a web-site $\}$ and u is a user interactively navigating the Web-site. The recommendation problem is to obtain the *wish-list* $I_u \in I$, which is a list of items that are ranked based on u's interests.

In general, to acquire a wish-list for a user, a recommendation process goes through three steps/phases:

1. Obtaining User Perceptions: Data about user perceptions such as navigation behaviors are collected. In some systems [8,7], these data need further processing for abstracting data which are used in the later phases.
2. Ranking the Items: The predicted user interests are utilized to provide the predicted user wish-list.
3. Adjusting user settings: The system acquires relevance feedback (or follow-up navigation behaviors) from the user and employs it to refine the user settings/profiles, which represent the user perceptions. On occasion, this phase is integrated into phase one.

Figure 1 illustrates the processing flow of Yoda. Suppose that music CDs are the items presented in a web-site. Yoda provides each active user a list of recommended CDs by analyzing his/her navigation behaviors. To generate the recommendations, during an offline process, Yoda obtains experts' recommendation (termed *experts' wish-lists*), which could be from human experts, clusters of user evaluations, or clusters of navigation patterns. Later, during the on-line recommendation process, the system first acquires the initial user profile, which is composed of a list of confidence values and a fuzzy

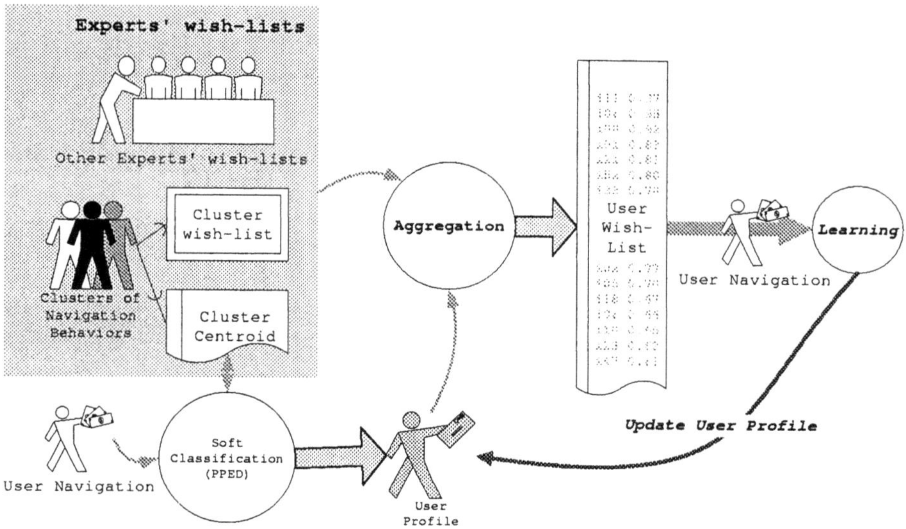

Fig. 1. Processing Flow of Yoda

cut, by softly classifying the user with clusters of navigation patterns. Note that the confidence values of the user toward other experts are not estimated at this step because the estimation process is comparably time consuming. Subsequently, Yoda uses the user profile to generate the customized recommendation (termed *user wish-list*) by weighted aggregation of the experts' wish-lists. Thereafter, the system improves and updates the user profiles as a background process by utilizing the follow-up user navigation behaviors and GA.

4 System Design

In this section, we provide a detailed description of Yoda's components. Since phase I is based on our previous work [18], here we elaborate more on phase II and III of Yoda.

4.1 Phase I - Obtaining User Perception

Yoda uses the client-side tracking mechanism proposed in [6] to capture view-time, hit-count, and sequence of visiting the web-pages (items) within a web-site. These features reflect users' interests on items. To analyze these features and infer the user interests, Yoda employs the *Feature Matrices (FM)* model, which we introduced in [18]. FM is a set of hyper-cube data structures that can represent various aggregated access features with any required precision. With FM, the patterns of both a single user and a cluster of users are modeled.

Here, Yoda uses FM to model the navigation patterns of the active users individually, and then the aggregated navigation pattern of each cluster is generated by clustering a collection of user navigation behaviors. Yoda also applies a similarity measure, termed *Projected Pure Euclidean Distance (PPED)* [18], to evaluate the similarity of a user navigation to a cluster navigation pattern.

Thus, Yoda quantifies the confidence value a user to each navigation-pattern cluster and initializes the corresponding user profile, which contains a list of confidence values to experts and a user perception standard (fuzzy cut). However, because the PPED method can only apply to FM model, Yoda cannot acquire the confidence values of a user's interests to the recommendation lists of other experts at this step.

4.2 Phase II -Ranking the Items

Two types of work in Yoda involve ranking the items. The first type is generating the experts' recommendations, which are lists of ranked items produced by either human experts, clusters of users, or clusters of navigation patterns. In our previous work [1], a content analysis technique was proposed to abstract common interests from navigation patterns. With this technique, the system can generate a list of ranked items for each navigation-pattern cluster. However, for the sake of simplicity, we briefly describe this technique and only focus on another type of ranking work - generating the user wish-list online. In order to properly describe this method, we first formally define some necessary terms.

Definition 1. An *item* is an instance of product, service, etc. that is presented in a web-site. Items are described by their *properties*, which are abstract perceptual features.

$$i = \{(p, \tilde{p}_i) \mid p \text{ is a property} \in P, \tilde{p}_i \text{ is a fuzzy set} \in F\} \in I \tag{1}$$

For example, for a music CD as an item, "styles" of the music, "ratings", and "popularity" can be considered as properties of the item. Since properties are perceptual we use fuzzy-sets to evaluate properties. ∎

Definition 2. A wish-list, I_x, for user/expert x is defined as:

$$I_x = \{(i, v_x(i)) | i \text{ is an item}, v_x(i) \in [0, 1]\} \tag{2}$$

where the *preference* value $v_x(i)$ measures the probability of item i be of interest to user/expert x. ∎

Definition 3. A cluster browse-list, B_k, for navigation-pattern cluster k is a list of items visited by all users in this cluster. ∎

A user profile is composed of two parts: user confidence data and user fuzzy cut value. The formal definition of user confidence data is as follows:

Definition 4. E denotes a set of experts in the system. U represents the set of users who have assigned reference confidence values to experts. π is a confidence value for a user u to an expert e; $\pi\ :\ o \in O,\ e \in E\ \ \rightarrow b_{o,e}$. Note that the value of $b_{o,e}$ is a form of human judgment and is represented as a fuzzy term.∎

Generating Navigation-Pattern Cluster Wish-lists Yoda represents the aggregated interests of the users in each cluster by a set of property values (PVs), termed *favorite PVs* of the cluster. The favorite PV, $F_p(k)$, identifies likelihood of the cluster k being interested in property p of the items and is extracted by applying a *voting procedure* to the *browse-list* of the cluster as follows:

$$\begin{aligned} C_{p,f}(k) &= \|\{i \mid i \in B_k, \tilde{p}_i = f\}\| \\ F_p(k) &= \max\{f \mid f \in F, C_{p,f}(k) = \max_{\forall f' \in F}\{C_{p,f'}(k)\}\} \end{aligned} \tag{3}$$

Example 1. Suppose the browse-list of cluster K is {A, B, G, K, Y, Z}, and the values of property "Rock" for the corresponding CDs are { (A, high), (B, high), (G, low), (K, medium), (Y, high), (Z, high) }. Because "high" has the maximum vote, the favorite PV of cluster K, $F_{Rock}(K)$, is "high".

Based on these extracted favorite PVs of the cluster k, Yoda can evaluate $v_k(i)$, preference value of an item i for cluster k, by quantifying the similarity between favorite PVs and property values associated with item i. The aggregation function used to compute $v_k(i)$ is:

$$\begin{aligned} G_f(k) &= \{p \mid f \in F,\ p \in P,\ F_p(k) = f\} \\ E_{k,f}(i) &= f \times \max\{\tilde{p}_i \mid p \in G_f(k)\} \\ v_k(i) &= \max\{E_{k,f}(i) \mid \forall f \in F\} \end{aligned} \tag{4}$$

Example 2. Suppose properties are grouped as $G_{medium}(K)$ = {Vocal, Soundtrack}, $G_{high}(K)$ ={Rock, Pop}, and $G_{low}(K)$ ={Classic}, and the item i is defined as { (Rock, low), (Pop, low), (Vocal, low), (Soundtrack, high), (Classic, medium)}. According to the equations above, the preference value $v_K(i)$ = max { (high × low), (medium × high), (low × low) } = (medium × high) = 0.75.

Generating User Wish-lists During the on-line recommendation process, Yoda aggregates the experts' wish-lists to generate the predicted user wish-list for the active user u. A fuzzy aggregation function is employed to measure and quantify the preference value $v_u(i)$ of each item i for the user u based on the user profile of user u. We use an optimized aggregation function with a triangular norm [19]. A triangular norm aggregation function g satisfy the following properties:

$$\begin{aligned} \text{Monotonicity: } & g(x,y) \le g(x',y') \text{ if } x \le x' \text{ and } y \le y' \\ \text{Commuatativity: } & g(x,y) = g(y,x) \\ \text{Associativity: } & g(g(x,y),z) = g(x,g(y,z)) \end{aligned}$$

With these properties, the query optimizer can replace the original query with a logically equivalent one and still obtain the exact same result. The optimized aggregation function we propose for Yoda is:

Definition 5. First, experts are grouped based on their reference confidence values assigned by user u.

$$G_f(u) = \{e \mid f \text{ is a fuzzy set} \in F,\ \pi_{u,e} = f\} \tag{5}$$

Then, the preference value $v_u(i)$ for item i is computed as:

$$\begin{aligned} E_{u,f}(i) &= f \times \max\{v_e(i) \mid e \in G_f(u)\} \\ v_u(i) &= \max\{E_{u,f}(i) \mid \forall f \in F\} \end{aligned} \tag{6}$$

∎

Basically, this aggregation function partitions the preference values into $\|F\|$ different subgroups according to the confidence values of the expert e. Subsequently, the system maintains a list of maximum preference values for all subgroups. Finally, the system computes the preferences of all items in the user wish-list by iterating through all subgroups. As compared to a naive weighted aggregation function with time complexity $O(\|E\| \times \|I\|)$ (where $\|E\|$ is the number of experts in the system) the complexity of the proposed aggregation function is $O(\|F\| \times \|I\|) = O(\|I\|)$, where $\|F\|$ is a small constant number representing the number of fuzzy terms.

To reduce the time complexity of generating the user wish-lists further, we apply a cut-off point on the expert wish-lists. Each shorten wish-list includes the N best-ranked items according to their preference values for the corresponding expert. In [19], Fagin has proposed an optimized algorithm, the A_0 algorithm, to retrieve N best items from a collection of subsets of items with time complexity proportional to N rather than total number of items. Here, by taking the subgroups of items (as described above) as the subsets, the A_0 algorithm can be incorporated into Yoda[1]. Applying the A_0 algorithm to generate a user wish-list with cut-off point N, we reduce the time complexity to $O(\|F\| \times \|N\|) = O(\|N\|)$, where $\|N\| \ll \|I\|$.

[1] Since our aggregation function is in triangular norm form, it satisfies the requirements of the A_0 algorithm.

4.3 Phase III -Adjusting User Settings

This learning mechanism is a background process performed at the same time that the users navigate the web-site. It employs GA for improving the list of confidence values by decoding the best chromosome to replace existing one in the system after its evolution. Users are not required to make additional effort to improve these confidence values. Yoda collects users' follow-up navigation behaviors and employs these behaviors as the goal of GA prior to the beginning of evolution[2]. Note that the learning mechanism is only triggered after receiving enough navigation data. In our implementation, it is activated when the number of navigated items is the same as that of the recommended items in the wish-list.

We first describe the method for transforming the navigation data to the relevance feedback needed in GA. Let FN be the set of follow-up navigated items and i be an item in FN. As described in Section 4.1, Yoda can capture the view-time, the hit-count and sequence about the items. Therefore, FN can be formally defined as:

$$FN = \{(i, v_t(i), v_s(i), v_h(i)) | i :\in I, v_t(i) : \text{view-time of } i, \\ v_s(i) : \text{sequence of } i \text{ in reverse order}, v_h(i) : \text{hit-count of } i\} \quad (7)$$

Assuming that users only navigate potentially desired items, the preferences of items can be estimated from navigation behaviors. That is, the users are more interested in the items that are navigated earlier, accesses more often, or viewed for longer periods of time. As a result, the feedback preference $\bar{v}_u(i)$ of the navigated item i from user u's perspective could be estimated based on the navigation data by using Equation (9).

$$\begin{aligned} \omega_f &: \text{the importance weight of feature } f \\ \mu_f &: \text{the mean of navigation data in feature } f \\ \sigma_f &: \text{the standard deviation of navigation data in feature } f \\ \psi_f &= \begin{cases} \frac{v_f(i)}{\mu_f + 3\times\sigma_f} & \text{if } f(i) \le (\mu_f + 3 \times \sigma_f) \\ 1 & \text{if } v_f(i) > (\mu_f + 3 \times \sigma_f) \end{cases} \quad (8) \\ \bar{v}_u(i) &= (\omega_s \times \psi_s) \times (\omega_h \times \psi_h) \times (\omega_t \times \psi_t) \quad (9) \end{aligned}$$

Note that for the normalization purpose, we use $(\mu_f + 3 \times \sigma_f)$ as the upper bound in Equation (8). This upper bound can prevent the affect from outliers [21] of the navigation data.

[2] Note that GA would converge per evolution process and there is no guarantee that it converges across several evolutions if the user's navigation behavior is inconsistent. However, in general, no learning mechanism can deal with inconsistent behaviors

Subsequently, we explain the coding design for GAs in our learning mechanism. The chromosomes represent a possible user profile. Two types of records are involved in the genes. One is user confidence information with k records, where k is the number of experts in the system. The value of the ith gene is an integer in $[0, L-1]$, where L is the number of fuzzy terms used in the system, and denotes the user's confidence level to expert i. The other is a user fuzzy cut value which is associated with the $(k+1)$th gene. The value of fuzzy cut is $(t+1)/L$, where $t \in [0, L-1]$ is the value of this gene.

For example, suppose that there are 50 experts and 8 different fuzzy terms in the system, there will be 51 genes per chromosome where the first 50 genes represent the corresponding confidence values to the experts, and the last gene represents the value of the user fuzzy cut. Additionally, after decoding, the value of 0 in gene i indicates that the confidence level to user i is "none" and the value of 6 in gene 51 indicates that the value of fuzzy cut is $(6+1)/8 = 0.875$. Likewise, after encoding, "full" confidence level to user i is represented by a number 7 in gene i and the 0.75 fuzzy cut is denoted by a number 5 in gene 51.

This coding method can guarantee a one-to-one mapping of profiles to chromosomes. That is, a chromosome will be decoded to one and only one legal user profile, and a user profile will be encoded to one and only one chromosome. Consequently, the solution space will be equal to the searching space in GA. This implies that our coding method is effective.

Next, we describe our GA fitness function, which heavily utilizes the preference list B estimated by our converting method. The fitness function first decodes the chromosome into a confidence list and a fuzzy cut value. Then, it obtains the user wish-list Q according to the profile using Equation (6). In other words, this process needs to interact with the system for obtaining experts' wish-lists. Finally, it generates the fitness value by measuring the similarity between Q and B. The similarity values are computed by Equation (12) which is based on two measurements. Equation (10) evaluates the similarity on ranking, and Equation (11) measures the average satisfaction of the user wish-list.

$$Q = \{(i, v_u(i)) | v_u(i)) \in [0,1]\}$$

$$B = \{(i, \bar{v}_u(i)) | \bar{v}_u(i) \in [0,1]\}$$

$$\text{Cos } \theta(Q, B) = \frac{\sum_i v_u(i) \times \bar{v}_u(i)}{\sqrt{\sum_i v_u(i)^2 \times \sum \bar{v}_u(i)^2}} \tag{10}$$

$$Avg(Q, B) = \frac{\sum_{i \in Q} \bar{v}_u(i)}{\|Q\|} \tag{11}$$

$$\text{Similarity}(Q, B) = \text{Cos } \theta(Q, B) + 3 \times Avg(B, Q) \tag{12}$$

In summary, once the learning process is triggered, the learning mechanism first converts the navigation behaviors to relevance feedback. Next, it encodes the corresponding confidence list to a chromosome and randomly generates other chromosomes as the initial population. Subsequently, GA iteratively discover better user profiles until it achieves the terminal condition such as the fitness value of one chromosome being 1 or the generation number being 200. In the end, the learning mechanism decodes the best chromosome to a confidence list and a fuzzy cut value for replacing the current data.

5 Performance Evaluation

In this section, we first describe our experimental setup and benchmarking method in Section 5.1. Subsequently, the details of our experimental results are discussed in Section 5.2.

5.1 Experimental Methodology

We developed a GA for Yoda using SUGAL [20] for its wide range of operators and data types. Yoda is implemented in C and on top of Microsoft Access 2000, which is running on a Pentium II 233MHZ processor with Microsoft NT4.0.

Parameter	Definition
M	Number of items in the web-site
N	The cut-off point (number of items in a user wish-list)
F	Number of fuzzy terms
E	Number of experts
O	Number of known experts ($E \geq O$)
K	Number of navigation-pattern clusters ($O \geq K$)
P	Percentage of interesting items within the item set
U	Number of users

Table 1. Benchmarking Parameters

In order to populate data for evaluation purposes, we propose a parametric algorithm to simulate various benchmarks (see Table 5.1). The benchmarking method maintains a list of preference values (denoted as $\mathring{A}_0$) that contains the perfect knowledge about items of interest to the active users. This is performed as follows. First, the algorithm randomly generates E experts and populates the preference information to an expert matrix $\bar{E}_0$. The cell $\bar{e}(i,j) \in \bar{E}_0$ represents the preference values for item j by expert i. Note that among these experts, there are K navigation-pattern clusters. Each cluster comprises a browse-list, a list of favorite PVs, and a pattern of navigation as the cluster centroid.

Next, the system randomly generates a list of confidence values $\ddot{\pi}$ and a fuzzy cut value for each active user. Each confidence value is represented by a fuzzy term, which is an integer in the range of $[0, 7]$. Finally, the system populates the preference values to $\mathring{A}_0$ by aggregating $\ddot{\pi}$ and $\bar{E}_0$ using Equation (6).

To simulate imperfect user feedback during the GA, all perfect knowledge will be tuned in a noisy process. Based on the preference values in this imperfect knowledge, the system then randomly selects a set of items and assigned feature values as the user navigation behaviors. These feature values are generated by a reverse procedure of Equation (11) . For example, the higher the preference value of an item is, the longer periods of view time is assigned to this item. Finally, the system reinitializes the user profile by assigning K imperfect confidence values of navigation-pattern clusters and a fuzzy cut value to the imperfect user profile.

5.2 Experimental Results

We conducted several sets of experiments to verify our system performances and to compare the results of different GA parameter settings. In these experiments, we observed a significant margin of improvement after incorporating the GA in matching the user expectations in various settings. It is also shown that the performance improvement of our learning mechanism is independent of the number of users. Moreover, the improvement is linearly increased with the number of items. However, due to the space limit, in this paper, we only stress the improvements achieved by applying our learning mechanism.

The results shown for each set of experiments are averaged over twenty runs, where each run is executed with different seeds for the random generator functions. The parameter settings of GA operators [20,17] are: population size=30, one-point crossover, tournament selection, keep the elitism, and mutation rate = 0.25. The benchmark settings of the following figures, i.e., the number of items, the number of cut-off point, the number of fuzzy terms, the number of experts, and the number of navigation-pattern clusters, are fixed at $M = 5000$, $N = 100$, $F = 8$, $E = 50$, $K = 10$, and $P = 5\%$, respectively.

Figure 2 demonstrates the improvements achieved by our learning mechanism. The X-axis of Figure 2 depicts the number of generations. The Y-axis of Figure 2.a illustrates the similarity distance (between query results and perfect user feedback) computed by Equation (10). The Y-axis of Figure 2.b represents average satisfaction computed by Equation (11), respectively. In this experiment, Figure 2 indicates that the accuracy of wish-lists improves drastically after incorporating the learning mechanism. As observed, the average satisfaction increases nearly 50% within ten generations of the evolution, and the similarity on ranking improves 100% after 40 generations of learning. Overall, in the majority of our experiments, GA can acquire nearly ideal user profiles, i.e, the rankings in the retrieval wish-list has 90% similarity to those in the perfect wish-list, within 40 generations. It should be noticed that Yoda

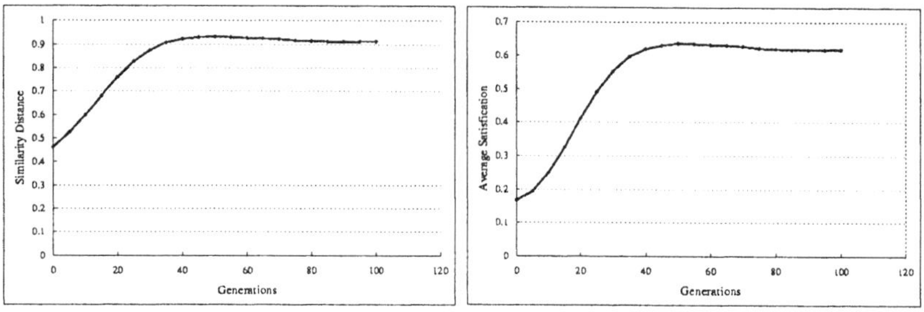

a. Similarity distance b. Average satisfaction

Fig. 2. The system improvement

only recommends the top 100 items for users and also only receives feedbacks about 100 items from users, where the set of feedback items and the set of recommended items are not identical. In other words, GA needs to search for ideal user profiles based on 2% of information. These results suggest that our learning mechanism is efficient and can greatly improve user profiles.

Since GA only has 2% information for learning, the limited information might restrict the learning ability. This problem was also observed in the experiments. In Figure 2, the accuracy of wish-lists slightly decreases after 50 generations of learning. The reason is that the learning mechanism is constrained by the limited feedbacks. To illustrate, consider the following example. Assume user *U* likes most of the items recommended by expert *A*. However, because the recommendation system only recommends few items and user *U* does not have the chance to know expert *A*'s recommendations, the learning mechanism has no ability to discover the relationship between *A* and *U*. Generally, this problem can be alleviated by several evolutions.

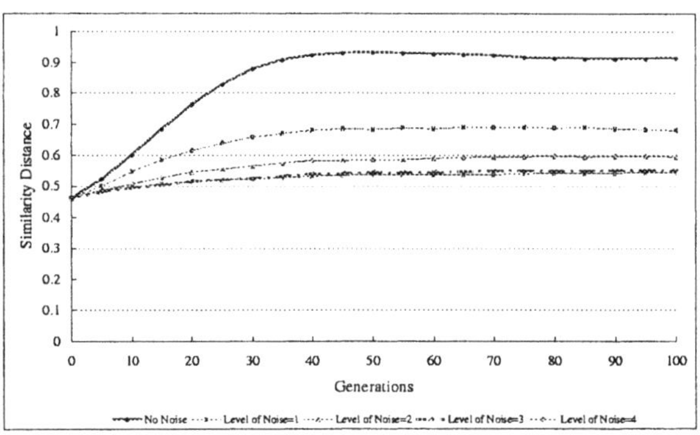

Fig. 3. Impact of noise

In order to compare the system performance when the user relevance feedbacks are imperfect, we introduce five different noise levels in the experiments of Figure 3, where noise level 0 represents perfect feedback and noise level 10 represents complete chaos. The X-axis is the number of generations and the Y-axis depicts the similarity distance (between query results and perfect user feedback) computed by Equation (10). As revealed by Figure 3, although the noise levels affect the accuracy of results, our learning mechanism still improves the quality of user profiles in the range of 20% to 50%. This figure indicates that our learning mechanism has the ability to tolerate noises during the learning process.

6 Conclusion

We proposed a recommendation system to reduce the information overload problem in e-commerce. However, this system heavily relies on user profiles for providing accurate recommendation lists. The system accuracy may decline if user profiles are inaccurate. Therefore, we introduced a learning mechanism that utilizes the users' navigation behaviors to improve the profiles automatically using genetic algorithms. The experimental results indicated that the accuracy of results significantly increased up to 100% by our GA-based learning mechanism. It also demonstrated that our learning mechanism has the ability of tolerating noises during learning processes and improvement is in the range of 20% to 50% depending on the noise level.

References

1. Shahabi C., Banaei-Kashani F., Chen Y.-S., McLeod D., (2001) Yoda: An Accurate and Scalable Web-based Recommendation System. In Proceedings of Sixth International Conference on Cooperative Information Systems (CoopIS 2001)
2. Moukas A., (1996) Amalthea: Information discovery and filtering using a multiagent evolving ecosystem. In Proceedings of 1st Int. Conf. on The Practical Applications of Intelligent Agents and MultiAgent Technology (PAAM)
3. Sheth B., (1993) Evolving Agents for Personalized Information Filtering. In Proceedings of the Ninth IEEE Conference on Artificial Intelligence for Applications
4. Holland J., (1975) Adaption in Natural and Artificial Systems. University of Michigan Press, Ann Arbor, Michigan
5. Konstan J., Miller B., Maltz D., Herlocker J., Gordon L., Riedl J., (1997) Applying Collaborative Filtering to Usenet News. In: Communications of the ACM (40) 3
6. Shahabi C., Zarkesh A.M., Adibi J., Shah V., (1997) Knowledge Discovery from Users Web Page Navigation. In Proceedings of the IEEE RIDE97 Workshop
7. Sarwar B., Karypis G., Konstan J., Riedl J. (2000) Application of Dimensionality Reduction in Recommender System – A Case Study. In Proceedings of ACM WebKDD 2000 Web Mining for e-Commerce Workshop
8. Kitts B., Freed D., Vrieze M., (2000)Cross-sell, a fast promotion-tunable customer-item recommendation method based on conditionally independent probabilities. In Proceedings of the sixth ACM SIGKDD international conference on Knowledge discovery and data mining, pp. 437-446

9. Breese J., Heckerman D., Kadie C. (1998) Empirical Analysis of Predictive Algorithms for Collaborative Filtering. In Proceedings of the Fourteenth Conference on Uncertainty in Artificial Intelligence, pp. 43-52
10. Sarwar B., Karypis G., Konstan J., Riedl J., (2000) Analysis of Recommendation Algorithms for e-Commerce. In Proceedings of ACM e-Commerce 2000 Conference, 2000.
11. Balabanovi M., Shoham Y., (1997) Fab, content-based, collaborative recommendation. In: Communications of the ACM, Vol 40(3), pp. 66-72
12. Resnick P., Iacovou N., Suchak M., Bergstrom P., Riedl J., (1994) GroupLens, An Open Architecture for Collaborative Filtering of Netnews. In Proceedings of ACM conference on Cumputer-Supported Cooperative Work, pp. 175-186
13. Good N., Schafer J., Konstan J., Borchers J., Sarwar B., Herlocker J., Riedl J., (1999) Combining Collaborative Filtering with Personal Agents for Better Recommendations. In Proceedings of the 1999 Conference of the American Association of Artifical Intelligence, pp. 439-446
14. Pazzani M., Billsus D., (1997) Learning and Revising User profiles: The Indentification of Interesting Web Sites. In: Machine Learning, Vol 27, pp. 313-331
15. Tan A., Teo C., (1998) Learning User Profiles for Personalized Information Dissemination. In Proceedings of Int'l Joint Conf. on Neural Network, pp. 183-188
16. Lam W., Mukhopadhyay S., Mostafa J., Palakal M., (1996) Detection of Shifts in User Interests for Personalized Information Filtering, In Proceedings of the 19th Int'l ACM-SIGIR Conf on Research and Development in Information Retrieval, pp. 317-325
17. Goldberg D.E., (1989) Genetic Algorithms in Search, Optimisation, and Machine Learning. Addison-Wesley, Wokingham, England
18. Shahabi C., Banaei-Kashani F., Faruque J., Faisal A., (2001) Feature Matrices: A Model for Efficient and Anonymous Web Usage Mining, In Proceedings of EC-Web 2001
19. Fagin R., (1996) Combining Fuzzy Information from Multiple Systems. In Proceedings of Fifteenth ACM Symposyum on Principles of Database Systems
20. Hunter A., (1995) Sugal Programming manual. http://www.trajan-software.demon.co.uk/sugal.htm
21. Knorr, E., R. Ng, and V. Tucakov., (2000) Distance-Based Outliers: Algorithms and Applications. The VLDB Journal, 8(3),pp. 237-253

Part 4 Fuzzy Logic

Automatic Web User Profiling and Personalization Using Robust Fuzzy Relational Clustering

Olfa Nasraoui[1], Raghu Krishnapuram[2], Anupam Joshi[3], and Tapan Kamdar[3]

[1] Department of Electrical and Computer Engineering, The University of Memphis, Memphis TN 38152, USA,
[2] IBM India Research Lab, Block 1, Indian Institute of Technology, Hauz Khas, New Delhi 110016, India
[3] Department of Computer Science and Electrical Engineering University of Maryland - Baltimore County, Baltimore, MD 21250, USA

Abstract. The proliferation of information on the world wide Web has made the personalization of this information space a necessity. Personalization of content returned from a Web site is a desired feature that can enhance server performance improve system design, and lead to wise marketing decisions in electronic commerce. Mining typical user profiles from the vast amount of historical data stored in access logs is an important component of Web personalization. In the absence of *a priori* knowledge, unsupervised or clustering methods seem to be ideally suited to categorize the usage behavior of Web surfers. In this chapter, we present a framework for mining typical user profiles from server acces logs based on robust fuzzy relational clustering. As a by-product of the clustering process that generates robust profiles, associations between different URL addresses on a given site can easily be inferred. In general, the URLs that are present in the same profile tend to be visited together in the same session or form a large *itemset*. Finally, we present a personalization system that uses previously mined profiles to automatically generate a Web page containing URLs the user might be interested in. Our personalization approach is based on profiles computed from the prior traversal patterns of the users on the website and do not involve providing any declarative private information or the user to log in.

1 Introduction

One of the data repositories, affecting every aspect of our life lately, is the World Wide Web. In addition to its ever-expanding size and lack of structure, the WWW has not been responsive to user preferences and interests. A user looking for some specific information has to wade through a morass of information, get bombarded with irrelevant information, and often lose track of their initial objective. One way to deal with this problem is through personalization. Personalization can either be done via information brokers (e.g. Web search engines), or in an *end-to-end* manner by making Web sites adaptive. Initial work in this area has basically focused on creating recommender systems. The Firefly system [41] attempted to provide CDs that best match a user's professed interests. The Webwatcher project [2] at CMU highlights hyperlinks in a page based on the declared interests and the path traversal of a user as well as the path traversals of previous users with similar interests. W^3IQ [18,19] and PHOAKS [44] have sought to use cooperative information retrieval techniques for personalization. "Mining" information from the user's interaction is another approach towards personalization. Perkowitz and Etzioni [33,34] proposed adapting Web pages based on a user's traversal pattern. The standard K-Means algorithm was used to cluster users's traversal paths in [40]. In [6], associations and sequential patterns between web transactions are discovered based on the Apriori algorithm [1]. There is also a recent body of work [3] which seeks to transform the Web into a more structured, database like entity and then using standard OLAP techniques on it [32]. It is important to mention that most of the above efforts have relied on relatively simple techniques which can be inadequate for real user profile data since they are neither resilient to the "noise" typically found in user traversal patterns, nor able to handle the uncertainties and fuzziness inherent in Web data. To deal with the fuzzy nature of Web data and to automatically determine the number of clusters, Nasraoui et al. [24,29] proposed to extract profiles using an unsupervised relational clustering algorithm based on the competitive agglomeration algorithm [10]. In their work, they have also proposed formal definitions for the Web user profile as well as quantitative evaluation measures. Also, to handle possibly unknown noise contamination rates in Web data, Nasraoui et al [28] have proposed mining the Web log data using a fuzzy relational clustering algorithm based on a robust estimator. In this work, they have also extended the formal definition of a Web user profile and its quantitative evaluation measures to a "robust" user profile and "robust" evaluation measures.

A related topic that has been recently gaining momentum is the idea that we can learn much about users and customers by tracking and analyzing their *clickstreams*, which is of great importance in e-commerce.

In the absence of any *a priori* knowledge, unsupervised classification or clustering methods seem to be ideally suited to analyze the semi-structured log data of user accesses by categorizing them into automatically generated classes of user session profiles. We define the notion of a "user session" as being a temporally compact sequence of web accesses by a user. The goal of our Web mining is to categorize these sessions. In this light, Web mining can be viewed as a special case of the more general problem of knowledge discovery in databases [9]. We define a new distance measure between two Web sessions that captures the organization of a Web site. This organizational information is inferred directly from the URLs.

Web mining involves data that is mildly to severely corrupted with "noise". Outliers and incomplete data can easily occur in the data set due to a wide variety of reasons inherent to Web browsing and logging. Moreover, the noise contamination rate and the scale of the data is rarely known in advance. For example, consider the situation where we are analyzing log entries to discover typical information access patterns. Clearly, there is a significant percentage of time (sometimes as large as 20-30 percent) that a user is simply "browsing" the Web and does not follow any particular pattern.

Categories in most data mining tasks are rarely well separated. The class partition is best described by fuzzy memberships [5], particularly along the overlapping borders. Specifically, in Web mining, certain access patterns may be regarded as belonging to more than one class with different degrees instead of belonging to only one class. Also, at times, it will be necessary to work with relational[1] data because it is intuitively and conceptually easier to describe the relation or similarity between two objects than to map them to numerical features. In fact, determining the nature and number of features is itself very challenging. This problem is particularly accute when the data contains nonnumeric fields. This means that relational clustering methods are expected to be highly beneficial in Web mining. As will be explained later, Web sessions are too complex to convert to simple numerical features. Hence, clustering the user sessions could be tackled by exploiting inter-session similarities within a relational framework.

For all these reasons, we present robust fuzzy relational methods to cluster the user sessions based on their pair-wise dissimilarities, and illustrate their use in extracting user profiles from real log data. The Relational Fuzzy $C-$ Maximal Density Estimator (RFC−MDE) [30] and the Robust Fuzzy C Medoids (FCMdd) can deal with complex and subjective distance/similarity measures which are not restricted to be Euclidean. The web sites for the department of Computer Engineering and Computer Sciences at the University of Missouri, as well as that of the department of Computer Sciences and Electrical Engineering at the University of Maryland-Baltimore County were used as testbeds for our algorithms which successfully analyzed server access logs and obtained typical session profiles of users. The performance of our techniques was superior to that of the Non Euclidean Relational Fuzzy C-Means (NERF) [16].

We also note that as a by-product of our clustering process, associations between different URL addresses on a given site can easily be inferred from the resulting robust profiles. In general, the URLs that are present in the same profile tend to be visited together in the same session, i. e., they form a large item set. These item sets are similar to the ones computed by the Apriori algorithm [1], and have been applied to mining associations and sequential patterns between web transactions in [6]. However, unlike the latter, our method mines typical users profiles as a primary goal, and the discovered associations resulting from this profile extraction come with no additional computation. The biggest advantage of our approach is that clustering results do not depend on the goodness or completeness of any pre-discovered

[1] Note that this term is used in its statistical sense, not in its database sense

associations. Some of these associations (ones with low support) can be very hard and time consuming to discover from Web session data.

The rest of the chapter is organized as follows. In Section 2, we present a framework for Web usage mining based on clustering the Web user sessions. In Section 3, we present an overview of relational clustering algorithms. In Section 3.1, we present the Relational Fuzzy C Maximal Density Estimator (RFC–MDE), and illustrate its performance in extracting robust session profiles from the access log files of several real Web sites. In Section 4 we present the Robust Fuzzy C Medoids (FCMdd) algorithm as well as a low-complexity version of it, and use it to extract typical session profiles from real access log files. Finally, in Section 6, we present the conclusions.

2 The Knowledge Discovery Process of Web Session Profiling

2.1 Extracting Web User Sessions

The access log for a given Web server consists of a record of all files accessed by users. Each log entry consists of: (i) User's IP address, (ii) Access time, (iii) URL of the page accessed, $\cdots$, etc. A user session consists of accesses originating from the same IP address within a predefined time period. Each URL in the site is assigned a unique number $j \in \{1, \ldots, N_U\}$, where N_U is the total number of valid URLs. Thus, the ith user session is encoded as an N_U-dimensional binary attribute vector $\mathbf{s}^{(i)}$ with the property

$$s_j^{(i)} = \begin{cases} 1 \text{ if the user accessed the } j^{th} \text{ URL during the } i^{th} \text{ session} \\ 0 \text{ otherwise} \end{cases}$$

The ensemble of all N_S sessions extracted from the server log file is denoted $\mathcal{S}$.

2.2 Assessing Web User Session Similarity

The similarity measure between two user-sessions: $\mathbf{s}^{(k)}$ and $\mathbf{s}^{(l)}$ relies on two sub-measures [29, 30]. The first measure which ignores the site structure is given by $S_{1,kl} = \frac{\sum_{i=1}^{N_u} s_i^{(k)} s_i^{(l)}}{\sqrt{\sum_{i=1}^{N_u} s_i^{(k)}} \sqrt{\sum_{i=1}^{N_u} s_i^{(l)}}}$. The second similarity measure requires the pre-computation of the similarities at the structural URL level that will be used in the computation of the similarity at the session level.

The entire Web site is modeled as a tree with the nodes representing different URL's. The tree is similar to that of a directory where an edge connects one node to another if the URL corresponding to the latter is hierarchically located under that of the former, The "syntactic" similarity between the ith and j^{th} URLs is defined as $S_u(i,j) = \min\left(1, \frac{|p_i \cap p_j|}{\max(1, \max(|p_i|,|p_j|)-1)}\right)$, where p_i denotes the path traversed from the root node (main page) to the node corresponding to the ith URL, and $|p_i|$ indicates the length of this path.

Note that this similarity which lies in [0, 1] basically measures the amount of overlap between the paths of the two URLs. This overlap is inferred directly from the URL address string by exploiting the one-to-one mapping between the address and the site topology. The pairwise URL similarities should be computed only once offline for a particular Web site prior to any clustering. Now the similarity on the session level which incorporates the syntactic URL similarities is computed by $S_{2,kl} = \frac{\sum_{i=1}^{N_U}\sum_{j=1}^{N_U} s_i^{(k)} s_j^{(l)} S_u(i,j)}{\sum_{i=1}^{N_U} s_i^{(k)} \sum_{j=1}^{N_U} s_j^{(l)}}$. The final similarity given by a maximally optimisitc aggregation of $S_{1,kl}$ and $S_{2,kl}$ is $S_{kl} = \max(S_{1,kl}, S_{2,kl})$. Finally, this similarity is mapped to the dissimilarity measure $d_s^2(k,l) = (1 - S_{kl})^2$. This dissimilarity measure satisfies the desirable properties: $d_s^2(k,k) = 0$, $d_s^2(k,l) >= 0\ \forall k,l$, and $d_s^2(k,l) = d_s^2(l,k)\ \forall k,l$. However, unlike a metric distance it violates the triangular inequality in some cases. For instance, the dissimilarity between the sessions {/courses/cecs345/syllabus} and {/courses/cecs345} is zero. So is the dissimilarity between {/courses/cecs345} and {/courses/cecs401}. However, the dissimilarity between {/courses/cecs345/syllabus} and {/courses/cecs401} is not zero (it is 1/4). This illustrates a desirable property for profiling sessions which is that the dissimilarity becomes more stringent as the accessed URLs get farther from the root because the amount of specificity in user interest increases correspondingly.

2.3 Clustering Web User Sessions

After pre-computing all pairwise dissimilarities, the extracted sessions can be clustered using relational clustering. We will present two robust fuzzy relational clustering techniques that can handle the noisy and fuzzy nature of Web usage data in Sections 3.1 and 4.

2.4 Interpretation and Evaluation of the Results

The results of clustering the user session data are interpreted using the following quantitative measures [30]. First, the user sessions are assigned to the closest clusters based on the computed distances, d_{ik}, from the ith cluster to the kth session. This creates C clusters $\mathcal{X}_i = \left\{ \mathbf{s}^{(k)} \in \mathcal{S} \mid d_{ik} < d_{jk}\ \forall j \neq i \right\}$, for $1 \leq i \leq C$.

The sessions in cluster $\mathcal{X}_i$ are summarized by a typical session "profile" vector [30] $\mathbf{P}_i = \left(P_{i1}, \ldots, P_{iN_U}\right)^t$. The components of $\mathbf{P}_i$ are URL relevence weights, estimated by the probability of access of each URL during the sessions of $\mathcal{X}_i$ as follows

$$P_{ij} = p\left(\mathbf{s}_j^{(k)} = 1 | \mathbf{s}_j^{(k)} \in \mathcal{X}_i\right) = \frac{|\mathcal{X}_{i_j}|}{|\mathcal{X}_i|}, \tag{1}$$

where $\mathcal{X}_{i_j} = \left\{ \mathbf{s}^{(k)} \in \mathcal{X}_i \mid s_j^{(k)} > 0 \right\}$. The URL weights P_{ij} measure the significance of a given URL to the ith profile. Besides summarizing profiles, the components of the profile vector can be used to recognize an invalid profile which has no strong or frequent access pattern. For such a profile, all the URL weights will be low.

Several classical cluster validity measures can be used to assess the goodness of the partition. The intra-cluster or within-cluster distance represents an average of the distances between all pairs of sessions within the ith cluster, and is given by $\overline{D}_{Wi} = \frac{\sum_{\mathbf{s}^{(k)} \in \mathcal{X}_i} \sum_{\mathbf{s}^{(l)} \in \mathcal{X}_i, l \neq k} d_{kl}^2}{|\mathcal{X}_i|(|\mathcal{X}_i|-1)}$. This is inversely related to the compactness or goodness of a cluster. A good guideline to use when evaluating clusters based on the intra-cluster distances is to compare these values to the total average pairwise distance of all sessions. The latter corresponds to the intra-cluster distance if all the user sessions were assigned to one cluster (i.e., no category information is used). Also it is important to recall that all distances are in $[0, 1]$. The inter-cluster or between-cluster distance represents an average of the distances between sessions from the ith cluster and sessions from the jth cluster, and is given by $\overline{D}_{Bij} = \frac{\sum_{\mathbf{s}^{(k)} \in \mathcal{X}_i} \sum_{\mathbf{s}^{(l)} \in \mathcal{X}_j} d_{kl}^2}{|\mathcal{X}_i||\mathcal{X}_j|}$. For a good partition, the inter-cluster distances should be high because they measure the separation between clusters.

3 Relational Clustering

The term "relational data" refers to the situation where we have only numerical values representing the degrees of similarity or relation between the pairs of objects in the data set. In contrast, "object data" refers to the the situation where the objects to be clustered are explicitly represented by vectors $\mathbf{x}_i \in \Re^p$. Algorithms that generate partitions of relational data are usually referred to as relational clustering algorithms. Relational clustering is more general in the sense that it is applicable to situations in which the objects to be clustered cannot be represented by numerical features. For example, we can use relational clustering algorithms to cluster URLs (Universal Resource Locators) if we can define a dissimilarity measure to quantify the degree of resemblance between pairs of URLs. The pair-wise dissimilarities are usually stored in the form of a matrix called the dissimilarity matrix.

One of the most popular relational clustering algorithms is the SAHN (Sequential Agglomerative Hierarchical Non-overlapping) model [42] which is a bottom-up approach that generates crisp clusters by sequentially merging pairs of clusters that are closest to each other in each step. Depending on how "closeness" between clusters is defined, the SAHN model gives rise to single, complete and average linkage algorithms. A variation of this algorithm can be found in [13]. Another well-known relational clustering algorithm is PAM (Partitioning Around Medoids) due to Kaufman and Rousseeuw [21].

This algorithm is based on finding k representative objects (also known as *medoids* [20]) from the data set in such a way that the sum of the within cluster dissimilarities is minimized. A modified version of PAM called CLARA (Clustering LARge Applications) to handle large data sets was also proposed by Kaufman and Rousseeuw [21]. Ng and Han [31] propose another variation of CLARA called CLARANS. This algorithm tries to make the search for the k representative objects (medoids) more efficient by considering candidate sets of k medoids in the neighborhood of the current set of k medoids. However, CLARANS is not designed for relational data. Finally, it is also interesting to note that Fu [11] suggested a technique very similar to the k medoid technique in the context of clustering string patterns generated by grammars in syntactic pattern recognition. Some of the more recent algorithms for relational clustering include [12], [35], [43], and [4].

SAHN, PAM, CLARA and CLARANS generate crisp clusters. When the clusters are not well defined (i.e., when they overlap) we may desire fuzzy clusters. Two of the early fuzzy relational clustering algorithms are the ones due to Ruspini [39] and Diday [8]. Other notable algorithms include Roubens' Fuzzy Non Metric Model or FNM [36], Windham's Association Prototype Model or AP [45], Hathaway & Bezdek's Relational Fuzzy c-Means [17], and Kaufman & Rousseeuw's Fuzzy Analysis or FANNY [21]. Recently, Nasraoui et al. [24, 29] presented an unsupervised relational clustering algorithm based on the competitive agglomeration algorithm [10].

3.1 The Relational Fuzzy $C-$ Maximal Density Estimator

It is known that for complex data sets containing overlapping clusters, fuzzy partitions model the data better than their crisp counterparts. In particular, fuzzy memberships are richer than crisp memberships in describing the degrees of belonging of data points lying in the areas of overlap. Moreover, fuzzy partitions generally make the optimization process less prone to local or suboptimal solutions. Let $\mathcal{X} = \{\mathbf{x}_j \mid j = 1, \ldots, N\}$ be a set of feature vectors in an $n-$dimensional feature space with coordinate axis labels $x_1, x_2, \ldots, x_n$, where $\mathbf{x}_j = (x_{j1}, x_{j2}, \ldots, x_{jn})$. Let θ represent the parameters to be estimated. With a fuzzy partition, a data point $\mathbf{x}_j$ belongs to each cluster, $\mathcal{X}_i$, to a varying degree called fuzzy membership u_{ij}. A fuzzy partiton must satisfy the following constraints [5],

$$0 \leq u_{ij} \leq 1$$

$$\sum_{i=1}^{C} u_{ij} = 1 \ \forall j = 1 \cdots N$$

$$0 \leq \sum_{j=1}^{N} u_{ij} \leq N \ \forall i = 1 \cdots C$$

Using fuzzy memberships offers other advantages in terms of smoothing the surface of the objective function and reducing its discontinuity [25], thus making the problem analytically more tractable. The Maximal Density Estimator (MDE) [26] is a new robust estimator that is free of any presuppositions about the noise proportion. One way to use a fuzzy partition while estimating the cluster parameters with the MDE is to use the following criterion

$$\min_{\Theta,\sigma_i,u_{ij}} \left\{ J = \sum_{i=1}^{C}\sum_{j=1}^{N} u_{ij}^m w_{ij} \frac{d_{ij}^2}{\sigma_i} - \alpha \sum_{i=1}^{C}\sum_{j=1}^{N} u_{ij}^m w_{ij} \right\}, \tag{2}$$

where $m \in [1, \infty)$ is a fuzzifier parameter that controls the degree of fuzziness of the resulting partition, with values closer to 1 corresponding to crisper partitions, and w_{ij} is given by

$$w_{ij} = \exp \frac{-d_{ij}^2}{2\sigma_i}. \tag{3}$$

In (2), d_{ij}^2 is the residual of data point $\mathbf{x}_j$ with respect to the fit computed from the ith cluster prototype θ_i, and w_{ij} is a positive weight associated with point $\mathbf{x}_j$. The weight w_{ij} can be considered as the degree of membership of data point $\mathbf{x}_j$ in the inlier set or the set of good points associated with the ith cluster. The first term of this objective function tries to minimize the scaled residuals of the good points. The second term of this objective function tries to use as many good points (inliers) as possible in the estimation process, via their high weights. Thus the combined effect is to optimize the density, i.e., the ratio of the total number of good points to the volume. We choose the value of α to balance the two terms. In 2-D, we choose $\alpha = 1$. For the general n-dimensional case α should be close to n, since the ratio of the first term to the second term approaches the average of a χ^2 distribution for Gaussian data. Finally, we should note that d_j^2 should be a suitable distance measure, tailored to detect desired shapes, such as the Euclidean distance for spherical clusters, or the Gustafson-Kessel (GK) distance [14] for ellipsoidal clusters characterized by a covariance matrix, etc.

Since each cluster is independent of the rest, it is easy to derive the optimal update equations for the parameters for each cluster. The scale parameter of the ith cluster is given by

$$\sigma_i = \frac{1}{(2+\alpha)} \frac{\sum_{j=1}^{N} u_{ij}^m w_{ij} d_{ij}^4}{\sum_{j=1}^{N} u_{ij}^m w_{ij} d_{ij}^2}. \tag{4}$$

To find the optimal prototype parameters θ_i of the ith cluster, we set

$$\frac{\partial J}{\partial \theta_i} = \frac{1}{\sigma_i} \sum_{\mathbf{x}_j \in \mathcal{X}_i} u_{ij}^m w_{ij} \frac{\partial d_{ij}^2}{\partial \theta_i} = \mathbf{0}.$$

For instance for the case of location estimation, d_{ij}^2 is the squared Euclidean distance $d_{ij}^2 = ||\mathbf{x}_j - \mathbf{c}_i||^2$, and the center $\mathbf{c}_i$ is given by

$$\mathbf{c}_i = \frac{\sum_{j=1}^{N} u_{ij}^m w_{ij} \mathbf{x}_j}{\sum_{j=1}^{N} u_{ij}^m w_{ij}} \tag{5}$$

To simplify the algorithm, we de-couple the robust parameter estimation process via the robust weights, w_{ij}, from the partitionning process, via the memberships, u_{ij}. Since the parameter estimates in (5) which optimize (2) are already robust, we use the simpler Fuzzy c-Means [5, 39] objective function to update the memberships u_{ij} in each iteration as follows:

$$u_{ij} = \frac{\left(\frac{1}{d_{ij}^2}\right)^{\frac{1}{m-1}}}{\sum_{k=1}^{C} \left(\frac{1}{d_{kj}^2}\right)^{\frac{1}{m-1}}}. \tag{6}$$

Therefore, the optimization process will consist of alternating updates of the memberships, as given by (6), and the cluster centers and scale parameters as given by (5) and (4). We call the resulting clustering algorithm the Fuzzy $C-$ Maximal Density Estimator (F$C-$MDE).

The F$C-$MDE algorithm was originally formulated to deal with object or feature data only. For relational applications, F$C-$MDE must be extended so that it can work on relational data. First, the squared Euclidean distance, $d_{ik}^2 = ||\mathbf{x}_k - \mathbf{c}_i||^2$, from feature vector $\mathbf{x}_k$ to the center of the ith cluster, $\mathbf{c}_i$, is written in terms of the relation matrix $\mathbf{R}$ as follows [16]:

$$d_{ik}^2 = (\mathbf{R}\mathbf{v}_i)_k - \mathbf{v}_i^t \mathbf{R} \mathbf{v}_i / 2. \tag{7}$$

Here, $\mathbf{R} = [R_{jk}]$ is the dissimilarity between $\mathbf{x}_j$ and $\mathbf{x}_k$, and $\mathbf{v}_i$ is the membership vector defined by

$$\mathbf{v}_i = \frac{\left(u_{i1}^m w_{i1}, \ldots, u_{iN}^m w_{iN}\right)^t}{\sum_{j=1}^{N} u_{ij}^m w_{ij}}. \tag{8}$$

Equation (7) allows the computation of the distance between the data points and cluster prototypes in each iteration when only the relational data, $\mathbf{R}$, are given. Therefore, a relational dual of F$C-$MDE exists for the special case where the object data and relational data satisfy

$$\mathbf{R} = [R_{jk}] = ||\mathbf{x}_j - \mathbf{x}_k||^2 \tag{9}$$

This means that even when only relational data is available in the form of an $N \times N$ relation matrix, the relational dual of F$C-$MDE is expected to perform in an equivalent way to the F$C-$MDE provided that the relation matrix, $\mathbf{R}$, is Euclidean, i.e., there exists a set of N points in $\mathcal{R}^{N-1}$, called a realization of $\mathbf{R}$, satisfying (9).

When a realization does not exist for the relation matrix, $\mathbf{R}$, some of the distances computed using (7) may be negative. To overcome this problem, we use the β-spread transform [16] to convert a non-Euclidean matrix $\mathbf{R}$ into an Euclidean Matrix $\mathbf{R}_\beta$ as follows

$$\mathbf{R}_\beta = \mathbf{R} + \beta\,(\mathbf{M} - \mathbf{I}) \tag{10}$$

where β is a suitably chosen scalar, $\mathbf{I} \in \mathcal{R}^{n\times n}$ is the identity matrix and $\mathbf{M} \in \mathcal{R}^{n\times n}$ satisfies $M_{jj} = 1$ for $1 \le i, j \le n$. The distances d_{ik}^2 must be checked in every iteration for negativity, which indicates a non-Euclidean relation matrix. In that case, the β-spread transform should be applied with a suitable value of β to make the d_{ik}^2 positive again. An underestimate for the lower bound on β was derived [16] and related to the necessary shift that is needed to make the distances positive. This result can be summarized as

$$\Delta\beta = \max_{i,k}\{-2d_{ik}^2/\left\|\mathbf{v}_j - \mathbf{e}_k\right\|^2\}, \tag{11}$$

where $\mathbf{e}_k$ denotes the kth column of the identity matrix. An alternative approach [21] to this problem imposes Kuhn-Tucker conditions to ensure positivity of the memberships. The resulting Relational F$C-$MDE algorithm (RF$C-$MDE) can deal with complex and subjective dissimilarity/similarity measures which are not restricted to be Euclidean or metric. The RF$C-$MDE algorithm is summarized below:

The Relational Fuzzy C− Maximal Density Estimator (RFC−MDE)

Fix the number of clusters C;
Pick C distinct random rows from relation matrix to serve as the initial implicit prototypes, this results in initial distances d_{ik}^2 for $1 \le i \le C$;
Repeat
 Compute membership vectors $\mathbf{v}_i$ for $1 \le i \le C$ using (8);
 Compute $d_{ik}^2 = (\mathbf{R}_\beta \mathbf{v}_i)_k - \mathbf{v}_i^t \mathbf{R}_\beta \mathbf{v}_i/2$ for $1 \le i \le C$ and $1 \le k \le N_S$;
 If ($d_{ik}^2 < 0$ for any i and k) then {
  Compute $\Delta\beta$ by using (11);
  Update $d_{ik}^2 \leftarrow d_{ik}^2 + (\Delta\beta/2) * \left\|\mathbf{v}_j - \mathbf{e}_k\right\|^2$ for $1 \le i \le C$ and $1 \le k \le N_S$;
  Update $\beta = \beta + \Delta\beta$;
 }
 Compute robust weights w_{ik} for $1 \le i \le C$ and $1 \le k \le N_S$, using (3);
 Compute scale parameters σ_i for $1 \le i \le C$ using (4);
Until (*memberships stabilize*).

3.2 Experimental Results

The Web mining procedure described in Section 2 was used to extract typical user session profiles from the log data of the Web sites of two departments at two different universities during 1998. We first describe the results for the department of Computer Engineering and Computer Sciences at the University of Missouri, Columbia. The log data from accesses to the server during a period of 12 days was used. After filtering out irrelevent entries, the data was segmented into 1703 sessions. The maximum elapsed time between two consecutive accesses in the same session was set to 45 minutes. The number of distinct URLs accessed in valid entries was 369. The initial distance values d_{ik}^2 were obtained by randomly choosing C rows, for $1 \leq i \leq C$, from the relation matrix and computing the fuzzy memberships using (6), which treats the transactions corresponding to the selected rows as initial prototypes.

After clustering the relational data with RFC−MDE and $C = 35$, the sessions were assigned to the clusters in a minimum distance classifier sense. As a result, only 15 clusters that had cardinalities exceeding 30 were kept, hence making a sufficiently strong profile. Table 1 illustrates four profiles computed using (1), where only the significant URLs ($P_{ij} \geq 0.15$) are displayed, and the individual components are displayed in the format {P_{ij} - j^{th} URL}. The sessions were assigned to the closest cluster and the session clusters or profiles were examined qualitatively. The results are summarized in Table 2, which also lists the cardinality and the intra-cluster distance for all clusters.

Table 1. Examples of Profiles Discovered by RFC−MDE from Missouri Data

i	$\mathbf{P}_i$
4	{.78 - /cecs_computer.class} {.96 - /courses.html} {.99 - /courses_index.html} {.96 - /courses100.html} {.34 - /courses300.html} {.2 - /courses_webpg.html} {.28 - /courses200.html} {.87 - /}
7	{.47 - /cecs_computer.class} {0.85 - /degrees_undergrad.html} {0.84 - /degrees_index.html} {0.85 - /bsce.html} {0.46 - /bscs.html} {0.32 - /bacs.html} {0.31 - /courses.html} {0.31 - /courses_index.html} {0.31 - /courses100.html} {0.21 - /courses300.html} {0.18 - /courses200.html} {0.84 - /degrees.html} {0.22 - /general.html} {0.22 - /general_index.html} {0.22 - /facts.html} {0.16 - /research.html} {0.65 - /}
13	{.18 - /~shi} {.64 - /~shi/cecs345} {.38 - /~shi/cecs345/java_examples} {.19 - /~shi/cecs345/references.html} {.20 - /~shi/cecs345/Lectures/05.html} {.20 - /~shi/cecs345/Lectures/06.html} {.29 - /~shi/cecs345/Lectures/07.html} {.18 - /~shi/cecs345/Projects/1.html}

The results show that RFC−MDE succeeded in delineating many different profiles in the user sessions. Except for the 14th cluster, all clusters correspond to real profiles reflecting distinct user interests. The profiles fol-

Table 2. Summary of RFC−MDE User Session Profiles for Missouri Data

i	$\lvert\mathcal{X}_i\rvert$	description	$\overline{D}_{Wi}$
1	56	Professor 1's course pages	0.15
2	33	Access statistics pages	0.1
3	64	Site manager's pages	0.13
4	206	General course inquiries	0.2
5	94	main page, people, faculty, research and degree pages	0.68
6	141	cecs352 course pages	0.24
7	68	Undergraduate degree and general course inquiries	0.3
8	66	Accesses to adminstrator's pages	0.24
9	162	Accesses to the cecs227 class pages	0.25
10	62	Professor 2's main page and research papers	0.29
11	64	Sessions combining Dr Joshi's courses and research pages	0.66
12	191	Short sessions mostly limited to main page and class list	0.26
13	142	Professor 3's cecs345 general course enquiries	0.35
14	119	Mixture of unrelated accesses that don't make a strong profile	0.92
15	152	Dr. Saab's course pages	0.55

lowed the access patterns of typical users – the general "outside visitor" is captured in profiles 5 and 12, prospective students in profile 4 and 9, students in CECS352 in profile 6, etc. The goodness of these clusters is recognizable through their low intra-cluster distances (considerably lower than the total average pairwise session distance of 0.9), and their high inter-cluster distances (the majority between .9 and 1). Note that many sessions that do not belong to any profile are lumped in the 14th profile which is easily recognized as a spurious cluster by using the quantitative evaluation measures. In fact, this particular cluster had no significant URLs ($P_{ij} < 0.15$ for all j) and its intra-cluster distance (0.92) was even higher than the total average pairwise distance of all sessions. In addition to the intra-cluster distance, the robust weights, w_{ij}, are extremely useful for extracting the core members of each class, as well as for distinguishing between strong and spurious profiles. In fact, only the core members of each cluster are expected to have a significant robust weight. For example when only sessions with weights exceeding 0.04 are considered, profiles Nos. 5, 14, and 15 end up having less than 10 members, hence making weak profiles. Note that the spurious cluster No. 14 was eliminated by this method as all its members have low robust weights. Also, several sessions were identified as noise with respect to certain profiles because of their low weights. For example, the following two sessions from profile No. 13, having low robust weights, were considered as noise:

{/courses400.html, /people_index.html, /~shi/publications, /~shi/cecs345, /~joshi/scipad}

{/~shi/cecs345, /~saab/cecs303/private, /~saab/cecs303/private/solution,

/~saab/cecs303/private/solution/hw1.html}

As can be seen, these sessions do not have a specific interest in the 13th profile which concerns Dr Shi's pages.

The Non Euclidean Relational Fuzzy $C-$Means (NERF) [16] was also used to cluster the sessions relation matrix, and resulted in only 12 significant profiles, as shown in Table 3. RF$C-$MDE fared better than NERF in the sense that the spurious cluster corresponding to the 12th cluster found by NERF (which corresponds to the 14th profile found by RF$C-$MDE) had 339 more sessions. Also, NERF completely missed the clusters corresponding to the 11th and 15th profiles. Moreover, as can be inferred from the higher cardinality and the average intra-cluster distance for comparable profiles (such as the 5th profiles found by RF$C-$MDE and NERF), NERF's clusters tend to contain more irrelevent sessions or noise. Unlike in the case of RF$C-$MDE, we cannot distinguish noise in the profiles obtained by NERF because it has no robust weights. This is because the fuzzy memberships, u_{ij}, are relative, and regardless of whether a data point is noisy, its memberships across all classes always sum to one, i.e., $\sum_{i=1}^{C} u_{ij} = 1 \; \forall j = 1 \cdots N$.

We also note that as a by-product of the clustering process, associations between different URL addresses on a given site can easily be inferred from the resulting robust profiles. In general, the URLs that are present in the same profile tend to be visited together in the same session. For example, by looking at the 7th profile in Table 1, we can deduce that the URLs making up that profile tend to co-occur or form a large item set, similar to the ones computed by the Apriori algorithm [1]. Such item sets can be applied to mining associations and sequential patterns between web transactions in [6]. However, unlike the latter, our method mines typical users profiles as a primary goal, and the discovered associations resulting from this profile extraction come with no additional computation.

Table 3. Summary of NERF User Session Profiles for Missouri Data

i	$\lvert\mathcal{X}_i\rvert$	description	$\overline{D}_{Wi}$
1	70	Professor 1's pages	0.2
2	34	Access statistics pages	0.12
3	64	Site manager's pages	0.13
4	213	General course inquiries	0.21
5	109	Main page, people, research, and faculty pages	0.78
6	163	cecs352 course pages	0.28
7	69	Undergraduate degree and general course inquiries	0.31
8	66	Accesses to adminstrator's pages	0.24
9	172	Accesses to the cecs227 class pages	0.28
10	80	Professor 2's main page and research papers	0.35
11	206	Short sessions mostly limited to main page and class list	0.29
12	458	Mixture of unrelated accesses	0.87

The next experiment consists of extracting typical user session profiles from the log data of the Web site for the Computer Science department at the University of Maryland, Baltimore County during 1998. The log data from accesses to the server during a period of 6 hours in the late evening was used. After filtering out irrelevent entries, the data was segmented into 678 sessions. The maximum elapsed time between two consecutive accesses in the same session was set to 45 minutes. The number of distinct URLs accessed in valid entries was 1681.

After clustering the relational data with RFC−MDE and $C = 35$, the sessions were assigned to the clusters in a minimum distance classifier sense. As a result, only 12 clusters that had cardinalities exceeding 10 were kept, i.e., those making a sufficiently strong profile. Table 4 illustrates four profiles computed using (1), where only the significant URLs ($P_{ij} \geq 0.15$) are displayed, and the individual components are displayed in the format $\{P_{ij}$ - j^{th} URL$\}$. The sessions were assigned to the closest cluster and the session clusters or profiles were examined qualitatively. The results are summarized in Table 5, which also lists the cardinality and the intra-cluster distance for all clusters.

Table 4. Examples of Profiles Discovered by RFC−MDE from Maryland Data

i	$\mathbf{P}_i$
2	{.25 - /~mshadl1/Other_Links.html} {.75 - /~mshadl1/profiler.html} {.17 - /~mshadl1/Episode_Guide.html}
4	{.24 - /courses/undergraduate/201/fall98/lectures/index.shtml} {.26 - /courses/undergraduate/201/fall98/projects/index.shtml} {.21 - /courses/undergraduate/201/fall98/projects/p4/index.shtml} {.21 - /courses/undergraduate/201/fall98}
8	{.68 - /~sli2/tetris} {.77 - /~sli2/directory.html} {.67 - /~sli2/tetris/content.html} {.19 - /~sli2/cube/content.html}
9	{.45 - /agents} {0.19 - /agents/news}
12	{.98 - /} {.19 - /people/faculty/faculty.shtml}

The results show that RFC−MDE succeeded in delineating many different profiles in the user sessions. Except for the 11th cluster, all clusters correspond to real profiles reflecting distinct user interests. The profiles seem to reflect the intersts of leisurly users that browse the world wide Web in the late evening, as most profiles reflect an interest in free internet games offered by some of the department's graduate students (Profiles No. 2, 5, 6, and 8). Also profile No. 10 reflects an interest in a large set of pictures of a famous supermodel, posted on a graduate student's homepage. Note that many sessions that do not belong to any profile are lumped in the 11th profile which is easily recognized as a spurious cluster by using the quantitative evaluation measures. In fact, this particular cluster had no significant URLs

Table 5. Summary of RFC−MDE User Session Profiles for Maryland Data

i	$\|\mathcal{X}_i\|$	description	$\overline{D}_{Wi}$
1	13	Graduate course and degree enquieries (/www/courses/graduate) and (/www/graduate)	0.78
2	48	Accesses to ˜mshadl1 pages (graduate student's web page about the Hit TV series "Profiler")	0.49
3	20	Accesses to ˜sletscl pages (a page about model ceramic cottages)	0.64
4	58	inquiries about undergraduate course No. 201	0.81
5	27	Accesses to ˜sli2 pages, particularly (/˜sli2/cube) (a free game offered by a graduate student)	0.43
6	20	Accesses to (/ etoton1/games) (a free game offered by another graduate student)	0.27
7	15	Accesses to / ebert (professor) pages	0.68
8	79	Accesses to ˜sli2 pages, particularly (/˜sli2/tetris) (a free game offered by a graduate student)	0.55
9	58	inquiries about agents (/agents) (The Intelligent Software Agents page)	0.71
10	19	Accesses to (/ rmobar/Claudia.html) (Supermodel pictures offered by a graduate student)	0.35
11	200	Mixture of unrelated accesses that don't make a strong profile	0.99
12	42	Short sessions mostly limited to main page and faculty list	0.66

($P_{ij} < 0.15$ for all j) and its intra-cluster distance (0.99) was even higher than the total average pairwise distance of all sessions (0.98). In addition to the intra-cluster distance, the robust weights, w_{ij}, are extremely useful for extracting the core members of each class, as well as for distinguishing between strong and spurious profiles. In fact, only the core members of each cluster are expected to have a significant robust weight. For example when only sessions with weights exceeding 0.029 are considered, only profiles Nos. 5, 6, 8, 9, 10, and 12 still have more than 10 members, hence making a strong profile. Note that the weak profile No. 11 was eliminated as all its members have low robust weight. Also the following session from profile No. 5, having low robust weight, was considered as noise, obviously, because it is not clear that the user's interest relates to that of the 5th profile:

{/˜sli2/cube/cube.html, /˜evans/Hemingway1.html,
/˜cef/science96/drift.html}

The Non Euclidean Relational Fuzzy C−Means (NERF) [16] was also used to cluster the sessions relation matrix, and resulted in only 4 significant profiles, as shown in Table 6. RFC−MDE fared better than NERF in the sense that the spurious cluster (No. 3) found by NERF, which corresponds to the 11th profile found by RFC−MDE, had 264 more sessions. Also, NERF completely missed the clusters corresponding to the 3rd, 4th, 7th, 8th, 9th, and

10th profiles, and lumped the 2nd and 6th profiles found by RFC−MDE into a single cluster (This corresponds to the 3rd profile found by NERF). Moreover, as can be inferred from the higher cardinality and the average intra-cluster distance for comparable profiles (such as the 5th and 1st profiles found by RFC−MDE and NERF respectively), NERF's clusters tend to contain more irrelevent sessions or noise.

As in the previous experiment with the University of Missouri data, We note that as a by-product of the clustering process, associations between different URL addresses on the UMBC site can easily be inferred from the resulting robust profiles. In general, the URLs that are present in the same profile tend to be visited together in the same session.

Table 6. Summary of NERF User Session Profiles for Maryland Data

i	$\|\mathcal{X}_i\|$	description	$\overline{D}_{Wi}$
1	13	Graduate enquieries (/www/courses/graduate) and (/www/graduate)	0.78
2	112	Accesses to ˜sli2 pages, particularly (/˜sli2/cube)	0.62
3	66	Accesses to (˜mshadl1) and (/ etoton1/games)	0.67
4	464	Mixture of unrelated accesses that don't make a strong profile	0.99
5	35	Short sessions mostly limited to main page	0.58

4 The Relational Fuzzy c Medoids Algorithm (FCMdd)

Let $X = \{\mathbf{x}_i | i = 1, 2, \ldots, n\}$ be a set of n objects. Each object may or may not be represented by a feature vector. Let $r(\mathbf{x}_i, \mathbf{x}_j)$ denote the dissimilarity between object $\mathbf{x}_i$ and object $\mathbf{x}_j$. Let $\mathbf{V} = \{\mathbf{v}_1, \mathbf{v}_2, \ldots, \mathbf{v}_c\}, \mathbf{v}_i \in X$ represent a subset of X with cardinality c, i.e., $\mathbf{V}$ is a c-subset of X. Let X^c represent the set of all c-subsets $\mathbf{V}$ of X. The Fuzzy c Medoids Algorithm (FCMdd) minimizes:

$$J_m(\mathbf{V}; X) = \sum_{j=1}^{n} \sum_{i=1}^{c} u_{ij}^m \, r(\mathbf{x}_j, \mathbf{v}_i), \tag{12}$$

where the minimization is performed over all $\mathbf{V}$ in X^c. In (12), u_{ij} represents the fuzzy [5], or possibilistic [15, 23] membership of $\mathbf{x}_j$ in cluster i. The membership u_{ij} can be defined heuristically in many different ways. For example, we can use the FCM [5] membership model given by:

$$u_{ij} = \frac{\left(\frac{1}{r(\mathbf{x}_j, \mathbf{v}_i)}\right)^{1/(m-1)}}{\sum_{k=1}^{c} \left(\frac{1}{r(\mathbf{x}_j, \mathbf{v}_k)}\right)^{1/(m-1)}}, \tag{13}$$

where $m \in [1, \infty)$ is the "fuzzifier". Since u_{ij} is a function of the dissimilarities $r(\mathbf{x}_j, \mathbf{v}_k)$, it can be eliminated from (12). This is the reason J_m is shown as a function of $\mathbf{V}$ alone. When (12) is minimized, the $\mathbf{V}$ corresponding to the solution generates a fuzzy or possibilistic partition via an equation such as (13). However, (12) cannot be minimized via the alternating optimization technique, because the necessary conditions cannot be derived by differentiating it with respect to the medoids. (Note that the solution space is discrete.) Thus, strictly speaking, an exhaustive search over X^c needs to be used. However, following Fu's [11] heuristic algorithm for a crisp version of (12), we describe the following fuzzy algorithm (FCMdd) that minimizes (12).

The Fuzzy c-Medoids Algorithm (FCMdd)

Fix the number of clusters c; Set $iter = 0$;
Pick initial medoids $\mathbf{V} = \{\mathbf{v}_1, \mathbf{v}_2, \ldots, \mathbf{v}_c\}$ from X^c;
Repeat
  Compute memberships u_{ij} for $i = 1, 2, \ldots, c$ and
    $j = 1, 2, \ldots, n$, by using (13); (A)
  Store the current medoids: $\mathbf{V}^{old} = \mathbf{V}$;
  Compute the new medoids $\mathbf{v}_i$ for $i = 1, 2, \ldots, c$:
    $q = \underset{1 \le k \le n}{\text{argmin}} \sum_{j=1}^{n} u_{ij}^m \, r(\mathbf{x}_k, \mathbf{x}_j); \quad \mathbf{v}_i = \mathbf{x}_q;$ (B)
  $iter = iter + 1$;
Until $\left(\mathbf{V}^{old} = \mathbf{V} \text{ or } iter = MAX\_ITER\right)$.

The crisp version of FCMdd above, which we call the Hard c Medoids (HcMdd) algorithm, can be obtained by replacing step (A) with:

$$q = \underset{1 \le k \le c}{\text{argmin}}\; r(\mathbf{x}_j, \mathbf{v}_k); \quad u_{ij} = \begin{cases} 1 & \text{if } i = q \\ 0 & \text{otherwise} \end{cases} \tag{14}$$

The above algorithm falls in the category of Alternating Cluster Estimation [38] paradigm, and is not *guaranteed* to find the global minimum. It is advisable to try many random initializations to increase the reliability of the results. We have experimented with three different ways of initializing the medoids. The first way is to pick all the medoid candidates randomly. We call this method Initialization I. The second way is to pick the first candidate as the object that is most central to the data set, and then pick each successive one by one in such a way that each one is most dissimilar to all the medoids that have already been picked. This makes the initial medoids evenly distributed. We refer to this procedure as Initialization II.

Initialization II for FCMdd

Fix the number of medoids $c > 1$;
Compute the first medoid:
$q = \underset{1 \le j \le n}{\operatorname{argmin}} \sum_{i=1}^{n} r(\mathbf{x}_j, \mathbf{x}_i); \qquad \mathbf{v}_1 = \mathbf{x}_q;$
Set $V = \{\mathbf{v}_1\}$, $iter = 1$;
Repeat
$iter = iter + 1$;
$q = \underset{1 \le i \le n; \mathbf{x}_i \notin V}{\operatorname{argmax}} \ \min_{1 \le k \le |V|} r(\mathbf{v}_k, \mathbf{x}_i); \qquad \mathbf{v}_{iter} = \mathbf{x}_q;$
$V = V \cup \{\mathbf{v}_{iter}\}$;
Until $(iter = c)$.

For a given data set, the initialization produced by Initialization II is always fixed. Sometimes a bit of randomness might be desirable. In the third initialization strategy, we add randomness by picking the first medoid candidate randomly. The rest of the medoids are selected the same way as in Initialization II. We call this method Initialization III. The computational complexity of Initialization I, II and III are $\mathcal{O}(c)$, $\mathcal{O}(nc^2)$ and $\mathcal{O}(nc^2)$ respectively. We found that both Initialization II and III work well in practice.

The fuzzifier m in FCMdd determines the degree of fuzziness of the resulting clusters. Since the medoid always has a membership of 1 in the cluster, raising its membership to the power m has no effect. Thus, when m is high, the mobility of the medoids from iteration to iteration may be lost, because all memberships become very small except the one corresponding to the current medoid. For this reason, we recommend a value between 1 and 1.5 for m.

It can be seen from step (B) of FCMdd that the complexity of the algorithm is $\mathcal{O}(n^2)$, where n is the number of input objects. However, this is too expensive for most Web mining applications. To overcome this problem, we can modify step (B) of FCMdd so that it examines only a subset of objects while updating the medoid for cluster i. The subset we choose is the set of p objects in X that correspond to the top p highest membership values in cluster i. We denote this subset by $X_{(p)i}$. The subsets $X_{(p)i}$, $i = 1, 2, \ldots, c$, can be identified during the membership updating step, i.e., in step (A) of the algorithm. This increases the complexity of step (A) to $\mathcal{O}(ncp)$. However, the complexity of step (B) is reduced to $\mathcal{O}(ncp)$. Therefore, the overall complexity is linear in the number of objects. The value of p should be proportional to the dimensionality d of the data, e.g. $2d$. However, when the data is relational, d has no meaning. In such cases, p could be chosen to be much smaller than the average number (n/c) of points in a cluster. The modified FCMdd algorithm is summarized below.

Linearized Fuzzy c-Medoids Algorithm (LFCMdd)

Fix the number of clusters c; Set iter = 0;
Pick the initial set of medoids $\mathbf{V} = \{\mathbf{v}_1, \mathbf{v}_2, \ldots, \mathbf{v}_c\}$ from X^c;
Repeat
Compute memberships u_{ij} for $i = 1, 2, \ldots, c$, and $j = 1, 2, \ldots, n$, by using (13) and identify $X_{(p)i}$, $i = 1, 2, \ldots, c$. (A)
Store the current medoids: $\mathbf{V}^{old} = \mathbf{V}$;
Compute the new medoids $\mathbf{v}_i$ for $i = 1, 2, \ldots, c$:
$q = \operatorname{argmin}_{\mathbf{x}_k \in X_{(p)i}} \sum_{j=1}^{n} u_{ij}^m \, r(\mathbf{x}_k, \mathbf{x}_j)$ $\quad \mathbf{v}_i = \mathbf{x}_q$; (B)
$iter = iter + 1$;
Until $(\mathbf{V}^{old} = \mathbf{V}$ or $iter = MAX\_ITER)$.

4.1 Robust Versions of FCMdd

It is well-known that algorithms that minimize a Least-Squares type objective function are not robust [7, 37]. In other words, a single outlier object could lead to a very unintuitive clustering result. To overcome this problem, we design an objective function for a robust version of FCMdd based on the Least Trimmed Squares idea [22, 37], we use the membership function in (13). Substituting the expression for u_{ij} in (13) into (12), we obtain:

$$J_m(\mathbf{V}; \mathbf{X}) = \sum_{j=1}^{n} \left(\sum_{i=1}^{c} (r(\mathbf{x}_j, \mathbf{v}_i))^{1/(1-m)} \right)^{1-m} = \sum_{j=1}^{n} h_j, \tag{15}$$

where

$$h_j = \left(\sum_{i=1}^{c} (r(\mathbf{x}_j, \mathbf{v}_i))^{1/(1-m)} \right)^{1-m} \tag{16}$$

is $1/c$ times the harmonic mean of the dissimilarities $\{r(\mathbf{x}_j, \mathbf{v}_i)) : i = 1, \ldots, c\}$ when $m = 2$. The objective/criterion function of the Robust Fuzzy c Medoids (RFCMdd) algorithm is obtained by modifying (15) as follows:

$$J_m^T(\mathbf{V}; \mathbf{X}) = \sum_{k=1}^{s} h_{k:n}. \tag{17}$$

In (17), $h_{k:n}$ represents the k-th item when $h_j, j = 1, 2, \ldots, n$, are arranged in ascending order, and $s < n$. The value of s is chosen depending on how many objects we would like to disregard in the clustering process. This allows the clustering algorithm to ignore outlier objects while minimizing the objective function. For example, when $s = n/2$, 50% of the objects are not considered in the clustering process, and the objective function is minimized when we pick c medoids in such a way that the sum of the harmonic-mean dissimilarities of 50% of the objects is as small as possible. We can design the following heuristic algorithm to minimize (17).

The Robust Fuzzy c Medoids Algorithm (RFCMdd)

Fix the number of clusters c, and the fuzzifier m;
Pick the initial medoids $\mathbf{V} = \{\mathbf{v}_1, \mathbf{v}_2, \ldots, \mathbf{v}_c\}$ from X^c;
iter = 0;
Repeat
  Compute harmonic dissimilarities h_j for $j = 1, 2, \ldots, n$, using (16);
  Sort h_j, $j = 1, 2, \ldots, n$ to create $h_{j:n}$;
  Keep the s objects $\mathbf{x}_{1:n}, \ldots, \mathbf{x}_{s:n}$, corresponding to the first s $h_{j:n}$;
  Compute memberships $u_{ij:n}$ for $i = 1, 2, \ldots, c$ and $j : n = 1, 2, \ldots, s$, by using (13), and identify $X_{(p)i}$, $i = 1, 2, \ldots, c$;
  Store the current medoids: $\mathbf{V}^{old} = \mathbf{V}$;
  Compute the new medoids $\mathbf{v}_i$ for $i = 1, 2, \ldots, c$:
  $q = \underset{\mathbf{x}_{k:n} \in X_{(p)i}}{\operatorname{argmin}} \sum_{j=1}^{s} u_{ij:n}^{m} \, r(\mathbf{x}_{k:n}, \mathbf{x}_{j:n}); \qquad \mathbf{v}_i = \mathbf{x}_q;$
  $iter = iter + 1$;
Until $\left(\mathbf{V}^{old} = \mathbf{V} \text{ or } iter = MAX\_ITER\right)$.

As mentioned above, the choice of the retention ratio, s/n, should reflect the percentage of noise in the data. If the noise proportion is higher than 50%, we cannot guarantee that we will obtain the correct estimates for the parameters such as cluster center, variance, etc [7, 37]. A common approach in robust statistics is to assume that the noise proportion is 50% and then apply a correction to the estimate *after* the parameters have been (robustly) estimated [37]. For a known distribution (such as a Gaussian), the correction is given by a simple formula. In our application, since the data is relational, such corrections can be difficult to apply, except in a heuristic manner. Another option is to estimate the retention ratio when it is not known in advance. When estimation is not possible, our recommendation is that we estimate or pick a lowerbound for retention ratio and use it. This will at least ensure that the estimates are not affected by outliers. It is also possible to optimize the objective function with respect to the retension ratio. See for example [28, 30].

Interestingly, the worst-case complexity of the RFCMdd algorithm still remains $\mathcal{O}(n\log n)$. This is a good result, considering that robust algorithms are very expensive. A robust fuzzy clustering algorithm based on the Least Median of Squares idea, presented in [27], can easily me extended to relational clustering as well. In this case we simply replace the summation in (17) by the median. In other words, we use

$$J_m^M(\mathbf{V}; \mathbf{X}) = \underset{1 \le k \le n}{\operatorname{median}} \, h_{k:n}. \tag{18}$$

A genetic algorithm was used to optimize this criterion in [27].

4.2 Experimental Results

To validate the capacity of our algorithms to extract user access patterns, we ran several experiments comparing FCMdd with NERF . Both the naive and the linearized implementations of FCMdd were used. The experiments were done on a number of Web server logs obtained from servers at the University of Maryland - Baltimore County (UMBC). We report here a subset of our experimental results, on log sizes that represent a quarter days activity to five days of activity in April 2000, on the UMBC CSEE Web server. Instead of reporting the number of hits in each log, we report here the number of sessions generated from a log since the clustering algorithm operates on the sessions. In the case of FCMdd, we overspecify the number of clusters to be 50. The same number of clusters (50) was used for NERF as well.

The intracluster distance for most clusters (average 0.343) was much smaller than the intercluster distance (average, 0.996), although there are a few exceptions, such as cluster 0 (0.998). This cluster represented an aggregation of all course related URLs.

Given that in the linearized implementation, we are using only a fraction of the possible medoid candidates at each update step, one might expect that the clusters formed may not be as good as the regular implementation. However, we found that the LFCMdd generated better clusters than the regular implementation for many of our logs. In fact, the average intra cluster distance was 0.343 for the linearized version as opposed to 0.435 for the regular implementation. We speculate that this is because of the "local" nature of the search used by the linearized version. The linearized version confines its search for the medoid of a cluster to the neighborhood of the current medoid. This means that given a good initialization, this method can find good "localized" clusters. The regular implementation does a more global search and sometimes could get stuck in strange minima.

We provide brief descriptions of the clusters generated by our algorithm. Table 7 lists some of the clusters found. Recall that the clusters were generated by overspecifying the number of clusters to be 50 and then determining the actual number c_{actual} using the procedure described in Section 2.4. When the cardinality of a cluster is too low (in our case when less than 30), the cluster was considered as not having enough support, and thus was not listed. For illustration purposes, we show here the top level URLs found, and in the table show the sum of the strengths of the underlying URLs. For instance, if a cluster has the URL ~plusquel/ with strength 0.8 and ~plusquel/cmsc310 with strength 0.7, we will report it here as ~plusquel with strength 1.5.

The clusters seemed fairly consistent across logs worth several days. In other words, similar (though not identical) clusters were formed as we mined different sized logs from the same time period. In our analysis, we chose to disregard clusters that had a very small cardinality (number of sessions in them). In traditional data mining jargon, one would say that there was not enough support for such clusters. We also ignored those clusters that did not have a strong URL profile as explained in Section 2.4.

- Clusters 0 (/agentslist/) and 20 (/agents/) contain user sessions that accessed the pages maintained by the Agents group at UMBC.
- Cluster 2 (/help/oracle/) represents user sessions that accessed the help pages of oracle8, likely to be from students enrolled in the undergraduate and graduate database courses.
- Cluster 6 (/www/) represents user sessions that accessed an older version of the CSEE Web pages.
- Cluster 9 (/471/) represents users who want to access the CMSC 471 course pages. It contains hits to pages containing current information, lectures and notes.
- Clusters 11 (/cgi-bin/) represents access to the queries provided on the server using CGI scripts.
- Cluster 19 (/~ugrad) represents users who accessed Web pages that provides brochures and admission information for undergraduates.
- Clusters 21 (/courses/) contains user sessions that access information about the courses offered by the CS department. Given the enrollment differences, a larger support is found for /courses/undergrad/ as opposed to /courses/graduate/, as expected.
- Clusters 3 (/~kalpakis), 13 (/~qlu2) and 18 (/~mikeg) correspond to user sessions that accessed home pages of individual users.
- The remaining lusters have cardinalities that are too small to be included in the study.

5 Creating Personalized Web Pages Using Adaptive Web Servers

Traditionally, adaptive Web site development has been limited to the use of data obtained from the user by filling out "registration" type forms. Sites such as http://my.netscape.com/ and http://my.cnn.com/ create a personalized Web page, based only on such declarative information. Typically, these sites list all possible categories of information and leave it to the user to select or de-select a particular category of information. The user can also decide the layout by placing items of relative importance above other items. Intelligence derived from tracking a single user can be used to create adaptive Web pages that show his/her interests as well as recommend similar pages. Amazon.com uses collaborative filtering to direct customers to items bought by other customers who purchased the same item. These methods either use declarative information or track a single user to obtain profiles. These methods have raised privacy concerns since they often deal with personal and identifying information.

Table 7. CSEE Logs Analysis using Linear FCMdd Algorithm (clusters with more than 30 sessions)

Cluster	Cardinal	URLs	URLs	Deg
0 - /agentslist/	628	3864	{/agentslist/*}	1.511
			{/agentslist/archive/*}	1.449
2 - /help/oracle8/	41	241	{/help/*}	6.976
			{/help/oracle8/*}	6.585
			{/help/oracle8/server803*}	4.488
			{/help/oracle8/server803/ A54654_01/*}	1.098
3 - /~kalpakis/	46	137	{/~kalpakis/*}	3.543
			{/~kalpakis/Courses/*}	1.761
			{/~kalpakis/Courses/441/*}	1.326
6 -/www/	32	104	{/www/*}	3.156
			{/www/graduate/*}	2.531
			{/www/graduate/rpg/*}	1.156
9 -/471/	60	893	{/471/*}	14.167
			{/471/current/*}	5.45
			{/471/current/lectures/*}	4.333
			{/471/lectures/*}	5.25
			{/471/lectures/uninformed-search/*}	1.05
			{/471/notes/*}	3.333
			{/471/notes/7/*}	1.05
11 -/cgi-bin/	76	358	{/cgi-bin/*}	4.171
			{/cgi-bin/raw?url=http:/*}	3.776
			{/agents/*}	2.697
13 -/~qlu2/	49	12	{/~qlu2/*}	1.837
16 -/~sli2/	236	203	{/~sli2/*}	13.86
			{/~sli2/cube/*}	9.932
			{/~sli2/plot*}	2.085
18 -/~mikeg/	81	90	{/~mikeg/*}	3.012
20 -/agents/	466	1544	{/agents/*}	3.406
21 -/courses/	1048	3443	{/courses/*}	7.889
			{/courses/undergraduate/*}	6.776
			{/courses/undergraduate/201/*}	2.512

Our work uses a very simple way to profile users without revealing any personal information about them. In our system, an apache module places a cookie on the users machine. This cookie is generated using the *mod_usertrack* option which generates a random unique number for a user and places it as the cookie on the users machine. The logs generated also do not contain user ids as *identd* is not used when a hit is registered. Hence, creating a mapping between user ids and their cookie information is also not possible. A user visiting a Web page, is viewed as one of the users belonging to a cluster which has behavior patterns similar to his or her own. This method has the advantage of not revealing any private profile information about a user, but at the same time generating a *personalized* page for the user.

Assume that the user is interested in the class pages for CMSC 771 and CMSC 661. This information is inferred from her inclusion in the groups of users frequenting the pages for CMSC 771 and CMSC 661. Thus the list of URLs, she might be interested in is compiled on the basis of the groups, she belongs to. Page titles and snippets for the URL are also displayed along with the link to the page to make her task of identifying the page simpler. Thus, a user coming to the UMBC CS page would be shown a lists of URLs which she frequents on the UMBC CS server. A link to the default CS page is also provided, in case the user is interested in looking up some information not presented on his personal page.

Recent experiments in comparing the usage of IP addresses verses cookies have concluded cookies to generate more accurate user sessions than IP addresses.

Cookies are unique to a user and are placed on the user's machine, the first time the user accesses the particular Web server. Every access to the Web server after the first hit, registers the hit belonging to the user's cookie. No mapping between a user and a cookie is maintained, hence keeping the users identification unknown.

5.1 Experimental Setup of Personalizing Tool and Results

The module is coded in Mod Perl and runs on Apache HTTP Server 1.2.5. Cookies with a unique number were generated using the *mod_usertrack* module and placed on the user's machine. Every hit on the website registers an entry on the server logs along with the cookie information.

Session files consisting of the unique session numbers and the cookie related to the particular session were generated. Clusters are generated for the Web logs using the sessions. A cluster file consists of the mapping of the session number and the cluster it belongs to. Having assigned sessions to a cluster, profiles have to be generated for each cluster. A profile for a cluster is defined as the most common URLs belonging to sessions, which in turn belong to the cluster. An apache module generates a Web page on the fly for a user coming to the site. The user's cookie is examined to determine the sessions corresponding to his or her traversal patterns. If no cookie is present or if no matching sessions for the cookie are found, the user is shown the default page. Otherwise, further processing is carried out to generate their personalized page.

For each session matching the cookie, corresponding clusters are obtained. A user might have multiple sessions recorded in the logs. Different sessions could point to different clusters i.e. traversal patterns or may point to the same cluster. In case of different traversal patterns, URLs from different clusters are displayed on the personalized page, grouped by their appearance in the clusters. A snippet of information is also provided along with the link to the page.

Clusters for the experiment were generated from logs obtained from servers at the Computer Science Department at UMBC. In the snapshot provided, the user falls into multiple categories. The user accesses the pages related to Knowledge Query and Manipulation Language (KQML), the pages related to the CIKM 2000 conference and also the pages related to the 471 class at UMBC. These different categories denote the different *modes* in which the user uses the CS Web pages. A user might show a single traversal pattern on a Web server or a pattern which is a combination of different traversal patterns. Figure 1 shows links related to the user's traversal pattern on the CS server.

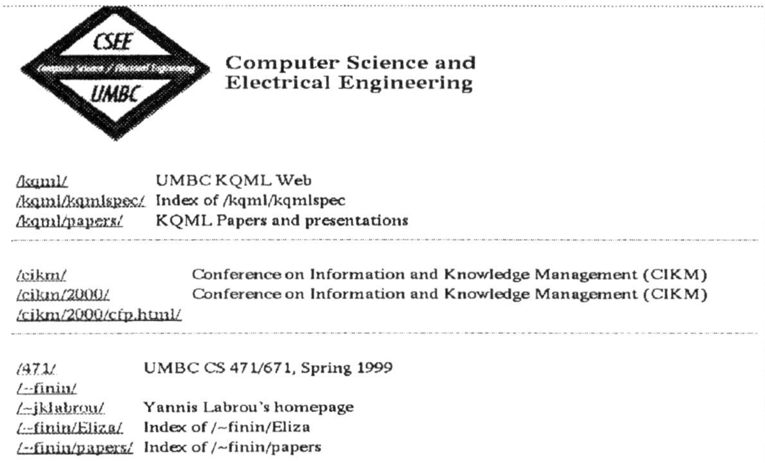

Fig. 1. Adaptive Web page for a Web user

6 Conclusions

We have presented a new approach for the automatic discovery of user session profiles in Web log data based on robust fuzzy relational clustering. We defined the notion of a "user session" as being a temporally compact sequence of Web accesses by a user. A new similarity measure to analyze session profiles is presented which captures both the individual URLs in a profile as well as the structure of the site. we have presented new relational fuzzy clustering algorithms (RFCMdd and RFC−MDE) that have the capacity to handle complex noisy and fuzzy Web usage data, and used them to successfully cluster the sessions extracted from real server access logs into typical user session profiles, and even to identify the noisy sessions and profiles. The resulting clusters are evaluated subjectively, as well as based on standard statistical criteria. The criteria used were the intra-cluster and inter-cluster distances, and the significance of the components of a session "profile" vector which also summarizes the typical sessions in each cluster. Our experiments on real data sets showed that our approach outperformed NERF in extracting profiles from the Web access logs, and in identifying noisy sessions.

We also presented an approach to personalize the Web space by generating pages dynamically based on off-line clustering of Web logs. Web logs were sessionized using cookies. These adaptive Web pages can reduce network traffic by directly showing a user to the page of his or her interest without them having to look around for it. Such an approach also mitigates the issue of security since no personal or declarative information is obtained from a user to present "personalized" pages. In ongoing work, we are examining the scalability of the system and extending it to examine logs and add results in an incremental fashion to existing results. Also, a study as to whether the users find such personalized pages to be relevant and to what extent, is being carried out.

Note that in some applications, the frequency of accesses to a Web page (or alternately, the viewing time) within the same session may be important. In that case, the definition of $\mathbf{s}_j^{(k)}$ should be modified to the number of times the jth URL is accessed in the kth session (or alternately, some measure of relative viewing time). In ongoing experiments, we are also looking into a multi-resolution profiling approach where clustering is applied recursively on the profiles found in previous runs.

Acknowledgements

Partial support of this work by the National Science Foundation Grants IIS 9800899 and IIS 9801711 is gratefully acknowledged. This work was also partially supported by a Faculty Research Initiation Grant from the University of Memphis to Olfa Nasraoui.

References

1. R. Agrawal and R. Srikant. Fast algorithms for mining association rules. In *Proceedings of the 20th VLDB Conference*, pages 487–499, Santiago, Chile, 1994.
2. R. Armstrong, T. Joachims D. Freitag, and T. Mitchell. Webwatcher: A learning apprentice for the World Wide Web. In *Proceedings of the AAAI Spring Symposium on Information Gathering from Heterogeneous, Distributed Environments*, pages 6–13, Stanford, CA, March 1995.
3. G. Arocena and A. Mendelz. Weboql: Restructuring documents, databases, and web. In *Proc. IEEE Intl. Conf. Data Engineering '98*. IEEE Press, 1998.
4. P. Bajcsy and N. Ahuja. Location- and density-based hierarchical clustering using similarity analysis. *IEEE Transactions on Pattern Analysis and Machine Intelligence*, 20:1011–1015, 1998.

5. J. C. Bezdek. *Pattern Recognition with Fuzzy Objective Function Algorithms.* Plenum Press, New York, 1981.
6. R. Cooley, B. Mobasher, and J. Srivasta. Web Mining: Information and pattern discovery on the World Wide Web. In *Proc. IEEE Intl. Conf. Tools with AI*, pages 558–567, Newport Beach, CA, 1997.
7. R. N. Davé and R. Krishnapuram. Robust clustering methods: A unified view. *IEEE Transactions on Fuzzy Systems*, 5(2):270–293, 1997.
8. E. Diday. La methode des nuees dynamiques. *Rev. Stat. Appliquee*, XIX(2):19–34, 1975.
9. U. Fayad, G. Piatetsky-Shapiro, and P. Smyth. From data mining to knowledge discovery: An overview. In U. Fayad, G. Piatetsky-Shapiro, P. Smyth, and R. Uthurusamy, editors, *Advances in Knowledge Discovery and Data Mining.* AAAI/MIT Press, 1996.
10. H. Frigui and R. Krishnapuram. Clustering by competitive agglomeration. *Pattern Recognition*, 30(7):1223–1232, 1997.
11. K. S. Fu. *Syntactic Pattern Recognition and Applications.* Academic Press, San Diego, CA, 1982.
12. K. C. Gowda and E. Diday. Symbolic clustering using a new similarity measure. *IEEE Transactions on Systems, Man, and Cybernetics*, 20:368–377, 1992.
13. S. Guha, R. Rastogi, and K. Shim. CURE: An efficient algorithm for large databases. In *Proceedings of SIGMOD '98*, pages 73–84, Seattle, June 1998.
14. D. E. Gustafson and W. C. Kessel. Fuzzy clustering with the fuzzy covariance matrix. In *Proccedings of IEEE CDC*, pages 761–766, San Diego, California, 1979.
15. R. J. Hathaway and J. C. Bezdek. Switching regression models and fuzzy clustering. *IEEE Transactions on Fuzzy Systems*, 1(3):195–204, 1993.
16. R. J. Hathaway and J. C. Bezdek. NERF c-means: Non-Euclidean relational fuzzy clustering. *Pattern Recognition*, 27:429–437, 1994.
17. R.J. Hathaway, J.W. Devenport, and J.C. Bezdek. Relational dual of the c-means clustering algorithms. *Pattern Recognition*, 22(2):205–212, 1989.
18. A. Joshi, C. Punyapu, and P. Karnam. Personalization and asynchronicity to support mobile web access. In *Proc. Workshop on Web Information and Data Management, 7th Intl. Conf. on Information and Knowledge Management*, November 1998.
19. A. Joshi, S. Weerawarana, and E. Houstis. On disconnected browsing of distributed information. In *Proceedings of IEEE Intl. Workshop on Research Issues in Data Engineering (RIDE)*, pages 101–108, Birmingham, UK, 1997.
20. L. Kaufman and P. J. Rousseeuw. Clustering by means of medoids. In Y. Dodge, editor, *Statistical Data Analysis Based on the L_1 Norm*, pages 405–416. North Holland/Elsevier, Amsterdam, 1987.
21. L. Kaufman and P. J. Rousseeuw. *Finding Groups in Data, An Itroduction to Cluster Analysis.* John Wiley & Sons, Brussels, Belgium, 1990.
22. J. Kim, R. Krishnapuram, and R. N. Davé. Application of the least trimmed squares technique to prototype-based clustering. *Pattern Recognition Letters*, 17:633–641, 1996.
23. R. Krishnapuram and J. M. Keller. A possibilistic approach to clustering. *IEEE Transactions on Fuzzy Systems*, 1(2):98–110, 1993.
24. O. Nasraoui, H. Frigui, R. Krishnapuram, and A. Joshi. Mining web access logs using relational competitive fuzzy clustering. In *Eighth International Fuzzy Systems Association Congress*, Hsinchu, Taiwan, Aug. 1999.

25. O. Nasraoui and R. Krishnapuram. Crisp interpretation of fuzzy and possibilistic clustering algorithms. In *3rd European Congress on Intelligent Techniques and Soft Computing*, volume 3, pages 1312–1318, Aachen, Germany, Aug. 1995.
26. O. Nasraoui and R. Krishnapuram. A robust estimator based on density and scale optimization, and its application to clustering. In *IEEE International Conference on Fuzzy Systems*, pages 1031–1035, New Orleans, LA, Sep. 1996.
27. O. Nasraoui and R. Krishnapuram. A genetic algorithm for robust clustering based on a fuzzy least median of squares criterion. In *Proceedings of NAFIPS'97*, pages 217–221, Syracuse, NY, Sept. 1997.
28. O. Nasraoui and R. Krishnapuram. Mining web access logs using a relational clustering algorithm based on a robust estimator. In *Proc. of the Eighth International World Wide Web Conference*, pages 40–41, Toronto, 1999.
29. O. Nasraoui, R. Krishnapuram, H. Frigui, and Joshi A. Extracting web user profiles using relational competitive fuzzy clustering. *International Journal on Artificial Intelligence Tools*, 9(4):509–526, 2000.
30. O. Nasraoui, R. Krishnapuram, and A. Joshi. Relational clustering based on a new robust estimator with application to web mining. In *Proceedings of the North American Fuzzy Information Society*, pages 705–709, New York City, 1999.
31. R. T. Ng and J. Han. Efficient and effective clustering methods for spatial data mining. In *Proceedings of the 20th VLDB Conference*, pages 144–155, Santiago, Chile, Sept. 1994.
32. O.Zaiane and J. Han. Webml: Querying the world-wide web for resources and knowledge. In *Proc. Workshop on Web Information and Data Management*, 7th *Intl. Conf. on Information and Knowledge Management*, 1998.
33. M. Perkowitz and O. Etzioni. Adaptive web sites: an ai challenge. In *Proc. Intl. Joint Conf. on AI - IJCAI97*, 1997.
34. M. Perkowitz and O. Etzioni. Adaptive web sites: Automatically synthesizing web pages. In *Proc. AAAI 98*, 1998.
35. G. D. Ramkumar and A. Swami. Clustering data without distance functions. *Bulletin of the IEEE Computer Society Technical Committee on Data Engineering*, 21:9–14, 1998.
36. M. Roubens. Pattern classification problems and fuzzy sets. *Fuzzy Sets and Systems*, 1:239–253, 1978.
37. P. J. Rousseeuw and A. M. Leroy. *Robust Regression and Outlier Detection.* John Wiley and Sons, New York, 1987.
38. T. A. Runkler and J. C. Bezdek. ACE: A tool for clustering and rule extraction. *IEEE Transactions on Fuzzy Systems*, 1999.
39. E. H. Ruspini. Numerical methods for fuzzy clustering. *Information Science*, 2:319–350, 1970.
40. C. Shahabi, A. M. Zarkesh, J. Abidi, and V. Shah. Knowledge discovery from user's web-page navigation. In *Proceedings of the IEEE Intl. Workshop on Research Issues in Data Engineering (RIDE)*, pages 20–29, Birmingham, UK, 1997.
41. U. Shardanand and P. Maes. Social information filetering: Algorithms for automating 'word of mouth'. In *Proc. CHI'95 Conference on Human Factors in Computing Systems*, New York, 1995. ACM Press.
42. P. H. A. Sneath and R. R. Sokal. *Numerical Taxonomy - The Principles and Practice of Numerical Classification.* W. H. Freeman, San Francisco, 1973.

43. Y. El Sonbaty and M. A. Ismail. Fuzzy clustering for symbolic data. *IEEE Transactions on Fuzzy Systems*, 6:195–204, 1998.
44. L. Terveen, W. Hill, and B. Amento. PHOAKS - a system for sharing recommendations. *Communications of the ACM*, 40(3):59–62, 1997.
45. M. P. Windham. Numerical classification of proximity data with assignment measures. *Journal of Classification*, 2:157–172, 1985.

Fuzzy Quantifiable Trust in Secure E-Commerce

Daniel W Manchala

Xerox Research and Technology, Xerox Corporation

Abstract. Traditional models of trust between vendors and buyers fall short of requirements for an electronic marketplace, where anonymous transactions cross territorial and legal boundaries as well as traditional value chain structures. Fuzzy quantifications of trust may offer better evaluations of transaction risk in this environment.
How do we set measurement criteria to make these distinctions? One way is to quantify *trust*. This fundamental concept in managing commercial risk refers broadly to the assurance that someone or something will act in exactly the way you expect. Research on this problem in e-commerce has focused on *authentication*— that is, associating a public key with its owner [11]. However, all these models were based on *transitive trust* along a transaction path of entities that trust the key to different extents. E-commerce, on the other hand, requires *mutual trust* among a vendor, a customer, and all transaction intermediaries. This article introduces a notion of fuzzy quantifiable trust and then develops models that can use these metrics to verify e-commerce transactions in ways that might be able to satisfy the requirements of mutual trust. The article attempts to define fuzzy quantifiable trust for an e-commerce infrastructure.

1 Risk Evaluation with Trust Metrics

Although no single unit of measure is adequate to the definition of trust, several dependent variables, such as cost, can be used to describe it. These variables in turn influence action protocols that can be used to evaluate the risk involved in an e-commerce transaction. The article describes several variables used to calculate the overall risk on a transaction. These include the cost on a transaction, transaction history over the participants, indemnity, etc.

Several entities are involved in an e-commerce transaction. Risk is evaluated at each of the major entities (nodes) involved in the transaction. Other entities involved in the transaction might provide a fuzzy referral. Based on the fuzzy information gathered by each of the major transacting entities, suitable trust actions are triggered that catalyses the transaction to complete. These actions include various kinds of verification that in turn grant, deny, request-guardian-referral or guarantor-referral.

The following sections illustrate fuzzy processing of information in an e-commerce transaction using two examples.

1.1 Internet Commerce Printing

In this example, several users send a request to print copies of user-supplied documents to a commercial print shop server that distributes both the print requests and user-supplied documents to various printers at different locations[6]. The print request details the number of copies to be printed, whether to print as black and white or as color, the paper size and quality, and the desired print location. For instance, someone planning to give a conference presentation in Washington, D.C., might send a print request from Los Angeles to a commercial print shop, asking that the presentation copies be available at the conference location in Washington on a specified date and time. The print shop makes the arrangements and collects payment. Various electronic payment mechanisms including digital cash [2], electronic cheques [10], charging the customer's credit card [13] or account [4] or even an automatable payment selection process [3] may be used upon completing the print task.

1.2 Internet Stock Trading

In this example, several traders buy and sell stocks from a stock exchange through a stockbroker. Each stockbroker collects information on how many shares or bonds to trade and at what time and price from each of the traders. The broker collects a certain fee for the services and attempts to trade on behalf of the traders based on each trader's constraints. The broker may also help in online trade transaction services by providing timely stock price information based on the trader's profile of what shares are owned and how much profit would be made when sold at a particular time. Most of these kinds of transactions take place today using the Transaction Layer Security (TLS) [6] protocol and may use identification certificates such as the X.509 certificate [7].

2 Transaction Based Risk

In this section we define a few terms used in this document to introduce formal constructs that represent and reason transaction based risk.

2.1 Notation and Definitions

Transacting Entity: Any entity that engages itself in an electronic commerce transaction is a transacting entity. This entity could be a customer (C), a vendor (V), a broker (B), an intelligent agent (IA), a payment server or any intermediary (for example a trusted intermediary TI).

Trust Authority: Trust matrices are used to evaluate the trust on a certain transaction or on the next set of transactions. Unless these trust matrices are protected against manipulation and are maintained by certain authorities, transacting entities cannot *trust* them. These authorities are called Trust Authorities (TA). Transacting entities use trust protocols to access these trust matrices. A TA maintains trust matrices by updating them based on the information they receive from each completed transaction. The TA should be able to provide proof to trust matrix updates using non-repudiation services. In addition, it should be able to provide upon request to each of the transacting entities the level of trust (index) that could be placed on a certain transaction.

Agreement Framework φ: A relationship binding all the transacting entities involved in a single set of transactions. The relationship usually includes various policies for conducting transactions and is usually placed at a TA. Each set of transactions is interpreted based on the policy, and the results are used to update trust matrices [12].

Threshold θ: A measure of trust below which a transacting entity is fully trusted and hence the transaction need not be verified.

Belief β: The possibility that the next set of transactions is fully trust-worthy and hence would yield complete revenue.

Merge Operator: Arithmetic operator that acts on two trust relations to yield a single trust relation which reflects the trust between two neighboring entities involved in the transaction. This is used for trust propagation.

Transaction σ: A transaction is defined as consisting of a set of transaction entities π, a set of end transaction entities $\omega \subseteq \pi$, a set of protocol paths γ, each path identified by a set of transaction entities, a set of states δ = {*fail, success, attack, in-progress*}, mode of operation μ = {*purchase, trust-index, preventive, recovery, correction*}, acknowledgement messages τ_a = {*complete, complaint, query, suspicion*}, trading messages τ_b and an agreement framework φ. Therefore, $\sigma = (\pi,\omega,\gamma,\delta,\mu,\tau,\varphi)$. Note that under anonymous mode, $\omega = \pi$.

Semantic Relationship: A semantic relationship exists between two trust variable sets X and Y *iff* the elements of the relationship X x Y quantifiably measures trust, the current state of the entity can be represented by one of the elements of X, the state of the current transaction set can be represented by one of the elements of Y and the policy of the agreement framework AF set up at the trust authority TA honors the action Z between X and Y.

The trust variable set *Transaction History* is semantically related to another trust variable set *Number of Microtransactions* since the current state of one of the transacting entities (a customer) can be represented by *Transaction History* and the state of the current transaction set is represented by *Number of Microtransactions*. However, the trust variable set "*Transaction History*" may or may not be related to "*Cost of Transaction*". This depends upon the policy dictated by the action Z as to whether it is "*Verification of a Transaction*" or "*Price of Goods*" set by the agreement framework AF implying whether this relationship should have the action Z of verifying a transaction or setting the price of goods respectively.

Trust Variable	Measurement Bands				
Key Mechanism	Investigative Order	Dual Key	Public Key	One-way Hash	Simple Hash
Verification Frequency	Every Transaction	Smaller Intervals	Medium Sized Intervals	Widely Spaced Intervals	Large Variation
Loyalty	First time Customers	Low	Transfer	Good	Very Good
Cost of Transaction	Expensive	Highcost	Medium Cost	Small Cost	Negligible

Fig. 1. Relationship between certain Trust Variables and Trust Actions.

As shown in Figure 1, transactions involving negligible cost use a simple hash or a password scheme. Expensive transactions require an OOB (out of band) technique such as a background investigation. For example, this may involve calling up and contacting references. Similarly, the frequency on verification of negligible cost transactions may imply that the verification between two consecutive microtransactions could be large. On the other hand, every expensive transaction may have to be verified. Thus verification frequency and secure key-mechanism employed depends upon loyal status of customer, transaction cost and etc.

Definition 2.1 Electronic Commerce Trust Relationship ECTR: A trust variable set X is ECT related to another trust variable set Y if there exists a semantic relationship between the two sets over an action Z. An ECTR is represented by a trust matrix T.

$$T = \{((x, y), z) \mid (x, y) \in X\text{x}Y, z \in Z\} \quad (1)$$

Example: Consider Figure 2, which describes a transaction based trust matrix with the *Transaction History* of a certain customer on the y-axis, and the *Cost of Transaction* on the x-axis. *Transaction History* of a customer is a statistical quantity that is computed by taking into account several previous transactions of a customer. To a certain extent this resembles the credit history of a consumer. Transaction history can by restricted to a certain class of products, one trust matrix for each class; examples of classes being groceries, books, accounting software, mathematical software, etc. From the figure, one can infer that no matter what the cost of a single transaction is, every transaction is verified (for authenticity, proof of origin, etc.) for customers with the worst transaction history. However, not every transaction needs to be verified or checked for low (micro or small) cost transactions if the customer happens to have an excellent transaction history. A single matrix entity represented by the letter 'V' signifies that each and every transaction should be verified. All entities, which do not have a 'V', are grouped into a zone called the *Trust Zone.* Transactions in the *Trust Zone* need not be verified. The boundary of a trust zone is called a trust contour.

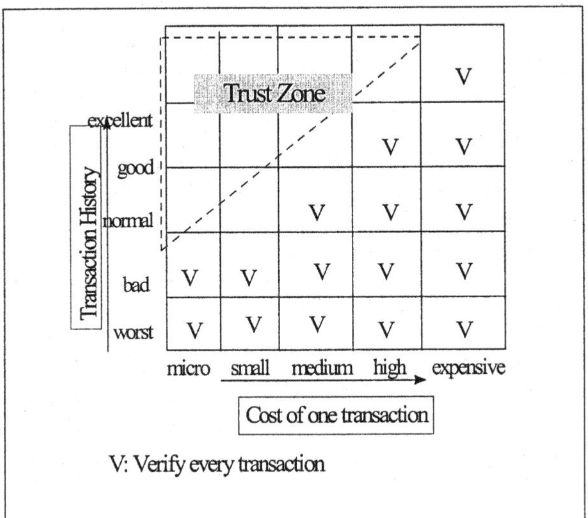

Fig. 2. Trust Matrix between *Cost of Transaction*, and *Transaction History.*

Axiom 2.1: Trust Zone is bounded.

Explanation: The transacting capability of a customer A is bounded by a trust contour within which transactions can occur without verification. The customer cannot make purchases beyond what the vendor can sell, neither can the vendor have a price tag on too small a cost of item whose value is a fraction of a micro-transaction in which case the item is free of cost; hence cost of transaction is bounded by the limits set on the trust matrix. Trust is extended only to a small set of customers whose transaction history is within limits. A customer's transaction history is thus bounded.

3 Fuzzy Trust Models

The relationship between trust variables and actions could best be represented using trust models. The article first starts with Boolean trust models along with its inaccurate prediction and defines fuzzy trust models and how these models could be used effectively to determine the value of a transaction with each of the transacting entities.

Interactions between the transacting entities lead us to redefine the fuzzy values at each node using certain propagation algorithms. The distributed nature of these fuzzy evaluations together with an intelligent update of customer or vendor values poses significant challenges both in design and management.

It is useful to provide linguistic terms like micro-cost transaction, excellent transaction history, etc., to describe trust variables like cost of transaction or transaction history which enables transacting entities to easily describe their measurement units. Such description could be in the form of rules on which computations could be made using fuzzy expert systems [11]. The actions may also have to be weighted to make a meaningful difference between the various degrees of measurement. For example, it does not make sense to verify a transaction for a person with the worst transaction history when purchasing a high cost transaction to the same extent as a person with good history when purchasing a low-cost transaction. These verification strengths should be weighted.

Definition 3.1 Weighted Trust Surface WTS and Fuzzy Trust Surface FTS: The WTS of an ECTR is defined as the surface defined by the elements of T that are below and under a certain threshold θ. A FTS is generated by replacing the numeric values by fuzzy subsets of linguistic values. The value of θ is derived by taking into account the loss of the current set of transactions being amortized by the revenue on the previous sets of transactions and a belief β on the revenue on future sets of transactions.

Example: Figure 3 explains how more trust is placed on customers who have a good transaction history compared to one who has a worst transaction history when both make excessively large number of micro-transactions by verifying transactions at regularly spaced intervals. For example, a customer having excellent transaction history has one in fifty (*V/50*) transactions verified for transactions done in a session when the number of transactions are excessively large in number. For a customer with worst transaction history, not only is each and every transaction verified, but each and every transaction may be verified thoroughly (probably by consulting other vendors, trusted intermediaries, previous transactions, etc.). This may be represented by a stronger *V*, say *20V*. Thus a weighted trust surface is formed with peaks at *20V* and valleys at *V/70*. The so formed weighed trust matrix is still cumbersome, since it is difficult to play with numbers; and what exactly does *20V* mean compared to say *10V*. Developing a fuzzy logic based [16] trust matrix (Figure 4) using linguistic terms allows easy interpretation of the matrix entities. Fuzzy trust matrix can be replaced by a set of fuzzy membership functions that could be useful in reasoning.

Definition 3.2 Zadeh's Compositional Rule of Inference: Let $R(x)$, $R(x, y)$ and $R(y)$ where $x \in X$, $(x, y) \in XxY$, and $y \in Y$ be fuzzy relations in X, XxY and Y respectively. Let A and B denote particular fuzzy sets in X and XxY. Then the compositional rule of inference asserts that the solution of $R(x) = A$ and $R(x, y) = B$ is given by $R(y) = AoB$ where AoB is the composition of A and B [17].

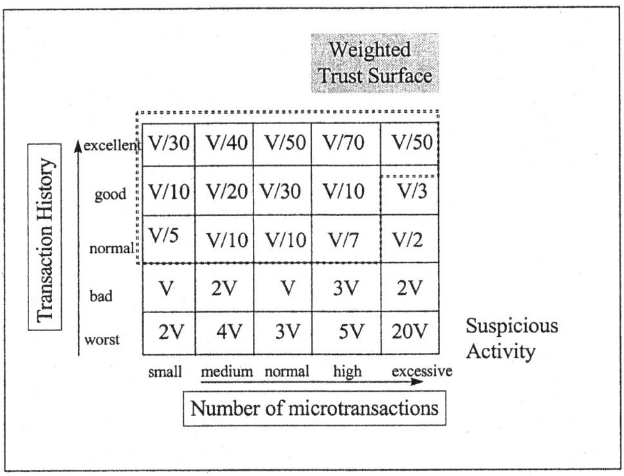

Fig. 3. Weighted Verification of Transactions.

Application 3.1 Fuzzy Logic Inference: Let A and B be fuzzy sets defined over X and Y respectively. A fuzzy rule $A \rightarrow B$ is first transformed into fuzzy relation $R_{A \rightarrow B}$ that represents a correlation between A and B and is defined as [16].

$$\mu_R(x, y) = \min(\mu_A(x), \mu_B(y));\ x \in X, y \in Y. \tag{2}$$

Given a fact A' and a rule $A \rightarrow B$, applying Zadeh's compositional rule gives

$$
\begin{aligned}
B' &= A' \circ R_{A \to B} \\
\mu_{B'}(y) &= \max_x \min(\mu_{A'}(x), \mu_R(x, y)) \\
&= \min(\alpha, \mu_B(y)) \text{ where } \alpha = \max \min(\mu_{A'}(x), \mu_A(x)).
\end{aligned} \tag{3}
$$

Fuzzy logic inference is used in building fuzzy expert systems to reason on trust parameters.

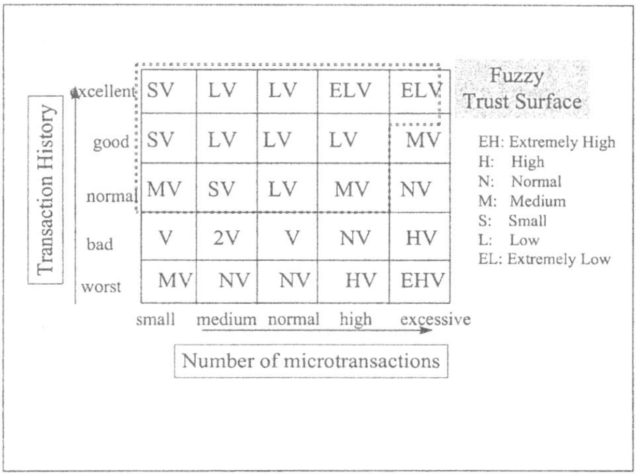

Fig. 4. A Fuzzy Trust Matrix

4 Commerce Related Attacks and Fuzzy Models

This section presents a number of commerce related attacks; how attacks can be detected, prevented, corrected, and how recovery from loss due to such attacks can be made possible. A transaction can be in any one of the following states: {*fail, success, in-progress, attack*}. A transaction is said to be successfully complete when the trust authority TA receives a *complete* acknowledgement from the end transacting entities ω. This does not guarantee that the current transaction will not switch to an attack state. The TI or TA may determine that the transaction is under attack and may transition the state of the transaction from success to attack state. A transaction is said to be in in-progress if the TA has not received a complete acknowledgement from the end transacting entities. A transaction is said to have failed if it has not received a complete message during the time allocated for the transaction (*trans-time*) defined in the agreement framework to complete or it receives a *complaint* or *suspicion* acknowledgement from one of the transacting entities. If the cause of the failure is due to a *complaint* or *suspicion*, the transaction is said to be under attack; the state of the transaction transitions from *in-progress* (or *fail*) to *attack*. When the transaction is in *attack* state, the transaction switches from its current mode (*buy, sell*, etc) to *preventive* mode to prevent the attacker from causing further damage due to the transaction by enabling stronger verification. The transacting entities are in a suspended state and cannot continue to process transactions while the transaction is in *preventive* mode. The transaction can simultaneously spawn off into other modes in parallel to perform loss *recovery* to recover from transaction losses if possible and *correction* to enable the victims to resume from suspended state. The following sections present a few attack scenarios and how they can be prevented or corrected using fuzzy models.

4.1 Stolen Token

Known security techniques using cryptographic methods is capable of preventing password sniffing over the wire thus preventing the theft of passwords or identity as they travel across the wire. Such security provides little benefit if the identity in the form of password or token (smart card or the computer that stores identity certificates) is stolen. Once stolen, the illegitimate customer impersonates the genuine customer and makes transactions over the Internet. Note that the impersonating customer may be making payments for goods bought, but these payments are not genuine since they were stolen from the genuine customer. Hence, in-time payments may not constitute enough proof of genuineness of the customer for this commerce-related attack. The best that could possibly be done is to limit the loss. Trust matrices could be used to reduce such loss or minimize risk involved in transactions.

One of the benefits of using trust matrices is that it limits an impersonator to make purchases only as much as the person whom is being impersonated could purchase. In other words, if the authorized person cannot purchase expensive goods, then the impersonator cannot purchase expensive goods.

Theorem 4.1: An impersonator X cannot cheat more than what the authorized person A can transact.

Proof: The transacting capability of a customer A is bounded by a trust contour within which transactions can occur without verification (Axiom 3.1). Any transaction that falls outside the trust contour subjects itself to verification upon which the impersonator X or the customer A has to provide *other* authentication and authorization information. Hence the impersonator's transactions are bounded by the customer's trust boundary. Any impersonator trying to make such a transaction would fail.

Lemma 4.1: The customer or the impersonator will have to improve their trustworthiness to make transactions outside the current trust boundary.

Detection by analyzing spending pattern: The observed characteristic of impersonators who steal tokens is to make as many purchases without detection as soon as possible before the theft/loss of the token is reported to the trust authority. For a not-so-frequent user, detecting a theft/loss of token is not fast enough to prevent the impersonator from making substantially large number of transactions. Usually, the spending pattern of the impersonator reveals the genuineness of the user. The trusted intermediaries or authorities, by observing these purchase patterns might detect such fraud before the genuine customer can detect.

Prevention by Timer-Delay Key Recovery: Once a suspicious spending pattern has been detected, further loss can be prevented by delaying the key delivery [14] to the impersonating customer. Key delivery is delayed until the receiving customer (genuine or impersonating) provides more secret-sensitive (bio-metrics, zero knowledge proofs, etc) information not contained in the stolen smart card or computer.

Correction and Transaction Recovery: Once identity is re-established, a new token is issued to the customer. Losses to the customer and vendor are covered under the agreement framework. However, recovery of information or services from the impersonator cannot be recovered or is rather hard, if the impersonator disappears soon after discovery.

Definition 4.1 Dynamic ECTR: An ECTR between X and Y over Z is said to be dynamic if the values of the elements of the trust matrix T it represents vary with respect to a parameter K.

Example: Figure 5 denotes a trust matrix between the "Transaction History", and the "Number of Transactions". From the figure, one can infer that mutual trust gets established with increased number of transactions. Conducting commerce by transacting many (suitably large number) transactions implies the loyalty of a customer to a particular vendor or trusted intermediary. However, an excessively large number of transactions should trigger suspicious activity. When a suspicious activity is triggered, every transaction is verified no matter what the Transaction History of the customer might be. Such a transaction activity might occur when a malicious intruder steals or confiscates the authentication token (smart card, computer with an installed private key), and impersonates the original owner (legal transacting entity). This is indicated in the trust matrix by placing a V in the entire column that represents excessive transactions (except for a customer who has excellent transaction history). Eventhough the trust matrix infers that customers who make excessively large number of transactions should be checked and verified, it ignores the fact that most customers in this category are indeed trustworthy and only certain customers who make excessively large number of transactions within a short span of time or in spurts should be verified. The parameter K is time over a certain set of transactions.

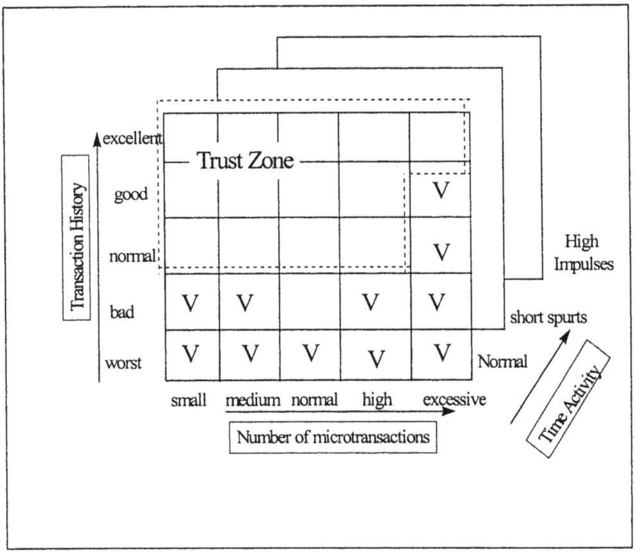

Fig. 5. Trust Matrix between *Number of Transactions*, and *Transaction History* w.r.t *Time Activity*.

4.2 Contour Discovery

One of the main weaknesses with the fuzzy trust matrices is its being prone to contour discovery attacks. An impersonating customer could try to discover the trust zone and make transactions such that none of the transactions could come under scrutiny that might enable the discovery of the impersonating character. An impersonator can discover the safe contour (trust boundaries) by watching several transactions between a trusted customer and the transacting vendor and thus expose the privacy held by the person. The impersonator can later replay similar types of transactions and receive free goods. The impersonator can thus cheat the vendor (and reduce the trustworthiness of the customer) by making several transactions within the discovered trust boundary. Once the contour has been discovered, the impersonator can perform extremely large number of transactions without making any payments. The impersonator can later disappear from the Internet just when discovered.

***Definition 4.2 Privacy Exposure*:** Discovery of the safe contour (trust boundaries) by watching several transactions between a trusted customer and the transacting vendor for a later replay thus exposing the commerce related trust privacy held by the person.

***Definition 4.3 Trust Regain Time/Period & Invalidated Contour*:** Amount of time defined in the agreement framework during which the trust contour is invalidated making each transaction to be verified before committing the transaction.

The vendor at that instant has no other choice but to declare the customer as having been impersonated. The vendor can continue to verify every transaction for a certain pre-determined trust-regain time, thus making the transaction-processing-time of each transaction time consuming during the trust regain period. Other security measures like creating new encryption keys for the trust base (set of trust matrices) are taken to prevent further attacks by the same impersonator.

Prevention by Random Perturbation: Prevention of contour discovery attacks can be achieved by using an audited trust zone i.e.; transactions within the trust zone are verified randomly instead of committing the transaction without security checks for authentication, authorization or trust.

Definition 4.4 Audited Trust Zone: A Trust Zone is said to be audited if the transactions in the Trust Zone could be randomly verified i.e., the transactions can be randomly selected for verification.

We therefore have:

V = 0	if transaction falls into trust zone and trust zone is in non-audited mode.
V = 1	if transaction lies outside the trust zone i.e. every transaction is verified.
V = R	a random number if transaction is in trust zone. Trust zone is in audited mode.

Within the trust region, the probability of verification is one-half, a transaction is either verified or not verified. Attackers may sometimes take a chance at this probability. In order to control the probability of verification, randomization can be modulated. As shown in the Figure below, region R_1 may be verified 70% of the time, whereas region R_3 may be verified 30% to 50% of the time varying with respect to time. Similar random modulation techniques have been applied to statistical data bases [1]; the reference also describes other techniques used for security control of statistical databases.

Definition 4.5 Random Modulated Fuzzy Set: The result of a fuzzy logic composition is modulated by a randomly generated number in order to preserve the audit properties of the trust contour. Thus, from application 4.1:

$$\begin{aligned} \mu_{B'}(y) &= \theta \otimes \max_x \min(\mu_{A'}(x), \mu_R(x, y)) \\ &= \theta \otimes \min(\alpha, \mu_B(y)) \end{aligned} \tag{4}$$

where $\alpha = \max \min (\mu_{A'}(x), \mu_A(x))$, θ is a random number, and $\otimes$ is a modulation operator that represents probability of selection.

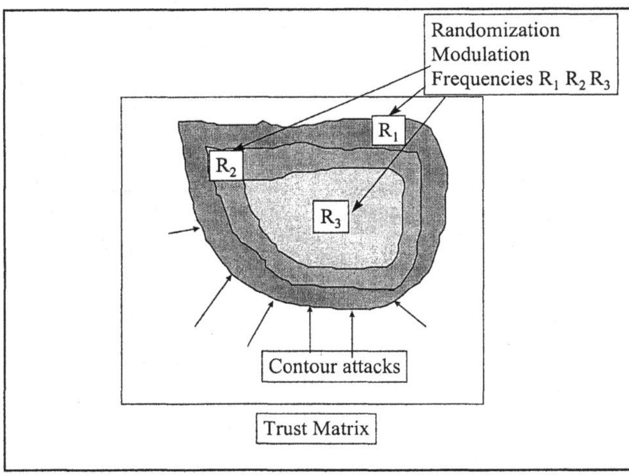

Fig. 6. Contour Attacks and Random Modulation on a Trust Matrix

4.3 Trust Manipulation

There is always a fear on part of the transacting entities that a malicious entity may destroy the trust threshold. For example, a malicious entity acting as a vendor may try to perform commerce with a customer having good reputation and later inform the trust authority of having not made genuine payments. A similar activity may destroy a vendor's reputation by a malicious customer. The customer may purchase several goods, but yet complain of low quality or defective goods. This reduces the trust index of the vendor. Even if transactions do not take place, malicious vendors or customers may influence changing the trust index of an honest transacting entity. Prevention of such activities can only be done by using suitable cryptographic protocols that provide a non-repudiable proof of completeness of transaction. These protocols should include proper identification techniques (authentication).

Definition 4.6: Trust Threshold Violation. Manipulation of the trust database by posting several illegitimate transactions with the intent of destroying a transacting entity's trust reputation and affecting the trust threshold thereby changing the trust index.

Detection, Correction, Prevention and Recovery: The use of strong cryptographic protocols [15] are used to prevent the occurrence of such attacks. These attacks are detected by an unusual change in overall trust index over a certain period of time and a sudden drop in trust threshold over a few transactions. To prevent further attacks, as a correctional method, the transacting entity is marked and trust index violation due to that entity is closely monitored. Once such an attack is detected, the victims trust index can easily be recovered using rollback techniques. This is one of the only attacks whose damage can be recovered.

4.4 Bogus Transactions

There are several occasions when a transacting entity may try to duplicate a transaction either by replaying the cost or type of transaction; this occurs especially when proper authentication procedures have not been followed, and provision has been made for reuse of cached security information. Such situations might occur when the transacting entities decide to forego strong authentication and encryption in favor of efficiency for micro to medium cost transactions. For example, a malicious entity could watch a set of transactions and observe the pattern of costs. This usually occurs for electronic services like CPU usage. It may then try to purchase services whose value is equal to the median cost of the set of transactions, and perhaps exactly the same as the transaction that was recently transacted. The unsuspecting vendor may bill this as a duplicate entry when actually a malicious entity made use of the CPU by using it for exactly the same time as a previous legal transaction. Intelligent agents are capable of controlling the exact CPU usage of procedures that wish to use a CPU. The best way to prevent such bogus transactions is to modulate the CPU price (vary it randomly around a mean value).

5 Propagation of Trust

Generally in the world of electronic commerce, a customer may need to interact with several trusted intermediaries before actually contacting the vendor. Some of these intermediaries may or may not have had a trusted relationship between them. In cases where a trusted relation (like a set of trusted matrices) did not exist previously, a default relation is set between them. Otherwise, the existing relations are invoked to participate in the commerce exchange. There are several factors contributing to affect the relationships between two trusted parties.

As an example, let us consider Figure 7, which is an interaction diagram [8], that places trust matrices as a trust relationship between two entities. Thus there is a trust relationship between the customer and the trusted intermediary (TI), and there is another trust relationship between the trusted intermediary and the broker. The number of these trust relationships increases with the number of trusted intermediaries that go between the customer and the vendor. In order to form an overall trust relationship that govern the transactions between the customer and the vendor, the trust relationships between the customer and the vendor (called the chain of trust relationships) should be *reduced* to a single overall trust relationship, that takes into account each and every relationship. The process of reducing the chain of trust relationships into a single relationship is accomplished as follows:

1. Convert the interaction diagram into a sequencing diagram. This can be done using Ketchpel's approach [8].
2. The sequencing diagram places trust relationships near merge operators. Merging operators are those operators that help in reducing two trust relationships into one. Example of merge operators includes convolution, min, max, composition, average, etc. The details of the merge operator that should be used are governed by the policies of the trusted entities, and any other intermediaries (for example, brokers).
3. Using the merging operators, trust relationships are combined recursively until a single relationship is obtained.

Figure 8 shows a sequence diagram created from an interaction diagram. The trust relationships are reduced at the site of the merge operators.

Definition 5.1 Trust Relationship Merger: The merger of two ECTRs is defined by a set of operators as follows: Let R and S be two ECTRs in the same product space X x Y. The merger * is

$$\mu_{R*S}(x, y) = {}_{y}^{*}\{\mu_R(x, y), \mu_S(x, y)\}, (x, y) \in X \times Y. \ \forall\, x \text{ over } y. \tag{5}$$

Here * could be any of {min, max, -, product, average}.

Example: As an example, consider the trust matrix shown on the left-hand side of Figure 9 to be the one that exists between the customer and the trusted intermediary. The variables used in the matrix are transaction history, and number of micro-transactions. On the right hand side, a similar trust matrix is used between the trusted intermediary and the broker. This reflects the relationship that exists between these two parties. The variables used could be the number of microtransactions, and a satisfaction index. Satisfaction index could indicate the average transaction history of the customers in a category, or a quantity that the trusted intermediary determines based on the satisfaction report it has from its customers. A merge operator in this case could be one that uses the matrix on the RHS to lessen the verification risk used by the matrix on the LHS. It could be a subtraction, a min operator on the two quantities, or an averaging operator, or a combination of operators. The resulting matrix with some of the entities filled is shown in Figure 10.

When merging two matrices, different operators could be applied to different rows. For example, if the matrix entities on the LHS matrix in Figure 9 are represented by the variable x, and the matrix entities on the RHS matrix in Figure 10 are represented by the variable y, operators like x-y, $min(x, y)$ are applied to the different rows to obtain the matrix entities in Figure 10.

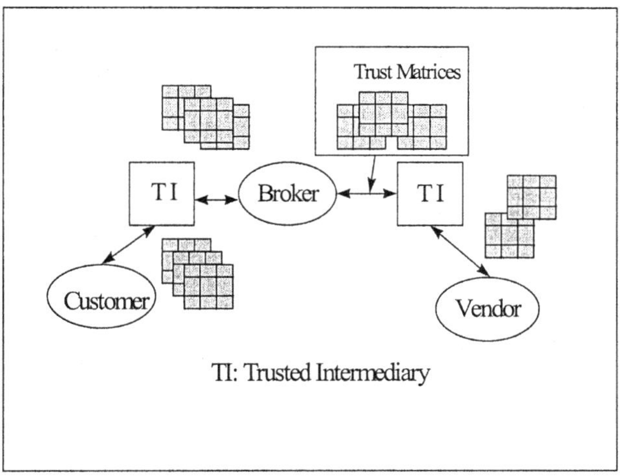

Fig. 7. A Trust Relationship Shown as a Set of Trusted Matrices between Two Entities.

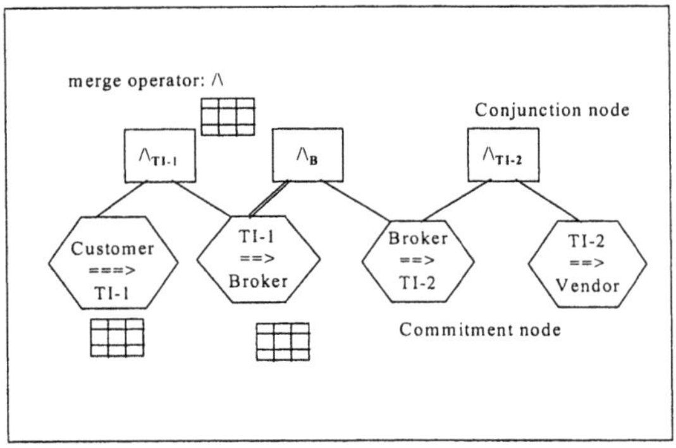

Fig. 8. A Sequence Diagram Indicating the Use of Merge Operators

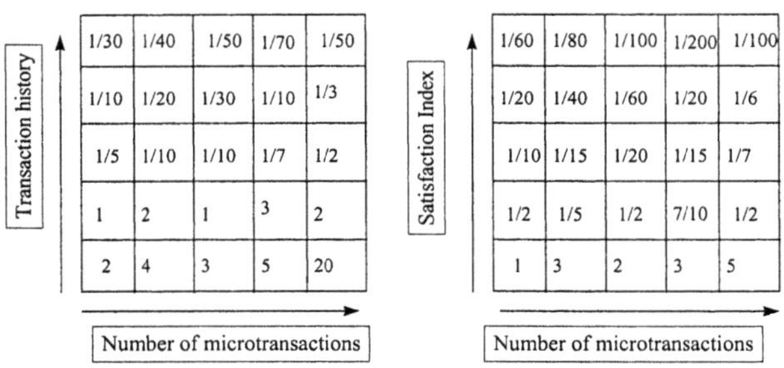

Fig. 9. Related Trust Matrices in the Two Relationships

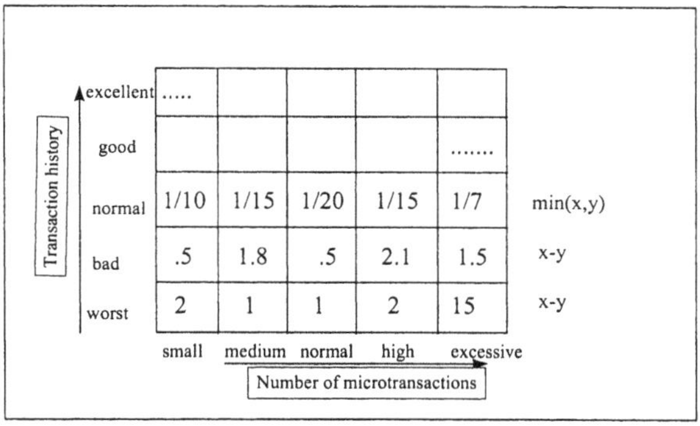

Fig. 10. Trust Matrix formed by Merging the Two Trust Matrices in Figure 11.

6 Conclusions

Existing models based on the credit card system model measures trust as a function of credit history. These are statistical in nature, and are based on a customer's credit record. They do not support a possibility theoretic approach. They do not address issues like on-line payment verification, and cannot suitably be used for electronic commerce. The approach presented in this paper provides a unique and novel technique to determine payment verification of transactions, yet randomizing the effort to avoid the unnecessary computation costs involved in verifying each and every transaction. The paper makes a careful analysis of commerce-related attacks and threats and discusses solutions to prevent and correct them. Solutions to these attacks cannot possibly be solved by cryptographic methods alone. As part of future work, attacks based on anonymous mode of operation would be studied and corrective and preventive methods for recovery and survival will be researched.

References

1. Adam NR, Wortmann JC (1989) Security Control Methods for Statistical Databases: A Comparative Study. ACM Computing Surveys 21: 515-556
2. Chaum D, Pedersen TP (1993) Wallet Databases with Observers. Advances in Cryptology-Cypto'92

3. Chung E, Dardailler E (1997) Joint Electronic Payment Initiative, W3C-Note, http://www.w3.org/TR/NOTE-jepi
4. Cox B, Sirbu M, Tygar JD (1995) NetBill Security and Transaction Protocol. Proceedings of the 1st USENIX Workshop on Electronic Commerce, pp. 77-88
5. deBry R. et al., (1999) Internet Printing Protocol—Model and Semantics, Version 1.0. RFC 2566, available at ftp://ftp.isi.edu/in-notes/rfc2566.txt. More information on IPP can be found at http://www.ietf.org/html.charters/ipp-charter.html
6. Dierks T, Allen C (1999) The TLS Protocol Version 1, RFC-2246, http://www.ietf.org/rfc/rfc2246.txt
7. ITU-T Recommendation X.509 (1997): Information Technology - Open Systems Interconnection - The Directory: Authentication Framework
8. Ketchpel S, Garcia HM (1996) Making Trust Explicit in Distributed Commerce Transactions, 16th International Conference on Distributed Computing Systems (ICDCS '96), Hong Kong
9. Knowledge Systems Laboratory, FuzzyCLIPS, User's Guide. Institute of Information Technology, National Research Council, Canada
10. Neuman BC, Medvinsky G (1995) Requirements for Network Payment: The NetCheque Perspective, In: Proceedings of IEEE Compcom '95
11. Reiter MK and Stubblebine SG (1997) Toward Acceptable Metrics of Authentication, In: Proceedings of the IEEE Symposium on Security and Privacy, Oakland, pp.10-20
12. Roscheisen M, Winograd T (1996) A Communication Agreement Framework of Access/Action Control. Proceedings of the IEEE Symposium on Security and Privacy, Oakland
13. SET (2000) Secure Electronic Transactions, http://www.mastercard.com/set
14. Su J, Manchala DW (1997) Building Trust for Distributed Commerce Transactions, In: 17th International Conference on Distributed Computing Systems (ICDCS '97), Baltimore, pp. 322-329
15. Su J, Manchala DW (1999) Trust Vs. Threats: Recovery and Survival in Electronic Commerce, In: 19th International Conference on Distributed Computing Systems (ICDCS '99), Austin, pp. 126-133
16. Zadeh L (1978) Fuzzy sets as a basis for a theory of possibility, Fuzzy Sets and Systems, 1:3-28
17. Zimmerman H J (1991) Fuzzy Set Theory - And Its Applications, 2nd Revised Edition, Kluwer Academic, Boston

Fuzzy Similarity in E-Commerce Domains

Adam Niewiadomski [1], Piotr S. Szczepaniak [1, 2]

[1] Institute of Computer Science, Technical University of Lodz
Sterlinga 16/18, 90-217 Lodz, Poland
[2] Systems Research Institute, Polish Academy of Sciences
Newelska 6, 01-447 Warsaw, Poland

Abstract: This chapter focuses on application of a fuzzy similarity measure of textual records to services available within the e-commerce. Firstly, concepts for comparison of natural language words and sentences rooted in the theory of fuzzy sets, and in the concept of fuzzy relation in particular, are presented. Then, on two examples of application to the e-commerce domain, the aspect of the user-friendliness of the approach is demonstrated.

Keywords: fuzzy set, fuzzy similarity measure, text comparison

1 Introduction

Within the e-commerce, two quite natural tendencies clash: the need for standardization and the desire for flexibility. The only reasonable outcome of this conflict can be partial standardization or – in other words – restricted flexibility. It is particularly visible within the domain of Business-to-Customer (B-to-C) communication. Communication performed in the Business-to-Administration (B-to-A) and Business-to-Business (B-to-B) domains is usually easier to formalize and it runs with the use of a highly specialized terminology and strictly defined procedures.

In this chapter, some new ideas based on natural language processing for establishing a user-friendly interface applicable to the Business-to-Customer domain are presented. The method uses fuzzy relations to compare textual documents on their similarity. This is the method which allows the customer to navigate effectively within the huge number of products offered over diverse Web services. The fuzziness in the sense of Zadeh [4] is sufficient to establish the proposed method for text similarity analysis. The new original method presented below, simple and effective, is believed to complete also natural language intuitions.

2 Basic definitions

2.1 Fuzzy set

The concept of a fuzzy set was introduced by Zadeh in 1965 [4]. He added a positive real number from the [0,1] interval interpreted as a "membership level (or degree)" to each element of a considered space. Formally, a fuzzy set A in a non-empty space $\boldsymbol{X}$ is a set of ordered pairs

$$A = \{<x, \mu_A(x)>: x \in \boldsymbol{X}\}\,, \tag{2.1}$$

where $\mu_A: \boldsymbol{X} \to [0,1]$ – the membership function.

Let us present the concept of a fuzzy set with a simple example.

Example

Let $\boldsymbol{X} = \{\ \mathbf{0, 1, 2, 3, 4, 5, 6, 7, 8, 9}\ \}$. Fuzzy set A is to characterize the non-crisp predicate *small pair digit*:

$$A = \{<\mathbf{0}, 1.0>, <\mathbf{2}, 0.8>, <\mathbf{4}, 0.5>, <\mathbf{6}, 0.3>, <\mathbf{8}, 0>\}$$

2.2 Fuzzy relation

A fuzzy relation can be defined on the basis of (2.1), cf.[3]. Fuzzy relation R in the Cartesian product of two non-empty spaces $\boldsymbol{X}$ and $\boldsymbol{Y}$ is a set of pairs:

$$R = \{<(x, y), \mu_R(x, y)>: x \in \boldsymbol{X},\ y \in \boldsymbol{Y}\}\,, \tag{2.2}$$

where μ_R: $\boldsymbol{X} \times \boldsymbol{Y} \to [0,1]$ is the membership function. The positive real number $\mu_R(x, y)$ is usually interpreted as a degree of connection between x and y.

If it has the following properties:

a) reflexivity, if and only if
$$\mu_R(x, x) = 1 \qquad \forall x \in \boldsymbol{X} \tag{2.3}$$

b) symmetry, if and only if
$$\mu_R(x, y) = \mu_R(y, x) \qquad \forall x, y \in \boldsymbol{X}, \tag{2.4}$$

a fuzzy relation is called a „neighbourhood relation" and can be interpreted as a model of non-transitive similarity.

3 Text similarity

3.1 Comparison of words

It might be useful if a software procedure was able to relate words which are similar to each other but not identical. Since no such result can be achieved with the use of the classical identity relation, a fuzzy relation on $\boldsymbol{S}$ – the set of all words within the universe of discourse, for example a considered language or dictionary – is proposed:

$$RS = \{(<s_1, s_2>, \mu_{RS}(s_1, s_2)):\ s_1, s_2 \in \boldsymbol{S}\}\ . \tag{3.1}$$

Let the membership function $\mu_{RS}: \boldsymbol{S} \times \boldsymbol{S} \rightarrow [0,1]$ be of the form

$$\mu_{RS}(s_1, s_2) = \frac{2}{(N^2 + N)} \sum_{i=1}^{N(s_1)} \sum_{j=1}^{N(s_1)-i+1} h(i,j) \quad \forall s_1, s_2 \in \boldsymbol{S}\,, \tag{3.2}$$

where:
$N(s_1)$, $N(s_2)$ – the number of letters in words s_1, s_2, respectively;
$N = \max\{N(s_1), N(s_2)\}$ – the maximum of $N(s_1)$, $N(s_2)$;
$h(i, j) = 1$ if a subsequence, containing i letters of word s_1 and beginning from its j-th position in s_1, appears at least once in word s_2; otherwise $h(i, j) = 0$;
$h(i, j) = 0$ also if $i > N(s_2)$ or $i > N(s_1)$;

Note that $0{,}5\,(N^2 + N)$ is the number of possible subsequences to be considered.

Example
Comparison of words:
s_1 = "PROGRAMMER" and s_2 = "PROGRAMMING".

Here

$$\mu_{RS}(s_1, s_2) = \frac{2}{(121+11)} \sum_{i=1}^{11} \sum_{j=1}^{11-i+1} h(i,j) =$$

$$= \frac{9+7+6+5+4+3+2+1}{66} \approx 0{,}561\ , \tag{3.3}$$

because in s_2 there are:

nine one-element subsequences of s_1 (P, R, O, G, R, A, M, M, R);

seven two-element subsquences of s_1 (PR, RO, OG, GR, RA, AM, MM);

six three-element subsequences of s_1 (PRO, ROG, OGR, GRA, RAM, AMM), etc., and the longest subseqeunce of s_1 which can also be found in s_2 is 'PROGRAMM' consisting of eight letters.

The following operation is proposed to make *RS* symmetrical (in the sense of (2.4)) for any pair of words:

$$\mu_{RSsym}(s_1, s_2) = \{\ \mu_{RS}(s_1, s_2)\ ,\ \mu_{RS}(s_2, s_1)\ \}\ . \tag{3.4}$$

3.2 Comparison of sentences

Having the procedure for comparison of words, it is possible to compute the similarity for any pair of sentences. Let us introduce the fuzzy relation on $\boldsymbol{Z}$ – the set of all sentences within the considered language:

$$RZ = \{(<z_1, z_2>, \mu_{RZ}(z_1, z_2)) \colon z_1, z_2 \in \boldsymbol{Z}\ \}\ , \tag{3.5}$$

with the membership function $\mu_{RZ}\colon \boldsymbol{Z} \times \boldsymbol{Z} \rightarrow [0,1]$ of the form

$$\mu_{RZ}(z_1, z_2) = \frac{1}{N} \sum_{i=1}^{N(z_1)} \max_{j \in \{1,..,N(z_2)\}} \mu_{RSsym}(s_i, s_j)\ , \tag{3.6}$$

where:

s_i – i-th word in the sentence z_1 ;
s_j – j-th word in the sentence z_2 ;
$\mu_{RS}(s_i, s_j)$ – the value of the μ_{RS} function for the pair (s_i, s_j) ;
$N(z_1)$, $N(z_2)$ – the number of words in sentences z_1, z_2 ;
$N = \max\{\ N(z_1), N(z_2)\ \}$ – the number of words in the longer of the two compared sentences.

To make *RZ* symmetrical for any pair of words, the operation analogous to (3.4) is used:

$$\mu_{RZsym}(z_1, z_2) = \{\ \mu_{RZ}(z_1, z_2)\ ,\ \mu_{RZ}(z_2, z_1)\ \}\ . \tag{3.7}$$

Example

Comparison of sentences:
z_1 = JOHN WALKS , and z_2= IS JOHN WALKING, $N(z_1) = 2$, $N(z_2)=N=3$.

Through (3.6) there is:

$$\mu_{RZ}(z_1, z_2) = \frac{1}{3} \sum_{i=1}^{3} \max_{j \in \{1,2,3\}} (\mu_{RSsym}(s_i, s_j))\ .$$

Thus the final result is of the form

$$\mu_{RZ}(z_1, z_2) = \frac{0{,}067 + 1 + 0{,}357}{3} \approx 0{,}457$$

where

$0{,}067$ is max $\{\mu_{RSSym}(\text{JOHN, IS}), \mu_{RSSym}(\text{WALKS, IS})\}$;

$1{,}0$ is max $\{\mu_{RSSym}(\text{JOHN, JOHN}), \mu_{RSSym}(\text{WALKS, JOHN})\}$;

$0{,}357$ is max $\{\mu_{RSSym}(\text{JOHN, WALKING}), \mu_{RSSym}(\text{WALKS, WALKING})\}$;

4 Application of similarity measures in *e-commerce* domains

4.1 Bookshop on-line

In the recent years the so called "electronic shopping" (e-shopping) has become a very popular Web service. Various e-firms are vitally interested in selling their products, and this is why almost each of them places a proper purchase form in its site. Such a form consists of a set of fields to make it possible for the user (and – *in spe* – client) to specify name and requested properties of a desired product, and of course a credit card number.

Obviously, the moment of clicking the submit button by the user confirming this way his/her will of buying something is the last lap of a long, boring and partially unstructured process, referred to as in the natural language - "decision making".

First of all, the customer wants to find out as much as it is possible on all the products he/she considers as the object of transaction. It should be noted that the typical user does not usually have sufficient knowledge and lacks proper terminology, so he/she cannot state precisely enough what he/she is actually looking for. His/her question may contain grammar mistakes, slang names of products or imprecise technical parameters. In view of this fact, computer procedures should be able to perform a process of intelligent acquisition of information from the user. "Fuzzy similarity" presented here is one of possible approaches which may be useful. Its application to searching the resources in electronic bookshops or libraries is described below.

The set of data on products offered by a firm may be given in the form of a standard simple database (see Table 4.1).

Title	*Author*	*Editor's note*
Catch 22	Joseph Heller	Joseph Heller was born in 1923 in New York, Brooklyn....
Picture this	Joseph Heller	The name Joseph Heller is well known to many readers and editors...
Cyberiada	St. Lem	-

Table 4.1: Sample textual database for e-bookshop

The comparison of records from the database with user's query may be performed according to the formula

$$\mu(z,r_j) = \frac{\sum_{i=1}^{n} w_i \cdot \mu_i(z_i, r_{ji})}{\sum_{i=1}^{n} w_i} \tag{4.1}$$

where: z – user's query;
z_i – i-th field of user's query;
r_j – j-th record in the database;
r_{ji} – i-th field of j-th record in the database;
w_i – the weight of i-th field of the record and of the query;
μ_i – the similarity between the i-th fields of the query and the record, e.g. computed with (3.2) and (3.4) for single words, or with (3.6) and (3.7) for sentences (sets of words).

The sample comparison of user's query (z) to a database record (r_1) is

$z = \{ z_1 =$ Catch 22, $z_2 =$ J. Heller, $z_3 =$ ""},

$r_1 = \{ r_{11} =$ Catch 22, $r_{12} =$ Joseph Heller, $r_{13} =$ Joseph Heller was born in 1923 in New York, Brooklyn....},

$w_1 = w_2 = w_3 = 1$.

Thus

$$\mu(z,r_1) = \frac{\sum_{i=1}^{4} w_i \cdot \mu_i(z_i, r_{ji})}{3} = 0{,}508\,,$$

where:

$\mu_1(z_1, r_{11}) = 1{,}0$;
$\mu_2(z_2, r_{12}) = 0{,}524$;
$\mu_3(z_3, r_{13}) = 0{,}0$.

The value of the similarity level can be now compared with other values (for other records) in the database being searched. The final result can be expressed as a ranking of a given number of the records found to be the most similar to a given query.

4.2 Frequently asked questions

Frequently Asked Questions are well known to every user of the Web. Almost each business website is supported by the answering system to make the information exchange user-friendlier. "Netsurfers" usually ask about products advertised in the site, about additional data on them, etc. Of course it is impossible to publish all relevant data in the site, nevertheless they are often requested for by users. *FAQ* systems give a chance to webmasters to solve this problem.

The authors of [1] place the *FAQ* problem in the *Case-Based Reasoning* domain. Obviously each question from a user can be treated as a separate *casus* and handled in the proper way, basing on the knowledge stored in the system database. On the other hand, the soft computing methods may assist the *CBR* systems [2] and make them more intelligent. Here, the following application of fuzzy similarity to *FAQ* is proposed.

Let us treat user's request as a natural language sentence, not necessarily formed and built as a typical question. Two examples of such requests are given below

„Where's some info on HP DeskJet 690 ?"

or

„My printer does not work; out of paper" .

It is seen that the database of the cases should be an integral component of the *FAQ* system. The difference between a "typical" *CBR* database and *FAQ* database is that the former stores data of various types (numerical, textual, logical, hyperlinks, etc.), while the records in the latter are of the form:

{ *ID*, *Question*, *URL* } ,

A sample *FAQ* database may be of the form given below:

ID	*Question*	*URL*
1	Fuzzy and non-sharp letters in the printing	http://www.mysite.com/toner.htm
2	How can I set the width of margins in a printed document ?	http://www.mysite.com/printing.htm
3	Hewlett Packard printer installation	http://www.hp.com/first_install.asp

Table 4.2: Sample database for *FAQ* system

Let the *FAQ* system compare a case to user's query according to the formula

$$\mu(\{s_1,..,s_n\},\{p_1,..,p_k\}) = \frac{1}{n}\sum_{i=1}^{n} \max_{j\in\{1,..,k\}} g(s_i,p_j) \tag{4.2}$$

where: $s_1, \ldots, s_n$ – words in user's query;
$p_1, \ldots, p_k$ – words in the case description from database;
g – function for words similarity computed with (3.2).

Generally, using fuzzy similarity the response system works according to the following algorithm:

1. Determine the user's query – the set of words of the form: $\{ s_1, \ldots s_n \}$.

2. Choose the accuracy level for the comparison : μ_0.
3. Compare the query to all records from the database; take the maximum of the similarity degrees $\mu_1, \mu_2, \ldots\ldots, \mu_k$.

4. **IF** at least one record in the database is similar to the query with a degree $\mu_i \quad \mu_0$
   THEN go to 5;

   ELSE
   i. send an e-message including the unhandled query to the Webmaster
   ii. go to 6 .

5. Recommend a few (for instance: three) Websites with answers to URL.
6. **STOP**

The fuzzy similarity method is a useful and easy "tool" for *FAQ* systems. The following advantages should be pointed out:

- The user does not need to know technical terms or vocabulary.
- The user may use natural, non-official, and non-structured language while exchanging information.
- The process of querying runs in a very convenient and "safe" interface – the WWW form.
- The response system is user-friendly – non-complicated WWW sites as answers (similarity to HELP systems).

The described method enables handling of user's requests expressed in a natural language *via* Internet. Moreover the gist of the method is widely supported with *Case-Based Reasoning* systems details. In particular, the B-to-C services may benefit from its application.

5 Conclusions

So far, in textual database searching the methods used for text comparison have been based mainly on the classical identity relation, according to which two given texts are either identical or not. The application of fuzzy relations enables formalization of the human language intuition concerning similarity of textual information. The new, to the authors' knowledge, measures for comparison of natural language texts increase the chance that a user who does not know exact names of the products that he/she is looking for will be able to find a set of keywords similar to the one he needs in the Web.

The described solution is not sensitive to grammatical mistakes or other misshaped language constructions. Moreover, the implementation of the fuzzy similarity method is not troublesome at all.

References

1. Lenz M., Hübner A., Kunze M. (1998). *Textual CBR* . In: Lenz M., Bartsch-Spörl B., Burkhard H.-D., Wess S. (Eds.) (1998): *Case-Based Reasoning Technology. From Foundations to Applications.* Springer Verlag, Berlin, Heidelberg.
2. Pal S.K., Dillon T.S., Yeung D.S. (Eds.) (2001): *Soft Computing in Case Based Reasoning*. Springer-Verlag, London.
3. Pedrycz W., Gomide F. (1998): *An Introduction to Fuzzy Sets; Analysis and Design.* A Bradford Book, The MIT Press, Cambridge, Massachusetts and London, England.
4. Zadeh (1965). *Fuzzy sets.* Information and Control, **8**, pp. 338-353.

Part 5 CBR and Agents

Agencies of Agents for Logistic Applications

Sonali Banerjee

4339 Coventry Ct
Union City
CA 94587-5900

Abstract. This paper presents an overview of current trends in Electronic Business (E-business), and discusses how an enterprise can use the Electronic Marketspace to its strategic advantage.
In this paper, we define an agency to be a multi-agent system created by integrating agents selected from a library of reusable agents that have formed a federation. A federation of agents comprises of a set of registered agents, which are themselves complete knowledge-based systems. The set of agents may be heterogeneous with respect to long-term knowledge, solution-evaluation criteria, or goals, as well as languages, algorithms, hardware requirements, etc.
An agency-based framework is presented for E-business in the domain of logistics and supply systems. To support the integration of heterogeneous and reusable agents into functional agent sets, a framework for the coalition of cooperating agents is needed. The role of cooperative information agents is discussed within the context of E-business.
Conflict is an integral part of problem solving in multi-agent systems and is often the focal point of interaction among agents. Rules about agent interaction can be used to mediate, mitigate or avoid conflict and as a control structure for agent activity to ensure global coherence of the agent set. This can be achieved by an executive agent that has an overall perspective of the other agents in the federation.
A facilitator, providing query and result refinement, together with, decision making tools that can be customized to take advantage of specific agents and agent-set characteristics, while maintaining a global view of the problem that needs to be solved can be integrated with the adoption of the agent architecture discussed here. The effectiveness of the facilitator as a coordination mechanism is in the specification of the rules that guide the task or service agents in problem solving and the meta-rules which instantiates appropriate knowledge sources. Several scenarios, with the prototype facilitator has been considered as proof of this concept.
Such logistic systems enjoy wide acceptance in commercial and military application domains, as witnessed by the phenomenal growth in Internet stocks for companies such as Amazon.com. We show how agent-based systems provide scalable, configurable and evolutionary solutions for such applications.

1 Introduction

The rapid strides made in computer science and information technology has enabled business organizations to reach new customers and open new markets in an electronic marketspace. Doing business electronically is more cost-effective than building new stores or warehouses and hiring more people to run them. The Internet and World Wide Web has made it easier to give or get information, share crucial business data, and build better business relationships. It has streamlined processes, simplified sharing of critical data and lowered organizational barriers – to reach beyond a company's walls and into the operations of its customers, suppliers and business partners. Commerce in an interactive world provides customized goods and services based on a trail of previous activity and preferences. This in turn, makes it possible for customers to have more options, effective input and on-line demos. It also allows customers to "try before they buy" and involves them in product design and delivery. Virtual tours and three dimensional simulation allow customers to become familiar with a product even before its purchase. Collaborative tools allow customers to provide design input to manufacturers across the globe. Package tracking systems allow customers and manufacturers to go on-line and find out details about the status and delivery of the products they have ordered.

For a smooth transition from traditional ways of doing business, to doing business electronically, it becomes necessary to establish a compelling Internet presence preferrably one that is a natural extension of the existing physical business. This requires tight integration of existing business systems and practices along with the creation of Internet commerce solutions. In order to attract customers, boost customer confidence, establish relationships and retain customers, these solutions should be robust. To be competetive in the marketplace, these solutions must be dynamic so that they can quickly change to market conditions and variables in the marketspace. The solutions should be secure for obvious reasons. They must be scalable and extensible to accommodate future growth.

In order to satisfy all these requirements, an organizations should adopt an integrated system architecture that can be built on pre-existing resources and can evolve within a well-defined electronic-business(e-business) strategy. Putting the right components in place – in constructing e-business sites – creates a solid foundation that can support ongoing business expansion. Software agents[1] that are human proxies can be used to capture experiences and best practices and leverage them in the construction of an e-business presence. An agent architecture, that is scalable is, therefore, the ideal solution for logistic applications.

2 Infrastructural Requirements of Logistic Applications

The components required to support the various aspects of logistic applications and the technology available to support them is discussed in this Section. Here, we address the infrastructure required for conducting business electronically. These requirements are general and apply to most enterprises that have legacy systems and also access information on the Internet. We discuss the data and information constructs required for business communications, as well as, the notion of confidentiality and security as they pertain to logistics on the Internet. We briefly touch upon electronic cataloguing and transportation handlers before discussing our experience with interactive transaction management. Finally, we introduce the notion of customization based on data mining of customer experience and feedback.

2.1 Data Interchange

Traditionally, Electronic Data Interchange (EDI) has been used to conduct online business-to-business commerce using Value Added Networks (VANs). EDI provides the standards and services needed to perform electronic transactions such as purchase orders. Most electronic commerce (e-commerce) software products use EDI based applications and are processed in a synchronized batch mode. Typically, EDI software extracts flat files from mainframe financial or order processing systems and translates the data into EDI standard forms that are then transmitted as large batches of EDI forms over a dedicated phone line or a VAN. However, EDI software needs to synchronize protocols with all the partners' systems and the X12 format used in EDI, is rigid and complex, making new applications difficult to implement. Also, EDI on VANs lack the ability to do spontaneous online transactions. Furthermore, connectivity and proliferation is limited to other users of the EDI format and software tools that are compatible.

The Internet has had a tremendous impact on e-commerce because it enables continuous, around-the-clock, easy contact with clients and customers distributed throughout the world. It has opened up the customer base as well as supplier bases. Today, tools are available that meld traditional EDI with the Internet so that companies with EDI software can do business with companies on the web that do not have EDI. These products lets companies that do not have conventional EDI software use Web browsers to talk to EDI software. This is a significant improvement over traditional EDI based on VANs.

2.2 Security

There are confidentiality and security issues that must be addressed before the Internet can be used in large-scale automated business applications. Securing the

Web and Internet has been a major roadblock in the advancement of electronic commerce.

The most prevalent security tool, public key encryption ensures confidentiality, authentication, data integrity and non-repudiation of origin and return. The technology used, encloses transactions into encrypted envelopes and electronically seals them so that only parties with the encryption key can view the contents of the envelopes that are sent securely over the Internet . However, all partners must install the same software and coordinate their upgrade cycles. Alternatively, wrappers are available to convert conventional EDI software into secure formats, such as the Secure socket layer (SSL) encryption protocol which is specially suited to Internet-based transactions.

The Internet has built firewalls, to protect individual networks from attacks by hackers, but the TCP/IP protocol suite used by all computers connected to the Internet is fundamentally lacking in security services at the lower layers of the protocol stack - within TCP, IP and transmission protocols such as Ethernet. This allows such problems as eavesdropping, password "sniffing", data modification, spoofing and repudiation to occur.

To secure the Internet, the protocol architecture of IP includes an Authentication Header (AH) which provides authenticity and integrity using the message-digest algorithm(MD5) [2] and Encapsulating Security Payload (ESP) [3] which provides confidentiality using the Data Encryption Standard (DES) algorithm [4] A number of session-layer protocols have been proposed within the Internet Engineering Task Force (IETF) to support distribution of keys for use with almost any TCP/IP application. The most significant of these are the Simple Key Exchange Protocol (SKEP), Photuris and the Internet Security Association and Key Management Protocol (ISAKMP). The IETF has proposed Privacy-Enhanced Mail (PEM) and MIME Object Security Services (MOSS) to provide application-layer security [5].

The World Wide Web consortium (W3C) [6] currently has provided an HTTP extension designed to identify different payment types over the Internet using the Protocol Extension Protocol (PEP). In its Joint Electronic Payment Initiative (JEPI) it aims at creating a framework for interoperability among various payment methods. JEPI would use the Universal Payment Preamble, a proposed negotiation standard for different payment methods such as Secure Electronic Transaction (SET) enabled software. The JEPI, by using the Universal Payment Preamble, would enable transactions using multiple protocols to interoperate over the Internet.

Another technique used in payment system for Internet users is based on email callbacks [7]. It uses the existing Internet protocols and instead of using cryptography, a high-level protocol is used. The protocol involves looking up the Personal Identification Number (PIN) in its database and finding the email address of the payer. An email message is then sent asking the payer to confirm the commitment to pay with a "yes", "no" or "fraud". Only on receipt of a "yes" reply is the financial transaction actually initiated. Since the Virtual PIN is useless off the Internet and requires email confirmation on the Internet, transactions are unaffected by simple attacks such as "sniffing". The valuable financial token, such as credit card numbers, account information, etc. , never appear on the Internet messages but are linked to the Virtual PIN after being retrieved from the database.

It may be concluded therefore, that even though the Internet is an open medium and inherently is not secure, several tools are available to provide secured transactions over the Internet.

As more companies conduct their business over the Internet, the infrastructure and standards required, for commercial payment software, are being established. Commerce Net [8] is a consortium of 200 companies and organizations dedicated to promoting Internet commerce. It is an association to exchange logistics information and establish standards for electronic commerce on the Internet. They have proposed the Secure HTTP (S-HTTP) protocol to provide confidentiality, data integrity and authentication for business transactions.

2.3 Electronic Catalogin

Most organizations today have their web page on the World Wide Web (WWW) which provides up-to-date information about the company and its products. Several organizations have used the Internet to publish and maintain electronic catalogs, automate their transactions and established business-to-business(B2B) or business-to-customer (B2C) links. Catalog software has helped to streamline the process of publishing online catalogs with capabilities for tracking and personalizing catalog sales.

2.4 Transportation Handlers

Transportation and freight companies with Web sites allow shippers to track the status of packages and provide real-time, on-line shipment information. Software or hardware based automated shipping systems that allows organizations to place, track and bill their own orders in-house are extensively used for the delivery of goods and products. Usually the software can be downloaded to desktops to schedule pickups,as well as, to track and confirm deliveries. Several Internet based transportation services allow customers to prepare shipping labels from the Web without additional software or help from representatives of the transportation handler.

2.5 Interactive Transaction Management

Today, there are several commercially available tools for Internet transactions and service providers specializing in e-Business. These interactive order management systems provide an Internet commerce "shell" or "store-front". Typically, these include software, often a web server with a "distributed shared services architecture" that separates the management of a business transaction from that of its content. The software deals with the actual transaction. This includes taking orders and other information through a firewall that connects the organization to the Web, automating the actual mechanics of placing the order from the WEB browser, transferring that order from a Web server to the vendors' order-entry and processing system; tracking state, local and federal taxes; calculating shipping charges; interfacing with accounting systems, etc. Most of the available software support all HTTP browsers, including those that support security protocols SSL or (PCT). By centrally managing the authentication and authorization of end users and installing an access management and reporting application designed to provide a simple and cost-effective way of building user authentication, authorization and session tracking, companies can securely and centrally manage business transactions using content on multiple distributed Web servers. This architecture can be used to collaborate in a distributed work environment, secure payment, complete order management, provide online customer service, provide information in a controlled environment (B2B) and forge business partner relationships.

2.6 Customization

One of the main advantages of using the electronic media is the ease with which goods and services can be tailored to the requirements and preferences of the customer. The customer experience often determines whether a customer will come back Therefore, it would be prudent to include in the e-business infrastructure, a personalization engine through which customers can define their preferences, such as which departments they frequent, which product types interest them, and what they consider a suitable price range. This allows businesses to present tailored information to individual customers. Consumer preferences and buying patterns are often tracked in a database, which forms the basis for ongoing analysis, building profiles and tracking customer behavior. To leverage this data, there should be predefined reports for gathering information on hits, product sales information, sales demographics, and so forth. With this information, businesses can simultaneously attract new customers of the particular demographic group and market more effectively to their existing customers. When customers request information, the response can be built on the fly and presented to the user through a Web browser. Therefore, the customer always gets information that is correct and up-to-date without having to wait for someone to 'get back with the information.' The personalization tool may be used in conjunction with storefronts and payment systems, to establish tracking and reporting mechanisms for data mining and customer profiling. By gathering data and using algorithms that govern each customer's purchasing and decision-making tendencies, the tool becomes, in effect, an intelligent agent playing the role as an analyst.

3 Agents in Logistic Applications

The dictionary defines an agent as one that acts on behalf of another. The word agent has been used in several contexts such as an insurance agent(representative), a chemical agent(substance causing change), an investigative agent(having authority to act), etc. While software agents are subservient to humans, they are often expected to have several characteristics normally atributed to humans. A software agent is generally thought of as a program which is autonomous, goal driven, adaptive, intelligent, mobile, proactive, reactive and robust. An intelligent agent is an attempt to model a software agent after human cognitive behavior.

Logistic applications require access to diverse data residing in multiple, autonomous, heterogeneous databases and the tools to integrate that data into coherent information that can be used by the enterprise. The problem is complicated by the fact that the data may by multimedia with diverse temporal and spatial granularity [9,10,11,12] and stored in diverse formats [13]. The semantics of the data may conflict across multiple sources and the data may be of uncertain quality, and the reliability of the source may be questionable.

Agents are useful in e-business logistics because they are goal driven adaptive[14] problem solvers[15] and therefore act as 'catalysts' that are pro-active. They can make contact and establish connections. They can negotiate and facilitate interactions. They can disseminate information to a wide audience or automatically target information to those interested [16]. Intelligent autonomous software agents may be used to filter information [17], integrate information from heterogeneous sources [18, 19], automate stereotypical behavior and regulate transactions for efficient business interactions [20]. The use of agents removes the need of having the user initiate all tasks explicitly and to monitor all events. An agent system could provide a common interface for the entire business process. Agents can be configured automatically with appropriate knowledge bases (ontologies), task-specific information, negotiation and communication protocols for its mission

One of the main reasons for choosing an agent architecture is that it can scale, is modular, robust, composable and configurable. Furthermore, by modeling software agents to behave like human agents, consumer resistance to change from traditional environments to virtual environments is likely to be overcome.

Using agents for e-Business increases productivity by allowing processes to be done in parallel. The increased throughput becomes critical to performance with greater proliferation of business on the Internet. Available infrastructure can be leveraged to build agents. Each agent is relatively simple and hardy with known abilities, although, sometimes (as in viruses), these abilities may not be declared. For a seamless connection between enterprises for a particular logistic application, these agents can be combined to form agent systems. This enables the application system requirements for a particular application to be built (and altered) fairly rapidly.

3.1 Types and Organizations of Agents

Although agents have been given human attributes and are assumed to be adaptive to some degree, in general, an agent is a program that is specialized to perform a particular task. As such, an agent may be classified on the basis of the role it plays in the overall organization. Based on our research, we have identified the following types of agents :

Executive Agent — is a *coordinator* for a group of agents. It is informed of significant events. A significant event can lead to the activation of new agents. For example, if the enterprise is notified of disaster-relief request, then the executive agent would coordinate with other agents in implementing the relief scenario.

User Agents — acts on behalf of a user, and is responsible for assisting users: 1) in browsing catalogs and information holdings such as the information repository, 2) in the intelligent formulation of queries, and 3) in the planning of tasks within a mission-specific scenario such as provisioning logistic support for a disaster relief effort.

Real-time Agents — are mission-specific, defined and configured to process incoming data, and update the appropriate database or notify the appropriate users. The real-time agents are autonomous, communicate with each other using a pre-defined protocol. Real-time agents are responsible for monitoring the external environment, interacting with other systems, or acting on inputs from users. When an event is detected by a real-time agent, it is signaled to the relevant agents.

Facilitation Agents — provide intelligent dictionary and object location services. For example a facilitation agent might accept a request from the Executive Agent to find all *external* providers of 'antibiotics,' and it might respond with the pharmaceutical producers and suppliers for the region in question. Other agents such as *knowledge rovers* (defined below) could then arrange for the items to be requisitioned, retrieved, and paid for. A knowledge rover could also post a request for bids, accept responses, make contracts, and provision the requested items.

Mediation Agents — are configured to assist in the integration of information from multiple data and information sources, having diverse data formats, different meanings, differing time units, and providing differing levels of information quality. Mediators [21,22,23] are configured to accept queries from the Executive, translate the queries into the query language of the appropriate database system, accept the retrieved result, integrate it with results from other sources, and return the information to the Executive for presentation to the User Interface Agent.

Active View Agents — are created to monitor real-time events from the environment or from databases, and to use these events to initiate actions that will result in the update and synchronization of objects in the Data Warehouse and also in local views maintained at user workstations. These agents are configured to perform very specialized monitoring tasks and have a collection of rules and actions that can be executed in response to events and conditions that occur in the environment or in the databases.

Information Curators — are responsible for the quality of information in the information repository. They assist in evolving the data and knowledge bases associated with enterprise information resources. They work with knowledge rovers to incorporate newly discovered resources into the information repositories.

Knowledge Rovers[24,25] — travel from desktop-to-desktop at the discretion of the sender. These intelligent agents execute remotely, gather data, make decisions, take corrective actions, and report. They can also modify themselves, collaborate and initiate or terminate other processes. Password security and access restrictions prevent agents from unauthorized use and travel. They may be used, for example, to identify which vendors have a specific item on hand. This would involve obtaining information from several vendors. The knowledge rover dispatches *field agents* to specific sites to get the relevant information. If the knowledge rover gets similar information from more than one source, it may ask a *mediator*[26,27,28,29,30,31,32,33,34] to resolve the inconsistency. The knowledge rover reports back to the Executive Agent. The rovers are also responsible for Internet resource discovery. These new information sources and their data are analyzed to determine the adequacy, quality and reliability of retrieved information and whether it should be incorporated into the information repository.

Field Agents — are *specialized* agents that have expertise in a certain domain, (for example, pharmaceuticals), and knowledge about domain-specific information holdings at one or more sites. For example, a field agent could be tasked to monitor all aspects of a single item, say an 'antibiotic' produced by several manufactures and distributed by several vendors. They negotiate with the local systems through their *wrapper*, or Federation Interface Manager, retrieve appropriate data, and forward it to the appropriate requesting agent.

An agent system consists of a single agent or multiple agents. Although it might seem that single agent systems would be simpler than multiagent systems, the opposite is in fact true. Distributing control among multiple agents allows each agent to be simpler. The agents in the multi-agent system could be organized in a number of ways.

Principles of organizational theory can be used to model the multi-agent system, define inter-agent interaction and structure the organization of agents. Irrespective of the organization of the agents in the system, there are several issues with multi-agent systems that need to be addressed. These are discussed later in this paper.

The various forms of organizations of multiple agents, may be generalized into three categories, namely, homogeneous non-communicating agents, heterogeneous non-communicating agents and communicating agents with any degree of heterogeneity. As the agent organization becomes more complex, it introduces new issues and complications. If a task can be accomplished with non-communicating agents, then adding communication only makes the system more difficult to design and implement. The type of multiagent system to be used depends on the characteristics and uncertainty in the domain. The simplest possible system that is effective within the domain should be used. Domain characteristics to consider include: the number of agents; the amount of time that may be allocated to each agent (real-time domain?); whether or not new goals arrive dynamically; the cost of communication (in terms of time and resources); the cost of failure (in terms of time and resources) and user involvement. Analysis indicates that there are three different sources of uncertainty in a domain [35]. The transitions in the domain itself might be non-deterministic; agents might not know the actions of other agents; and agents might not know the outcomes of their own actions.

The simplest multi-agent system consists of homogeneous non-communicating agents. All agents have the same internal structure including goals, domain knowledge, and possible actions. They also have the same procedure for selecting among their actions. The only differences among agents are their inputs, the actual actions they take and possibly their location. Although the agents have identical capabilities and decision procedures, they may have limited information about each other's internal state and sensory inputs. Thus they may not be able to predict each other's actions. Several information retrieval and information filtering agents(for example, the research prototype, meta-crawler and the commercial product Copernicus) have this kind of an architecture.

Heterogeneous agents in a multi-agent domain add a great deal of potential power at the price of added complexity. Agents might be heterogeneous in any of a number of ways, from having different goals to having different domain models and actions. When agents have similar goals but different abilities, they can be organized into teams. Each agent then plays a separate role within the team. A benevolent team of agents that are heterogeneous with respect to their abilities, together with the method for assigning different agents to different roles, can completely represent most logistic applications. The method for task assignment might be obvious if the agents are very specific and can each only do one thing. If the method is sophisticated enough to capture the various scenarios, minimal human interaction is required in the agent driven logistic application.

The full power of a multi-agent system can be realized when, the ability for agents to communicate with one another, is added. With the aid of communication, agents can coordinate effectively. Communication, without the aid of any centralized agent, helps avoid bottlenecks and long queues for resources, by allowing the heterogeneous agents to post constraints to each other's scheduler.

3.2 Issues Involved in Multiagent Systems

A crucial problem in multi-agent systems is that of balancing the autonomy of individual agents with the co-ordination required between agents in order to efficiently complete complex tasks. In a multi-agent environment coordination is required because there are dependencies between the agents' actions. There is a need to meet global constraints, and generally, no one agent has sufficient competence, resources or information to solve the entire problem. This problem is compounded and complicated by issues of goal and task partitioning, load balancing and resource balancing. The system is also constrained by the deontic requirements of the agents in the system.

Coordination involves actors performing interdependent activities that achieve tasks, and therefore, its analysis includes task decomposition, resource allocation, synchronization, group decision making, communication and the preparation of common objectives. The major issues that need to be addressed therefore are: distributed planning and coalition formation, negotiation mechanisms and the protocols by which agents can coordinate and manage commitments. Problems with communication, synchronization, resource utilization, time constraints, failures in commitment and task completion, need to be resolved when the agent system is being designed.

An important aspect of heterogeneous agent systems is whether agents are benevolent or competitive. In an environment where we have multiple agents concurrently performing multiple tasks, we require a mechanism by which we can regulate the sequence in which tasks are performed so as to optimize productivity. Even if they have different goals, they may be co-operative towards each other or they may actively try to inhibit each other. An agent may be co-operative by design, if it can serve its own self-interest by establishing a reputation for being cooperative. The challenge here is to obtain and maintain coordination between the autonomous co-operating agents that are working towards the common and/or individual (possibly conflicting) goals. This requires us to determine how to model an agent's activities and how to detect dependencies between those activities. With heterogeneous agents, the problem of modeling others is very complex. The goals, actions, and domain knowledge of the other agents may be unknown and thus need modeling. Without communication, agents are forced to model each other strictly through observation.

Coordination may be defined as the process of managing dependencies between activities in order to avoid conflicts while having maximum concurrency. In general, co-ordination between agents can be assigned a positive value based on the statistical measure of the ratio of tasks successfully completed to the total number of tasks that the agent has participated in. When there are controversies or unconstructive competitions, the interaction between agents may be said to be negative. The net contribution of all the working teams will then depend on the signs of the interactions. If the interaction between agents is positive, the agents in the system are said to be in cooperation. When working on a task up against another cooperative agent, the two can benefit from a sense of trust for each other. Co-operation is also an issue when certain resources are required simultaneously by the competing agents. Designers of multi-agent systems with limited resources must decide how the agents will share the resources. Several of these agents can then form coalitions in order to concurrently perform a more complex task. Such a coalition of agents, each of which is specialized in its particular task, which together can commit to a more complex task is called an agency. More about agencies is presented later in this paper.

Agent coalitions may be formed through deliberated means using planning algorithms and load balancing, reactive means based on perception of the various other autonomous agents in the system; proactive means by the spontaneous formation of coalitions with the autonomous agents themselves taking the initiative or competitive means which are market based and use a measure of cost-benefit analysis. Each of these forms of coalition formation have there own advantages and disadvantages. If coalitions are formed based on a planning algorithm, an executive agent or controller is required. Further, it requires that all participating agents, atleast temporarily, surrender autonomy to the executive agent. This architecture is simple to visualize and use and can be very efficient in some cases. However, with this architecture, the system has a bottleneck and the performance and robustness of the system depends heavily on the performance of the executive agent. Coalitions based on reactive algorithms, do away with this problem but are. in general, slower. Such coalitions are also more vulnerable to rogue agents. Coalitions based on proactive algorithms also do not have the bottleneck and are somewhat less vulnerable but tasks which involve high cost or low reward may remain undone since no agent may take it on. Coalitions formed on the basis of market conditions uses a combination of proactive and reactive algorithms and also take into consideration additional motivating factors and long term goals such as alliance formation between agents. Such coalitions are more effective in some situations but the overhead in computational complexity can make it slow and inefficient. Also, development, maintenance and rescaling of such agents, is more difficult.

Another problem is regarding control. Controls on the agents may be enforced through access control mechanisms, by task re-assignment or agent termination. These decisions may be made by monitoring resource consumption or may be based on performance criteria. The control mechanism to be used, depends on the overall architecture of the agent system. The control mechanism should take into account the communication between agent, the mechanism and effects of interrupting a task and the cost of reassigning tasks.

3.3 Agencies

Communicating agents that are co-operative can be organized into federations to perform tasks that are too large or complex for a single agent. Rather than a monolithic system, a federated approach to the Intelligent Integration of Information using cooperating agents is more robust and scalable to the needs of information integration for e-business and logistic operations.

An agency is a subset of a federation of trusted agents, each with specific goals and a specific functional role. The agents within the agency can communicate with each other within a defined vocabulary. In order to have interoperable systems for added flexibility, the agents may communicate in XML so that the vocabulary is extendible depending on future requirements. This framework and architecture is modular, scalable, and fosters the creation of virtual enterprises, in logistics and similar application domains.

4 Agents For E-Business and Logistic Applications

Most enterprises have legacy systems and also access information on the Internet. Commerce on the Internet requires the ability to access diverse data residing in multiple, autonomous, heterogeneous databases and integrate or fuse that data into coherent information that can be used by the enterprise. The problem is complicated by the fact that the data may by multimedia with diverse temporal and spatial granularity and stored in diverse formats. The semantics of the data may conflict across multiple sources and the data may be of uncertain quality, and the reliability of the source may be questionable.

Most enterprises have legacy systems and also access information on the Internet. Commerce on the Internet requires the ability to access diverse data residing in multiple, autonomous, heterogeneous databases and integrate or fuse that data into coherent information that can be used by the enterprise. The problem is complicated by the fact that the data may by multimedia with diverse temporal and spatial granularity and stored in diverse formats. The semantics of the data may conflict across multiple sources and the data may be of uncertain quality, and the reliability of the source may be questionable.

With the widespread use of the Internet and world wide web (WWW), we have a complex, evolutionary, dynamic, distributed electronic market and the concepts of a global village. Information is easily available online but needs to be properly interpreted and processed in order to negotiate and conduct business. Multiple copies of knowledge and data, possibly in differing formats, may have to be maintained by any application system that uses information from the web. There are several facets to the heterogeneity of information in systems: syntactic, control and semantic. Syntactic heterogeneity refers to the different formats currently used to represent both knowledge and data. Control heterogeneity refers to the many reasoning mechanisms for intelligent systems including induction, deduction, analogy, case-based reasoning, etc. Semantic heterogeneity arises from disagreement on the meaning, interpretation and intended use of related knowledge and data. With different knowledge representations, information about the same thing is represented in different ways in the knowledge database. Such alternative views are helpful in making semantic leaps that result in "discovery" and automated "creativity". Agents can be used to gather and process information and monitoring/ active view agents can provide alerts, based on user-specified critical events, conditions, or new/pertinent information and knowledge. Syntactic differences in information can be resolved by translation agents given the computational equivalence of the representation formalisms. Problem-solving can then be a cooperative endeavor of several agents. Cooperative information agents play a major role in the Electronic Marketspace by: Coping with the different styles and interfaces to different marketplaces; Eliminating repetitive tasks; Eliminating the need to have the user initiate all tasks (and monitor all events) explicitly; Enabling interoperability of software that perform different tasks (by providing a communication medium).

Therefore, rather than a monolithic application system, a federated approach to integration of information using cooperating intelligent agents, is more amenable to the needs of information integration requirements of e-business logistics. Agents with domain-specific knowledge can provide services, such as, access, query formulation, facilitation, brokerage, mediation, integration, wrapping, etc., that enable the modern enterprise to realize its information management needs, while serving its users in a timely, efficient and cost-effective manner. Commercially available and existing (legacy)software infrastructure can be "wrapped" in to develop field agent that can interact with the other agents in the system. Thus, a system of cooperating information agents, each having the requisite knowledge to perform its tasks within the larger problem-solving framework would provide a flexible architecture for the business application.

The advantage of using Agents for building e-business and logistic applications is that they are composable and configurable so that the application system requirements for a particular enterprise can be built fairly rapidly. The agent system would provide the infrastructure needed for a seamless connection of enterprises and would serve as an "engine" or "shell" for transactions between databases involved in the different commerce applications. The system should be designed to contain everything that software developers and system and network administrators would need to construct, launch, receive and manage the intelligent agents in the application they develop. Specifically, the system should provide an integrated development environment, an agent manager interface and sample agents. The development environment may includes an editor (preferably visual), an agent scripting language (preferably featuring OLE and HTML support), debugging tools, sample source code, and perhaps a help system. Today there are some commercially available systems which may be deployed, relatively easily, as a logistic application.

5 System Architecture

In this Section, we propose an agency-based architecture for the Electronic Marketspace. The overall architecture of the application consists of a collection of cooperating agencies, each consisting of cooperating agents.

Each agency performs a specific functional role in the Marketspace. Therefore, each agency can be considered as a collection of cooperating autonomous agents with particular expertise. The same agent may "register" and be a part of more than one agency.

At the heart of the system is an executive agent that acts as a facilitator in the organization. The executive agent is XML based and consists of a registration interface and an attribute information repository. The function of the executive agent is to rate the performance of agents and to determine if a registered agent can join an agency. It also implements a request-response service. A client sends its request through the front end input interface. The back-end services responds to this request and sends back to the client the response through an output table. The executive agent also acts as a structured mediator to co-ordinate the actions of the registered agents within the agencies. The executive agent essentially orchestrates the calling sequence and parameter passing of various 'registered' agents while trying to reach a specific predetermined goal.

Individual agents can dynamically join and leave the system as long as their behavior is known to the executive agent or mediator and the agent types conform to their predefined behavior (specialized for some task and committed to assigned tasks). Also it is required that the agent completes all tasks in the queue to which it has committed. The configuration of agents at any time is managed as a back-end engine(in the executive agent) that is transparent to the system user. The agents themselves may be scattered across several servers and behind firewalls, provided they reside in a predetermined location reachable by the facilitator. All agents are assumed to be reliable and trustworthy - that is, they are committed to perform assigned tasks and behave in the way expected by the executive agent. All tasks assigned are either completed in a given time period or an error message is sent to indicate why the task could not be completed or the task is aborted after an allotted time(failure).

Agent communication is based upon a request-response protocol and is strictly agent-to- agent. There is no broadcasting of messages and an agent cannot eavesdrop on conversation between other agents. The conversation space for communication between agent is well-defined and all agents conform to a specific vocabulary known to and specified by the facilitator.

The 'registration' process is an establishment of trusted relationships. It is represented as an update to a configuration file. Sources may take a proactive role by advertising their capabilities but these must be ratified using the registration interface which involves including the addresses of desired sources. At the time of registration, meta-data is provided to ensure co-operation. Pre-defined criteria may be applied so that the information / business is reliable and dependable. The language and vocabulary of these sources can be made to conform to the system by using wrappers or message translators/transducers if the message exchange semantic is well known but we assume in our system the finally wrapped/transduced agent speaks XML

6 Case Study of an Agent Based Just-in-time Delivery System

We have adopted the Agency-based architecture and tailored it to the current vision of the prototypical Electronic Marketspace concept. The architecture developed here, is agency based and is designed to take advantage of the extensive World Wide Web network.

This electronic system is designed primarily to eliminate the need for a large military warehouse of food, clothing and pharmaceuticals for the different supply sites. Since this has strategic implications, it is very important to closely monitor transactions, track the supply of critical items and be able to take necessary corrective action in a timely fashion. This is done automatically by the deployment of special rovers, called sentinels that monitor the system, inform logisticians and decision-makers and trigger alternative contingency plans to take care of a possible crisis. Figure 1 is an overview of the entire system.

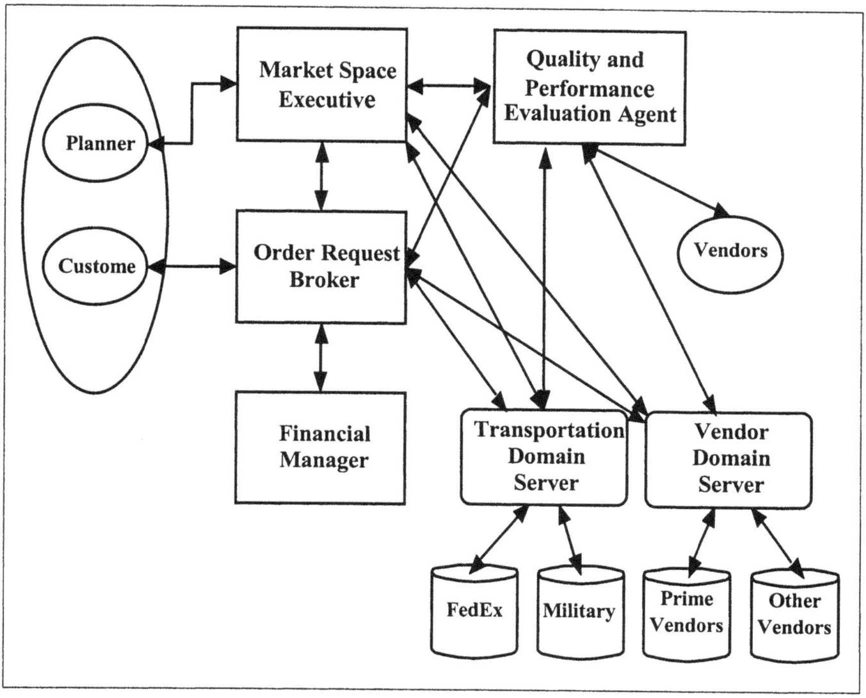

Figure 1: Vision for the prototypical Electronic Market Space

Each agency in the architecture is a multi-layered agent or a federation of agents with a specific goal and functional role in the marketspace. Therefore each can be considered as a collection of cooperating autonomous agents with particular expertise. A detailed version of the architecture with the various agents and sentinels is shown in Figure 2.

The following discussion outlines the constituent agents and the role they play.

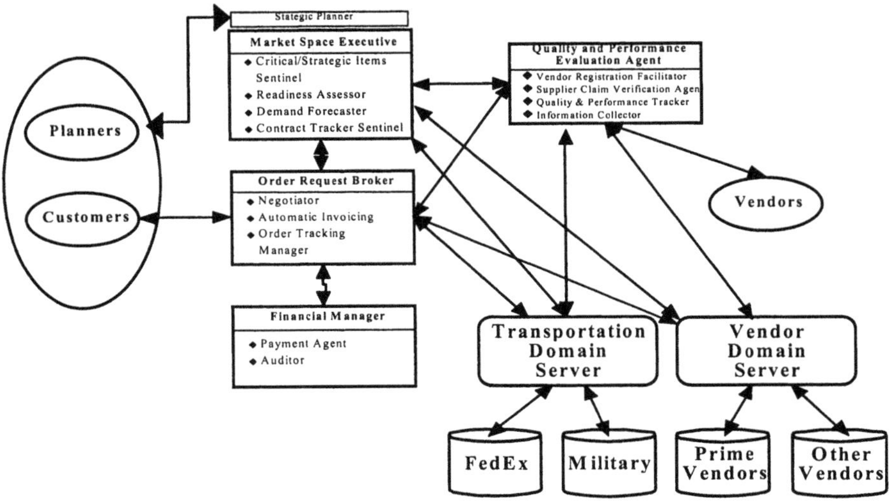

Figure 2: Detailed Architecture for the prototypical Electronic Marketspace

7 Marketspace Executive

This agency handles planning and monitoring of the marketspace. It ensures that probable crisis situations are detected early and avoided by taking suitable action. This also acts as an interface for the organization's planners and strategists who are aware of the long term goals, expectations and strategies.

7.1 Strategic Planner

The strategic planner is the interface to the marketspace executive agency. It allows the user to provide domain knowledge, define long term plans and objectives of the system, define rules and constraints, identify critical items and situations that need to be monitored, define the cause-effect relationships, establish rules and course of action for the sentinels, and obtain reports on all aspects of the system at any time. The desired features of the interface would be to provide heuristic support for all information searching scenarios and providing suggestions for building better queries.

7.2 Sentinel to Track Critical/Strategic Items

This agent consists of a group of daemons which continuously monitor the state of the system, tracking the critical and strategic items .

7.3 Readiness Assessor Sentinel

This agent ensures that strategic plans can be fulfilled by the resources. It is a daemon that ensure that crisis situations are avoided and contingency plans are in place in critical situations.

7.4 Demand Forecasting Manager

This agent breaks down plans into resources and material that need to be provided. It also builds the contract terms necessary to maintain the inventory.

7.5 Sentinel Tracking Contract Terms

This agent is a daemon that monitors the system to alert against any deviation from the contracts made so that necessary alerts are flagged and triggers are fired. This allows the system to detect any deviation from plans already in place so that necessary action can be taken in a timely fashion to ensure crisis control.

8 Order Request Broker

This agency handles the day-to-day functions of the marketspace. It ensures that transactions run smoothly without interruptions and takes corrective action to undo any inconsistency (roll-back). This also acts as an interface for the human operators who perform the individual transactions by providing optimized mapping of customer order to system transactions, suggestion on building better queries to the user (query refinement), improving overall order fulfillment and delivery turn around time. It also enables the creation of personalized user profiles. This agency may be considered to have the following agents:

8.1 Negotiator

This agent provides optimized broker-supplier mapping, and also negotiates with registered suppliers to form contracts in accordance with the specifications and terms specified by the customer.

8.2 Automatic Invoicing

This agent receives supplies and requests payment. It consults a database that contains records of contracts made and supplies obtained against these contracts. It acknowledges the receipt of merchandise based on UPC code scans and a contract identification code which indicates the partial or complete fulfillment of a particular contract. On the receipt of merchandise it sends a request for payment to the appropriate agent in the financial broker.

8.3 Order Tracking Manager

This agent takes over the contract after negotiations have been completed by the negotiator. It tracks progress made and maintains contact with the supplier in order to ensure that the contract is fulfilled according to schedule. If any problem is indicated by the supplier, this agent sends the pertinent information to the sentinel in the in the marketspace executive agency which tracks contract terms. It also communicates with the quality and performance tracker in the quality and performance evaluation agent.

9 Financial Broker

An area vital to the electronic commerce architecture is a secure payment scheme. There are a number of institutions and organizations involved in research to develop not only a secure form of payment but also to make the Internet a secure place for such a business transaction. Some of the major institutions include CyberCash[36], DigiCash[37], First Virtual Bank [38] and many more. Besides the security issues that need to be addressed, a viable interface has to be developed to make payments for purchases with a pay-on-delivery paradigm in mind. This would involve automated invoicing, electronic transfer of funds and performing audits.

The financial broker is the agency that handles the financial transactions of the organization. It consists of the following agents:

9.1 Electronic Invoice Payment and Funds Transfer Agent

This agent removes the need for invoices to be prepared and approved. When the automatic invoicing agent acknowledges the receipt of merchandise corresponding to a particular contract, funds are automatically transferred to the supplier account and records of the financial transaction are sent to the auditor. Depending on the contract terms, the payment may be made incrementally as items are delivered or deferred until the order is completed.

9.2 Auditor

This agent maintains records of all the financial transactions and performs audits.

10 Quality & Performance Evaluation Agent

This agency provides directory services and tracks performance of the vendors. It tracks the measure of the level of confidence in different suppliers - based on previous history, verifies supplier claims and obtains referrals. The agency consists of the following agents:

10.1 Vendor Registration Facilitator

This agent enables new vendors to make their services available to the client. The agent serves as a broker and establishes the communication between the vendor and the customer.

10.2 Supplier Claim Verification Agent

The services that this agent provides include the verification of supplier authenticity by obtaining and checking references. Small contracts in non-critical areas may be recommended (to the negotiator in the order request broker) by this agent in order to build trust in a newly registered vendor.

10.3 Quality & Performance Tracker

The service that this agent provides includes extraction of information and updating the knowledge stored in the supplier-meta-database. As the system is put into use, a variety of information such as previous product specification, user preferences, suppliers used, services used etc. is logged at this tracker site. Data mining techniques are used to extract relationships between the queries, suppliers and clients. Information obtained from the order request broker is used to come up with an evaluation of vendor performance. This evaluation is taken into consideration by the negotiator in the order request broker when selecting a vendor for a new contract.

11 Customer Scenarios

This section presents examples of scenarios showing how the agent community would cooperate in providing information to logistic users.

Customer	Example Scenario	Related Breakthrough concepts	Highlights
92 Airborne	Deploying to Bosnia where floods have caused an outbreak of cholera. Assumptions: Supplies are prepackaged and delivered prior to deployment; Information is available.	Automated Readiness Models available to the Marketspace Executive; Electronic Cataloging; Data Warehousing; Information Sharing; Electronic commerce and communication.	Soldier on the ground in Bosnia uses laptop computer to hook up to a satellite and access the protypical electronic marketspace; Searches electronic catalogs for price, delivery, stock availability, etc; Orders directly from vendor; With insight into logistics requirements from operations plans and readiness models, the system anticipates requisitions models, and facilitates orders rather than reacting from "Ground Zero"; In-place business arrangements facilitate delivery of goods without scrambling. Examples: A soldier can type in "cholera" or "Bosnia/ wintertime" and obtain a list of suggested items to order from the table of equipment (TOE) from the readiness model; Soldier requests either generic - "aspirin" or specific brand such as BAYER or ALLEVE.
Florida National Guard Unit	Deploying troops for hurricane emergency relief. Assumptions: 1. Supplies are not prepackaged. 2. Transporting supplies is more difficult. 3. National Guard requirements are not	Electronic cataloging; Data warehousing; Automated readiness models available to the Marketspace; Information	Guardsman in Florida uses laptop computer to hook up to satellite and access prototypical electronic marketspace; Searches electronic catalogs for price, delivery, stock availability, etc; Orders directly from vendor; The organization uses historical supply models and requirements;

	usually covered under typical business arrangements. Improvisation is key to success.	sharing; Electronic commerce.	Prime Vendor information is available in data warehouses; The organization explores piggybacking on existing business arrangements.
Army Base	Reserves being activated	Information Sharing; Automated Readiness Models available to the Marketspace; Data Warehousing; Real Time Processing; Shared Production.	External: Customer contacts one source to get support for a given mission and the organization's ability to fulfill needs. Internal: Type in "cold, desert" to determine requirements, recommendations, incidentals for all needs, now and in the future; System reports stock on hand; Stock immediately available is determined and shared production helps evaluate options for remaining requirements; Asset balances updated real-time as stock is allocated; Web site is culmination of all information needed.
Air Force Base (AFB)	Out-of-stock condition: Prime vendor in same town. Goal: Get stock from prime vendor to AFB.	Information Sharing; Electronic Commerce using established Business Arrangements; Electronic Catalogs; Data Warehousing;	External Perspective: Customer wants one contact (either prime vendor or the organization) for guaranteed receipt of goods within hours. Internal Perspective: Prime vendor relationship established via "Best Value" Procurement; Real-time processing of requirements; Funds verified; Violations flagged and turned around immediately; Vendor and Order Request Broker are notified automatically via "intelligent gateway" ; Requisition visible to contractor so he/she can ship goods; Requisition automatically re-edited to reflect alternate supplier if Prime Vendor cannot deliver; Information sharing within the system provides flexibility and automated intelligence to best determine where stock should come from; Delivery order validated against contract terms, processed automatically against contract, sent electronically to contractor, updated

			automatically and simultaneously to reflect new totals - signed electronically; Information on past performance automatically recorded; Best shipping strategy determined by automatically evaluating excess stock on hand and customer priority; Contract terms (e.g. delivery schedule) are strictly monitored and enforced.

12 Information Flow

This Section discusses the flow of information required in order for the different agents to perform correctly. Information exchange takes place by sending messages from one agent or object to another. The flow of information is critical to the agent performance. In this section we discuss the different types of messages and the routes that they follow.

Source of Information	**Information Description**	**Receiver of Information**
Customer Strategic planner	Order info (requisitions, priorities, etc.)	Marketspace Executive Negotiator Supplier Claim verification Agent
Customer	Order ratification	Negotiator
Supplier Claim verification Agent Established business arrangements from vendor database	Supply Sources	Readiness Accessor Strategic planner User
Readiness Assessor	Recommended alternative sources of supply prioritized to meet user order criteria	Strategic planner
Vendor database	Historic contract and vendor performance info	Strategic planner Demand forecaster
Order Request Broker	Contract and vendor performance info	Strategic Planner Quality and Performance tracker Vendor database
Vendor database	Historic vendor performance measures and uncertainties Vendor's expected contract performance parameters	Readiness Assessor
Quality & Performance Tracker	Dynamic, real-time vendor performance	Readiness Assessor

	estimates and uncertainties/confidence levels Tradeoff relationships between vendor cost/price and performance	
Demand Forecaster	Demand data over the course of the planning scenario Demand priorities established	Strategic planner
Strategic Planner Negotiator Readiness Assessor	Customer ordering criteria Real-time requisitions Subset of established business relationships that meet legal and regulatory conditions	Negotiator
Negotiator	Running contracts	Order Tracking Manager Quality & Performance Tracker Automatic Invoicing
Automatic Invoicing	Partial fulfillment of contract	Payment Agent Quality & Performance Tracker Order tracking Manager
Demand Forecaster	Estimated risk of completing the transaction	Strategic Planner
Readiness Assessor	Best supply support alternative for demand Prioritized list of alternative supply support Measure of fit with customer ordering criteria	Strategic Planner
Order tracking Manager	deviation from schedule delays in delivery incomplete fulfillment of contract	Quality & Performance Tracker
Payment Agent	Record of funds transferred	Auditor
Vendor	Electronic Catalog Payment methods	Vendor Registration Facilitator
Supplier claim Verification agent	New supplier information	Readiness Assessor Vendor database
Readiness Assessor Strategic Planner	Information about unconventional requirements	Information Collector

13 Conclusion

In nondeterministic systems such as logistic applications, software agents that intelligently anticipate, adapt and actively seek ways to support users in the marketplace are indispensable. It is possible to model a logistic application in a way that allows each logical block to be handled by a relatively simple agency. Agency-based architectures increases productivity by allowing processes to be done in parallel. An executive agent in the agency-based architecture maintains control and ensures co-ordination among agents through established communication protocols. This makes it possible to address issues of goal partitioning and load-balancing. This results in scalable, robust applications that can be tailored for high performance in the given domain.

This paper has presented the current state of information technology in the area of e-commerce logistics. Traditional tools as well as those used to leverage the Internet and World Wide Web for e-business has been discussed. We have briefly examined some of the commercial software tools and techniques currently available. We have presented an information architecture consisting of the information interface, management and gathering layers. Intelligent active services are presented for each layer and the role of the agents in the agency is discussed. The architecture presented represents a *family* of cooperating intelligent agents that may be configured to support decision makers as well as enterprise tasks in various scenarios. These agents play specific roles within an enterprise information architecture, supporting users, maintaining active views, mediating between users and heterogeneous data sources, refining data into knowledge, and roaming the global information infrastructure seeking, locating, negotiating for and retrieving data and knowledge specific to their mission.

The communication and synchronization issues among agents is the subject of continuing research. Further work needs to be done to make the protocols for inter-agent communication more thorough and robust. Adapting the architecture to use the Agent Communication Language (ACL) allows interoperability between the agents, prevents task duplication and allows task exchange and sharing of partial results.

This paper represents the current architectural *vision* for our research activities, and we continue to work toward that vision.

References

1. Genesereth, M. and S.P. Ketchpel (1994), *Software Agents.* Communications of the ACM, **37**(7): p. 48-53.
2. Metzger, P.a.S., W (1995), *IP Authentication using Keyed MD5.* Internet RFC 1828, Proposed Standards.
3. Atkinson, R. (1995) , *IP Encapsulating Security Payload.* Internet RFC 1827, Proposed Standards.
4. Metzger, P., Karn, P and Simpson, W (1995), *The ESP DES-CBC Transform.* Internet RFC 1829, Proposed Standards.
5. Bhimani (1996), *Securing the commercial Internet.* Communications of the ACM,: p. 29-35.
6. Berners-Lee, T., et al.(1994), *The World-Wide Web.* Communications of the ACM, **37**(8): p. 76—82.
7. Borenstein, N.S. (1996), *Perils and pitfalls of practical cybercommerce.* Communications of the ACM, **39**(June): p. 36-44.
8. CommerceNET, *http://www.commerce.net/.*
9. Klusch, M. and O. Shehory (1996). *Coalition Formation Among Rational Information Agents.* in *Seventh European Workshop on Modelling Autonomous Agents in a Multi-Agent World (MAAMAW-96).* Eindhoven, Netherlands: Springer-Verlag.
10. Maes, P., ed.(1990) *Designing Autonomous Agents: Theory and Practice from Biology to Engineering and Back.* Special Issues of Robotics and Autonomous Systems, The MIT Press: Cambridge, MA, London, England. 194.
11. G. Wiederhold, S. Jajodia, and W. Litwin (1991), "Dealing with Granularity of Time in Temporal Databases," in Lecture Notes in Computer Science, vol. 498, R. Anderson and others, Eds.: Springer- Verlag, pp. 124-140.
12. G. Wiederhold, S. Jajodia, and W. Litwin (1993), "Integrating Temporal Data in a Heterogeneous Environment," in Temporal Databases: Theory, Design, and Implementation, A. U. Tansel, S. Jajodia, and others, Eds.: Benjamin/Cummings, pp. 563-579.
13. G. Wiederhold (1996), "Foreword to Special Issue on the Intelligent Integration of Information," Journal of Intelligent Information Systems, vol. 6, 2/3, pp. 93-97.
14. Decker, Keith; Sycara, Katia (1997), Intelligent adaptive Information Agents. Jour. of Intelligent Info. Systems, 9,239-260.
15. R. Davis and R. Smith (1983), "Negotiation as a Metaphor for Distributed Problem Solving," *Artificial Intelligence*, vol. 20, pp. 63-109.
16. P. Maes, T. Darrell, B. Blumberg, and A. Pentland (1996), "The ALIVE System: Wireless, Full-Body Interaction with Autonomous Agents," ACM Multimedia Systems.
17. K.-Y. Lai and T. W. Malone (1991), "Object Lens: Letting End-Users Create Cooperative Work Applications," presented at Proceedings of CHI'91.
18. L. Kerschberg (1997), "Knowledge Rovers: Cooperative Intelligent Agent Support for Enterprise Information Architectures," in Cooperative

Information Agents, vol. 1202, Lecture Notes in Artificial Intelligence, P. Kandzia and M. Klusch, Eds. Berlin: Springer-Verlag, pp. 79-100.

19. L. Kerschberg (1997), "The Role of Intelligent Agents in Advanced Information Systems," in Advanced in Databases, vol. 1271, Lecture Notes in Computer Science, C. Small, P. Douglas, R. Johnson, P. King, and N. Martin, Eds. London: Springer-Verlag, pp. 1-22.
20. S. Jajodia and L. Kerschberg (1997), "Advanced Transaction Models and Architectures," . Norwall, MA: Kluwer Academic Publishers.
21. S. Dao and B. Perry (1996), "Information Mediation in Cyberspace: Scalable Methods for Declarative Information Networks," *Journal of Intelligent Information Systems*, vol. 6, 2/3, pp. 131-150.
22. G. Wiederhold (1992), "The Roles of Artificial Intelligence in Information Systems," *Journal of Intelligent Information Systems*, vol. 1, pp. 35-56.
23. G. Wiederhold (1996), "Foreword to Special Issue on the Intelligent Integration of Information," *Journal of Intelligent Information Systems*, vol. 6, 2/3, pp. 93-97.
24. Kerschberg, L. (1996), *et al.*, *Knowledge Rovers: A Family of Configurable Software Agents*, in *Proposal Funded by DARPA's Advanced Logistics Program.*, Center for Information Systems Integration and Evolution, George Mason University, URL: http://www.isse.gmu.edu/KRG/: Fairfax, VA.
25. Kerschberg, L. (1997), *Knowledge Rovers: Cooperative Intelligent Agent Support for Enterprise Information Architectures*, in *Lecture Notes in Computer Science*, M. Klusch, Editor., Springer-Verlag.
26. A. Motro (1990), "FLEX: A Tolerant and Cooperative User Interface to Databases," *IEEE Transactions on Knowledge and Data Engineering*, vol. 2, pp. 231-246.
27. A. Motro (1993), "Accommodating Imprecision in Database Systems: Issues and Solutions," In *Multidatabase Systems: An Advanced Solution to Global Information Sharing*, A. R. Hurson, M. W. Bright, and S. Pakzad, Eds.: IEEE Computer Society Press, pp. 381-386.
28. A. Motro (1993), "A Formal Framework for Integrating Inconsistent Answers from Multiple Information Sources," Department of Information and Software Systems Engineering, George Mason University, Fairfax, VA, Technical Report ISSE-TR-93-106.
29. A. Motro (1994), "Intensional Answers to Database Queries," *IEEE Transactions on Knowledge and Data Engineering*, vol. 6, pp. 444-454.
30. A. Motro (1994), "Management of Uncertainty in Database Systems," In *Modern Database Systems: The Object Model, Interoperability and Beyond*, W. Kim, Ed.: Addison-Wesley Publishing Company/ACM Press.
31. A. Motro (1995), "Multiplex: A Formal Model for Multidatabases and Its Implementation," ISSE Department, George Mason University, Fairfax, VA, Technical Report ISSE-TR-95-10.
32. A. Motro (1995), "Responding with Knowledge," In *Advances in Databases and Artificial Intelligence, Vol. 1: The Landscape of Intelligence in Database and Information Systems*, vol. 1, L. Delcambre and F. Petry, Eds.: JAI Press.
33. A. Motro, D. Marks, and S. Jajodia (1994), "Aggregation in Relational Databases: Controlled Disclosure of Sensitive Information," European Symposium on Research in Computer Security.

34. A. Motro and P. Smets (1996), "Uncertainty Management in Information Systems: from Needs to Solutions," . Norwall, MA: Kluwer Academic Publishers, pp. 48
35. K. S. Decker (1995), "Environment Centered Analysis and Design of Coordination Mechanisms," in Ph.D. Thesis, Department of Computer Science. Amherst, MA,: University of Massachusetts.
36. Cybercash, *http://tear.cybercash.com/*.
37. Digicash, *http://cybercash.com/*.
38. Bank, F.V., *http://www.fv.com/*.

Intelligent Customer Support for Product Selection with Case-Based Reasoning

Ralph Bergmann[1], Sascha Schmitt[2], Armin Stahl[2]

[1] University of Hildesheim, Germany
[2] University of Kaiserslautern, Germany

Abstract. Current product-oriented database search facilities are widely used on the Internet but recognized as limited in capability for intelligent sales support. The vision of intelligent knowledgeable virtual sales agents is to incorporate more knowledge about products, customers, and the sales process into an electronic shop. This chapter describes a knowledge-based technology called case-based reasoning (CBR) and shows how it can be adapted and applied for developing intelligent virtual sales agents. To emphasize the advantages for our approach, we implemented several applications, some of which are in daily use.

1 Introduction

Electronic commerce offers a huge variety of application areas nowadays. Much effort is put into research and exploration of these areas. However, research to address one of the most important problems, responsive online sales support, has generated only few promising approaches. Most electronic catalogs and online shops still do not explore the interactivity available on the Web. On most sites, the searching and indexing capabilities provide only little more support than their printed counterparts. While these search functions are considered quite important by the online sellers, the quality of the retrieval results is miserable [7]. The key to enhancing search quality, and more generally, to approach the vision of intelligent knowledgeable virtual sales agents, is to incorporate more knowledge about products, customers, and the sales process into the sales agent.

Driven by the challenge to improve Internet-based electronic commerce, Case-Based Reasoning (CBR) technology emerged as a new important area [3, 5, 17, 19, 20]. The main role for CBR in electronic commerce is intelligent customer support for the task to select a product that is most appropriate for the customer's demands. Currently, several applications of this kind have been implemented and are accessible on the Web already.

In this chapter, we give an overview of the methods for intelligent customer support that have been developed starting from the CBR idea. First, the next section gives a brief overview of the general electronic commerce scenario and the role of intelligent customer support. Then, we introduce the basic CBR idea as the starting point. Based on this, Sect. 4 describes an application and specialization of CBR for intelligent customer support. Finally, we present two different concrete application examples.

2 The Electronic Commerce Scenario

In conventional electronic commerce scenarios, only computers represent the companies. Electronic sales agents act in substitution for human sales clerks in the different phases of the online sales.

2.1 The Electronic Commerce Transaction Phases

From a customer's point of view, the classical sales transaction consists of the three main steps: *information*, *agreement*, and *settlement* [16]. These steps are often extended by a fourth one *after-sales* [8].

In case of electronically supported sales transactions resp. transactions processed via electronic media like the Internet, we consider a slightly different model of three consecutive high-level business processes: *pre-sales*, *sales*, and *after-sales* [19]. Each of these processes is described on a more detailed level by several sales transaction phases, which is depicted in Fig. 1. In these phases we regard the customer's view on the problem. The sales person's view would certainly look different.

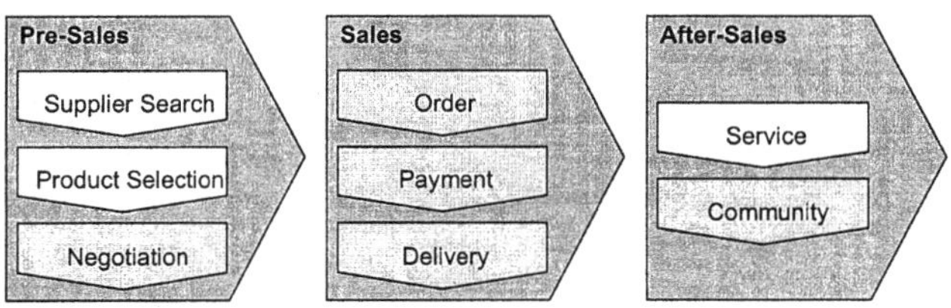

Fig. 1. Transaction Phases in Electronic Commerce.

In the pre-sales phase, three processes are identified. The customer will usually start the transaction by looking for a supplier who will possibly be able to solve her/his problem resp. fulfill her/his requirements (*supplier search*). This can either be a supplier-focussed search, i.e. the customer knows already the supplier and is just looking for more specific information, or a problem-oriented search, i.e. the customer does not know the supplier yet. Having identified one or more suppliers, available information will be collected and compared. This process also has to identify all information relevant for the customer's buying decision. The overall aim of this process is to present products that will be selected by the customer (*product selection*). Product properties are often most relevant for this decision. In complex decision situations, it is possible to further support the customer during product search. This process does not only have to solve the problem of fixed product selection but also the problem of configuration of products by the customer (cf. Sect. 4.3). The last process considered as part of the pre-sales phase is the negotiation about prices and conditions for buying. The succeeding sales phase consists of the *ordering* resp. order placement for the selected products and the decision for an adequate way of *payment* and *delivery*. The additional after-sales processes *service* and *community* try to increase the degreee of customer satisfaction and/or to bind the customer stronger to the supplier. The aim is also to increase the customer's benefit of deploying the product.

Depending on the offered products in the electronic shop and the target customer groups, the individual sales phases will be more or less strongly supported by the sales agent. In this chapter, we deal with the aspect of intelligent customer support. How this can be realized is exemplarily shown on the basis of the product selection process, at which we take a more detailed look in the ensuing subsection.

2.2 Steps Involved in Product Selection

The general product selection process can be subdivided into four phases:

1. *Dialog*: Interactive acquisition of customer's wishes.
2. *Retrieval*: Selection of appropriate products from the product base.
3. *Customization*: Modify the retrieved product to better fulfill the customer's wish.
4. *Product Presentation*: Show the product to the customer and possibly explain why the product is appropriate.

During the *dialog* phase (cf. Sect. 4.1), the customer's demands and wishes have to be captured interactively with the customer and formalized by the system. Based on this information, the electronic sales system processes the *retrieval* phase (cf. Sect. 4.2) to select appropriate products from the product database, which are then presented to the customer. Before or even within the *presentation* phase (cf. Sect. 4.4), a *customization* phase (cf. Sect. 4.3) can be possibly invoked, either to automatically adapt the found products or also interactively adapt them with the customer's control. These four phases do not necessarily have to be processed one after the other but they can interweave, which will even be the usual way. Furthermore, the phases might be iterated.

To provide intelligent customer support appropriate technology is needed. Case-Based Reasoning, CBR, is a well-established technology that qualifies for such a purpose. This has already been proven in several applications. CBR is especially suited for supporting not only the product selection process but also the supplier search and service processes. The following section gives a brief introduction into CBR technology and later sections show its potentials especially in the field of electronic commerce.

3 Fundamental Technology: Case-Based Reasoning

In this section, we describe the basics of the fundamental technology used to realize the intelligent customer support for product selection, namely Case-Based Reasoning (CBR).

The basic idea of CBR is to solve new problems by comparing them to problems already solved [1, 3, 10, 12]. The key assumption is that if two problems are similar then their solutions are probably also similar.

3.1 The CBR Concept: Using Old Solutions for New Problems

Old problems and their solutions are stored in a database of cases — the *case base.* Often, the cases are stored as collections of attribute-value pairs, but for complex tasks it is useful to explicitly represent the hierarchical structure of the cases by describing them as structured objects, using inheritance, object decomposition, and possibly other relations between the object parts.

When a new problem has to be solved, the CBR system searches for the most similar old problem within the case base. The solution to this old problem can be adapted to more precisely meet the requirements of the new problem. Fig. 2 illustrates the steps taken in a Case-Based Reasoning system.

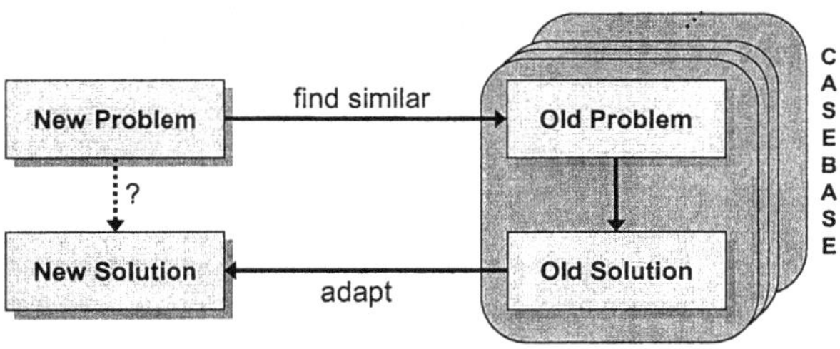

Fig. 2. General Processing within a CBR System.

For applying CBR to product search in electronic commerce, the cases are descriptions of products. The problem description in a case is a specification of a single product and possible demands the product can satisfy. The solution to the problem is an unambiguous reference to the product. For configurable products such as computers, automobiles, complex machines, and so on, the solution is not only the part number, but also possibly the entire configuration. When a customer enters a query, i.e., a description of a desired product, the query is regarded as a new problem and the CBR system tries to solve it by comparing it to the cases in the case base.

3.2 Similarity Measures

To be able to find a *similar* old problem in the case base, CBR systems must have more specific domain knowledge built into them than ordinary database systems. The main part of this additional knowledge is encoded in a *similarity measure*, a function that assesses the similarity of a given query to the cases in the case base. The similarity values are ordinal values that are often normalized to the interval [0, 1]. A value of 0 means "does not satisfy the query at all" and a value of 1 says "that's exactly what you asked for".

To understand how such a similarity measure is used to find the best solutions for a given problem, consider the cases being represented as a fixed length vector of n attributes. These attributes can have numerical values or their values can be arranged to reflect some kind of order.

The problem space can be seen as a n-dimensional space where similar problems are placed closely together. The term "close" is defined by the similarity measure, e.g., in Fig. 3 the circle around the query Q indicates a region with "close" cases defined by a particular similarity threshold. When a new problem is presented to the system, the similarity to all the cases in the case base is calculated. The cases within a similarity range of a certain threshold (or sometimes a fixed number of similar cases) are then presented to the user, i.e. in our scenario to the customer.

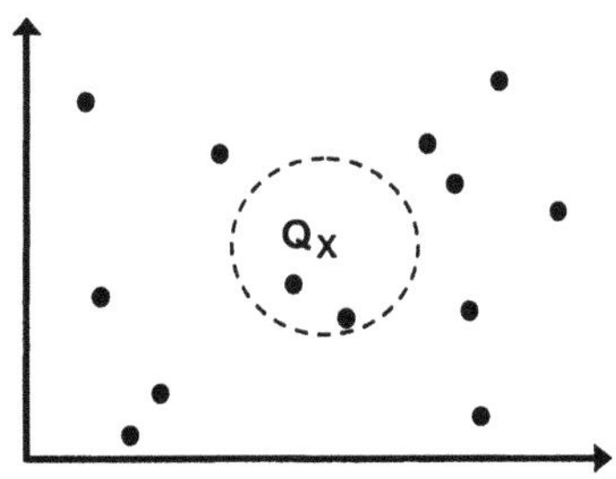

Fig. 3. Cases Distributed over the n-dimensional Problem Space.

The usual approach to define such a similarity measure is to start with so-called *local* similarity measures for all the attributes. For numerical attributes a simple approach is to calculate the difference between the query value and the value of the case and normalize the result to the interval [0, 1], for example, by applying the formula $1 - (d / (d + 1))$ to the difference d. However, most attributes require specialized functions because the similarity function must reflect the domain knowledge about to what degree a deviation of an attribute value can be tolerated since the case (or here the product) is still useful.

In real-world applications not all attribute values are numerical values. A case description very often contains boolean or symbolic attributes. In such cases, a table that defines the similarities for all possible pairs of attribute values can describe the local similarity measure. Even more complex attribute types such as taxonomy types or complex objects are sometimes required.

Once the local similarity functions are defined, the global similarity of two cases must be derived from the local similarities. The usual way to do this is to apply a weighted sum to all the local similarities. Consider a query q is described by the attributes $q_1, \ldots, q_n$ and a case c is described by $c_1, \ldots, c_n$, where attribute values with corresponding indices belong to the same attribute. The similarity σ between q and c can be calculated from the local similarities σ_i as follows:

$$\sigma(q,c) = \sum_{i=1}^{n} w_i \sigma_i(q_i, c_i)$$

where

$$\sum_{i=1}^{n} w_i = 1 \text{ and } w_i \geq 0 \text{ for all } i.$$

Although the weights w_i have to be assessed by a domain expert, they can be manipulated by the customer to express individual preferences.

This general method of defining a similarity measure as a weighted sum can be modified and refined in many ways. In general, the computation of the similarity measure depends on the data model and the type of application. A simple weighted sum is not always adequate. For example, non-linear dependencies between the weights can cause the relevance of a certain feature to depend on the values of other features. CBR offers a number of possible solutions to account for such non-linear similarity measures.

Finding a suitable similarity measure is often the most critical part of the design and implementation of a CBR system. Once a good similarity measure has been found and implemented, maintaining a CBR system is rather easy. Typically, neither the similarity measure nor the domain model need to be changed for a long time compared to the knowledge bases of other types of expert systems. Often, the only part that undergoes significant changes over time is the case base.

3.3 Adaptation

Some CBR systems do not only support the retrieval of old solutions but they also adapt solutions to the new problem and thus create new solutions that differ from the old ones. This is particularly important when the solution space is large with respect to the number of cases that can be expected to be in the case base. To implement the adaptation step, the knowledge needed to perform the solution modification must be represented in some suitable form in the CBR system. Depending on the application domain, the adaptation process can be more or less complicated. Bergmann and Wilke [2] describe a classification of different adaptation methods and the knowledge required by them.

When applying CBR to product selection, adaptation is important for complex, configurable products. If there are many product variants (like for the configuration of personal computers, other technical equipment, or also, for example, for travel packages), we cannot develop a case base that explicitly stores each possible product configuration. Here, we must start from a limited set of typical base products from which one the initial product is chosen that is then adapted to better suit the customer's requirements.

4 Realizing Intelligent Product Selection

CBR is closely related to the field of database technology. The motivation for the need of the relatively new CBR technology instead of standard database systems in electronic commerce environments comes from the fact that ordinary database systems do not provide sales support. Customers searching for product information on the Web will be dissatisfied with a huge database of products and a database search engine on top of it because for using the system one needs very special knowledge. Only a customer who knows the product part number is assured of finding the desired information. However, if the customer is not looking for a specific part but for a product with particular qualities, the success of the search is much less certain. Unless being very familiar with the contents of the database, the customer will get either no answer to the query or an excess of answers that might not be sorted in any usable way. The situation is even more frustrating if the customer does not know exactly what qualities to look for.

An online catalog could provide intelligent sales support through a system that puts the knowledge of a shop assistant into its product selection component. The system would require enough domain knowledge about the products to be able to aid customers in their searches. Such a system would not only satisfy the customers but also help the manufacturer or broker to sell products. Case-Based Reasoning is one way to implement it.

Two essential properties distinguish this approach described from ordinary database systems: cases are compared using special similarity measures and they can be further customized after retrieval by using adaptation techniques. In contrast to the concept of equality, similarity does not follow an obvious semantics [4]. Different interpretations of similarity are possible and affect the functionality of the Case-Based Reasoning system. In electronic commerce applications, the similarity measures are used as a heuristic for the degree of customer satisfaction with the product. The better the similarity measures approximate the degree of satisfaction, the better are the product suggestions made by the electronic sales system.

In the following sections we discuss the single steps of the product selection process, introduced in Sect. 2.2, in more detail. We will show how to support these steps in an intelligent way by applying the Case-Base Reasoning technology.

4.1 Dialog

Online customers need information adequate to their demands instead of pure data. They want personalized advice and product offerings instead of simple possibilities for product search [18]. Gaining sufficient information from the customer but also providing her/him with information at the right place is the key. Resulting from this fact, an automated communication process is needed that simulates the sales dialog between customers and sales persons. In electronic commerce applications it is important to keep the effort for the customer to communicate with the sales system as low as possible. Different types of electronic sales sites can be found, e.g., portals, e-malls, e-shops, etc., dealing also with different kinds of products. There is a high potential that customers get easily lost. They are asked a wide range of questions about the whole spectrum of products on the e-site. They run into difficulties and at the end they get frustrated because of too many, too difficult, or redundant questions that lead to wrong or no results at all in the worst case. Unsatisfied customers can easily leave to the next electronic shop, which is only a mouse-click away. However, the system has to find out about the customer's demands, wishes, and requirements before it can search its database for adequate products. Since not all customers are the same, it is necessary to follow a personalized strategy, which offers one-to-one support. But, such strategies are still far away from being the standard in current electronic shops.

Dialog Categories in Electronic Commerce

According to the level of customer assistance offered during demand acquisition, currently available electronic sales systems can be classified in three different categories:

Catalog-based. Catalog-based systems offer very little guidance. They implement only browsing functionality like the customer would do with a traditional paper-based product catalog. Sometimes, full text search allows easier product navigation in the electronic shop.

Questionnaire-based. The next higher level of customer support is reached by questionnaire-based applications, which present a structured input mask or form of all product features resp. attributes. Such forms are a convenient way for experts to express their product wish in every detail but can be very hard to handle for inexperienced customers.

Dialog-based. The best customer support is reached by dialog-based applications. Such systems offer guidance by asking goal-directed questions and presenting product alternatives, to help the customer decide. The dialog can either be *static* or *dynamic*, depending on how the next interaction is decided. Static dialogs follow a pre-defined strategy, which is usually modeled in terms of a decision tree or a rule base. Dynamic dialogs decide at runtime which interaction to execute next, depending on the customer's previous answers and the currently available products. Dynamic dialogs offer the highest flexibility and come closest to one-to-one support. Dialog-based strategies are hardly found in commercial applications. First prototypes can be found, which follow a static strategy, but no dynamically interpreted dialog is applied.

We will focus on the dynamic dialogs because they are especially useful to bridge the knowledge gap that hinders communication between customer and sales system [13]. The customer has knowledge on her/his product wish, which has to be communicated to the system. There might be rather only an idea of the desired functionality the desired product should have than knowledge about technical aspects of specific products. Additionally, the customer's product wish may be incomplete since s/he may be undecided in some aspects of the product. The electronic sales system should help the customer to make a decision.

The task of the dialog system as part of the sales system is to decide which interaction, i.e. which question to ask, is most useful for finding adequate products to the current sales situation. One possible criterion is to determine the expected information gain of the interaction. An interaction that contributes much information leads to shorter dialogs, which implies less effort for the customer. It is also important that questions are chosen according to the customer's domain knowledge, i.e. they have to be easily understood. At this stage, a sales system based on CBR technology can profit from the information contained in the similarity measures.

Information Gain Measures for Dynamic Dialogs

In the context of electronic commerce, a question is relevant if it helps to discriminate between products the customer is willing to buy and unsatisfactory products. The more information is conveyed by a question, the better can the candidate products be separated. The exact amount of information gained depends on the answer to the question and the current set of available products. If, e.g., only red cars are available, the fact that the customer wants a red car does not help to narrow down the set of candidate products and does therefore not convey any valuable information. Since the information gain depends on the customer's answer to the question, which cannot be known in advance, only the expected information gain of a question can be calculated which is the weighted sum over all possible answers. A goal-directed, dynamic dialog strategy chooses questions with the highest expected information gain.

Recently, a couple of CBR approaches to automated sales dialogs have been suggested. The ideas that can be found have in common that their aim is the reduction of the number of questions (dialog length) a customer is asked by the sales system. While in this context mostly information gain measures based on entropy are proposed [6], measures based on similarity distributions are better suited for electronic commerce applications [9]. The similarity of a product represents the degree of customer satisfaction in a product. A similarity distribution with a great variance helps to discriminate between satisfying and unsatisfying products. An information gain measure that tries to optimize the variance of similarities in the current set of candidates, is the most direct way to find satisfactory products [9].

Customer-Adaptive Dialogs

Not all customers are the same. A real sales person is aware of this fact and treats each customer individually. If an electronic sales system is to offer one-to-one support, the chosen strategy has to adapt to each individual customer. This can be reached by, e.g., assigning individual attribute weights, making customized product suggestions, choosing questions that require minimal effort from the customer and can easily be understood.

All these adaptations require information about the customer. To obtain the customer's profile her/his reactions to dialog interactions can be observed. From these reactions, conclusions can be drawn on the customer's profile and predictions can be made for future reactions. Such an assessment of the customer can be implemented by utilizing, e.g., a Bayesian network like done by Kohlmaier et al. [9]. Dynamically obtaining the customer profile allows the system to react on changes in the customer's behavior. While solutions that are based on a stored profile would depend on correct information, a dynamically created profile is directly sensitive to the customer's behavior. If the customer changes her/his behavior during the dialog, the profile changes as well and the dialog strategy selects different questions, matching the new profile.

If one focuses on single attribute questions, the most important way to adapt to the customer is to pose questions that the customer can answer. Most traditional strategies trying to minimize the dialog length neglect the fact that a question will not be answered. The customer will also not answer an arbitrary amount of questions because s/he is only willing to invest a certain amount of effort in finding the desired products. If each question requires less effort to answer then in total more questions can be posed. But, if the questions that require less effort to answer convey less information, more questions are required in total to narrow down possible target products. A utility function has to balance between the effort required to answer a question and the expected information gain. The required effort can be estimated by the customer's reaction to the question and the probabilities of future reactions. In this way, a customer-adaptive dialog strategy can be implemented by selecting attribute questions with the highest expected utility value, which is derived from the combination of the probabilities and the similarity-influenced measure.

A dialog system selecting questions based on similarity influence is obviously strongly connected to the retrieval system.

4.2 Retrieval

Retrieval techniques from CBR have become very important techniques for realizing intelligent product recommendation agents. The core of such applications is a product database that describes the specific features of each available product. When applying CBR, this product database is treated as a case base, i.e., each product record in the database is interpreted as a case in a case base. During the retrieval phase, product cases are retrieved based on the *similarity* (see Sect. 3.2) between the product features and the requirements. The similarity encodes the knowledge to assess whether a product is suitable for the customer's requirements.

Similarity can be formalized through *similarity measures* that are modeled by combining several parameterizable *local similarity measures* for individual product features with a *global aggregation function*. Thereby global and individual preferences for product selection can be modeled. The main purpose of the retrieval component is to select from the product database a set of products with the highest similarity as computed by the similarity measure. In the area of CBR, several different similarity-based retrieval algorithms have been developed in the past. In the following, we want to give a short overview of the algorithms that are particularly suited to realize intelligent product selection. Here, the challenge is to realize *efficient* retrieval on a *large* and *highly dynamic* product database.

Complete Brute-Force Search

The complete brute-force search evaluates the similarity of each case from the case base with respect to the query and maintains a list that collects the best matching cases. This means, in our electronic commerce scenario the algorithm compares the customer's demands with every available product in the product database and computes a respective similarity value. The output is then a list of products ordered by these similarity values.

One advantage of this algorithm is obviously the low implementation effort. Another advantage is its *completeness* for every computable similarity measure, i.e., it can be guaranteed that the most similar product is found. However, if large databases are used or if many customers access the electronic shop at the same time the algorithm is unacceptable due to bad performance.

Case-Retrieval Nets

If the application requires a more efficient algorithm than the brute-force search, special index-based approaches can be applied. One such approach that is used by commercial CBR applications in the area of electronic commerce is based on case retrieval nets (CRNs) [11]. A case retrieval net is a directed graph with nodes representing cases as well as the so-called information entities (IEs) contained in the cases (e.g., the product attributes). These nodes are linked according to the degree to which they influence each other, i.e., through a local similarity. Given a set of cases, such a case retrieval net is constructed prior to retrieval. During retrieval, the IEs that occur in the current problem description are activated and this initial activation is propagated through the net. Cases that are activated at the end of this process are those selected by the retrieval approach.

The advantage of this approach compared with the brute-force search is the much better performance. However, to use a CRN the underlying graph structure has to be constructed offline and must be updated after every change in the product database. To manage this index structure for large databases the memory requirements of the algorithm are an important aspect to be considered.

Similarity-based Retrieval by Approximation with SQL Queries

Another approach that tries to avoid the disadvantages of the previously described retrieval algorithms is a similarity-based retrieval on top of relational databases [15]. The basic idea behind this approach is to approximate similarity-based retrieval with adequate SQL queries. Therefore, a special SQL query is constructed to retrieve a limited number of cases from the database. For these cases the exact similarity values are then computed by using the defined similarity measure. After that, the algorithm decides whether it is necessary to retrieve more cases from the database to find the most similar cases. In this case the previously SQL query will be relaxed to get the necessary cases. If enough cases are retrieved they are presented to the user ordered by the computed similarity values.

On the one hand, this approach avoids duplicating the case data or compiling index structures and is therefore ideal for huge case bases which are often subject to changes. On the other hand, it is also very efficient because the time-consuming similarity computation is restricted on a relatively small subset of the product database. The disadvantage of this approach is that the completeness of the retrieval cannot be guaranteed in general. This means, the most similar case is not necessarily included in the returned result list. However, this may be tolerated for product selection with huge databases because there are probably other returned products that are acceptable for the customer.

4.3 Customization

When selling products that allow modifications in order to satisfy the individual needs and wishes of a particular customer, an additional phase can be included into the overall product selection process. During this customization phase, the customer has the possibility to find a product that fulfills her/his specific demands even if the given product database does not contain such a product at all. Therefore, the best-matching product selected by the retrieval process before is used as a starting point. This product can be characterized as the best available standard product that is available within the given product database. In the case of very complex configurable products, the retrieved product can also represent a kind of minimal configuration that can be extended or modified to satisfy the customer demands. Then we can also call it *base product.*

To support the customization phase with intelligent software agents, approaches that have their origin in adaptation techniques from CBR can be applied. Which approaches are most suitable depends mainly on the structure of the products to be customized. Products that allow only limited modifications require usually different customization techniques than products that support wide configuration possibilities. For example, it is a significant difference whether a customer may only choose the color of a product or s/he may completely configure products such as holidays, insurance plans, or complex technical equipment. To be able to handle these different product types, two different customization approaches have been developed:

Operator-based Customization

The operator-based customization approach supports interactive modification of products by the customer. After a best-matching product has been retrieved and presented to the customer, a set of *customization operators* is provided, which may be applied to further customize the product. Each customization operator encodes a particular atomic way of adapting certain products. The description of such an operator contains

- a precondition that specifies under which circumstances the product can be modified,
- a set of parameters to specify the details of the customization,
- an action part specifying how the product is affected by the customization.

The result of the application of such an operator is a modified product that is presented to the customer. S/He has then to decide whether this product fulfills her/his demands or not. For the second case, the customization component may provide further customization operators in order to find a more suitable product. The currently presented product can then be characterized as an *intermediate product* of the entire customization process (see Fig. 4).

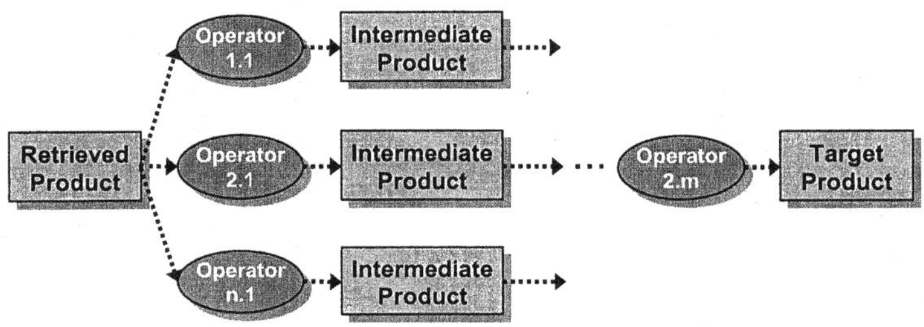

Fig. 4. Operator-based Customization.

By applying the described procedure, the customization component enables the customer to navigate through the space of available products and takes care of the applicability of operators, validity of parameter values, and the consistency of the adapted products.

In B2C scenarios, the operator-based approach is particularly suited to support products with limited customization capabilities since otherwise the set of applicable operators overstrains the customer. However, in B2B scenarios in which clients have expert knowledge about the products, the operator-based approach can be applied to more complex products as well.

Incremental Component Replacement

The incremental component replacement approach is particularly suited to complex products that require sophisticated customization. It is assumed that products are structured into sub-components, possibly in a hierarchical manner. Furthermore, product databases with some pre-configured base products and individual sub-components are required. After retrieving the best pre-configured base product with respect to the customer's requirements, the product is customized by incrementally replacing sub-components by more suitable ones. This customization process is organized as a cycle. Components with a low similarity (*weak components)*, i.e., components that do not fulfill the customer's requirements well enough, are candidates for being replaced. By recursively applying CBR at the level of sub-component, alternative components are selected from the product database. Then, the weak component is replaced by an alternative component and the validity of the resulting adapted product is checked. During this validation, constraints that exist between the different components are evaluated. Violation leads to backtracking to the component replacement step, giving the next best component a chance. This adaptation cycle is executed several times. In every run the overall suitability of the product is increased. An illustration of the described procedure is shown in Fig. 5.

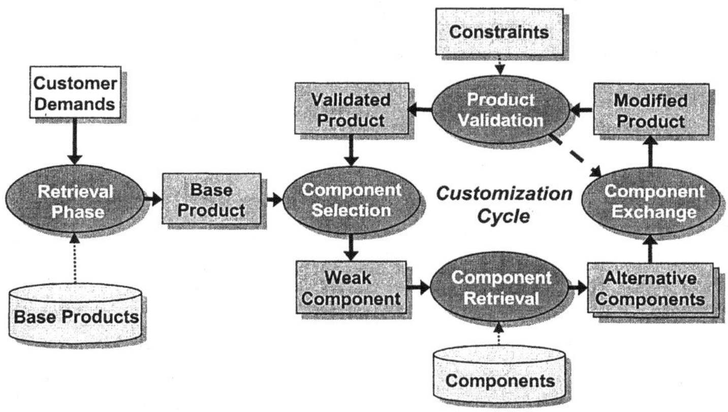

Fig. 5. Incremental Component Replacement.

Generally, we can notice that the adaptation cycle implements a hill-climbing search to solve a combination of a constraint satisfaction problem and an optimization problem for the product suitability (measured by the similarity). On the one hand, it has to find a combination of different components representing a working product, i.e., a product that fulfills all constraints. On the other hand, it has to find an optimal combination that fulfills the customer's demands as well as possible.

4.4 Product Presentation

After the product has been retrieved and possibly adapted, it must be presented to the user. First, it is important to present the right amount of product information. If the volume of information is too large, the user has to look at more information than s/he needs, which causes a cognitive effort for mental information filtering. Second, information should be presented in an appropriate way, i.e., such that it can be comprehended as fast as possible by the user.

The most simple approach to product presentation is to show a sorted list of products. The top ranked products are displayed, ordered according to their similarity. Each row shows a recommended product, including the similarity, the product identification, and some typical product features.

The next, more informative experience presentation approach not only shows some product information but the whole set of attributes on which the retrieval and customization depends. This helps the customer to better understand the reason why a certain product is proposed. This obviously increases the amount of information that needs to be displayed. In order to preserve the clearness of the presentation the information can be structured into several categories among which the customer can switch. The hypertext approach easily supports such a structuring. Additional information concerning the meaning of the product description can be linked to the individual attribute.

To increase the confidence in the reusability of the selected product, an explanation of the similarity ranking may be required. Since the similarity is based on the product attributes, this level provides the proper terms for such an explanation. A very simple and quite common approach is to explain the case selection through the local similarities related to the attributes. Depending on the degree of the local similarity, the values of the attributes of the cases are displayed in different color. More elaborated explanations of similarity can be given in the form of structured text. For each attribute a textual explanation is constructed that indicates the causes for a certain local similarity value. This explains the relation between the customer's wishes and the product features.

5 Applications

To emphasize the advantages for our approach, we implemented several applications some of which are in daily use. Detailed evaluations have been performed. Example applications are presented in the following two subsections.

5.1 Customer Support for Electro-Mechanical Components

We briefly sketch an example application for product search of parameterizable products. The application has been realized for the German company "Jola Spezialschalter K. Mattil & Co."[1] as part of the EC project SMARTSELL[2]. Jola produces thousands of electro-mechanical components and devices like floating and magnetic switches, level controls, liquid level indicators, moisture detectors for cooling ceilings, etc. Jola has realized that it needs a way to provide its customers, who are not technical experts, assisted access to the products.

The non-expert customer needs advice and has not yet or only a long time ago purchased Jola products. S/He needs an intelligent sales assistant that asks for

---

[1] www.jola-info.de

[2] Project No. 28835. Partners: Jola Spezialschalter K. Mattil & Co. GmbH (Prime Contractor - Germany), tec:inno GmbH (Germany), and Interactive Multimedia Systems – IMS (Ireland).

her/his requirements and recommends appropriate products. Within the SMARTSELL project, the assisted access search has been developed.

The behavior of the virtual sales assistant is closer to that of a human expert. Since communication is performed with an inexperienced customer, the focus of the dialog is not on technical details, but on the purpose of the products.

In order to be able to search products with respect to the above-mentioned purpose-oriented characteristics, the product modeling that is used by the case-based retrieval component describes each product in terms of these attributes. They represent knowledge about the purpose for which a particular product is applicable. The similarity measure used for case-based retrieval encodes to what degree a deviation from the ideal application scenario of a product is still acceptable. Fig. 6 shows the user interface of the virtual sales assistant for Jola.

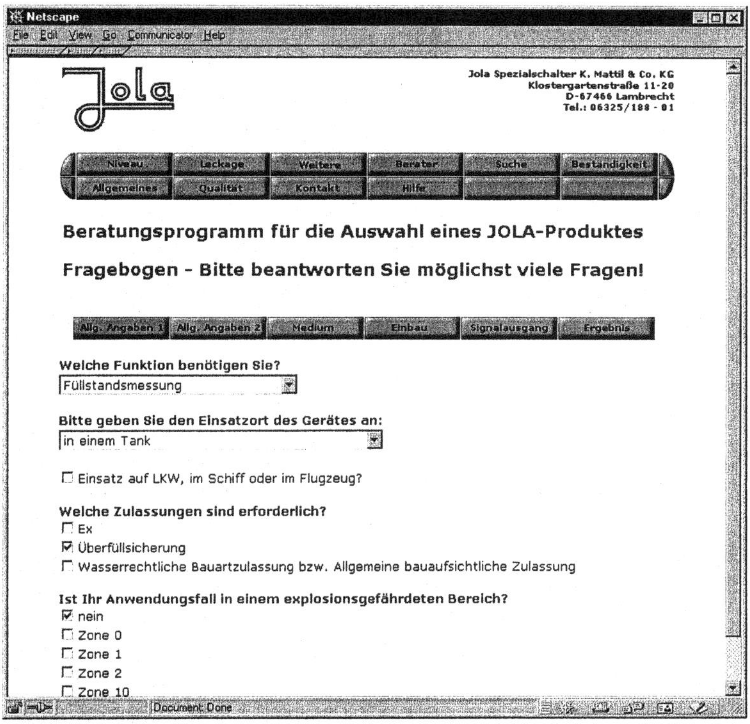

Fig. 6. The Jola Virtual Sales Assistant.

In general, customers of Jola are neither very knowledgeable about the product variety nor do they know which kind of product is appropriate to their problem. The use of these very special technical parts in industry is underlying specific constraints. Even if a product has been found for the customer's purposes, s/he might have further specifications like length limitations or there is a need for accessories. For some components, the latter are even indispensable. Suppose the retrieval system has returned a liquid level transmitter. For these types of switches, the customer has several possibilities for modifications. S/He can adapt the length of the shaft, the diameter of the screw-in-nipple, or the type of float of this switch. Furthermore, there are accessory components to choose like a transducer. Only depending on the latter component, further components can be chosen, e.g., a switching unit for signals and/or a display instrument. With the help of a customization service based on operators (see Sect. 4.3) it is possible to guide the customer, not being familiar with all the modification possibilities and constraints, to her/his target product.

5.2 Customer Support for Personal Computers

Customer support for personal computers is a very challenging task due to the large number of available components and the constraints that restrict the way in which these components can be combined. By applying the intelligent dialog and the incremental component replacement approach, comprehensive intelligent customer support can be implemented that is a significant improvement compared to the current e-shops run, e.g., by Dell, Transtec, Vobis, or Atelco.

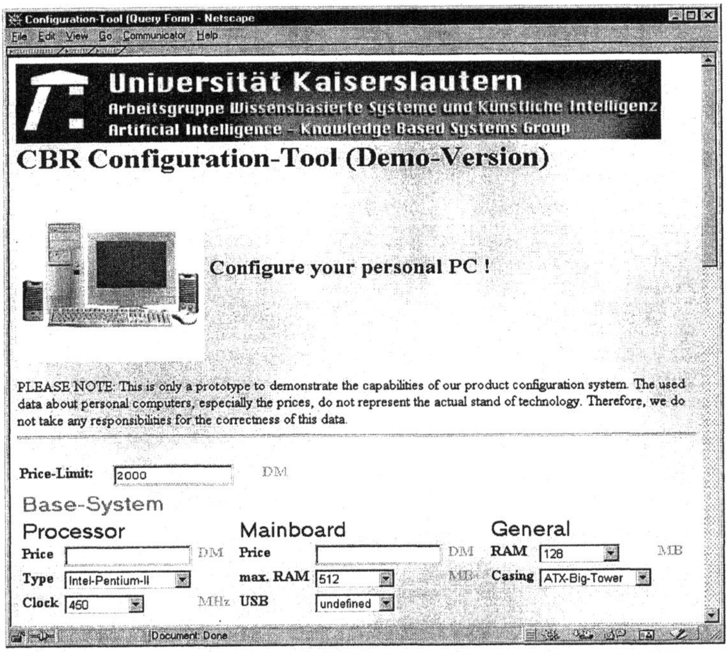

Fig. 7. A Prototypical System for Realizing Customer Support for Personal Computers.

To show the capabilities of these techniques, a first research prototype has been developed [17]. This prototype consists of a detailed model for the domain of personal computers using decomposition and inheritance relations. By decomposing the representation of the products, i.e. the personal computers, into separate representations for each component (e.g., the hard disk, the processor, etc.), the system gets important knowledge about the compositional structure of the products. Further, the system uses two different product databases. The first database consists of the descriptions of several pre-configured personal computers representing available base products. The second database contains the technical descriptions of the available components that can be used to configure a personal computer. To find a suitable personal computer with respect to the demands of a particular customer the system first performs a similarity-based retrieval on the base product database. If there is no adequate personal computer available, the system applies the incremental component replacement approach described in Sect. 4.3 to customize the best matching base product. Through replacing or adding components, the system finally configures a new personal computer that is presented to the customer as the best available product. To guarantee the technical functionality of this product, the system has also knowledge about the specific technical restrictions in the domain of personal computers. A part of the WWW-based user interface of the described prototype is shown in Fig. 7.

6 Conclusion

One of the core difficulties in setting up a customer-friendly electronic shop is caused by the large amount of knowledge involved in a sales process, which is unfortunately still neglected by most electronic shops. Therefore, many current shops appear more like a warehouse where one must exactly know what s/he wants and where to find it. When observing the traditional human-based sales scenario from a knowledge perspective, we can see that many kinds of knowledge play an important role:

- *knowledge about products*: product properties and technical specifications, application areas, product structure, compatibility with other products, prices, experience about faults, etc.
- *knowledge about clients*: requirements, wishes, preferences, shopping type, product experience, product language, cultural affiliation, etc.
- *strategic knowledge*: recommendation, communication, negotiation, sales, etc.

Typically, the vendor, distributor, or manufacturer is the only one who possesses the full knowledge about products. On the other hand, the client is the only one who possesses the client knowledge. This leads to what we call a knowledge gap [4], which must be bridged during the sales process.

In the traditional sales scenario, the human sales agent who makes use of her/his strategic knowledge to mediate between the client and the vendor bridges this knowledge gap. In the future, we expect the knowledge gap to grow significantly. This is due to the fact that products to be sold online will become much more complex. First, products are getting more complex in general and second, after online sales has focused on simple products it will move to the more complicated cases. Additionally, the number of products available for online sale will increase as well. Together, the amount of relevant product knowledge increases. On the other hand, the number of online shoppers is increasing and new classes of shoppers will discover the Internet. This, the increasing diversity of customer wishes and the demand for individually customized products, will increase the uncertainty on the seller's side about the customer and how s/he is best served. The resulting growth of the knowledge gap will become the critical problem for improving or at least maintaining the acceptance of online shopping in the near future. Knowledge-based technologies, in particular CBR, can help bridging this knowledge gap in electronic commerce. As we have shown in this chapter, they provide the means for automatic knowledge processing as part of an intelligent sales agent.

Acknowledgement

Some of the results presented in this chapter have been achieved as part of the ESPRIT project WEB**SELL**[3] (1998-2000). WEB**SELL** aimed at developing CBR techniques and tools for sales support for Internet-based electronic commerce.

References

1. Aamodt A, Plaza E (1994) Case-Based Reasoning: Foundational Issues, Methodological Variations, and System Approaches. In: AICOM, Vol. 7, No. 1, 1994
2. Bergmann R, Wilke W (1998) Towards a new formal model of transformational adaptation in case-based reasoning. In: Proc of the European Conference on Artificial Intelligence, ECAI-98, Brighton, United Kingdom
3. Bergmann R, Breen S, Göker M, Manago M, Wess S (1999) Developing Industrial Case-Based Reasoning Applications. The INRECA-Methodology. LNAI 1612, Springer Verlag
4. Bergmann R, Richter MM, Schmitt S, Stahl A, Vollrath I (2001) Utility-Oriented Matching: A New Research Direction for Case-Based Reasoning. In: Vollrath I, Schmitt S, Reimer U (eds) Proc of the 9th German Workshop on Case-Based Reasoning, GWCBR'01, Baden-Baden, Germany. In: Schnurr HP, Staab S, Studer R, Stumme G, Sure Y (Hrsg) Professionelles Wissensmanagement. Shaker Verlag
5. Cunningham P, Bergmann R, Schmitt S, Traphöner R, Breen S, Smyth B (2001) WEBSELL: Intelligent Sales Assistants for the World Wide Web. In: R. Weber, C. Gresse von Wangenheim (Eds.): Proc of the Workshop Program at the 4th International Conference on Case-Based Reasoning, ICCBR-2001, Vancouver, Canada, July 31, 2001. Workshop 3: Case-Based Reasoning in Electronic Commerce

---

[3] Project No. 27068. Partners: tec:inno GmbH (Prime Contractor - Germany), Adwired AG (Switzerland), Interactive Multimedia Systems – IMS (Ireland), IWT Magazin Verlags GmbH (Germany), Trinity College Dublin (Ireland), and the University of Kaiserslautern (Germany).

6. Doyle M, Cunningham P (2000) A Dynamic Approach to Reducing Dialog in On-Line Decision Guides. In: E. Blanzieri, L. Protinale (Eds.): Advances in Case-Based Reasoning. Proc. of the 5th European Workshop on Case-Based Reasoning, EWCBR 2000, Trento, Italy. LNAI 1898, Springer Verlag
7. Hagen PR (2000) Must search stink. The Forrester Report. June 2000
8. Klein S (1997) Kommerzielle elektronische Transaktionen: sektorale Struktur, Umfang und strategisches Potential. In: R. Werle, C. Lang (Eds.): Modell Internet. Entwicklungsperspektiven neuer Kommunikationsnetze. Campus, Frankfurt a M
9. Kohlmaier A, Schmitt S, Bergmann R (2001) A Similarity-based Approach to Attribute Selection in User-Adaptive Sales Dialogs. In: Aha DW, Watson I (eds) Case-Based Reasoning Research and Development. Proc of the 4th International Conference on Case-Based Reasoning, ICCBR-2001, Vancouver, Canada. LNAI 2080, Springer Verlag
10. Leake DB (1996) Case-Based Reasoning: Experiences, Lessons, and Future Directions. Menlo Park, CA: AAAI Press
11. Lenz M, Burkhard HD (1996) Case Retrieval Nets: Basic ideas and extensions. In: Görz G, Hölldobler S (eds) KI-96: Advances in Artificial Intelligence. LNAI 1137, Springer Verlag
12. Lenz M, Bartsch-Spörl B, Burkhard HD, Wess S (1998) Case-Based Reasoning Technology. From Foundations to Applications. Springer Verlag
13. Schmitt S, Bergmann R (2001) A Formal Approach to Dialogs with Online Customers. In: O'Keefe B, Loebbecke C, Gricar J, Pucihar A, Lenart G (eds) e-Everything: e-Commerce, e-Government, e-Household, e-Democracy. Proc of the 14th Bled Electronic Commerce Conference, Bled, Slovenia. vol 1: Research
14. Schmitt S, Maximini R, Landeck G, Hohwiller J (2000) Implementation of a Product Customization Module for CBR Systems in Electronic Commerce Environments. In: Göker M (ed) Proceedings of the 8th German Workshop on Case-Based Reasoning, GWCBR2000, Lämmerbuckel, Germany
15. Schumacher J, Bergmann R (2000) An effective approach for similarity-based retrieval on top of relational databases. In: Blanzieri E, Portinale L (eds) Advances in Case-Based Reasoning. Proc of the 5th European Workshop on Case-Based Reasoning, EWCBR 2000, Trento, Italy. LNAI 1898, Springer Verlag
16. Selz D, Schubert P (1998) Web Assessment - A Model for the Evaluation and Assessment of successful Electronic Commerce Applications. In: Proceedings of the 31st HICSS Conference, Hawaii, USA, vol IV
17. Stahl A, Bergmann R, Schmitt S (2000) A Customization Approach for Structured Products in Electronic Shops. In: Klein S, O'Keefe B, Gricar J, Podlogar M (eds) Electronic Commerce - The End of the Beginning. Proc of the 13th Bled Electronic Commerce Conference, Bled, Slovenia. vol 1: Research
18. Stolpmann M, Wess S (1999) Optimierung der Kundenbeziehung mit CBR-Systemen. Addison-Wesley
19. Wilke W (1998) Knowledge Management for Intelligent Sales Support in Electronic Commerce. Dissertation, University of Kaiserslautern, Germany
20. Wilke W, Lenz M, Wess S (1998) Case-Based Reasoning for Electronic Commerce. In: (Lenz et al. 1998)

Mobile Agent Based Auctionlike Negotiation in Internet Retail Commerce

XiaoFeng Wang[1], Xun Yi[2], Ramayya Krishnan[3], Chee Kheong Siew[2], and Pradeep K Khosla[1]

[1] Department of Electrical and Computer Engineering, Carnegie Mellon University, Pittsburgh PA 15213 USA, Email:xiaofeng@cs.cmu.edu
[2] Nanyang Technological University, Singapore
[3] Heinz School, Carnegie Mellon University, USA

Abstract. As an intelligent and agile software, mobile agent is promising to boost the flexibility and performance of current Internet retail commerce. However, due to the constrained computational resources and security concerns, current first-generation shopping agents have only limited capacities to conduct negotiation. On the other hand, though online auction exhibits attractive features for retail negotiation such as fairness and openness, it suffers from the problems such as reversed consumer-buyer relation and low performance. In this chapter, we present a novel trading scheme which combines together the favorable features of mobile agent and traditional English auction. The scheme implements an *auctionlike* negotiation protocol to rationalize the buyer-seller relation, keep the dominant strategies in the English auction and simplify the security measures to protect mobile trade agents during the trading process. Based on the protocol, an online learning algorithm supported by clustering techniques and fuzzy sets further helps to improve the system performance and flexibility. In this chapter, we report our in-depth research on the proposed scheme. Both theoretic and empirical results are presented.

1 Introduction

Online marketplaces open a new area for retail commerce. They offer traditional merchants an additional channel to advertise and sell products to customers, thus potentially increasing sales. Forrester Research estimates that online retail sales will reach 17 billion USD early this century [4]. Moreover, online markets are also more efficient than their physical-world counterparts thus lowering transaction costs for both merchants and consumers.

Consumer Buying Behavior (CBB) marketing research shows negotiation is an important stage for retail commerce. It's the stage where the price or other terms of the transaction are determined [6]. To automate online negotiation, intelligent agent is the best candidate. The features of personification and autonomy enable agents to simulate the process as it happens already between humans, and hence human negotiating strategies and approaches may be easier to translate into it [6]. Mobile agents further extend trading services to weak, mobile consumers and are promising to improve the flexibility, efficiency and performance of negotiation protocols at the same time.

In addition, since retail shopping always combines brokering and negotiation process together, mobile agent, characterized as an important online information collector, is deemed as the mediator to conduct automatic negotiation naturally.

Although great research efforts have been invested to the agent-mediated automatic negotiation [15,14,9], current first-generation shopping agents possess only limited bargaining capacities. The reasons come from two aspects. Firstly, automatic negotiation is a difficult procedure which needs complicated computation to infer rival's strategies. Whereas mobile agents usually only have limited computing resources. This makes them hard to compute rival's strategies while easy to be computed. Under the Internet retail scenario, online merchants usually have more resource than the shopping agents who are, therefore, at significant disadvantages. Secondly, mobile agents depend on server environment to run. Thus they have to expose codes and data to the hosts. In the hostile environment, this makes them vulnerable to information stealing and tampering from malicious hosts, which in turn jeopardizes mobile agents' qualifications as online negotiators.

As a special negotiation type, auction exhibits certain characteristics which fit well with intelligent mobile agents. In the English and second-price auctions, bidders have dominant strategy which is open to all the participants. That means all the bidders are free from the intentions to infer rivals' strategies thus saving the computing resource as well as ensuring the fairness during the negotiation. From auctioneers' point of view, they want to maximize their payoff. Different from what's in other types of negotiation, during auction, they may not at a disadvantage if the bidders divine their strategies [2]. Sometimes, the auctioneers even want to make the strategies publicly known to push up the final bid. This greatly reduces the confidential information that needs to protect during the trading. With such an open, simple and fair negotiation scheme, mobile agents can fully take advantage of their beneficial features to play active roles in automating the Internet trading.

However, current implementation of auction to the Internet retail commerce has exposed some of its unfavorable features. Guttman and Maes [5] point out these problems such as irrational consumer-seller relations and low performance. The introducing of centralized salesroom scheme also brings in new security concerns for mobile agent bidders, which actually impairs the advantages of auction itself.

Nowadays, consumers are much more in the driver's seat in the online market than in the physical-world market largely due to the dramatic reduction of search costs [11]. This increases the competition among retailers and forces them to positively differentiate themselves in value dimensions other than price. However, most of current online auctions (as in ebay, ubid, onsale, etc.,) are hosted by sellers[1]. Instead of merchants competing for consumer patronage, such auctions force consumers to compete with one another for a specific merchant offering. This brings in "winner's curse", which pushes up the winning bid above the product's market valuation. On the other hand, retailers often care less about profit on any given transaction and care more about long-term profitability. Customers' loss through the "winner's curse" actually destroys the relationship between retailers and customers, thus damaging the retailers' benefits in the long run.

Furthermore, the traditional online auctions have long delay between starting auctions and purchasing the product. This retards a large number of impatient or time-constrained consumers. In fact, the English and Yankee auction protocols are usually implemented over the Internet for several days. The passive role the auctioneer plays makes thing worse: She has to wait for a critical mass of bidders to complete the auction rather than actively search the potential bidders. This exacerbates time consuming during the auction. Since only the bidder(s) with highest valuations can purchase the auctioned good(s), the rest of the bidders (the majority) have to endure the long fruitless delays. Unlike the vendue of works of arts, this is quite annoying in retail commerce.

To improve auction performance, some people suggest dispatching agent bidders to a centralized salesroom to conduct the auction locally. However, this causes security problems. In order for a mobile agent to run, it must expose its data and code to the host environment. Therefore, if the auctioneer conspires with the owner of the salesroom, she can manipulate the auction to her advantage. This results in potential losses from the bidders' side.

In this chapter, we propose a novel trading scheme which can fully preserve the favorable features of traditional auction while effectively solve its defects with the mobile agent techniques. In our scheme, a Secure Agent-Mediated Auctionlike Negotiation (SAMAN) protocol [12] is implemented which keeps the fairness and openness features in the traditional English auction while rationalize the customer-merchant relation in retail commerce. The protocol further simplifies the security measures to protect mobile trade agents with the openness of auctions, asynchrony and redundancy of mobile agent scheme. Based on the protocol, an online learning algorithm [13] further helps customer agents to learn from their previous trading experience to discover the most appropriate vendors and thus improve the performance during the negotiation process.

We present the scheme and our theoretic and empirical studies on it as follows: Section 2 describes the general architecture; Section 3 presents the SAMAN protocol; Section 4 introduces a learning algorithm which helps mobile agents to improve the negotiation performance; Section 5 and 6 give out

[1] With some reversed auctions provided online, such auction schemes are not prevailing in retail market because customers usually tend to make their purchase decision only after enough comparisons.

theoretic analyses on the proposed scheme from the viewpoints of auction theory and security; Section 7 empirically investigates the learning algorithm; Section 8 concludes the whole paper.

2 Descriptions of the General Architecture

The whole agent-mediated Internet trading architecture is illustrated in the following figure:

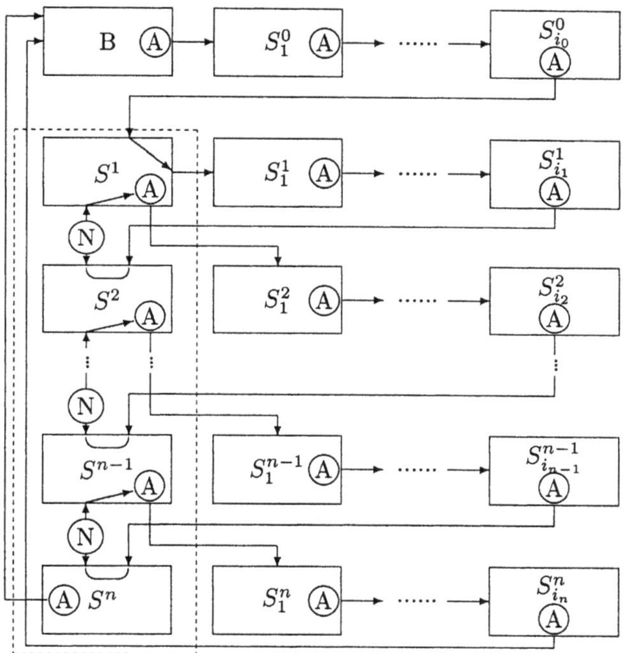

Fig 1: The Agent-mediated Internet Trading Architecture

In the above architecture, B denotes a buyer; S_i^j stands for a selle; A represents the intelligent trade agent and N refers to the auctionlike negotiation process.

As illustrated in figure 1, the trading process is carried out through the interactions among buyer, seller and mobile trade agents. The buyer has a devise called *agent home* (AH) which provides mobile trade agent service. To purchase produces online, the buyer can generate a mobile trade agent through the AH. From the trading experience accumulated in the AH, the agent figures out an "optimal" initial outsourcing plan according to the buyer's preferences. With the plan, mobile trade agents itinerate merchant servers to conduct an asynchronous, reversed auctionlike negotiation among the merchants. The negotiation is carried out in a two-merchant-one-round fashion. Two mobile trade agents (cloned at the early stage of the trading process) residing in two merchant servers act as auctioneers to control the negotiation process. Since such a negotiation runs asynchronously, the agents can tailor the number of rounds and the associated durance to the buyer's requirements.

After exhausted its initial plan, the mobile agent can refer to online catalogues to gather other potential merchants' information and further revise its original plan. At the end of the purchase, the buyer will evaluate the satisfaction of the overall trading experience and activate the AH to update the recommending vendor list through a learning algorithm.

Security problems in the trading architecture are tackled from both buyer and seller sides. The AH is equipped with security modules to authenticate the incoming agents, check the validation of trading results and conduct an investigation to prove a merchant server's malicious actions. Likewise, the seller should have security mechanism to authenticate the mobile agents getting into the server and encrypt the agents moving out to other hosts. Furthermore, each merchant is required to record certain *nonrepudiation evidence* from the mobile agent passed by in their local database for a period of time. Such evidence includes the agent's incoming and outing servers, time stamp, the merchant's signatures on the information provided to the agent and negotiation results. Once the buyer detects any illegal actions after agents return, she preserves the right to launch an investigation. Any seller who cannot provide correct non-repudiation evidence during the investigation will be deemed as a malicious breeder.

In the following two sections, we will introduce the SAMAN protocol and the learning algorithm to improve the performance of negotiation.

3 Secure Agent-Mediated Auctionlike Negotiation protocol

The SAMAN protocol is formally illustrated as follows:

Start Trading. The trading procedure starts when the buyer sends a trade agent out to purchase specified products or services. Just before this, the agent constructs its initial outsourcing plan by referring to a local database called vendor knowledge base (VKB). The VKB contains well-trimmed merchant information helping to improve the negotiation performance according to agents' previous experience. The maintenance of such a database is through a learning algorithm which we will introduce in the next section. The mobile trade agent is also equipped with the buyer's reserve price, i.e, the initial minimum bid (MB) and the minimum bid decrement (MBD).

Referring to figure 1, the trade agent A starts its purchasing trip over the Internet from buyer B, then one after another visits a series of seller servers $S_1^0, S_2^0, \cdots, S_{i_0}^0$ $(i_0 \geq 0)$, S^1 according to its plan. We suppose the first i_0

servers do not provide the required products or services and Server S^1 is the first one which can meet the purchase requirements with the price lower than the MB. Then the agent replaces the MB with S^1's price, clones itself, keeps one copy in the current server and continues to roam to the next seller.

Bidding Procedure. From the outsourcing plan, the agent chooses an unpassed seller and visits the server. Note that if the merchants on the initial plan run out, the agent will browse online catalogues to select new seller servers and add them to its visiting list.

We assume the agent further roams a series of seller servers $S_1^j, S_2^j, \cdots, S_{i_1}^j$ $(1 \leq j \leq n-1, i_1 \geq 0)$, S^{j+1} as shown in figure 1. These servers can be categorized into two types: Type I and Type II. Type I belongs to the sellers who cannot meet the purchase requirements or further lower the MB. Type II consists of all servers whose owners provide the desired products or service and are capable of lowering the MB.

For a Type II server, a negotiation procedure should be carried out between it (also called bidding server BS) and Server S^j (called waiting server WS) for the sale of the products or services. The agent who stays in the waiting server is called waiting agent (WA) and the agent who bids in the bidding server called bidding agent (BA). After negotiation, there are two possible results. One result is that the waiting server is still the winner of the competition. We call such a negotiation result as Result I. Another result is that the bidding server beats the waiting server and becomes the new waiting server. This negotiation result is called Result II.

Among the series of seller servers $S_1^j, S_2^j, \cdots, S_{i_1}^j, S^{j+1}$, only Server S^{j+1} is supposed to be a Type II server and the negotiation result between Server S^{j+1} and Server S^j is Result II. For other servers, even if they are Type II servers, the negotiation result between them and Server S^j is Result I.

The negotiation between a BS and WS (S^j) is performed in the following procedure:

1. The bidding agent (BA) sends a start-negotiation request to the waiting agent (WA). It includes the BS's current bid which must be lower than the current MB by integral times of the MBD and authentication information.
2. The WA authenticates the request. If correct, it passes the new bid to the WS and then continues the following procedure. Otherwise, it ignores the request.
3. The WS checks the current bid and makes its decision about whether to further lower the sale price or give up. If the decision is lowering price, the WS gives its new bid according to the bidding regulation (New bid must be lower than the current bid by integral times of the MBD), and then the WA replies the BA with a bidding response. If the decision is giving up, the procedure goes to 5.
4. The BA notifies the BS of the new bid. Then the BS has to make a decision on whether to further lower the sale price or give up. If it lowers

the price, the BS renders another bid to the BA who relays the bid to the WS through the WA. Then the procedure goes to 3. If it gives up, the procedure goes to 6.

5. Because the WS fails to further lower the price, it has to send a failure notification to the WA. The notification must include the BS's final bid and be stamped with the WS's digital signature. The WA sends the notification to the BA who passes it to the BS after authentication. The BS also signs on the notification and return it to the BA. The BA keeps a copy of the dually signed notification for itself and sends it back to the WA who will authenticate it and then reserves it as non-repudiation evidence. Both the BA and the WA replace the MB with the final bid. After that, the WA becomes a new BA and leaves the former WS to resume its information brokering task while the BA has to stay in the new WS as a new WA. Thus this round of negotiation ends. The process is illustrated in figure 2.

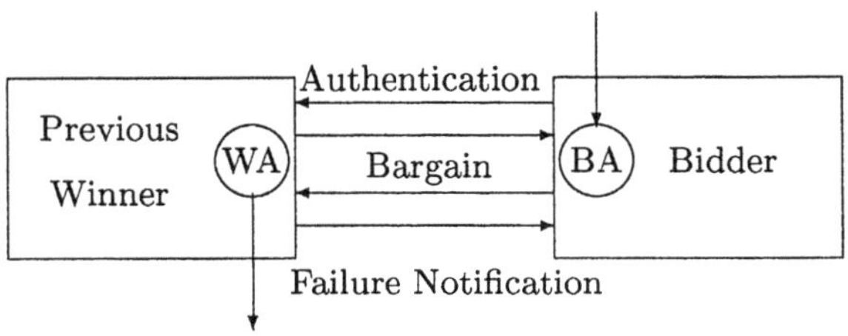

Fig 2: The negotiation process for Result II

6. Because the BS fails to lower the price, it sends a signed failure notification including the WS's final bid to the BA. The BA notifies the WA of the BS's decision. The latter checks the signature of the notification and then passes it to the WS. The WS dually signs on the notification and returns it to the WA. The WA keeps a copy for itself and sends the notification back to the BA. After checking the signature, the BA leaves the current server and roams to the next merchant according to the outsourcing plan. Both the BA and the WA have to update the MB before the end of this round. This illustrated in figure 3.

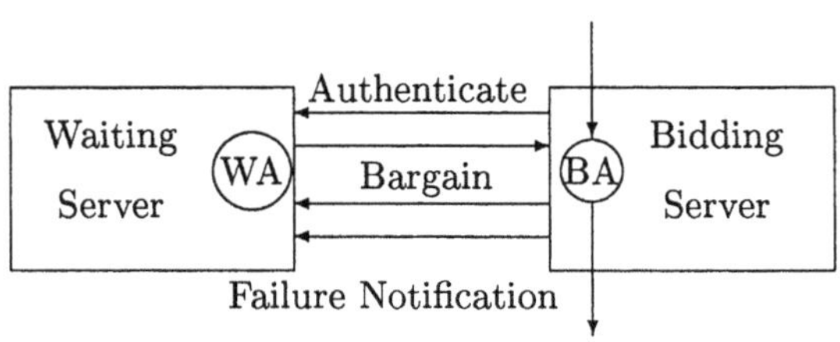

Fig 3: The negotiation process for Result I

In order to guarantee trade agent's security during the trading, every server agent visited must preserve non-repudiation evidence for the agent such as incoming and outgoing servers, the signed confirmation notification from the next server, etc. Therefore, once any illegal actions on mobile agents have been detected, merchants can use such information to prove their innocence.

Return of Trade Agent. The buyer can take control of the trading process by pre-setting termination conditions to a trade agent. These conditions usually include two aspects. One is the scale of the auction, i.e, the number of bidders the agents are required to visit. The other is the agent's lifetime. Therefore, once agents visited enough bidders or their lifetime was expired, they must return to the AH.

Once the termination conditions are met, both the BA and the WA must return to the AH. Just before leaving, the WA may conduct some additional trading actions such as completing some early steps of payment protocol since the last WS is obviously the final winner.

After having received the BA and the WA, the AH checks the final price and merchants' signatures on the notifications for all the negotiation rounds. If no problem is found, the buyer contacts the merchant for the payment and delivery. Otherwise, she will not trust the trade agent and may launch an investigation to dig out the malicious server. To some weak user such as mobile users, they may simply discard the agent and restart the trading process.

The last step to complete the trading is evaluation. Following the buyer's feedback on the products or services, the AH uses a learning algorithm to update merchant information in the VKB. Such information will provide mobile trade agents for the next trading mission with "initial guesses" about the potentially optimal vendors. Our research shows: Visiting these merchants first will improve the negotiation performance in general.

4 Learning the Optimal Merchants

In general, the SAMAN protocol exhibits nice performance. In the traditional English auction, to lower down price for a MBD, the auctioneer has to broadcast the bid first and wait for bidders' responses. However, in the SAMAN, each message passing except the last two between the BS and the WS will lead to a MBD decrement in the price. This reduces the communication load during the negotiation. From the viewpoint of merchants (bidders), they do not need to participate the whole negotiation process. This is because the negotiation is carried out in an asynchronous way. A merchant joins the competition at the MB which reflects previous merchants' valuations. Likewise, as soon as the merchant exhausts her valuation, she will leave at once. Such a setting shortens the durance a merchant needs to know her chance to get the transaction. Details on the analysis can be referred from an extended version of [12].

From the buyers' perspective, they sense the negotiation delay from the expected time the mobile agents take to find two "optimal" bidders capable of lowering down the price to the bottom (the minimal bid obtainable in the marketplace). This is because the SAMAN protocol interleaves the bidding process with the merchant information gathering and the delay in finding ideal merchants is much longer than that of the pure bidding (especially with the SAMAN's superior performance in communication loads). Suppose the agents manage to figure out beforehand two merchants with the lowest valuations for the products or services. They can visit these two merchants at first and conduct one round negotiation to get the best price. Knowing about this, the buyer only needs to set a short lifetime for the agent with the confidence that the agents can bring back a decent price in such a short time. If, however, agents are not so lucky, they came across the merchants in a reversed way: Each merchant only can lower down the price for only one MBD. The buyer has to wait a long time to get the ideal results. Therefore, the knowledge about potential optimal retailers is important to improving the negotiation performance.

The purpose of the learning algorithm is to prepare knowledge about potentially optimal retailers for the incoming trading mission. Based on retailers' information obtained by trade agents, the AH can make generalisations to single out the most promising candidates to compose the reference list (initial outsourcing plan) for the next round of trading. With the increasing of knowledge and repetitive learning process, the reference list becomes more and more accurate and agents will solely rely on it to do the trading sooner or later.

Suppose the buyer purchases only one kind of product, such as bread, and each retailer has a static valuation for it. In this case: after every trading round, the AH inserts the records of newly discovered bread sellers into the VKB and sorts them in ascending order, according to their final prices. Before the next trading, the top 2 retailers will be put into the reference list since we know that so far, they can provide the cheapest bread. However, in the real world, buyers need to purchase products more than just bread. To establish a price sequence for every kind of goods is too storage intensive to be feasible. Thus, the problem now is how to find retailers selling other cheap commodities such as biscuit from the previous knowledge of bread sellers.

Often in practice, there exists certain relationship among the prices of different kinds of commodities. For example, the shops selling cheap bread usually have low valuations for biscuit. Thus, it should be beneficial to develop a method of prediction, that is, a procedure for selecting cheap biscuit sellers through evaluating their prices for bread. Based on such idea, we design a learning algorithm with the assumptions that (1) Merchant's valuations are correlated among the commodities we are interested in; (2) The coefficients of such correlation are uniform among different kinds of goods. The second assumption denotes that there is no special strong or weak relation between any two members in the product set of interest. For example, whether a retailer has cheap bread, or whether she sells cheap biscuit implies whether her milk is also cheap with the same probabilities. Therefore, the AH may predict the retailer's possible price rank (It is indeed a predicted valuation ranks) for milk by just averaging her previous price ranks for the bread and biscuit. The order of the combined price ranks should imply the possible order of merchants' valuations for milk.

However, since the above-mentioned price ranks only roughly indicate the possible order of retailers' milk prices, to strictly follow such order to find the best milk sellers is unreasonable. Actually, two retailers with minor difference in their price ranks may have the same milk prices or even a reversed price order. On the other hand, for the retailers who have high prices for bread and biscuit, there should be a way for them to improve their ranks through providing low prices for other commodities. From our daily life experience, we know that merchants can be divided into certain groups according to their general price levels. It is obvious that supermarkets usually sell cheaper items than big department stores. Similarly, merchants inside the VKB also can be classified by their price ranks. These who have the close price ranks should be in the same group. Before the trading for milk, the AH selects the promising sellers from every group in the following way: (1) Inside one group, each member has the same probability to be selected; (2) The number of the retailers selected from certain group depends on the general price rank of such group. This provides a more reasonable way to recommend retailers to the trade agent.

In our algorithm, the VKB is taken as a fuzzy set: "merchants selling the cheap products". The set is divided and assigned a membership function based on its members' price ranks. The membership function in term supplies the criterion to select the candidates to compose the reference list.

We describe the learning algorithm as follows:

Acquisition of Initial Knowledge

At the very beginning, the AH has no knowledge about the retailers. After the first trading round, the trade agent brings back retailers' prices (their lowest bids) $v_1, v_2, \cdots, v_n$. The AH processes the information in the following way:

- Generating Price Ranks: The AH creates a new record with a price rank (PR) for every retailer the trade agent has visited. The PR value for the ith retailer can be calculated as: $PR_i = \frac{v_i - v_L}{v_H - v_L}$, where v_H stands for the highest price obtained and v_L for the lowest price.
- Sorting: The AH sorts the records inside the VKB in the ascending order according to their PR values.

After that, the AH sets the trading round count (TRC) to 1 and computes the mean of all the PR values $\overline{PR}$ in the VKB.

Merge

The AH already has certain knowledge about the retailers in the VKB. After trade agents return, a merge process is executed to adjust the retailers' ranking according to the new retailer price information agents obtained. Let PR'_1, PR'_2,...,PR'_n be the PR values of the retailers agents just visited; PR_1, PR_2,...,PR_m be the PR values of the records insides the VKB. The formula to merge these two lists together are:

- For retailers inside both lists, their new PR values are computed using the formulae:

$$PR_{new} = \frac{PR \cdot TRC + PR'}{TRC + 1} \tag{1}$$

- For retailers who was just visited by agents but have no records inside VKB, their PR values are computed using the formulae:

$$PR_{new} = \frac{\overline{PR} \cdot TRC + PR'}{TRC + 1} \tag{2}$$

- For retailers who are inside VKB but not visited by agents in the last trading round, their new PR values are computed using the formulae:

$$PR_{new} = \frac{PR \cdot TRC + \overline{PR'}}{TRC + 1} \tag{3}$$

$\overline{PR'} = \frac{1}{n} \cdot \sum_{i=1}^{n} PR'_i$ is the mean of PR' list.

After the merge process, the AH sorts the records in the ascending order of the updated PR values and re-calculates their means. The TRC will be incremented by 1.

Constructing Fuzzy Sets

After every trading round, a fuzzy set [7], "merchants selling the cheap products", is constructed based on the PR values of the merchants who were visited by the trade agent. The purpose is to explore these retailers' potentials to become the promising candidates for the next trading. The construction of the fuzzy set is realised by calculating a membership grade for every record inside the VKB. Its procedure is as follows:

- Clustering: Clustering is performed on the VKB so as to categorise merchants into price groups (PG) according to the closeness of their PR values. The algorithm we take is a standard instance-based approach [1]. Details are as follows:
  1. Set $k = 0$; o_0= the PR value of the first record inside VKB.
  2. Starting from the first record, for every record inside VKB, let m= the PR value of the current record and then perform Step 3 to 6.
  3. If $k = 0$, then $MinValue = Threshold$ and go to Step 5.
  4. Calculate $MinValue = dist(m, o_k) = |m - o_k|$.

5. If $MinValue < Threshold$ then $o_k = \frac{o_k|PG_k|+m}{|PG_k|+1}$, $PG_k = PG_k \cup \{m\}$; else $k = k+1$, $o_k = m$, $PG_k = \{m\}$.
6. Let the next record be current record, and then go to Step 2.

In the above algorithm, $Threshold$ is a threshold value to divide group. It is usually given by experts. After clustering, the records inside VKB are divided into k PGs.

- Membership Grade: Since all the records inside the same PG have close PR values, they should be assigned the same membership grades. The membership grade (MG) for the ith records of the PG is calculated from their expected PR value, i.e., o_i, by using formulae:

$$MG_i = \frac{1 - o_i}{1 - o_1} \tag{4}$$

where, $1 \leq i \leq k$.

After assigned a membership grade, every merchant inside the VKB is characterised by her degree of belonging to the fuzzy set. In another word, the AH makes an estimation on her possibility to offer a low price in the incoming trading round. Therefore, based on the fuzzy set, the AH is able to prepare the initial knowledge for the next mission.

Formation of Reference List

To compose a reference list for the incoming trading round, actually, is an approximate reasoning [7] process with the form:

Rule1: If shop X sells Q items, then X is a R shop with support m
Rule2: If Y is an item of shop X, then Y is R
Fact: Y' is an item of X

Conclusion: Y' is R

We now present an example to show the use of this reasoning model. Let $Q = R = cheap$, $m = 0.65$, bread, milk and biscuit be three cheap items in shop A, and cake be an expensive item in A. By Rule 1, A is a cheap shop with support $m = 3/4 = 0.75$. By Rule 2, A's items are cheap. Now assume sugar be an item of A. So we can conclude: sugar is cheap in A with support 0.75. The shop A is possible to be selected.

We make such selections from the fuzzy set following the principles: (1) every record has the opportunity to be chosen; (2) the probability to be selected for a specific record depends on the membership grade of such record. The detailed procedure to establish the reference list is:

- According to the number of merchants already visited (reflecting the AH's confidence in the knowledge obtained) and the buyer's requirements on timeliness, the AH figures out the number of merchants n should be selected from the fuzzy set.
- Based on the above mentioned number n, the AH uses the following formulae to calculate the number of candidates (n_i) that should be chosen

from the ith price group PG_i:

$$n_i = Min(|PG_i|, n \cdot \frac{MG_i}{\sum_{j=1}^{k} MG_j}) \quad (5)$$

Where, $1 \leq i \leq k$.

- The AH randomly selects n_i merchants from PG_i and then combines all the selected merchants in the descending order of their membership grades to form the reference list.

The reference list will be taken as initial merchant knowledge for the trade agent in the next trading round.

To explain the above algorithm, we use following example. Suppose agents first visited retailers A, B, C, D to buy bread and then went to $A, B, C.E$ for biscuit. Their prices (final bids) for bread are: A : \$1.1, B : \$1.2, C : \$1.7, D : \$1.9; for biscuit are: A : \$2.0, B : \$2.1, C : \$2.5, E : \$2.8. Retailer A and B is in the reference list for purchase of biscuit.

After generating PR values, retailers' price differences for certain product are mapped to the interval 0 to 1. In our example, for bread: $PR_A = 0$, $PR_B = 0.125$,$PR_C = 0.75$, $PR_D = 1$; for biscuits: $PR'_A = 0, PR'_B = 0.125, PR'_C = 0.725, PR'_E = 1$. This makes it possible to combine them together. After purchase of biscuits, trade agents bring back a list of the retailers they have just visited. Among them, A, B and C have been visited by agents in the previous trading. AH uses formulae (2) to update their PRs:$PR_{new(A)} = 0, PR_{new(B)} = 0.125, PR_{new(C)} = 0.738$. Since for each retailer the averaging process must take all their previous PRs into consideration, TRC is used to count the number of the previous trading rounds. Retailer E has no records in the VKB. This means that AH is ignorant about her price rank for bread. In this case, we take the mean of all the PR values for bread as her old PR [2] and then average it with her current PR value for biscuits. Formulae (3) shows the case. $PR_{new(E)} = 0.734$. Retailer D has not been visited in the recent trading round. So the AH has no idea about her valuation for biscuits. Similarly, we assume her possible new PR is the mean of all the PR values for biscuit and then combine it to her old PR values as in (4): $PR_{new(D)} = 0.732$. After merging the PR lists for bread and biscuit, the VKB will be sorted as: A, B, D, E, C. To further discern the best retailers in the VKB, a fuzzy set will then be constructed based on these data. Through clustering, two price groups (PG_1 and PG_2) are formed:$PG_1\{A, B\}, PG_2\{C, D, E\}$. A membership grade for the merchants inside each price group can be calculated by formulae (5). Thus, the fuzzy set can be expressed as:

$$VKB = 1/A + 1/B + 0.283/C + 0.283/D + 0.283/E$$

[2] This is based on the assumption that E can take every PR value in the VKB with the same probability

Suppose the trade agent has a new mission of buying milk and there will be 3 merchants to be selected from VKB. Using formulae (6), AH finds two candidates should be chosen from PG_1 and the rest one can be randomly selected from C, D, E. The selection results will be composed as a reference list to instruct the agent for the purchase of milk.

After several learning rounds, the list of the optimal retailers that the AH suggests becomes more and more accurate. This improves the negotiation performance progressively. Experiment results in the following section present such process. An interesting finding is that the VKB actually becomes a personal purchase profile of a specific buyer. If a person often purchases bread, the list will provide more accurate information for bread sellers than that of biscuit or milk retailers. Actually, buyer's purchase preference is recorded in the VKB after several rounds of learning.

5 Fair, Open and Rational Negotiation Protocol

To analyze auction model, McAfee and McMillan [8] starts from four assumptions:

1. All the bidders are risk-neutral, as is the seller.
2. The independent private-values model holds.
3. The bidders are symmetric.
4. The final payment from the winning bidder to the seller depends on the bid alone.

The first assumption indicates bidders' risk attitudes. The second supposes bidders' valuation model. There are two types of valuation models [10]. One is the Independent Private-Values Model: bidder I's valuation v_i is drawn from a distribution F_i, and the draws are statistically independent; the other is the Common-Value Model: the item being bid for has a single objective, but unknown value V and bidders's valuations v_i are independently drawn from publicly known $G(v|V)$. The third supposes bidders' valuations are drawn from the same distribution. The last decides winning bidder's final payment.

Once all these assumptions hold, the model is called as the "benchmark model" [6].

In the proposed auctionlike negotiation protocol, the retailers take similar roles as bidders. Thus, we can suppose they are risk-neutral. Since all retailers know quite well about the cost of the products/service they want to sell, their value models are independent private ones. In the retail marketplace, the costs of certain products/services are usually drawn from the same bell-sized distribution (Normal Distribution). This manifests that all the retailers in the proposed protocol are symmetric. The last assumption obviously holds for the retail commerce.

From the above explanation, we know that the SAMAN protocol naturally satisfies the assumptions of the "benchmark model". Therefore, the protocol can be analyzed with the same method as for the traditional auction.

Consider all the merchants attending negotiation with the proposed protocol. Their costs for the products/services can be presented as $c_1, \cdots, c_n$ which are drawn independently from a Normal Distribution G with a density function g. Suppose c_1 is the lowest cost, c_2 is the second lowest, etc. The sequence is arranged in a non-decreasing way. In statistical terminology, c_i is called the $i - th$ order statistic, $i = 1, \cdots, n$. During the negotiation, merchants with different costs may bid in a random sequence. However, the one whose cost is c_1 will definitely win at last. The bidder with cost of c_2 will drop out of the bidding as soon as the descending price breaks her bottom line. Thus the lowest-cost individual wins the bidding and pays a price equal to the cost of her last remaining rival. The payoff the winner can obtain is $c_2 - c_1$. McAfee and McMillan [6] proved that the expected value of this payoff is given by the expectation of $\frac{G(c_1)}{g(c_1)}$. Thus the expectation of the final bid will be $c_1 + \frac{G(c_1)}{g(c_1)}$

Due to the uncertainty about rivals' valuations, the best strategy for a merchant to obtain such a payoff is to keep lowering down current bid by a small unit (i.e., one MBD) until the price gets down to her cost (valuation). This helps to avoid the possible losses coming from the over-depreciation. Obviously, the strategy is dominant in the SAMAN protocol. Even in the cases of risk-averse bidders, the conclusion still holds [8].

The above analysis shows that the proposed protocol is strategical analyous to a descending English auction. With the dominant equilibrium, all the participants are free from the intentions to counter-speculate others' strategies. Thus the computing resources are saved during the negotiation and the fairness of the traditional English auction is fully preserved.

From the buyer's point of view, she wants to get the item at as low price as possible. This intention is publicly known by all the parties involved. During the negotiation, mobile trade agents are similar to auctioneers. They need not to bring with themselves any negotiation information except the reserve price which actually, will be open to all the merchants to incur a bidding process. That means mobile agents have little confidential information to protect in the protocol. Such openness feature effectively mitigates the security concerns in the trading.

Compared with most online retail auctions, the SAMAN protocol takes a reversed auction setting in which buyers act as auctioneers and merchants compete each other for sell. This elimiates the "winner's curse" problem thus rationalizing the relation between the consumers and retailers in the retail commerce. Buyers can expect economic rent through revelation of their valuations. From the analysis above, we can see that the competition between merchants can reduce the bid to the second-last bidder's cost. Thus buyers can get the product or service at a low price. On the other hand, sellers are also benefited from the negotiation in the long run. Just like what is mentioned in the introduction, retailers often care less about profit on any given transaction and care more about long-term profitability which actually depends on consumers' satisfactions. The interests retailers give to customers will be paid back by the customers' repeat purchases and additional purchases. Even for the losers in a specific trading round, their behaviors will also be recorded by the trade agents and analyzed by the AH. Through purchase evaluation, they have the opportunities to be re-patronized in the future.

Although the proposed protocol is for price competition, the same scheme can be extended to multi-dimentional bargaining. That means, the merchants can compete on other qualities (such as brand, service and delivery) of certain product according to consumers' preferences. In this case, it is important for merchants to exhibit their features to every buyer regardless of whether she would make a purchase with them in the current trading round. This is because the consumers may come back in the future once they find a match-up between the merchant's features and their needs. Therefore, it is definitely to merchants' benefits to participate such a negotiation. The protocol gives them chances to establish their positive reputations.

The above discussions justify the SAMAN protocol as a fair, open and rational negotiation protocol for the Internet retail commerce.

6 Security Issues

A mobile trade agent has to run in a merchant server. The merchant, therefore, gets opportunities to decompose the agent and analyze its codes and data or even modify the agent to acquire illegal profits. Current consensus is that it is computationally impossible to protect mobile agents from malicious hosts. Instead of tackling the problem from a computational (difficult) point of view, current research [3] is looking at sociological means of enforcing good host behavior.

In the proposed SAMAN protocol, trade agent acts as auctioneer. Just as analyzed before, auctioneer in a traditional English auction has nothing to conceal from bidders. Actually it may be to her benefit to open her valuation to get better payoff. Therefore, the trade agents in the protocol have no confidential information to protect from host's scanning.

On the other hand, the malicious merchants also have little opportunity to tamper with trade agents without being detected. Since there is always a WA residing in the current winner's server, the malicious actions to delete the winner's information from the BA's data are easy to detect. The winner may want to change the MB to get higher payment. However, her signature on the failure notification carried by the BA will reveal this illegal action. Another kind of attack is to modify agent's routing list, thus leading the trade agent to "barren land" where it can hardly find any ideal bidders. The WS may have the intention to do this. To protect such an attack, we let the agent start information brokering only from the loser's server. The winner has to keep the agent until the end of the trading or the lost of her position as a waiting bidder. Since the loser gets no payoff while she takes the risk of being detected if she tampers with the agent (remember servers must preserve non-repudiation evidence in case of buyer's investigation), it is to her benefit to keep good behaviours.

After agents return, the AH will check the agents to validate the negotiation results. Once the AH suspects that the agents were tampered with, it can activate an investigation process which traces the non-repudiation evidence kept in each merchant server (connected as a chain with the pointers of *incoming*, *outgoing servers*) to find out the malicious merchant. Such a merchant will not only lose the transaction but also be punished by loss of the reputation which leads to financial losses in her future businesses.

7 Empirical Study on the Learning Algorithm

As discussed in section 4, the SAMAN protocol has superior performance in communication times and bidders' involvement delay in comparison with traditional English auction. In a negotiation round, each message passing between the WA and the BA except the last two causes a MBD decrement according to the bidders' dominant strategies in section 5. While in a traditional English auction, at least two broadcastings are needed (announcing the current MB and sending the new bids) to get the same result. With the SAMAN, at any time point, there are only two bidders inside the negotiation. This is totally different from English auctions in that many bidders have to present in the negotiation simultaneously. Therefore, the bidders' total involvement delay has been greatly reduced.

Another important index for negotiation performance: buyer's involvement delay[3] is managed through the learning algorithm presented in section 4. The algorithm makes use of agents' trading experience and merchants' final offers (their prices for the products or services) to accumulate merchants' statistical features. This helps to estimate the potentially optimal merchants according to the buyer's preference. By visiting these merchants first, the agents can greatly reduce the buyer's involvement delay.

In this section, we empirically study the proposed learning algorithm. Suppose we can sample the current minimal bid from trade agents at a series of equal-gap time points $t_{i=1\cdots n}$ over trading processes with the fixed time interval. v_i stands for the MB the agents obtained at t_i. Usually, the impact of information gathering (filtering merchant information to find appropriate

[3] An associated performance index is *negotiation quality* which calculates buyer's expected final payment given the probability distribution of their searching time. Obviously, this index and buyer's involvement delay are two sides of the same coin. Reducing one can reduce the other.

merchants and migrating the agent through merchant servers) to the performance of the whole negotiation process (buyer's involvement delay) is much larger than the message exchanging in a specific bidding round. Hence, in our experiment, we ignore the time consumed in each bidding round and assume that agents can immediately (almost) get the competition result for a pair of bidders. We further define *anytime price* (AP) as $AP = \frac{1}{n} \cdot \sum_{i=1}^{n} v_i$. The AP actually reflects the buyer's involvement delay[4] because: A low AP implies that agents came across merchants with low prices at the earlier stage of the negotiation while a large AP indicates that agents kept visiting merchants with high prices until the end of the negotiation process. With a low AP, the buyer can shorten the agents' lifetime with the confidence that they still can get a decent bargain; With a large AP, the buyer have to wait long enough to get the best price. Therefore, minimizing buyer's involvement delay can be achieved by minimizing the AP.

We carried out an experiment to justify the effectiveness of the proposed learning algorithm in reducing the AP. Our experimental data are composed of 10 types of computer products from 100 retailers, totally 1,000 samples. In order to compare the negotiation performance in the trading of different products, we mapped their price decreasing processes to the interval of 0 to 100. Our method is:

1. For each product, select the highest price H and the lowest price L.
2. For every price X between the H and L, calculate its utility value (U) as $U = \frac{X-L}{H-L} \cdot 100$

Then, we used U_i as the MB at the time point t_i to compute the overall AP.

Starting from an empty VKB, we took 10 trading rounds, each for a different product as one test round (TR). In every trading round, trade agents must visit 10 retailers. Some of them are from the VKB, others are randomly selected from a simulated online catalogue. After repetitive 10 independent TRs (Every TR has the same sequence of 10 trading missions. Totally 1,000 times of price inquiry in 10 TRs.), the expected AP of the $ith(1 \leq i \leq 10)$ trading round (an average on the AP values of the ith trading round through 10 independent TRs), i.e., $\overline{AP_i}$, is taken to represent the performance in this trading round. There are a total of 28 time points. Figure 4 shows the change of the $\overline{AP}$ during the trading round. The curve exhibits a roughly "anytime feature". That means the performance of the system is improving with time. The only exception is that $\overline{AP_4}$ is higher than $\overline{AP_3}$. This comes from the influence of various correlation coefficients among the products in the real life. However, in general, the experiment demonstrates that the AP during the trading can be effectively reduced with the learning algorithm. This leads to the improvement of the negotiation performance in terms of

[4] Actually, the AP is used to measure negotiation quality. However, since such a index is essentially the same as buyer's involvement delay, we can use it to model the latter

buyer's involvement delay because small APs and enough samples from the marketplace make the buyer confident enough to reduce the time agents required to search the merchants with little risk of compromising the quality of the final outcome.

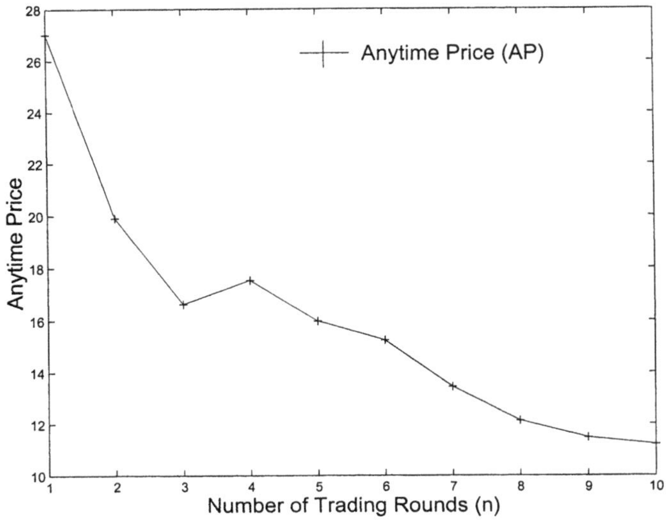

Fig 4: Reducing anytime price with the learning algorithm.

8 Conclusion

Mobile agent has great potentials to provide high performance, flexible and reliable automatic negotiation services to both online and mobile consumers given the obstacles to its practical implementations (such as security and resource limitation) being overcome. Meanwhile, although current online auctions possess many favorable characteristics, as retail negotiation protocols, they suffer from other problems such as irrational consumer-seller relation and low performance. In this chapter, we present a novel Internet negotiation scheme which takes advantage of the favorable features of both auctions and mobile agent techniques. Under a mobile agent based trading framework, a secure agent-mediated auctionlike negotiation (SAMAN) protocol is proposed to rationalize merchant-customer relation in the retail commerce and simplify the security measures to protect mobile trade agent. Based on the protocol, a learning algorithm with the techniques of clustering and fuzzy set is implemented to further improve the negotiation performance.

The proposed negotiation scheme has been studied theoretically and empirically. The theoretic analysis and experimental results are presented in the chapter to justify the effectiveness of the approach. In our future research, we are considering to apply other soft computing techniques such as game theoretic reputation mechanism to the system to further improve the reliability of the trading architecture. Moreover, practical implementation of the scheme to the wireless trading environment is also a promising investigation thrust.

References

1. Ada D, Kibler D, Albert M (1991) Instance-based learning algorithm. In: Proceedings of International conference of Machine learning
2. Beam C, Segev A, Shanthikumar G (1996) Electronic Negotiation through Internet-based Auctions. CITM Working Paper 96-WP-1019, available at http://haas.berkeley.edu/citm/wp-1019-summary.html
3. Borenstein N (1994) Email with a Mind of its Own: The Safe-Tcl Language for Enabled Mail. In: Proceedings of IFIP WG 65 Conference
4. Forrester Research Report (1997) On-Line Internet Spending
5. Guttman R, Maes P (1998) Cooperative vs. Competitive Multi-Agent Negotiations in Retail Electronic Commerce. In: Proceedings of the Second International Workshop on Cooperative Information Agents. Paris, France
6. Guttman R, Maes P (1998) Agent-mediated Integrative Negotiation for Retail Electronic Commerce. In: Proceedings of Workshop on Agent Mediated Electronic Trading. Minneapolis, Minnesota, USA
7. Klir G, Clair U, Yuan B (1997) Fuzzy set theory: foundations and applications. Prentice Hall
8. McAfee R P, McMillan J (1987) Auction and Bidding. Journal of Economic Literature:699-738
9. Sandholm T (1993) An Implementation of the Contract Net Protocol Based on Marginal Cost Calculations. In: Proceedings of the Eleventh National Conference on Artificial Intelligence. pp 256-262
10. Sanjiv R D, Rangarajan K. S (1997) Auction Theory: A Summary with Application to Treasury Markets. Working Paper 5873. National Bureau of Economic Research
11. Schewartz E, Webonomics (1997) Nine Essential Principle for Growing Your Bussiness on the World Wide Web. Broadway Books
12. Wang X F, Yi X, Lam K Y, Zhang C Q, Okamoto E (1999) Secure Agent-Mediated Auctionlike Negotiation protocol for Internet Retail Commerce. In: Proceedings of Workshop on Cooperative Information Agents. Springer-Verlag LNAI 1652 (An extended version of the paper is available at: www.cs.cmu.edu/~ xiaofeng/saman.pdf)
13. Wang X F, Zhang S C, Khosla P K, Kiliccote H, Zhang C Q, Lam K Y (2000) Anytime algorithm for agent-mediated merchant information gathering. In: Proceedings of ACM International Conference on Autonomous Agents. ACM press
14. Zeng D, Sycara K (1996) Bayesian Learning in Negotiation. In: Working Notes of the AAAI 1996 Stanford Spring Symposium Series on Adaptation, Coevolution, and Learning in Multiagent Systems
15. Zlotkin G, Rosenschein J S (1989) Negotiation and Task Sharing among Autonomous Agents in Cooperative Domains. In: Proceedings of the 11th International Joint Conference on Artificial Intelligence. Detroit, Michigan, pp 912-917

Subject Index

Author Index

Studies in Fuzziness and Soft Computing

B. Bouchon-Meunier, J. Gutierrez-Rios, L. Magdalena, R.R. Yager (Eds.)

Technologies for Constructing Intelligent Systems 1

Tasks

It deals with the theory behind the solutions to difficult problems in the construction of intelligent systems. Various methodologies for these cases are discussed, among which are fuzzy and network-based frameworks. Topics included in the book include fundamental issues in uncertainty, bayesian networks and other network methods.

2002. X, 404 pp. 83 figs., 47 tabs.
(Vol. 89) Hardcover **€ 74,95**; sFr 124,-
ISBN 3-7908-1454-7

B. Bouchon-Meunier, J. Gutierrez-Rios, L. Magdalena, R.R. Yager (Eds.)

Technologies for Constructing Intelligent Systems 2

Tools

Intelligent systems enhance the capacities made available by the internet. Topics in the book include preference modelling and decision making, learning, clustering and data mining.

2002. X, 429 pp. 61 figs., 24 tabs.
(Vol. 90) Hardcover **€ 74,95**; sFr 124,-
ISBN 3-7908-1455-5

C. Bertoluzza, M.A. Gil, D.A. Ralescu (Eds.)

Statistical Modeling, Analysis and Management of Fuzzy Data

The contributions in this book connect Probability Theory/Statistics and Fuzzy Set Theory in different ways. Some of these connections are either philosophical or theoretical in nature, but most of them state models and methods to work with fuzzy data.

2002. XIV, 309 pp. 29 figs., 9 tabs.
(Vol. 87) Hardcover **€ 64,95**; sFr 107,50
ISBN 3-7908-1440-7

M.B. Gorzalczany

Computational Intelligence Systems and Applications

Neuro-Fuzzy and Fuzzy Neural Synergisms

This presentation is preceded by a discussion of the main directions of synthesizing fuzzy sets, networks and genetic algorithms in the framework of designing CI systems.

2002. X, 364 pp. 147 figs., 21 tabs.
(Vol. 86) Hardcover **€ 69,95**; sFr 116,-
ISBN 3-7908-1439-3

You will find more information:

www.springer.de/studiesfuzziness/

Please order from
Springer · Customer Service
Haberstr. 7 · 69126 Heidelberg, Germany
Tel.: +49 (0) 6221-345-217/8 · Fax: +49 (0) 6221-345-229
e-mail: orders@springer.de
or through your bookseller

All prices are net-prices subject to local VAT, e.g. in Germany 7% VAT for books.
Prices and other details are subject to change without notice. d&p · BA-50659

Springer

GPSR Compliance
The European Union's (EU) General Product Safety Regulation (GPSR) is a set of rules that requires consumer products to be safe and our obligations to ensure this.

If you have any concerns about our products, you can contact us on

ProductSafety@springernature.com

In case Publisher is established outside the EU, the EU authorized representative is:

Springer Nature Customer Service Center GmbH
Europaplatz 3
69115 Heidelberg, Germany

www.ingramcontent.com/pod-product-compliance
Ingram Content Group UK Ltd.
Pitfield, Milton Keynes, MK11 3LW, UK
UKHW020133290926
15471UKWH00003B/448

* 9 7 8 3 6 6 2 0 0 3 1 0 7 *